The Early Church at Work and Worship

The Early Church
at Work and Worship

Volume 1
Ministry, Ordination, Covenant, and Canon

Everett Ferguson

James Clarke & Co

James Clarke & Co
P.O. Box 60
Cambridge
CB1 2NT
United Kingdom

www.jamesclarke.co
publishing@jamesclarke.co

ISBN: 978 0 227 17489 0

British Library Cataloguing in Publication Data
A record is available from the British Library

First published by James Clarke & Co, 2014

Copyright © Everett Ferguson, 2013

Published by arrangement
with Cascade Books

Contents

Contents

Acknowledgments

THE AUTHOR AND PUBLISHER are grateful to the original publications and publishers for permission to reprint articles. All used by permission.

1. "Images of the Church in Early Christian Literature." Previously unpublished.

2. "Attitudes to Schism at Nicaea." In *Schism, Heresy and Religious Protest*, edited by Derek Baker, 57–63. Studies in Church History 9. Cambridge: Cambridge University Press, 1972.

3. "A Note on Irenaeus, *Adversus Haereses* IV.8.3." In *Überlieferungsgeschichtliche Untersuchungen*, edited by Franz Paschke, 193–95. Texte und Untersuchungen 125. Berlin: Akademie Verlag, 1981.

4–7. "Ordination in the Ancient Church." *Restoration Quarterly* 4 (1960) 117–38; 5 (1961) 17–32, 67–82, 130–46.

8. "Selection and Installation to Office in Roman, Greek, Jewish, and Christian Antiquity." *Theologische Zeitschrift* 30 (1974) 273–84.

9. "Jewish and Christian Ordination: Some Observations" *Harvard Theological Review* 56 (1963) 13–19.

10. "Qumran and Codex D." *Revue d'Qumran* 8 (1972) 75–80.

11. "Origen and the Election of Bishops." *Church History* 43 (1974), 26–33.

12. "Eusebius and Ordination." *Journal of Ecclesiastical History* 13 (1962) 139–44.

13. "Laying on of Hands: Its Significance in Ordination." *Journal of Theological Studies* 26 (1975) 1–12.

14. "The Covenant Idea in the Second Century." In *Texts and Testaments: Critical Essays on the Bible and Early Church Fathers*, edited by W. Eugene March, 135–62. San Antonio: Trinity University Press, 1980.

15. "Justin Martyr on Jews, Christians, and the Covenant." In *Early Christianity in Context: Monuments and Documents*, edited by F. Manns and E. Alliata, 395–405. Jerusalem: Studium Biblicum Franciscanum, 1993.

16. "Canon Muratori: Date and Provenance." *Studia Patristica* 17 (1982) 677–83.

17. Review of G. M. Hahneman, *The Muratorian Fragment and the Development of the Canon* (Oxford: Clarendon, 1992), in *Journal of Theological Studies* n.s. 44 (1993) 691–97.

18. "Pseudepigraphy: Post-Canonical Letters." Delivered at the Seminar on the Development of Early Catholic Christianity, April 12, 1984. Previously unpublished.

19. "Factors Leading to the Selection and Closure of the New Testament Canon: A Survey of Some Recent Studies." In *The Canon Debate*, edited by Lee Martin McDonald and James A. Sanders, 295–320. Peabody, MA: Hendrickson, 2002.

Abbreviations

ANF	Ante-Nicene Fathers
BETL	Bibliotheca ephemeridum theologicarum Lovaniensium
BLE	*Bulletin de litteratur ecclesiastique*
CSEL	*Corpus Scriptorum Ecclesiasticorum Latinorum*
DAGR	*Dictionnaire des Antiquités Grecques et Romaines*, edited by Charles Daremberg et al. Paris: Hachette, 1873–1919
ERE	*Encyclopaedia of Religion and Ethics*. 13 vols. Edited by James Hastings. New York: Scribners, 1908–1927
FC	Fathers of the Church
GCS	Die griechische christliche Schriftsteler der ersten [drei] Jahrhunderte
HTR	*Harvard Theological Review*
JAC	*Jahrbuch für Antike und Christentum*
JBL	*Journal of Biblical Literature*
JECS	*Journal of Early Christian Studies*
JEH	*Journal of Ecclesiastical History*
JTS	*Journal of Theological Studies*
LCL	Loeb Classical Library
NHC	Nag Hammadi Codices
NIDNTT	*The New International Dictionary of New Testament Theology*. 4 vols. Edited by Colin Brown. Exeter: Paternoster, 1975–1978
NovT	*Novum Testamentum*

NovTSup	Supplements to Novum Testamentum
NPNF	Nicene and Post-Nicene Fathers
NTS	*New Testament Studies*
PG	*Patrologia graeca* (J. Migne)
PL	*Patrologia latina* (J. Migne)
ResQ	*Restoration Quarterly*
RevQ	*Revue de Qumrân*
RSR	*Recherches de science religieuse*
SecCent	*The Second Century*
StPatr	*Studia Patristica*
TDNT	*Theological Dictionary of the New Testament*
TDOT	*Theological Dictionary of the Old Testament*
TLZ	*Theologische Literturzeitung*
TU	*Texte und Untersuchungen zur Geschichte der altchristlichen Literatur*
WUNT	*Wissenschaftliche Untersuchungen zum Neuen Testament*
VC	*Vigiliae Christianae*
ZNW	*Zeitschrift für die neutestamentliche Wissenschaft*

1

Images of the Church in Early Christian Literature[1]

THE STUDY OF ECCLESIOLOGY often deals with the institutional, external aspects of the church. Less attention has been given to the nature or essence of the church. One approach many have found helpful in studying the essential nature of the church is by way of the images employed in reference to it.

The value of this approach in regard to the New Testament was demonstrated by Paul Minear's impressive and influential compilation of *Images of the Church in the New Testament* (1960). I covered the images used for the church in the New Testament in my book *The Church of Christ: A Biblical Ecclesiology for Today* (1996). Herwi Rikhof, *The Concept of the Church: A Methodological Inquiry into the Use of Metaphor in Ecclesiology* (1981), and Avery Dulles, *Models of the Church* (1987), examined imagery in contemporary theological discussion of the church. Less attention, however, has been given to the use of images for the church in Christian writers of the early centuries after the New Testament. Thomas Halton's collection of sources, *The Church* (1985), for the series Message of the Fathers of the Church (volume 4) gives only 10 out of 234 pages to

1. This paper is previously unpublished, but much of the content appears in my article on "Community and Worship" (2010). It began as a lecture at the International Reference Library for Biblical Research, Fort Worth, Texas, March 14, 2008, and at the Seminar on the Development of Early Catholic Christianity, Dallas Theological Seminary, April 3, 2008.

"The Images of the Church," noting the church as sheepfold, as edifice, as mother, as bride of Christ, and as the sheet let down from heaven in Peter's vision (Acts 10:9–16). E. Glenn Hinson's nearly contemporary collection of sources, *Understandings of the Church* (1986), for the series Sources of Early Christian Thought gives no explicit treatment of images for the church.

This situation changed somewhat with the massive, nearly 700 page, work of F. Ledegang, *Mysterium ecclesiae: Images of the Church and Its Members in Origen* (2001).[2] Ledegang's comprehensive study groups the scores of images and related terminology in the writings of Origen into six categories: body of Christ, bride of Christ, family, house and sanctuary, people of God, and "the earth and all that is in it." For this paper I will take Ledegang's six categories and give a passage from Origen and then some passages from Origen's chronological predecessors and contemporaries.

What is immediately evident in these images for the church is that they all emphasize the communal aspect of Christian faith and life. This communal emphasis stands in contrast to the individualistic approach of so many of the expressions of Christianity in the modern Western world. Most of these images are rooted in Biblical usage. They, furthermore, testify not only to the importance of the church in Christian thought, but also to the relation of the church to key theological concepts.

BODY

My approach is to give a passage from Origen and then some passages from his predecessors and contemporaries. Of Origen's extensive use of the body imagery I select one passage not from a commentary or homily that explicitly refers to its scriptural basis.

> We say that the divine Scriptures declare the body of Christ, animated by the Son of God, to be the whole church of God, and the members of this body—considered as a whole—to consist of those who are believers. Since, as a soul vivifies and moves the body . . . , so the Word, arousing and moving the whole body, the church, to the things that need to be done, moves also each

2. Other works to be noted are David Rankin, *Tertullian and the Church* (1995), with its chapter on "Tertullian's ecclesiological images" (65–90): ark, ship, camp, body of Christ, Trinity, Spirit, mother, bride, virgin, school, and sect; and G. G. Christo, *The Church's Identity Established through Images according to Saint John Chrysostom* (2006).

individual member belonging to the church, so that they do nothing apart from the Word.[3]

Origen in the context uses the analogy of the church to a body, animated by a soul, to support the union of the soul of Jesus, perfect man, with the eternal Word, Son of God; but he is drawing on 1 Cor 12:12 and 27 and Rom 12:4–5.

Origen's predecessor, Clement of Alexandria, made use of the body imagery for the church. In commenting on Ps 19:4–6, he quotes some who say that the "Lord's tabernacle is his body," but others say, "it is the church of the faithful."[4] Clement of Alexandria, like Origen, uses this imagery of the church as the body of Christ to reason back to the nature of Christ. He alludes to 1 Cor 12:12 with the words, "As a human being consisting of many members . . . is a combination of two—a body of faith and a soul of hope—so the Lord is of flesh and blood."[5] In an extended commentary on 1 Corinthians 6, Clement applies the language of body to the church; with special reference to verse 13 he says,

> The church of the Lord is figuratively speaking a body, the spiritual and holy chorus. Those who have been only called these things, but do not live according to the word, are fleshly. "But this spiritual body," that is the holy church, "is not for fornication" [1 Cor 6:13]. It is not fitting in any manner, however little, to abandon the gospel for the pagan life.[6]

The homily we know as *2 Clement*, wrongly ascribed to Clement of Rome, used the language of the church as the body of Christ to argue for the preexistence of the church. As Christ is preexistent, so is his body. The author stresses the close identification of the church with Christ, and he seems to take the body as the equivalent of the flesh of Christ. The result is an implicit argument against a Docetic/Gnostic disparagement of the flesh.

> I do not think you are ignorant that the church is the living body of Christ. For Scripture says, "God made the human being male and female" [Gen 1:27]. The male is Christ, and the female is the church. And you know that the Books and the Apostles say that the church is not [only] of the present time but is from the

---

3. *Against Celsus* 6.48. My translations follow existing translations, but modified.

4. *Prophetic Eclogues* 56.

5. *Instructor* 1.6.42.

6. *Miscellanies* 7.14.87.3. Cf. *Instructor* 1.5.22, "Believers are members of Christ."

> beginning. For it existed spiritually, as also did our Jesus. But he
> was manifested in these last days in order to save us. And the
> church, being spiritual, was manifested in the flesh of Christ . . .
> But if we say that the flesh is the church and the Spirit is Christ,
> then the one who abuses the flesh abuses Christ.[7]

Paul's image of the church as body of Christ must have worked itself into the Christian consciousness for it to be used so early for such different purposes from Paul's as to argue for the nature of Christ (Origen and Clement of Alexandria) and for the pre-existence of the church (*2 Clement*) as well as against sexual immorality (Clement of Alexandria and *2 Clement*).

BRIDE

Origen applies the imagery of the bride to the church in his *Commentary on the Song of Songs*. He connects the language of body with that of a bride. Commenting on Paul's words, "Our bodies are members of Christ," he explains,

> For when he says "our bodies," he shows that these bodies are
> the body of the bride; but when he mentions the "members of
> Christ," he indicates that these same bodies are the body of the
> Bridegroom.[8]

The words addressed by the Bridegroom to the bride in Song of Songs are "words spoken by Christ to the church."[9] They "can be understood as spoken of this present age, for even now the church is fair when she is near to Christ and imitates Christ."[10] Origen anticipates later individualistic spirituality in also applying the bridal imagery to the individual soul.

Methodius was a critic of Origen on some points of doctrine, but he shared with him the image of church as bride. Those who embrace the truth and are delivered from the evils of the flesh become "a church and help-meet of Christ, betrothed and given in marriage to him as a virgin, according to the apostle" [2 Cor 11:2].[11]

---

7. *2 Clement* 14.2–3, 4. Hermas, *Vision* 2.4 (2.8), says that the church was created first of all things.

8. *Commentary on the Song of Songs* 3.2 on 1:16.

9. *Commntary on the Song of Songs* 3.15 on 2:13–14.

10. *Commentary on the Song of Songs* 3.1 on 1:15.

11. *Banquet of the Ten Virgins* 3.8.

Clement of Alexandria applies the purity of the bride to the church avoiding heresies. He interprets Rom 7:2, 4 to mean Christians belong to Christ as "bride and church, which must be pure both from inner thoughts contrary to the truth and from outward temptations [heresies]."[12]

Tertullian stresses that the church as bride comes to Christ as a virgin. Against the proclamation by a bishop (whether in Rome or in Carthage is not clear) of forgiveness for the sins of adultery and fornication, the rigorist Tertullian, who considered these sins unforgiveable by the church, protests, "The church is a virgin! Far from Christ's betrothed be such a proclamation."[13]

MOTHER

The most important aspect of family imagery for the church in early Christianity was that of the mother. The image of the church as mother was one of the most popular in early Christianity, for which there is a comprehensive study by Joseph C. Plumpe, *Mater Ecclesia: An Inquiry into the Concept of the Church as Mother in Early Christianity* (1943).

Origen gave an allegorical interpretation of Prov 17:25 ("Foolish chilren are a grief to their father and bitterness to her who bore them"):

> The church is our mother, whom God the Father betrothed to himself as wife. For always through her he begets sons and daughters for himself. And such as are educated in the knowledge and wisdom of God are a joy to both God our Father and the mother church.[14]

Origen is precise here that the origin of Christians is with God the Father and not with the church. It is through the mother that God begets sons and daughters. Others were not always so careful and sometimes spoke as if the children (Christians) derived from the church; probably if pressed they would have acknowledged the theological priority of God.

Clement of Alexandria has a striking passage combining the imagery of virgin and mother for the church:

12. *Miscellanies* 3.12.80.

13. *On Modesty* 1.8; on the church as a virgin, also 18.11 and *On Monogamy* 11.2 ("virgin church betrothed to the one Christ") and *Against Marcion* 5.12.6. The church as bride of Christ in *On Monogamy* 5.7; *Against Marcion* 4.11.8; 5.18.9.

14. *PG* 17.201B.

> One is the universal Father, one also the universal Word, the Holy Spirit is one and the same everywhere, and one is the only virgin mother. I love to call her church. This one alone . . . is both virgin and mother, pure as a virgin, loving as a mother. She calls her children and nurses them with holy milk, the Word suited to infants.[15]

Clement seems to have Mary, the mother of Jesus, in mind with the language of virgin mother, but his reference is to the church, and so is implicitly an early instance of Mary as an image of the church. This passage is an early instance of adding the church to the usual Trinitarian confession of belief in Father, Son, and Holy Spirit, as in the Apostles and Nicene creeds. It is to be noted that the milk supplied by this mother to her children is not her own teachings but the universal Word. Shortly before this passage Clement said, "The mother draws to herself the children, and we seek our mother, the church."[16]

Methodius, in the same section quoted above on the church as bride, used the imagery of motherhood for the church. The church "conceives believers and gives them new birth by the washing of regeneration [Titus 3:5]," because Christ implants the spiritual seed that "is conceived and formed by the church, as by a woman, so as to give birth and nourishment to virtue."[17] Methodius, like Origen, is careful not to ascribe the generating power to the mother, but unlike Origen he ascribes the implanting of the spiritual seed to Christ and not to God (whose description as Father accords with Origen's language). Again, Methodius says that when the Word (Christ) begets in each one a true knowledge and faith, Christ is spiritually born in them: "Therefore, the church swells and travails in birth until Christ is formed in us [Gal 4:19]."[18]

Irenaeus, in his catechetical work *Demonstration* [or *Proof*] *of the Apostolic Preaching* 94, contrasts the church and the synagogue, "The Lord grants more children to the church than to the synagogue of the past."[19] Elsewhere he says against heretics that those "who do not partake of the Spirit [of God] are not nourished into life from the mother's breasts."[20]

15. *Instructor* 1.6.42.1.

16. *Instructor* 1.5.21; *Instructor* 3.12.99 says the same with reference to the church, "Let us children run to our good mother."

17. *Banquet of the Ten Virgins* 3.8.

18. *Banquet of the Ten Virgins* 8.8.

19. In chapter 98 Irenaeus says that the church throughout the world hands down the preaching of the truth to her children.

20. *Against Heresies* 3.24.1.

The *Letter of the Churches of Lyons and Vienne* provides one of the early uses of maternal imagery for the church. The letter speaks of those who in persecution had denied the faith and then came back to faith in this way: "There was great joy to the Virgin Mother, who had miscarried with them as though dead, and was receiving them back alive."[21] One of the Christians present signified this by making actions of giving birth.

Tertullian makes frequent use of the imagery of the church as mother. He employs the analogy of Adam to Christ as including Eve and the church:

> For as Adam was a figure of Christ, Adam's sleep shadowed out the death of Christ, who was going to sleep a mortal slumber, that from the wound inflicted on his side might in like manner [as Eve was formed], be typified the church, the true mother of the living.[22]

The language of Father and Son suggest a mother, and "our mother is the church."[23] Care for the martyrs in prison is described as the "provision which our lady mother the church makes from her bountiful breasts."[24] The statement in Gal 4:26 that the "Jerusalem above" "is our mother" prompts the comment that this is "the holy church in whom we have expressed our faith."[25]

Latin Christianity's fondness for the imagery of church as mother is seen in Cyprian, who refers to the church as mother more than thirty times.[26] For instance, in his argument against accepting baptism performed by heretics he makes the following argument:

> The Spirit cannot be received, unless he who receives it first exists. [His point is that one cannot receive the Spirit until first being reborn in the church.] As the birth of Christians is in baptism, and the generation and sanctification of baptism are with the one bride of Christ [the church], she alone is able spiritually to conceive and to give birth to sons to God. This being so,

---

21. Eusebius, *Church History* 5.1.45; cf. the allusion in 5.1.49.

22. *On the Soul* 43.

23. *On Prayer* 2. *On Monogamy* 7.9 parallels the "one Father, God," and "our mother, the church."

24. *To the Martyrs* 1.

25. *Against Marcion* 5.4.8. Ledegang, *Mysterium ecclesiae*, p. 206, takes this not as Tertullian's comment but as part of his quotation from Marcion, who thus becomes the first to call the church mother.

26. Plumpe, *Mater Ecclesia*, 81.

where and of what mother to whom is he born who is not a son
of the church? If one is to have God as his Father, he must first
have the church for a mother.[27]

On this basis Cyprian gave his famous declaration against schism, "He
can no longer have God for his Father who has not the church for his
mother."[28]

BUILDING/TEMPLE

Origen could speak of the church as a house. "The church is the house
of the Son of God." And again, "The church or the churches, then are the
houses of the Bridegroom and the bride, the houses of the soul and the
Word."[29]

Origen applies the language of the temple to the church mostly in
biblical passages about the temple. His commentary on John 2:13–17 includes these words:

> Jesus always finds some such in the temple. For in what we call
> the church, which is the house "of the living God, the pillar and
> ground of the truth [1 Tim 3:15]," when are there not some
> money-changers sitting . . . ?[30]

The continuation of the passage in John 2:19–21 prompts Origen in his
Commentary on John to combine the images of body and of temple, as
does the Gospel of John, for the church:

> If the body of Jesus is said to be his temple, it is worth asking
> whether we must take this in a singular manner, or must en-
> deavor to refer each of the things recorded about the temple
> anagogically to the saying about the body of Jesus, whether it
> be the body which he received from the virgin, or the church,
> which is said to be his body . . .
>
> One . . . will say that the body, understood in either way, has
> been called the temple because as the temple had the glory of
> God dwelling in it, so the Firstborn of all creation, being the im-
> age and glory of God, is properly said to be the temple bearing
> the image of God in respect to his body or the church. . . .

27. *Letters* 74.7.2.

28. *On the Unity of the Church* 6.

29. *Commentary on the Song of Songs* 3.3 on 1:17.

30. *Commentary on John* 10.23 (16).134.

> We shall attempt, however, to refer each of the statements
> which have reference to the temple anagogically to the churc . . .
> Then each of the living stones, will be a stone of the temple
> according to the worth of its life here.[31]

Here, as is usual with him, Origen quickly moves from the corporate use of the image to the individual believer. The biblical material offered a rich lode from which Origen could mine moral and spiritual teachings.

Clement of Alexandria repeated the argument of early Christian apologists against material temples, while applying the terminology of temple to the church and the assembly of God's people.

> Is it not the case that we do not rightly and truly circumscribe
> in any place the one who cannot be contained, nor do we con-
> fine in temples made with hands that which contains all things?
> What work of builders, stone cutters, and of handicraft can be
> holy? . . . If the sacred [ἱερὸν] is understood in a twofold way, of
> God himself and of a structure in his honor, is it not proper that
> we call holy the church, which according to full knowledge is
> for the honor of God, is of great worth, and is not constructed
> by human skill . . . but is fashioned by the will of God into a
> temple? For I do not call the place but the assembly of the elect
> the church.[32]

So, for Clement, in accord with the New Testament, God's temple now is not a place but the people assembled, the church.

For Tertullian, Christ, in contrast to the Jewish temple that was destroyed, "is the true temple of God."[33] But by extension Christians are "priests of the spiritual temple, that is of the church."[34] Alternatively, Christ was the rejected stone that became "the chief cornerstone," "accepted and elevated to the top place of the temple, even his church."[35] According to this imagery, it is the Holy Spirit who builds "the church, which is indeed the temple, household, and city of God."[36] The church is the spiritual

---

31. *Commentary on John* 10.39 (23).263–64, 267–68.

32. *Miscellanies* 7.5.28; *Miscellanies* 7.13.82 says with reference to 1 Cor 3:16 that "The temple is large, as the church, but small, as the human being." Ledegang, *Mysterium ecclesiae*, 320, lists Clement's varied use of the temple imagery: the cosmos, the soul of the Gnostic, the body, the body of Jesus, as well as the church.

33. *Against the Jews* 13.15. In *Against Marcion* 3.24, Christ is "the temple of God, and also the gate by whom heaven is entered."

34. *Against the Jews* 14.9.

35. *Against Marcion* 3.7.

36. *Against Marcion* 3.23.

temple, built upon Peter.[37] Individual Christians are themselves "temples of God, and altars, and lights, and sacred vessels."[38]

The theme of the spiritual temple replacing the physical temple in Jerusalem is expressed early in Christian literature by the *Epistle of Barnabas*, but the author applies it to the individual. The temple of the Lord is gloriously built when "having received the forgiveness of sins and having placed hope in his name, we became new." "Therefore God truly resides in our dwelling place."[39]

The church as a whole is the building in Hermas, but this time it is a tower and not a temple. In the elaborate parable of the tower in the *Similitudes* "the rock and the gate are the Son of God."[40] "The tower is the church," and the stones placed in the building are those who take the name of the Son of God and are clothed with the appropriate virtues.[41] In Hermas's *Visions* that open the *Shepherd*, it is also stated that "The tower which you see being built is the church," with the further comment that "the tower is built upon the waters" of baptism and "is founded on the word of the almighty and glorious name."[42]

PEOPLE OF GOD

Origen works with the theme of peoplehood quite extensively and in various ways. I select only one passage as illustrative of his approach. After contrasting the Egyptian people and the Israelite people and their respective priests, Origen addresses the congregation:

> Examining yourself, consider to which people you belong and the priesthood of which order you hold. If you still serve the carnal senses . . ., know that you are of the Egyptian people. But if you have before your eyes the Decalogue of the Law and the decade of the New Testament . . . and from that you offer tithes . . . "you are a true Israelite in whom there is no guile" (John 1:47).[43]

37. *On Monogamy* 8.

38. *On the Crown* 9.

39. *Barnabas* 16.8; the whole chapter is relevant.

40. *Similitudes* 9.12.1 (89).

41. *Similitudes* 9.13.1 (89); 9.13.4—15.6 (90–92).

42. *Visions* 3.3.3 and 5 (11).

43. *Homilies on Genesis* 16.6.

Here as elsewhere Origen identifies the true Christian people with the true Israel of Old Testament scripture.

In an extended discussion of different images for the children of God, Clement of Alexandria says that the Lord "calls us sometimes children, sometimes chickens, sometimes infants, and at other times sons and often little children, and a new people and a recent people."[44] Without expressly using the word church, Clement implies it in the language of a people. He makes the contrast, "the old race [Israel] was perverse and hard hearted," but "we the new people are tender as a child."[45] "Formerly the older people had an older covenant, and the law disciplined the people with fear, . . . but to the new and recent people a new covenant has been given, the Word has become flesh, and fear is turned into love."[46] The children of God "become a new, holy people, by regeneration."[47]

Alongside the word people Clement also uses the word "race" for Christians. Out of the Greek and Jewish peoples "there are gathered into one race of the saved people those who come to faith."[48]

Tertullian too develops the theme of the two peoples. He interpreted Gen 25:23 about the two nations and two peoples in the womb of Rebekah as referring to the older people of Israel (the Jews) and the later or lesser people, the Christians.[49] In all the nations now "dwells the people of the name of Christ."[50] Tertullian assigns the designation "third race" to pagan critics and rejects it (*To the Nations* 8).

Justin Martyr uses the language of people and race in reference to the church in succession to Israel: "After that Righteous One was put to death, we flourished as another people." He continues, "We are not only a people but also a holy people" and a people chosen by God.[51] He affirms of Christians that "We are the true high priestly race of God."[52]

44. *Instructor* 1.5.14.

45. *Instructor* 1.5.19.4.

46. *Instructor* 1.7.59.1. Cf. *Instructor* 1.5.20.3, "In contrast to the older people, the new and recent people have learned new blessings."

47. *Instructor* 1.6.32.4.

48. *Miscellanies* 6.5.42. Buell, *Why This New Race*.

49. *Against the Jews* 1.

50. *Against the Jews* 7.

51. *Dialogue with Trypho* 119.3–4. In 123 Justin quotes Old Testament passages to show that the church of the Gentiles is a new Israel, "counted worthy to be called a people" (123.1).

52. *Dialogue with Trypho* 116.3.

Early apologists presented Christians as a third (or fourth) race. The *Epistle to Diognetus* says that Christians in their religion "neither acknowledge those considered to be gods by the Greeks nor observe the superstition of the Jews," but are a "new race or way of life."[53] Aristides argues as follows: "It is evident to us, O King, that there are three classes of people in this world: the worshippers of those called gods by you, the Jews, and the Christians." The Syriac version gives four by dividing the worshippers of other gods into barbarians and Greeks to go with the Jews and Christians.[54]

ARK/SHIP

Among the images drawn from nature and objects in the world the ark or a ship is prominent. Origen was the first to work out the ark motif extensively in an ecclesiological sense.[55] In his Homilies on Genesis he drew lessons for the church from the instructions about the building of the ark. "This people, therefore, which is saved in the church, is compared to all those whether men or animals that are saved in the ark."[56] He continues by interpreting the different levels in the ark as degrees of progress in faith, and he takes Noah as an image of Christ.

> Therefore, Christ, the spiritual Noah, in his ark in which he frees the human race from destruction, that is, in his church, has established in its breadth the number fifty, the number of forgiveness.[57]

This association of the ark with salvation went back to 1 Pet 3:20–22 and was extensively employed in the early church,[58] but Origen explicitly connects the ark with the church.

---

53. *Epistle to Diognetus* 1. The *Preaching of Peter* said, "Do not worship as the Greeks," "neither worship as the Jews," but "worship in a new way by Christ"—quoted by Clement of Alexandria, *Miscellanies* 6.5.

54. *Apology* 2. The body of the apology proceeds by discussing the Chaldaeans ("barbarians" in the Syriac), who worship the elements, the Greeks, the Egyptians, then the Jews, and finally Christians.

55. Ledegang, *Mysterium ecclesiae*, 376, following his discussion of Origen's interpretations of the ark on 371–76.

56. *Homilies on Genesis* 2.3.

57. *Homilies on Genesis* 2.5. Fifty has the significance of forgiveness from the year of Jubilee and its release from debts.

58. Note Justin, *Dialogue with Trypho* 138.

Latin Christianity made much use of the analogy of the ark and the church. Callistus, bishop of Rome, argued that "the ark of Noah was a symbol of the church, in which were both dogs, wolves, and ravens," and so he alleged that those guilty of sin could remain in the church.[59] Tertullian alludes to this argument, referring to the different kinds of animals (raven, kite, dog, and serpent) in the ark as representing different types of people in the church, but he insists that no idolater was in the ark, so "Let there not be in the church what was not in the ark."[60] He had already anticipated the theme of the ark as a type of the church in his treatment of the flood in Noah's day as a type of baptism. "The dove is the Holy Spirit, sent forth from heaven, where is the church, a figure of the ark."[61]

Cyprian too argued from the ark as a type of the church: First Peter 3:20–21 proves that "the one ark of Noah was a type of the one church" and so only the baptism administered in the church (and not by schismatics) is valid; on this analogy those outside the church will perish.[62] Thereafter the analogy of the ark and the church was common.

Different from the image of the ark was the non-biblical image of a ship, which Origen does not connect with the church.[63] Hippolytus makes an elaborate development of the comparison.

> The "wings of the vessels" [Isa 18:1] are the churches; and the sea is the world, in which the church is set, like a ship tossed in the deep, but not destroyed; for she has with her the skilled pilot, Christ. And she bears in her midst also the trophy (which is erected) over death; for she carries with her the cross of the Lord. For her prow is the east, her stern is the west, and her hold is the south, and her tillers are the two Testaments; and the ropes that stretch around her are the love of Christ, which binds the church; and the net which she bears with her is the laver of the regeneration which renews believers . . . As the wind the Spirit from heaven is present, by whom those who believe are sealed. She has also anchors of iron accompanying her, that is the holy commandments of Christ himself, which are strong as iron. She also has sailors on the right and the left, assessors like the holy angels, by whom the church is always governed and defended. The ladder in her leading up to the sailyard is an

---

59. Hippolytus, *Refutation of All Heresies* 9.12(7).23.

60. *On Idolatry* 24.4.

61. *On Baptism* 8.4.

62. *Letters* 69.2.2; 75.15.

63. Ledegang, *Mysterium ecclesiae*, 643.

> emblem of the passion of Christ, which brings the faithful to the ascent to heaven. And the top sails aloft upon the yard are the company of prophets, martyrs, and apostles, who have entered into their rest in the kingdom of Christ.[64]

A similarly elaborate but different comparison of the ship to the church occurs in the Pseudo-Clementine literature:

> For the whole business of the church is like a great ship, bearing through a violent storm people who are of many places and who desire to inhabit the city of the good kingdom. Let, therefore, God be your shipmaster. Let the pilot be likened to Christ, the mate to the bishop, the sailors to the deacons, the midshipmen to the catechists, the multitude of the brothers to the passengers, the world to the sea, the foul winds to temptations, persecutions, and dangers . . . Let hypocrites be regarded as like to pirates . . . In order, therefore, that sailing with a fair wind you may safely reach the haven of the hoped-for city, pray so as to be heard. But prayers become audible by good deeds.[65]

The following chapter applies the comparison with specific exhortations to the different members of the church.

The earliest reference to a ship other than the ark as the church appears to be Tertullian, *On Baptism* 12. He was responding to those who suggested that "the apostles underwent a substitute for baptism when in the little ship they were engulfed by the waves." Tertullian replied that that was different from being "baptized by the rule of religion," and he then affirmed, "that little ship presented a type of the church, because on the sea, which means this present world, it is being tossed about by the waves, which mean persecutions and temptations." A modern scholar, Erik Peterson, has argued that the ship as a symbol of the church is a recasting of an older conception of Israel in an eschatological storm at sea. Such imagery could go back to a lost apocalyptic book.[66]

To return to my theses, this sampling of the rich variety of early Christian imagery for the church demonstrates the importance of the church in the experience and practice of early Christians.

---

64. *On Christ and Antichrist* 59.

65. Pseudo-Clement, *Letter of Clement to James* 14.

66. Peterson, "Das Schiff als Symbol der Kirche."

2

Attitudes to Schism
at the Council of Nicaea

THE COUNCIL OF NICAEA in AD 325 had to deal with disciplinary matters related to three schisms or heresies in addition to Arianism. The persons involved were the clergy among the followers of Meletius, Novatian, and Paul of Samosata.

The interpretation given in the standard history of the councils by Hefele and Leclercq[1] is that the fathers at Nicaea did not require a new ordination of Novatian and Meletian clergymen who returned to the Catholic Church. Their previous ordinations were valid but irregular. When this irregularity was corrected, the persons involved could then function in the clergy of the great Church. Later theory about the indelibility of ordination appears to have influenced unduly this interpretation.[2]

Let us look at the three main texts from the council. The fullest and least ambiguous is the synodal letter sent to the Egyptian and neighboring churches concerning the adherents of Meletius.

---

1. Hefele and Leclercq, *Histoire des conciles*, 1:576–87, 615–18. Translations of the canons are made from their text. See also Schroeder, *Disciplinary Decrees of the General Councils*; and Tanner and Albergio, eds., *Decrees of the Ecumenical Councils*.

2. Amann, "Réordinations," cols. 2390–92, sees some uncertainty in the thought of the fathers at Nicaea about the validity of the Novatian and Meletian ordinations, but rather than speak of a new ordination he says their clergy received a rite giving a guarantee of validity to their ordination. The later doctrine of the indelibility of ordination still influences an otherwise fine treatment of the sources.

> Since the synod was disposed to act kindly (for in strict justice he was worthy of no leniency), it was decreed that Meletius should remain in his own city and have no authority to make appointments [*procheirizesthai*][3] or to lay on hands [*cheirothetein*] or to appear in any city or village for this purpose, but should possess only the bare title of his rank [bishop]. Those who have been appointed [*katastathentas*] by him, after they have been confirmed by a more sacred ordination [*mystikōtera cheirotonia*], may on these conditions be fellowshipped and have their rank and officiate, but they shall be the inferiors of those enrolled [*exetazomenōn*] in each parish and church who have been appointed [*prokecheirismenōn*] by our most honourable colleague Alexander. These have no authority to make appointments [*procheirizesthai*] of persons pleasing to them or to propose names or to do anything without the permission of the bishop of the catholic and apostolic church serving under Alexander . . . If it should happen that any at that time in the church die, then those who have been recently received are to succeed to the office of the deceased, only if they appear worthy, and the people choose them, with the catholic bishop of Alexandria concurring in the election and ratifying it.[4]

The most frequently used word in the passage is *procheirizomai*. Instead of the older translation "nominate," I have rendered it "make appointments."[5] The idea of proposing names seems excluded by the word's usage alongside phrases literally meaning this.[6] The term might include designations of lower clergy whom a bishop selected directly, or it might mean the participation in or concurrence with an ordination by bishops or presbyters who did not directly engage in the laying on of hands.[7] Primary attention attaches to the use of the word *cheirothetein* ("to lay on hands"). There can be no doubt that the word means in this context "to lay on hands in ordination."[8]

---

3. Gelasius reads *Cheirotonein mēte cheirizein*.

4. The text with minor variants in wording is preserved in Socrates, *H.E.* I.9; Theodoret, *H.E.* I.ix.7ff; and Gelasius, *H.E.* II.33. My translation is made from Theodoret, ed. L. Parmentier and F. Schneidweiler in *GCS* (2nd ed.; Berlin 1954) 39–41.

5. Lampe, *A Patristic Greek Lexicon*, gives the meanings "put forward for office, appoint."

6. *hypoballein onomata* and *epilegesthai onomata*.

7. See Ferguson, "Eusebius and Ordination," 141ff.; see chap. 12 below.

8. Lampe cites more instances of this meaning than any other.

The key word for the thesis of this paper is *cheirotonia* ("ordination"). In requiring a more mystical (*mystikōtera*—shall we say "more sacramental"?) ordination, the council seems to speak clearly of its concept of ordination. Hefele takes *cheirotonia* here of benediction, which indeed he must in order to maintain his position. Such a singular use is wholly unparalleled in the early centuries and the interpretation is quite arbitrary. *Cheirotonia* here must mean "ordination," and the passage must mean that the Meletian clergy are to receive a new ordination. Note that before the former Meletian clergyman succeeded to a new charge in the catholic Church he must be elected by the people and have the approval of the patriarch of Alexandria, as would anyone else.

It is generally recognized that Nicaea accorded the same treatment to restored Novatians and to restored Meletians.[9] Since both groups were doctrinally orthodox and separated from the main Church on the grounds of moral rigorism, especially as regarded the reconciliation to the Church of apostates during persecution, a common policy was consistent. The decision on the Novatians is contained in canon 8.

> Concerning those who call themselves Cathari, if they [who are clerics] come over to the catholic and apostolic church, it is decreed by the holy and great synod that upon receiving a laying on of hands [*cheirothetoumenous*] they are to continue in the clergy . . . If, then, whether in villages or cities, all of the ordained [*cheirotonēthentes*] are found to be Cathari only, let them remain in the clergy and in the same rank in which they are found. But if some come over where there is a bishop or presbyter of the catholic church, it is evident that the bishop of the church has the rank of the episcopate; and the one named a bishop by those called Cathari has the honor of the presbytery, unless it seem fitting to the bishop to share with him the honor of his title. If this is not satisfactory, he shall provide for him a place as chorepiscopus or presbyter, in order that he may be seen to be of the clergy, and that there may not be two bishops in the city.

Commentators have differed over the significance of the "laying on of hands" in this text. Does the word mean "those who have previously received a laying on of hands in the Novatian sect"[10] or "those receiving a

9. Hefele and Leclercq, *Histoire des conciles*, 582; Bright, *Notes on the Canons of the First Four General Councils*, 26.

10. This was the view of Rufinus, the Greek commentators, and others—Hefele and Leclercq, *Histoire des conciles*, 583ff. I would suspect that Zonaras and Balsamon knew

laying on of hands on their return to the catholic Church"? The use of the present tense would favor the latter.[11] In either case the reference would be to a laying of hands on ecclesiastics, for it is only they who are in view. If the reference were to a Novatian imposition of hands, the ordination laying on of hands would be the obvious meaning. The council does use *cheirotonia*, ordination, for what Novatian clerics had received. If, however, we follow the Latin translators, then there is a question whether the laying on of hands pertained to the absolution of penitents, signifying their reconciliation to the fellowship of the Church,[12] or to a laying on of hands in ordination. Hefele and Leclercq rejected Gratian's interpretation requiring a reordination and chose the former interpretation, namely that Nicaea required a simple imposition of hands with the value of a benediction which restores the irregularity.[13]

William Bright's *Notes on the Canons of the First Four General Councils* nearly a century ago, although appearing to favor Hefele's view, gave the arguments in support of understanding the text as requiring a fresh ordination.[14] The *cheirothesia* family of words is not generally used of any laying on of hands other than that in ordination before the *Apostolic Constitutions*.[15] The earliest Greek writer to cite the canon, Theophilus of Alexandria at the end of the fourth century, understood the canon as enjoining a fresh ordination and substituted *cheirotonia* for *cheirothesia*.[16] This usage accords with that of the synodal letter about the Meletians.

Canon 19 about the followers of Paul of Samosata is conclusive that the Nicene bishops used *cheirothesia* for ordination.

> Concerning the Paulianists who have fled for refuge to the catholic church, it has been decreed that they must by all means

---

that the word meant ordination, but since reordination was no longer the practice in their time, they referred it to Novatian ordination.

11. Ibid. Hefele adds the point that the absence of the article and use of the pronoun with the participle favor this interpretation.

12. Coppens, *L'Imposition des mains*, chapter 5, for instances.

13. Hefele and Leclercq, *Histoire des conciles*, 583ff.

14. Bright, *Notes on the Canons of the First Four General Councils*, 25ff.

15. Turner, "*Cheirotonia, Cheirothesia, Epithesis Cheirōn*," 502. Eusebius, a participant at Nicaea, does not use the verb, but the one occurrence of the noun in his *Ecclesiastical History* refers to ordination (VI.xxiii.4).

16. "Since the great synod held at Nicaea decreed that the Novatians coming over to the church be ordained, do you ordain those who wish to come over to the church, if their life is upright and there is no objection," Theophilus, *Narratio de iis qui dicuntur Cathari*, PG 65 (1868) col. 446.

> be rebaptized. If any of them who in time past were found in
> the clergy and if they appear to be blameless and without re-
> proach, when they have been rebaptized, they are to be ordained
> [*cheirotoneisthōsan*] by the bishop of the catholic church. But if
> the examination finds them unfit, they are to be rejected. Like-
> wise in the case of their deaconesses and generally concerning
> those enrolled on the canon, the same policy shall be observed.
> We make mention of deaconesses enrolled on the list, since they
> do not have any laying on of hands [*cheirothesian*], that they arc
> numbered only among the laity.

Supposed difficulties have led to drastic solutions, such as removing the
last sentence as an interpolation made by someone embarrassed at the
possibility of deaconesses seemingly being counted in the clergy. This is
unnecessary, as is Hefele's suggestion, for which there is evidence, to read
"deacon" for the first occurrence of "deaconess." There is a "formal contradiction" with the end of the decree only if one understands kanōn as meaning "clergy." The canon or "roll" of the Church would have included any
special classes in the Church and benevolent cases as well as the clergy.[17]
The council is saying that the same procedure is to be followed in regard
to all the enrolled persons as is followed for the ordained. All may take
up the same position, if worthy, they had among the Paulianists, but they
have to go through the same process used in appointing the faithful to the
respective positions. *Cheirotonia* means ordination, as it does generally.
Cheirothesia is the laying on of hands in ordination. This act deaconcsses
do not receive,[18] hence they are technically "laity" although among the
enrolled persons of the Church. The council is at pains to specify the status
of deaconesses perhaps because of some special prominence among the
Paulianists.[19]

17. Canon 16 of Nicaea has only clergy in view, but Chalcedon, canon 2, illustrates
the broader meaning of *kanōn*. Cornelius's list of presbyters, deacons, subdeacons,
acolytes, exorcists, readers, doorkeepers, and widows (Eusebius, *H.E.* VI.xliii.II) would
constitute the "canon" of the church at Rome. Hippolytus, *Apostolic Tradition* I.x–xiv
takes up confessors, widows, readers, virgins, subdeacons, and those with the gift of
healing after the bishops, presbyters, and deacons. A similar explanation is given by
Schroeder, *Disciplinary Decrees of the General Councils*, 55–57.

18. *Apostolic Constitutions* VIII.xix–xx provides for a laying on of hands at the appointment of deaconesses. Cotsonis, "A Contribution to the Interpretation of the 19th
Canon of the First Ecumenical Council," takes the *cheirothesia* of benediction and not
the conferral of holy orders, but he does see the canon as implying that deaconesses
were canonically ordained like other members of the clergy. He explains the canon
as referring to some who took the habit at an early age and then were ordained later.

19. Eusebius, *H.E.* VII.xxx.10, 12ff. indicates something of the importance of

Since Paulianists were considered heretical in their view of the divine Trinity, their baptism in the triune name was not considered valid.[20] Since their baptism was not recognized, obviously their ordination was not. Silence about baptism in canon 8 implies that Novatians were not rebaptized.[21] If ordination was required of heretical Paulianist clergy, the same terminology must mean the same thing in the decisions relative to the schismatic Meletians and Novatians.

A look at the meaning of ordination in the fourth-century Church provides a further confirmation of the interpretation which has been given to these Nicene decisions. Ordination consisted of prayer and the laying on of hands. The act was understood as a blessing. The imposition of hands designated or marked out the person being ordained for divine favor which was invoked in the prayer. Laying on of hands in early Christian thought signified a blessing, and in ordination the prayer specified the blessing intended.[22] It was indeed the central feature and the imposition of hands was an accompaniment to the prayer.

A few passages will show the theological interpretation. "Blessed was he in being counted worthy to cover such a head with his hand and to bless so noble a soul with his voice" (*Life of Polycarp*, xi). Chrysostom defines the ordination as the prayer for God to bless: "[Luke] says not how, but simply that they were ordained by prayer; for this is the ordination. The hand of man is laid on, but God performs everything, and it is God's hand which touches the head of the one being ordained, if he is truly ordained."[23] Gregory of Nyssa in his sermon "On the Baptism of Christ" defines ordination as a change effected by benediction.[24] Jerome implies primacy for the prayer in his definition of the Greek word *cheirotonia*: "the ordination of the clergy which is accomplished not only at the verbal prayer but at the imposition of the hand (lest indeed in mockery someone be ordained ignorantly to the clergy by a secret prayer)."[25]

women in Paul's following.

20. Athanasius, *Orationes contra Arianos* II.xviii.41, 43.

21. Compare Arles, canon 8.

22. For a preliminary statement of the case see Ferguson, "Jewish and Christian Ordination," 15 (chap. 9 below). More fully developed in Ferguson "The Laying on of Hands" (chap. 13 below).

23. *Homilies xiv in Acts 6*, PG 60 (1862) col. 116. I have translated according to the punctuation that the Greek text seems to require.

24. *De baptismo Christi*, PG 46 (1863) col. 581d.

25. *In Isaiam* XVI.58, PL 24 (1865) col. 591.

Ordination thus was a particular kind of blessing. A new prayer for each ministry (deacon, presbyter, bishop) shows the specific nature of the ordination blessing. And the ordination was for service in a particular church.[26] The early Church expected a person to remain for life in the church where he was ordained. The frequent translations in the imperial Church called forth repeated protests in the canonical legislation against the practice, as already in Nicaea, canon 16.

It is not always clear whether a new ordination was involved in such translations. Since they often involved a promotion, such would be expected. But reordinations were performed where no promotion was involved. Apostolic Canons 68 decrees as follows:

> If any bishop, presbyter, or deacon receives a second ordination
> from any one, let him be deprived, and the person who ordained
> him, unless he can show that his former ordination was from
> the heretics; for those that are either baptized or ordained by
> such as these, can be neither Christians nor clergymen.

We may apply the rule, If somebody forbids it somebody is doing it. If there was a reordination in transferring a clergyman from one diocese to another, certainly there would have been in bringing him from a schismatic body to the catholic Church.

Hefele and Leclercq understood the Nicene fathers to use *cheirotonia* as equivalent to *cheirothesia*, meaning a benediction.[27] The situation is rather the reverse—*cheirothesia* supplied the meaning and content for ordination. The meaning of benediction is correct, but not in the weak or accommodative sense implied. There was not a "real" ordination earlier which now had to be regularized. *Cheirothesia* was used at Nicaea for the laying on of hands at ordination, because the meaning of ordination itself was a benediction for ministry. In view of this significance for the act, clearly a new act of ordination was required for reconciled schismatics before they could take up a ministry in the Church. This had nothing to do with any question of the "validity" of the former ordination. Such is a later and foreign concept to the terminology of Nicaea. Sacramental theology had not advanced as far about ordination as it had about baptism.

The readiness to accept schismatic clergymen into the clergy of the catholic Church was a realization that qualified leaders in the sect could be qualified leaders in the Church and that it was prudent in bringing such men back into the fellowship of the parent body to permit them

26. Chalcedon, canon 6.

27. Hefele and Leclercq, *Histoire des conciles*, 584, 617ff.

to continue in the honors to which they were accustomed. The council protected the rights of catholic clergy and the needs of good order. The council could not give schismatics a charge in the catholic Church without a new act of appointment to service. A simple reconciliation to the Church did not automatically guarantee one's ministry in the Church. There is no question of validity or non-validity of the previous appointment. Such questions were irrelevant, given the understanding of ordination which we have found in the fourth century, pre-Augustinian sources.

3

A Note on Irenaeus, *Adversus Haereses* IV.8.3

MARCEL RICHARD AND BERTRAND Hemmerdinger published in 1962 "Trois nouveaux fragments grecs de l'*Adversus Haereses* de Saint Irénée" (1962). It is appropriate that a tribute to M. Richard consider another passage from Irenaeus where the witnesses to his text give different readings.

The new edition of Books IV and V of *Adversus Haereses* under the supervision of Adelin Rousseau for Sources Chrétiennes in both the French translation and the Greek retroversion of IV.8.3 accepts the reading πᾶς βασιλευς δίκαιος ἱερατικὴν ἔχει ταξίν ("Every righteous king has the priestly order").[1] This is the reading of Johannes Damascenus, *Sacra Parallela* II.ii. Pseudo-Antonius Melissa, *Loci Communes* II.i, is not an independent witness, because the source of his book two is a recension of the *Sacra Parallela*.[2] This reading now has the significant support of the Armenian version. On the other hand, the Latin manuscript tradition reads *omnes enim justi sacerdotalem habent ordinem* ("All the righteous have the priestly order").

Transcriptional probability could be argued either way: Someone in the West could have had good reason for dropping a reference to the

---

1. I am following Sources Chrétiennes, vols. 100 and 152, 1965 and 1969, for the text and notes on readings. The passage cited is from vol. 100, p. 472.

2. Richard, "Florileges spirituels grecs."

priestly rank of kings, and someone in the East could have had good reason for adding such a reference.[3] The combination of the patristic and Armenian traditions is strong support for the Sources Chrétiennes reading. Nevertheless, the best witness to Irenaeus' text is Irenaeus himself, and to his argument we turn.

Irenaeus is arguing against Marcion that Abraham is included in the salvation of Christ, for the church is the seed of Abraham and receives the inheritance promised to him (IV.8.1). Furthermore, "Jesus' actions fulfilled and did not destroy the law, for in his healings and death he performed the work of the high priest" (IV.8.2). Jesus and his disciples did not break the law when they plucked the grain on the sabbath day. Irenaeus quotes Jesus' defense of his disciples on the basis of David's conduct in 1 Sam 21:1–6,[4] with the added comment, "justifying his disciples by the words of the Law and showing that it was lawful for the priests to act freely" (cf. Matt 12:5, "Or have you not read in the law how on the sabbath the priests in the temple profane the sabbath, and are guiltless?"). Then comes the disputed statement, "For David was recognized by God as a priest, although Saul was persecuting him, for every righteous (king) has the priestly order." David at the time was not the king, but he had been anointed. Irenaeus then extends the principle ("moreover") or gives a specific application to it ("indeed") by adding, "And all the apostles[5] of the Lord are priests." Irenaeus shows that statements about the Levites in the Old Testament were fulfilled in the conduct of Jesus' disciples in order to support the claim that "the disciples have the levitical inheritance" and so in their work in the Lord's temple they profane the sabbath but are blameless (IV.8.3).

According to Irenaeus' viewpoint David was regarded as a priest more because he was righteous than because he was a king. This may be seen from the equation which Irenaeus makes between disciples, priests, and the righteous in a passage which makes explicit reference to the one under study, V.34.3.[6] Irenaeus is arguing in Book V that all Christians can expect

---

3. For a classical parallel, note Isocrates 2.6, "Kingship, like priesthood, belongs to every man."

4. Irenaeus' quotation most nearly accords with Luke 6:3, 4 of the Synoptic sources, but his added comment shows that he has Matt 12:1–7 in mind.

5. The Armenian reads "disciples," and in view of Irenaeus' general usage (see the parallel cited below) he probably wrote μαθηταί. On the other hand, the context shows that Irenaeus had the apostles specifically in mind, so the Latin has correctly interpreted Irenaeus' thought.

6 The two passages have been brought together in studies of Irenaeus' thought, but without drawing conclusions from the latter about the reading of the former. Lawson, *The Biblical Theology of Saint Irenaeus*, 255. Cf. Dabin, *Le Sacerdoce Royal des Fidèles*,

a bodily resurrection and an enjoyment of a materialistic kingdom. There will be a "resurrection of the righteous" when the blessings announced to Israel are obtained by Christians because "we have shown a little above [V.32, but cf. also IV.8.1] that the seed of Abraham is the church" (V.34.1). The whole creation will experience a vast increase in productivity and according to the words of Dan 7:27, "the kingdom . . . is given to the saints of the Most High" (V.34.2). "These promises were announced not only to the prophets and fathers, but to the churches from among the Gentiles united with them." After quoting Jer 31:10–14 in which God promised to "magnify and feast the souls of the priesthood, the sons of Levi," Irenaeus makes a significant statement for this study: "Now we have shown in the preceding book that all the disciples of the Lord are Levites and priests who profane the sabbath in the temple but are without blame. Such promises clearly show the banquet on the creation in the kingdom of the righteous which God has promised to serve" (V.34.3).

Irenaeus makes reference back to the latter part of IV.8.3 summarized above. He refers specifically to the statement that "all the disciples (apostles) are priests" but proceeds to identify them with the righteous (who possess the kingdom). Here the meaning of disciples clearly includes all Christians, the church as the seed of Abraham. The thought of the kingship of the righteous is a further pointer to the earlier passage. Irenaeus cites Isa 32:1, "Behold a righteous king shall rule" in reference to Christ (V.34.4). Still his main attention is on the righteous persons who inherit the kingdom. "The righteous shall rule" (V.33.3). The association of the righteous with kingship and the disciples with priesthood suggests the linking of kingship and priesthood in 1 Pet 2:9 and Rev 1:6, but Irenaeus does not quote these passages.

These associations indicate that Irenaeus himself saw his emphasis in IV.8.3 to be on the priesthood of the righteous and not on the priesthood of the king. This conclusion is consistent with Irenaeus' view of the priestly function of the whole church. He describes prayer as the incense offered by the whole church to God: "Since therefore the name of the Son belongs to the Father and since the church sacrifices to God Almighty through Jesus Christ, he has well said, 'And in, every place incense and a pure sacrifice is offered in my name' [Mal 1:11]. Now John says in the Apocalypse [5:8] that incense offerings are the prayers of the saints" (IV.17.6). Of similar import is IV.18.6: "Thus he wills that we [the church] offer our gift at

---

511–12, for the acceptance of the Latin on the basis that David was given the privileges of a priest because he was righteous.

the altar frequently and without ceasing. There is, therefore, an altar in heaven, for our prayers and oblations are offered in that direction."

Within the same context and in a similar way Irenaeus treats the eucharist as an oblation of first fruits (bread and wine) offered by the whole church. Representative statements are the following: "This oblation the church has received from the apostles and offers to God throughout the whole world" (IV.17.6). "Therefore, the oblation of the church, which the Lord instructed to be offered throughout the whole world, is accounted by God a pure sacrifice and is acceptable to him" (IV.18.1). "Since, then, the church makes her offering with sincerity, her gift is rightly considered a pure sacrifice by God" and "The church alone offers this pure oblation to the Creator, offering to him with thanksgiving the things of his own creation" (IV.18.4). There must be some significance in the fact that Irenaeus speaks so often of the eucharist as the oblation of the church and not of a part of it. The church certainly stands in contrast to heretical sects, but Irenaeus' language is also in accord with a common view which saw the eucharistic sacrifice as the action of the whole Christian community.[7]

The sacrificial worship of prayer and eucharist by the church may be related to the concept of Christians as a priestly people. Although Irenaeus does not work it out, he apparently would regard the basis of the priesthood of Christians to be the anointing of the Holy Spirit received in baptism. The anointing of Christ is said by him to be the Holy Spirit. The following is his exposition of Ps 45:6, 6: "For the Son, as being God, receives from the Father, that is, from God, the throne of the everlasting kingdom, and the oil of anointing above His fellows. The oil of anointing is the Spirit, wherewith He has been anointed; and His fellows are prophets and righteous men and apostles, and all who receive the fellowship of His kingdom, that is to say, His disciples" (*Demonstration* 47).[8] This Holy Spirit becomes the possession of all Christians at baptism: "For such is the state of those who have believed, since in them continually abides the Holy Spirit, who was given by Him in baptism, and is retained by the receiver, if he walks in truth and holiness and righteousness and patient endurance" (*Demonstration* 42). One must notice in these passages about anointing the recurrence of the association of disciples, the righteous, and kingdom.

7. Congar, *Jalons pour une théologie du laïcat*, 277–79. Cf. p. 180 for the priesthood of the laity connected with baptism.

8. This and the following passage are quoted from the translation by Robinson, ed., (St. Irenaeus) *The Demonstration of the Apostolic Preaching*.

Even if Irenaeus wrote "king" in IV.8.3, I conclude that the Latin version has preserved the correct interpretation of the meaning of Irenaeus' words—all the righteous belong to the priesthood.

4

Ordination in the Ancient Church*

I: Greek, Roman, and Jewish Backgrounds

IN THIS STUDY ATTENTION will be given to the modes of selection and installation to office among the Romans, Greeks, and Jews. Later a detailed examination of the action and significance of ordination in the fourth century will be presented. Information concerning ordination will then be traced backwards so that the lines of evidence from the background and the foreground will be made to converge upon the New Testament. After an elucidation of the New Testament materials bearing on the subject the main themes of the study will be summarized and their relevance for today noted.

THE GRECO-ROMAN BACKGROUND

Roman Magistrates

The features of selection and installation of important magistrates at Rome in the last century of the Republic were determinative for the provincial towns established by Rome.[1]

---

1. We follow the definitive study of Mommsen, *Römisches Staatsrecht*, 1:578ff. The practices at Rome must be reconstructed from scattered literary references. The situation in the provinces, both confirming and clarifying procedures at Rome, is exemplified by the civil laws of Malaca in Spain at the end of the first century, *CIL* II, nos.

The chief magistrates were elected by the citizens; the voting was by the divisions of the citizenry known as centuries, with a majority in a century determining the vote of that century and a majority of the centuries determining the will of the assembly.[2] Entrance into office was conditioned on the *designatio,* an appointment to the office made by the presiding consul in the form of a *renuntiatio,* a proclamation of the outcome of the Election. Although bound by the outcome of the Election, he had great powers in accepting or rejecting candidates according to their qualifications. Extraordinary officers and lesser magistrates were appointed by a simple Naming to the function by the magistrate entitled to do so.

The entrance day of the magistrate was January I, and the office was passed to the person on the stated day. Although he was a private person up to the entrance day, the *designatus* was treated already as an officer, for declining the office had the same legal status as abdication.[3] The selection was the decisive thing.

There followed on the gaining of the office a two-fold confirmatory act. A magistrate could legally take office only if the gods were consulted. Hence, the new consul, for example, took the *auspices* on the morning of his first day in office. The purpose was to receive a favorable sign for the assumption of the office, but the very performance of the Auspication was an indication that the person had assumed office. Secondly, the assembly passed the *lex curiata de imperio* by which the community bound itself to obey the authority of the new officer within his competence. The *lex curiata* did not bestow the authority but rather set forth the same.[4]

A great amount of ceremony and formality marked the entrance (*inire*) into office. The office was not by them obtained, but rather was by them for the first time exercised, Usurpation (*usurpatio*) in the legal sense. After the first Auspication of the new consul, he put on the official dress and accompanied by lictors and friends went in solemn procession to the Capitol where he was seated in the curial chair (Solemn Seating). There he vowed to Jupiter that he had defended the state and offered sacrifice (Divine Invocation). The new consul then held a session of the Senate. Praetors, aediles, and quaestors similarly showed their entrance into

1963, 1964.

    2. See the article on "Voting," in *Oxford Classical Dictionary* (1949) 954.

    3. Mommsen, *Römisches Staatsrecht,* 1:590–91.

    4. Ibid., 590, 609. Here as elsewhere references to the original sources together with a translation of some of the more important may be found in the thesis.

office when they took their seat and first performed the function of office.[5] Within five days after assuming office the new magistrate had to present an Oath that he would observe the laws. The prevalence of the oath is seen in the fact that one was taken by the candidate when he announced his candidacy, when the proclamation of his election was made, and when he surrendered the office.[6]

Under the principate the power of the Emperor essentially limited the election-right even where the forms of Election were maintained. By the third century the manner in which emperors were in fact made became virtually a constitutional process. Following an Acclamation by the troops there was a proclamation and an Enthronement.[7]

In imperial times Porrection was known in appointment to office. A sword was given to the prefect to indicate his appointment.[8]

The following features are prominent in the appointment of the important civil officials in the Roman world: Election by the qualified voters with the important role played by the official presiding; the Invocation of the gods on the day of assuming office; the installation by Usurpation; the prevalence of Oath-taking; and the steady movement toward autocracy.

Roman Priesthoods

In the early Republican period the filling of all priestly colleges and sodalities was by Co-option.[9] However, certain lesser priests and religious functionaries were designated by the *Pontifex Maximus*. The latter was an elected official, chosen by a special assembly of seventeen of the tribes after a Nomination from their own number by the principal priests (*pontifices*). Later the same elective act by part of the tribes was inserted between Nomination and Co-option of the members of the four great priestly colleges. Nominations to the assembly convened for sacerdotal business were made by the respective colleges, which after the Election went through the form of Co-option. The Emperor's powers finally ended the independence of the priestly colleges although the old forms of Co-option remained.

---

5. Ibid., 615ff.

6. Ibid., 619–22. Steinwenter, "Ius iurandum," 1256–57.

7. Instinsky, *Bischofsstuhl und Kaiserthron*, 32ff.

8. Dio Cassius lxviiii.16.

9. For the Roman priesthoods, see Laing, "Priest, Priesthood (Roman)." The references on each class of the priestly personnel may be found in Wissowa, *Religion und Kultus der Römer*, 487.

Whether chosen by the members of a college, elected first by an assembly of the people, or designated by the *pontifex maximus,* the new priest had to be installed in his sacred function. The formal completion of Co-option came when the president of the college or sodality "called to sacred things" (*ad sacra vocabat*) the newly designated member, a constitutive Naming.[10]

Certain religious functionaries underwent an *inauguratio* (an Inauguration in the limited sense). The ceremony of Inauguration meant the declaration of the assent of the deity to the accomplished Election or Designation. In significance the *inauguratio* was the same as a magistrate's first taking of the auspices, the only difference being that in the latter case the official performed the function himself and in the former it was done for him by an augur. There is no evidence that *inauguratio,* or any other rite performed on the new priest, involved a change of state.[11]

The distinctive feature provided by the Roman priesthoods was their practice of Co-option.

Roman Associations

The officers of the Roman clubs were elected in an ordinary meeting by the vote of the members. The terms of office, as for civil officials, was customarily for one year, and re-election was permitted. The only ceremony attested for the induction into office is Oath-taking.[12]

Greek Magistrates

The Athenian constitution of the fourth century BC, for which the most evidence is available, may be taken as representative of Greek democracy.[13]

All important magistrates were selected either by Lot-taking (*klerosis*) or by Election (*cheirotonia*). The Lot was used for those positions the management of which every citizen possessed the ability, and the Lot-taking

10. Toutain, "Sacerdos. Rome," 945.

11. Wissowa, *Religion and Kultus der Römer,* 490. Cf. Nock, "Intrare sub Iugum," 108.

12. Liebenam, *Zur Geschichte und Organisation des Römischen Vereinswesens,* 199, 202.

13. Aristotle's *Constitution of Athens,* in the edition of Sandys, is the principal original source. Important studies include: Busolt, *Griechische Staatskunde;* and for this article, Siotis, "Die klassische und die christliche Cheirontonie."

emphasized that aspect of democracy which provides every one with the right to be chosen. *Cheirotonia* was voting by a show of hands, and the Election emphasized the right of every citizen to decide who was qualified to serve in certain specialized tasks.

The Election of officials occurred in an ordinary meeting of the Assembly. The meeting would open with prayer and sacrifice. The decision of the Council to place the Election on the agenda of the meeting of the Assembly would be presented. The supervision of the Election was in the hands of the nine chairmen (*proedroi*) for the day. The list of candidates was supplied either by the Nomination of friends or by announcement. There might be a preliminary vote to decide to proceed with the Election. At the appropriate time the Herald called for a show of hands for the respective candidates. The votes were counted and the report of the results was given and these results were ratified as a legal vote. Both were the assignment of the nine *proedroi*.

A distinctive feature of entrance into office in Athens was the Formal Scrutiny (*dokimasia*) which every official had to undergo at first of the civil year. The Scrutiny according to the law covered only the formal qualifications for the office, but in practice must have often covered the whole private and public life of the candidate. The Scrutiny was conducted by the presiding officer of the Assembly or of the law-court.

Next came the Oath-taking (*horkos*) by which the newly selected magistrate bound himself to rule according to the laws and to the best of his ability.[14]

Upon entrance into office Entrance-sacrifices were brought.[15] The details of the performance are obscure, but the idea seems to have been that one did not begin an important task without recourse to the gods, Divine Invocation.[16]

Greece differed from Rome in the extensive use of the Lot in filling magistracies. When Election was performed in Greece, the basic voting unit was the individual, and not a group. The Formal Scrutiny had a distinctive role in the Greek appointive process. Although Greece too had its sacrificial Invocation of the gods and Oath-taking, the ceremonies lack the elaboration and legal precision characteristic of Rome.

14. The Scrutiny and the Oath are described by Aristotle, *Ath. Pol.* 55.

15. Busolt, *Griechische Staatskunde*, 517, 518. The clearest statement comes from Demosthenes XIX.190.

16. Hild, in *DAGR*, 2:504.

Greek Priesthoods

In reference to the method of their selection Greek priesthoods may be placed in three categories: those following the civil analogy and filled by Election or Lot-taking, those closely connected with a given family and acquired by Inheritance, and those purchased.[17]

The ordinary civic priests were chosen by Election or by Lot-taking and served for one year. The use of lots was more common and could be interpreted as permitting the deity to choose his own minister.[18] The methods of voting and taking lots could be combined the field being narrowed by one means and the actual choice made by the other.[19]

Any number of circumstances may have brought a given family into especially close relationship with a given deity so that the service of that deity was reserved to members of the family; this was true even of civic cults. The rule of succession varied from family to family.

During the Hellenistic period in Asia Minor and the Islands there was a strong development of the practice of the purchase of priesthoods.[20] Purchase was sometimes combined with other methods of selection. The vendor was always the State.

The entrance into the functions of office by a newly chosen priest would be marked in some way with a certain ceremony, but "in classical antiquity most priesthoods did not, it seems, involve any solemn ordination or investiture."[21] Some Attic inscriptions mention Entrance-sacrifices. Priests of certain cults were also admitted by a form of initiation. At such a time the priest may have assumed any insignia of his office. The very paucity of the evidence is perhaps an indication that nothing unusual attached to the assumption of a priestly position in Greek religion.

---

17. Woodhouse, "Priest, Priesthood (Greek)," 305; Legrand, "Sacerdos. Grece," 938; Stengel, *Die griechischen Kultusaltertümer*, 44–46.

18. "As to the priests, we shall entrust it to the god himself to ensure his own good pleasure, by committing their appointment to the divine chance of the lot." Plato, *Laws* 759C.

19. A good example is supplied by Cicero, *Against Verres* ii.162. The comparison to Acts 1 is striking. The people narrowed the field by passing on the qualifications and then the divine choice was expressed through the Lot.

20. Nilsson, *Geschichte der griechischen Religion*, 2:74, 77ff. Sokolowski, "Partnership in the Lease of Cults in Greek Antiquity."

21. Nock, "Intrare sub Iugum."

Greek Associations

A special mode of appointment met with in the private associations of the Greeks is the Designation of an official by another, but this usually occurred only in the appointment of a lesser functionary by a higher officer. More common were appointments by Lot or by Election.[22] "The statutes of Greek guilds in Egypt during the imperial period open with an account of the Election of a president whose term was to run for a single year."[23] (Apparently Roman imperialism had not submerged local democratic traditions.) About the manner of Election by the members little information occurs, but the indications are that it was commonly by a show of hands.[24]

The installation of officers is spoken of in wholly general phrases in the overwhelming majority of cases. An Oath was taken in Attic colleges at the entrance into the association or into one of its offices. Sacrifices accompanied the entrance into office in some cases, as they did the laying down of office and all other important occasions.[25] The Oath-taking and Entrance-sacrifices are features that other phases of Greek life would lead us to expect, but the evidence is not sufficient to permit a generalization.

THE JEWISH BACKGROUND

Priests

The account of the installation of Aaron and his sons to the priesthood in Exodus 29 and Leviticus 8 gives the fullest description of installation to the priestly office. The seven-day ceremony, in the presence of the people, included the following elements: ceremonial washing, Investiture with the garments of the priesthood, Chrismation, and the performance of certain sacrifices which were accompanied by the placing of blood on the right ear, thumb, and the great toe and by the sprinkling of blood and oil on the person and garments of the new priest. There are several indications that the Investiture and the Chrismation were the basic elements in the ceremony (Exod 29:9c, 29; 40:14–15; Num 20:26–28).

---

22. Poland, *Geschichte des Griechischen Vereinswesens*, 416–17. A good introduction to the Greek associations in English is found in Tod, *Sidelights on Greek History*, chap. 3.

23. Boak, "The Organization of Guilds in Greco-Roman Egypt," 213.

24. Poland, *Geschichte des griechischen Vereinswesens*, 416–17.

25. Ibid., 253, 418, 499.

One set of passages suggests that all priests were anointed, whereas another set implies that Chrismation was limited to the high priest. That all priests received the oil is indicated by Exod 28:40–41; 30:30; 40:14–15 (but, do the latter two passages refer to the sons of Aaron as successors in the high priesthood?); Lev 7:36; 10:7; and Num 3:3. Nevertheless, the term the "anointed priest" seems to be a special term for the high priest (but this interpretation is not necessarily demanded in Leviticus 4), and anointing is given as the mark of Aaron's successor in Lev 6:22.[26] Apparently all priests could be spoken of as "anointed," but the "anointed priest" par excellence was the high priest. The account of the consecration of Aaron and his sons in Exodus 29 and Leviticus 8 does in fact make a distinction in the manner of the application of the oil. It is only sprinkled on Aaron's sons (and also on Aaron himself), whereas it is poured on Aaron's head (cf. Lev 21:10; Ps 133:2).

Several Pentateuchal statements indicate that Chrismation was to be used in the appointment of each new priest (Exod 29:29–30; 40:14–15). The virtual silence of sources outside the Old Testament leaves the question of what ceremony if any was in use in later times uncertain. Furthermore, it would appear that in the latter days of the Temple the high priest was no longer (or not always) anointed, for the Mishnah knows of high priests introduced to their office through the ceremony of Investiture.[27] The continuation of Chrismation into Hellenistic times is indicated by Dan 9:26 and 2 Macc 1:10. The Hasmonaean priest-kings, precisely because of the question of their legitimacy, would hardly have omitted the rite. Rather any abolition of Chrismation would have come in Herodian-Roman times.[28]

Christianity's break with the priestly traditions of the Old Testament is well symbolized by the absence of Chrismation in ordination until well into the Middle ages.[29]

26. For an analysis of the problem see Baudissin, "Priests and Levites," 83.

27. Such is the understanding of *Horajoth* 3:4 by Schürer, *Geschichte des Jüdischen Volkes*, 2:284. For the Mishnah, the English translation of Danby, *The Mishnah*, has been used. Only Investiture and Inaugural Usurpation in the installation of a new high priest are discussed in *b. Yoma* 12a, b. [Unless otherwise stated, references to the Babylonian Talmud are based on the edition of Epstein.] Josephus, *Ant.* xx.i, would indicate that Investiture was constitutive in making the high priest.

28. So Schürer, *Geschichte des Jüdischen Volkes*.

29. Ellard, *Ordination Anointings in the Western Church before 1000 A.D.*, 7–13, 104, finds the first evidence in the eighth century. At baptism there was a Chrismation at an early period, and Tertullian connects *this* ceremony with admission to the priesthood (*de Bapt.* 7).

The accounts of Exodus 29 and Leviticus 8 use words from the root *male'* ("to fill" or "to appoint") in reference to the installation of Aaron and his sons. The full form of the expression, "to fill the Hand," (Judg 17:5, 12), seems to have been the literal terminology for the installation of a priest. What was the hand filled with? The most attractive explanation, based on the "fill offering" of the Exodus and Leviticus texts, is that there was a handing over of sacrificial portions (Porrection) to the new priest. Consecration was meant thus to express that the priest was empowered to lay these pieces upon the altar, or, as the case may be, to take them for himself from the sacrifice as perquisites.[30] Leviticus 8:27 would lend support to this view. In most Old Testament passages, however, the word has lost any specific sense and means only "appoint."

Kings

Some data on the installation of kings is preserved in the stories of Saul and David in the books of Samuel. First, Saul was anointed privately by Samuel as an expression of the divine choice (1 Sam 10:1). The public selection took place by Lot in an assembly of the people (1 Sam 10:20–21). David, also, was designated to the kingship by Chrismation, and in this case the act was connected with the coming of the Spirit upon him (1 Sam 16:13–14). Chrismation is mentioned in later cases of disputed succession.

Coronation is mentioned (2 Kgs 11:12), but Chrismation seems to have been the rite with comparable significance to the coronations of pagan kings.

Prophets

By the nature of the prophetic office a regular mode of appointment would not be expected. As endowed with the Spirit of God, prophets could be spoken of as "anointed," but there is some question whether this was ever literally done.[31] In the Elijah–Elisha stories the mantle of the master was passed on to his successor (1 Kgs 19:19; 2 Kgs 2:6–15).[32]

---

30. Baudissin, "Priests and Levites," 70.

31. In 1 Kgs 19:16 Elijah is told to anoint Elisha, but no record is preserved of his doing so. Psalm 105:15 has reference to the Patriarchs but may imply an anointing of prophets (but with the Holy Spirit?). Isaiah 61:1 is metaphorical.

32. In *The Ascension of Isaiah*, according to the text adopted in the edition of Charles, *Apocrypha and Pseudepigrapha*, 43, there is reference to imposition of hands

Elders, Judges, and Rabbis—Old Testament Precedents

Gaster, in speaking of Jewish ordination, has observed that behind this institution lies a chapter of Jewish history which has not yet been elucidated—the appointment of judges.[33] The Old Testament passages speaking of the appointment of "judges and officers" in the land[34] give no indication of a mode of installation. The same applies to the elders, whose status appears to go back to the early tribal days of the Hebrews. The selection of seventy out of the elders to assist Moses is related in Num 11:16ff., a number which apparently was older in usage (Exod 24:1). The Sanhedrin of New Testament times was regarded as patterned on the institution of the seventy elders around Moses.[35]

The judges and the elders of Israel contributed to the picture of the rabbis in normative Judaism. The absence of a method of ordination in the texts relating to these people was supplied from the story of the appointment of Joshua in Num 27:15ff.[36] Deuteronomy 34:9 seems to look back to this incident, but the point immediately leaps to view that in Numbers Moses imposes hands on Joshua because he is a man "in whom is spirit" whereas in Deuteronomy Joshua has the "spirit of wisdom" because Moses has imposed his hands on him. Jewish commentators have seen no incongruity in the passages and have taken the "spirit of wisdom" (i.e. wisdom) as an added gift distinct from the "spirit" Joshua already possessed.[37]

on prophets: "And they [forty prophets] had come to salute him and to hear his words. And that he might place his hands upon them, and that they might prophesy and that he might hear their prophecy" (6:4–5). Charles ascribes this passage to a first-century Christian work. The significance of the act seems to be a benediction; cf. Coppens, *L'imposition des mains*, 3.

33. Gaster, "Ordination (Jewish)," 552.

34. Deut 16:18–20; 17:9; Exod 18:13ff.; 1 Chr 23:4; 26:29; 2 Chr 19:5–7.

35. *m. Sanhedrin* 1:6. There is no possibility of the two bodies possessing historical continuity (but local elders did have judicial functions—Deut 21:18–23). The Chronicler notes in the time of Jehoshaphat the appointment of a council of Levites, priests, and heads of families in Jerusalem to decide disputed cases (2 Chr 19:8ff.). It should be noted that the Mishnah passage speaks of the lesser councils of twenty-three elders in other cities, besides the great council in Jerusalem.

36. As the appointment of Joshua and of the seventy elders served as precedents in Judaism, so the appointment of Joshua and the consecration of the Levites (Numbers 8) are echoed in Acts 6 and 13. Daube, *New Testament and Rabbinic Judaism*, 237, 239. Farrer's chapter on the "Ministry in the New Testament" develops the analogies, but hardly establishes his theories from them.

37. Cf. Newman, *Semikhah*, 3. The one exception is the *Midrash Rabbah* to Num 15:25 (see edition of Freedman and Simon), which quotes the two passages side by side and seems to identify the "spirit of wisdom" with the "honor" of Moses and with

Coinciding with this view is the added consideration that the "because" in Deut 34:9 may be regarded as stating the evidence for and not the means of Joshua's wisdom.

The central feature of the Moses–Joshua episode is the Imposition of hands. The word used for the action of Moses is *samakh,* "to lean (one's hands) upon somebody or something." This word is to be distinguished from *śim,* and *shith,* "to place (one's hands)," which are the words used where a benediction is concerned (as notably in Gen 48:14ff.). The Septuagint has translated both *samakh* and *śim* by *epitithenai* (used for all types of Impositions of hands in the New Testament also) and *shith* by *epiballein.*[38] The placing of one's hands on another in benediction was accompanied by the spoken word usually in the form of prayer.[39] *Samakh* was a different act, meaning to lean so as to exert pressure.[40]

Samakh is used of witnesses laying their hands on the blasphemer who is to be stoned (Lev 24:14; cf. Susannah 34), of the person who brings an animal for sacrifice leaning upon it (Leviticus passim), and of the people consecrating the Levites (Num 8:10).

Although not significant in Jewish ordination, the consecration of the Levites was important as a precedent in early Christianity. Since the Levites replaced the first-born, the narrative speaks of their setting apart in sacrificial terms. All of the Israelites (or the elders as representatives?) laid hands on the Levites. Since this was the exclusion of a whole tribe, it was a non-repeatable act.

Efforts to find a common significance behind these usages of the act have not been notably successful. Elderenbosch has emphasized the ideas of solidarity and community, the giving of oneself so as to establish an identity, in the imposition of hands in the Old Testament.[41] This approach sounds good, but on application to the specific instances suffers the limitation of not being able to make a contribution to their understanding except in generalities. The interpretation in terms of "transference" has the

---

the "spirit" placed on the elders in Numbers 11.

38. Daube, *The New Testament and Rabbinic Judaism,* 224–29.

39. Lohse, *Die Ordination,* 16.

40. Cf. Amos 5:19. This meaning lay at the root of a Rabbinic controversy about whether an animal could be brought for sacrifice on a Sabbath or a festival, since work was invoived (*b. Hagigah* 16b). Although the Rabbis preserved the tradition of the action, it is to be noted that in the discussion the exertion of pressure was no longer derived from the meaning of *samakh.*

41. Elderenbosch, *De Oplegging der Handen,* chapter 3.

same defect.[42] It is easy to set up a general category, but a generalization does not aid in interpreting specific passages from which the generalization is drawn. If such diverse qualities as one's sins and one's gratitude could be transferred to the sin and peace offerings respectively, the act was hardly unambiguous. Moreover, there was no obvious transfer in the dedication of the Levites. Daube concludes that by pressing upon a person or animal one poured his personality into him or it, making a substitute.[43] But the case of the witnesses does not fit this frame of thinking, nor does the offering of a sacrifice. If the animal was a substitute, it represented the offerer in only one aspect (his sins or his feeling of gratitude); therefore, the distinction with *śim* breaks down, for this word is said by Daube to indicate the transference of something other than or less than the whole personality.

Lohse is probably right in concluding that there is no unified explanation for the Old Testament impositions of hands.[44] Indeed there is no necessity that there should be. Perhaps originally the act had a common root, but it could very easily acquire various connotations in different contexts. Furthermore, there is no basis for Behm's contention that a gesture must be unambiguous and have a definite meaning in a religion.[45] The history of religions is replete with actions that continue with a changed significance, or indeed with no significance save the sacredness which age imparts.

There is some confusion whether one or both hands were ordinarily employed in the rite. In the case of sacrificial animals where the subject is singular the singular "hand" is always used except in Lev 16:21 (where the consonantal text is singular but the context demands the plural). The rabbis, however, always spoke of the action in the plural, "hands." The evidence is more confused where persons are concerned. In Numbers 27 God tells Moses to impose his "hand" on Joshua; Moses is said to have imposed his "hands" on him. In the New Testament the plural is used in the great majority of cases, even of the action of one person. It would seem that no distinction was made, and in later times the practice gravitated toward the use of both hands.[46]

42. E.g., Behm, *Die Handauflegung im Urchristentum*, 139.

43. Daube, *The New Testament and Rabbinic Judaism*, 226–27.

44. Lohse, *Die Ordination*, 25.

45. Behm, *Die Handauflegung im Urchristentum*, 135.

46. Philo, contrary to Old Testament usage, in speaking of a person's sacrifices says that he lays on "hands" (*Spec. Leg.* i.203). The Septuagint, although generally following the number of Hebrew, sometimes changes the singular to the plural, as it does in Lev

Elders and Rabbis—the Rabbinic Literature

The Babylonian Talmud uses words from the *samakh* root for ordination, whereas the Palestinian Talmud uses *minnuy,* a general word for any kind of installation into an office. We are warranted in taking both terms as having the same meaning.[47] Lohse suggests that because *semikah* can have more than one usage *semikuth* came to be used exclusively for ordination,[48] but this is not certain. *Semikuth* is brought into conjunction with the *semikah zekenim* in three passages. Although Strack-Billerbeck take the latter to refer to "ordination to be elders,"[49] it seems better to take the phrase as equivalent to the imposition of the elders' hands in connection with a sacrifice for the sins of the community (Lev 4:15).[50]

The halakic midrash to Numbers understands the installation of Joshua as an example of Rabbinic ordination:

> God said to Moses: Give Joshua an interpreter (i.e. make Joshua a lecturing teacher at whose side an interpreter stands), so that he questions, and lectures, and makes decisions as long as you still live; if you depart from the world, the Israelites may not say: During the life of his teacher (Moses) he gave no decisions, and now he does. Moses had Joshua to stand up from the ground (on which he had sat before him up to that time as his student) and he set him before himself on the seat (as enjoying equal privileges) . . .[51]

A passage from the Palestinian Talmud describing the changes in the ordaining authority provides a good framework for the history of Jewish ordination during the early centuries of the Christian era:

> Originally, every one (*i.e.* every teacher) ordained his own pupils, thus R. Johanan b. Zakkai ordained R. Eliezer and R.

3:2, 8, 13. The plural is the common form in Greek Christian writers, but the singular is more often utilized by Latin writes (who generally show considerable indebtedness to the literal text of the Old Testament). See the references in Galtier, "Imposition des mains," 1305.

47. Strack and Billerbeck, *Kommentar zum Neuen Testament,* 2:648.

48. Lohse, *Die Ordination,* 28–29.

49. Strack and Billerbeck, *Kommentar zum Neuen Testament,* 2:653.

50. So Lohse, *Die Ordination,* 28; and Newman, *Semikhah,* 3–4. With the precedent of the biblical text and the Mishnah (*Sanhedrin* 1:3) before them it does not seem possible that the Talmudists reversed the usage.

51. *Sifre Numbers* 27:18, 20 from the quotation in Strack and Billerbeck, *Kommentar zum Neuen Testament,* 2:647–48.

Joshua, R. Joshua ordained R. Akiba, R. Akiba ordained R. Meir and R. Simeon. They were anxious to honor this house (the house of the Nasi) and declared that if the Beth Din ordained without the approval of the Nasi the ordination was not valid, but if a Nasi ordained without the knowledge of the Beth Din the Semikah was valid; then again they made a regulation that ordination should be performed with the mutual approval of the Beth Din and the Nasi.[52]

With the mention of R. Johanan b. Zakkai (d. about A.D. 80) this passage gives the first case of ordination in which names are recorded. The Babylonian Talmud preserves a story of a scholar ordaining his students during the war under Hadrian.[53]

The Palestinian Talmud is probably right in saying that the change from an individual teacher to the Nasi ("Patriarch" or "President") was made to do honor to his house. Most scholars ascribe this change to the time after the Hadrianic war, presumably under R. Gamaliel II, by AD 140. This centralization may have been part of the re-organization in those troubled times. The limitation of the Nasi's authority so that the approval of the council was required is usually ascribed to the third century at the time of R. Judah II.[54]

The essential part of early Rabbinic ordinations appears to have been the Imposition of hands. However, Rabbinic literature preserves no express mention of this rite in ordination earlier than about AD 380, and here in a context denying its necessity but apparently indicating that it was formerly so regarded.[55] The evidences adduced in Strack-Billerbeck seem conclusive that the Imposition of hands was performed and was the center of the rite of ordination: the name itself which is based on the Old Testament word used in the imposition of hands; the explanations of Moses' installation of Joshua which is interpreted according to the views held of a scholar's ordination; and the later denials of the necessity of this act, implying a previous practice.[56] We may add another argument: the

---

52. *p. Sanhedrin* 1, 19a, 43, following the translation of Newman, *Semikhah*, 13–14.

53. *b. Sanhedrin* 13b–14a.

54. Newman, *Semikhah*, 19–20.

55. "R. Aha, the son of Raba, asked R. Ashi: Is ordination effected by the literal laying on of hands?—[No,] he answered; it is by the conferring of the degree: He is designated by the title of Rabbi and granted the authority to adjudicate cases of kenas" (fines)." *b. Sanhedrin* 13b.

56. Strack and Billerbeck, *Kommentar zum Neuen Testament*, 2:654.

connection made by the rabbis between ordination and the imposition of hands in sacrifice.

Verbal Naming later replaced the practice of Imposition of hands. As Newman argues, the question of why a change was made points to the time when the change was made. The Imposition of hands was dropped in the time of Hadrian when ordination was restricted to the Nasi. Ordination was no longer an individual but a communal affair.[57] The new circumstances and the new ceremony called for a new name, and thus *minnuy* became the usual term in Palestine.

While ordination was performed by Imposition of hands, the act would have involved leaning upon the ordained so as to exert pressure.[58] When appointment by Naming came into use, the essential feature was the giving of the title "Rabbi." The sources also suggest an Investiture and Inaugural Usurpation such as giving a public discourse.[59]

There was a requirement that three ordained men be present for conferring ordination on another, but the rule itself puzzled the Talmudic interpreters.[60] The accounts of ordination make it clear that only one was the principal, so the other two must have been assistants or witnesses.

What was the meaning attached to ordination in Judaism? The leadership and authority of the rabbis were especially associated with judicial questions arising from the Law. This association points to the origin of rabbinic ordinations in the judges and in the greater and lesser Sanhedrins of pre-Christian times. Newman devotes a whole chapter to the "exclusive jurisdiction of the ordained."[61] An examination of this list of prerogatives of the ordained scholar in Judaism is instructive: They settled financial disputes, inflicted fines, established the calendar, released the first-born animal for profane use by reason of disqualifying blemishes, annulled vows, and originally inflicted corporal and capital punishment.

The impression of the ordained rabbi as a religious judge is strengthened by two further considerations. First, there is the principle, "There is no ordination outside Palestine," meaning that ordination could not be conferred outside the holy land.[62] The very existence of such a regulation

---

57. Newman, *Semikhah*, 104–10. Cf. also Lauterbach, "Ordination," 428–30.

58. Daube interprets the *Sifre* on Num 27:23 as likening the imposition of hands to pressing upon a full vessel (or to make a full vessel [*The New Testament and Rabbinic Judaism*, 231]).

59. Newman, *Semikhah*, 117–23.

60. *b. Sanhedrin* 13a, b.

61. Newman, *Semikhah*, 24–64.

62. *b. Sanhedrin* 14a; *p. Bikkurim* 3, 65d (quoted in ibid., 103).

indicates that ordination was rooted in the juridical life of the Jewish people in their homeland and was not a spiritual principle necessary to the religious life of the Diaspora. That the Babylonian exilarch (*resh galutha*) granted authorizations, sometimes called "ordinations," does not change the principle, rather it speaks of the legal status attained by Jewry in that region. The terminology for ordination was never changed in Babylonia because ordination never had its full meaning there. The second consideration is the granting of part and conditional ordinations.[63] Ordinarily, ordination conferred an equal status, and when a teacher ordained his student, this would have been the case.[64] But authorizations to decide ritual questions or act as a judge can be limited to certain cases or certain times. In cases of full ordination the ordination was apparently considered irrevocable.[65]

Other concepts besides the juridical one were associated with the rabbinate, but we have dwelt on the legal aspect because it indicates clearly the difference between Christian and Jewish ordination. Christian ordination had no comparable legal or juridical purpose. Ehrhardt calls attention to two subsidiary differences between Rabbinic and Christian ordination. The former required the presence of three, and this is a later feature of Christian ordination for which there is no early evidence. Moreover, Rabbinic ordination conferred an equal status, something not true of all Christian ordinations. A related problem to the latter would be the renewed laying on of hands in episcopal consecration of one already a presbyter—this would have been contrary to a Jewish rule against repeating the act.[66]

Ehrhardt claims that in early Judaism the transference of the Spirit was admitted and was connected with the Imposition of hands.[67] This is far from a general opinion among scholars. Davies states as follows: "It is precarious also to assume that Rabbinic ordination by the laying on of hands in the first century was meant to signify the transmission of the Holy Spirit."[68] Daube also declares that the imparting of the Spirit was

---

63. Bases for these are discussed in *b. Sanhedrin* 5a and *p. Hagigah* 1, 76a.

64. See Strack and Billerbeck, *Kommentar zum Neuen Testament*, 2:647, on *Sifre* on Num 27:18.

65. *b. Sanhedrin* 30b. Cf. Newman, *Semikhah*, 98.

66. Ehrhardt, "Jewish and Christian Ordination," 132, 134–35.

67. Ibid., 137.

68. Davies, *Paul and Rabbinic Judaism*, 213.

not Rabbinic ordination.[69] The Rabbinic comments on Num 27:18 and Deut 34:9 would appear to be conclusive evidence for the negative. The only passage this writer has found which would connect the Imposition of hands with the giving of the Spirit is a quite late homiletic midrash on Numbers 27.[70] Otherwise, Jewish writers stress that in Numbers 11 God made the transfer.[71] Numbers 27 has no transfer of the Spirit, and in the interpretations the emphasis is on the "honor" Joshua received in being designated Moses' successor.[72] Significantly, little is made of the Deuteronomy passage that does make a connection between spirit and the Imposition of hands. What little is said stresses that Joshua had, not Spirit, but wisdom from Moses. The "spirit of wisdom" passed down among Jewish scholars was that which a student learned from his teacher.

It has been noted above that at ordination the title of "rabbi" was given. There is evidence to suggest that originally "elder" (*zaqen*) was the status conferred in ordination. Lauterbach asserts that persons ordained to the Sanhedrin bore the title of *zaqen*, and he gives as evidence a passage in *b. Sanhedrin* 14a where this word is referred to the ordained.[73] Furthermore, the Talmudic statements which link the laying on of the hands of the elders in a communal sacrifice with ordination imply that "elders" are involved in both cases. The comments on Numbers 11 make the transition from the "elders" of the text to ordained teachers directly.[74] One of the texts denying ordination "outside the Land" speaks of it as ordination of elders.[75] Two passages referring to the later ordination by Naming speak of this as "appointment to be elders."[76] The term "elder"

69. Daube, *The New Testament and Rabbinic Judaism*, 241.

70. *Midrash Rabbah, Numbers* 15:25.

71. Not even Philo, *de Gigantibus* 24–25, is an exception to this, although it is the main passage to which Ehrhardt appeals, in spite of his skepticism about Philo's value for views held by Palestinian Jews ("Jewish and Christian Ordination," 131). Justin, *Dial.* 49, confuses Num 11:17 with Num 27:18 and Deut 34:9 in a way not found in Jewish sources. Nevertheless, even if Justin is reproducing some rabbi's exegesis, the transfer of Moses' spirit to Joshua is not ascribed to the Imposition of hands but to a separate act by God.

72. "Authority" is the happy rendering of the RSV. Both the Old Testament text and the Rabbinic interpretations show that the transfer involves Moses' authority or prestige (the Latin *auctoritas* would seem exactly to represent the Hebrew "honor" or "majesty" in this instance).

73. Lauterbach, "Ordination," 428.

74. *Sifre* Numbers 11:16 (quoted in Lohse, *Die Ordination*, 42).

75. *p. Bikkurim* 3.

76. *p. Megilloth* 1, 72b, and *Hagigah* 76c, in Strack and Billerbeck, *Kommentar zum*

(indicating dignity more than age) forges another link between ordination and the judicial aspects of Jewish life, for the term was the designation for the members of the councils in each community. It would appear to have been an early title for the ordained that enjoyed a revival in later times. The term, "rabbi," on the other hand, is first used as a *title* in reference to the disciples of Johanan ben Zakkai.[77] The Gospels show "rabbi" as a respectful form of address to a teacher, but are an evidence against its usage at that time for ordained teachers. "Rabbi" apparently acquired official connotations only at the time we also hear of the first ordinations performed by individual teachers.

Can Rabbinic ordination be traced to the time before AD 70? There is point in Newman's observation that the Talmud would not have tolerated any innovations such as R. Ashi's decision that laying on of hands by the qualifier was not necessary, or the introduction of part-ordination, if the Old Testament story of Moses and Joshua had been considered binding in all its details.[78] His doubts raise the more important question whether ordination by a scholar through the Imposition of hands would, or could, have been abandoned if it was an institution of long standing.[79] Moreover, there seems no reason why *individual* ordination could not have spread outside Palestine, and, if it was an old institution, the probability is that it would have done so.

In the face of these presumptions an effort has been made to break through the wall in our evidence raised at the time of the Jewish revolt, AD 66–70. Lohse has made the most persistent effort of recent times,[80] but his evidence has been answered by Ehrhardt.[81] We are left with no clear evidence for Rabbinic ordination before 70 and a presumption against it.

Neuen Testament, 2:655.

77. Moore, *Judaism*, 3:15.

78. Newman, *Semikhah*, 5. Newman notes the differences between the Moses–Joshua episode and Rabbinic ordination.

79. Ibid., 104–10. Newman points out that the proscription of ordination by Hadrian mentioned in Rabbinic sources would not account for a failure to resume Imposition of hands.

80. Lohse, *Die Ordination*, esp. 43.

81. Ehrhardt, "Jewish and Christian Ordination," 130ff.

Elders and the Sanhedrin

The term "elder" offers the one solid indication of ordination in earlier times. Ehrhardt has advanced a thesis which we would like to elaborate further. The main points of this thesis are as follows: ordination before 70 was the solemn ritual of admission to the Jerusalem Sanhedrin; in the time of Jesus the main rite in Jewish ordination was not the Imposition of hands but a Solemn Seating; the Imposition of hands rose to prominence in the troubled times, 70–135, when the precedent of Numbers 27 had to be stressed against Numbers 11 in the need for private ordination.[82] Although evidence is lacking for ordination of rabbis by Imposition of hands before 70, the same is not true for ordination to the Sanhedrin by Solemn Seating.

It is surprising that earlier investigators have not been impressed that all of the earliest descriptions of ordination make the key feature of the Seating the ordinand on the teaching chair. The *Sifre* to Numbers 27,[83] which was quoted earlier, says nothing about the Imposition of hands except as it appears in the citation of the biblical text. The central feature of the description is Moses raising Joshua up and Seating him on a chair. The same description holds true for the passage cited by Lohse[84] for support of Jewish ordination going back to pre-Christian times, *Assumption of Moses* 12:2. Discussing the appointment of Joshua, the text says, "And Moses took his hands and raised him into the seat before him.[85] Ehrhardt also finds support for Solemn Seating being the central concept of Jewish ordination in the words of Jesus about the scribes and Pharisees in Matt 23:2, they "sit in Moses' seat."[86] Lohse also cites texts from the *Sifre* on Deuteronomy where *yashabh* (in the form "cause to be seated") is used of ordination.[87]

82. Ibid., 125–38.

83. This work is part of the Halakic Midrash by the Tannaim to which Moore gives the first importance for determining second-century Jewish thought, especially as that thought preserved older traditions. Moore, *Judaism*, 1:133.

84. Lohse, *Die Ordination*, 30.

85. From Charles, ed., *Apocrypha and Pseudepigrapha*. Charles dates the work in the early part of the first century.

86. The background of the teaching and judging chairs of the Sanhedrin favors a non-eschatological interpretation of Matt 19:28.

87. Lohse, *Die Ordination*, 33. Cf. *p. Bikkurim* 3, 65d.

Probably the most significant passage on Jewish ordination is a statement from the Mishnah which should serve to certify the rest of the evidence.[88]

> The Sanhedrin was arranged like the half of a round threshing-floor so that they all might see one another. Before them stood the two scribes of the judges . . .
>
> Before them sat three rows of disciples of the Sages, and each knew his proper place. If they needed to appoint another as judge, they appointed him from the first row, and one from the second row came into the first row, and one from the third row came into the second; and they chose yet another from the congregation and set him in the third row. He did not sit in the place of the former, but he sat in the place that was proper for him.[89]

Samakh is the verb translated "appoint," and it is distinguished in the passage from "chose." The technical meaning "ordain" would seem to be definite. This word may further suggest a laying on of hands; what is significant is that taking the appropriate seat on the Sanhedrin represented one's admission to that body.

Apparently the same procedure was employed for the lesser Sanhedrins, or councils of judges. In the Babylonian Talmud (*Sanhedrin* 17b) the number one hundred twenty is given as the minimum population of a city in order that it may qualify for a Sanhedrin. In arriving at this number the commentator first counts the twenty-three members of a minor Sanhedrin, and then lists three rows of twenty-three who must sit before the council. There is no need to carry the arithmetic further; this much shows that the major Sanhedrin was the pattern for the lesser ones and presumably vacancies would be filled by both bodies in the same way as outlined in the Mishnah.

It may well be that Imposition of hands was part of the ceremony of ordination to a Sanhedrin. It may even have been that rabbis used the rite in the private "graduation exercises" of their pupils before AD 70. The evidence, however, is lacking. Ehrhardt's statement that "private ordination was, at any rate, not officially recognized before AD 70, but was a transient phase in the troubled times between AD 70 and 135, and not the true

---

88. Again we have a second-century source that collects earlier traditional material. Lohse (*Die Ordination*, 30–31) says this passage must refer to the time of centralization in the second century. The extent to which contemporary material is included in the Mishnah is debatable. It is more reasonable to take this passage for what it purports to be; a description of the Sanhedrin that was prior to the destruction of 70.

89. *m. Sanhedrin* 4:3–4.

origin of rabbinical ordination," is correct. The juridical nature of Rabbinic ordination is explained by its intention to continue the Sanhedrin. The Jewish background gives prominence to an act often overlooked in discussions of ordination—Solemn Seating.

Community and Synagogue Officers in the Diaspora

The liturgical functions of the Jewish synagogue, at home and abroad, were in the hands of a "chief of the synagogue" (*rosh hakeneseth, archisynagogos*) and a "servant" of the synagogue (*chazan, hyperetes*). No information exists in regard to their selection and installation.[90]

Distinct from these cult officials were the community rulers. At the legal head of Palestinian communities were local sanhedrins whose members were ordained and wore the title *zaqen*. Although a certain variety appears, non-Palestinian Jewish communities also had a collegiate body in charge of their administrative affairs. Inscriptions from the diaspora show a multiplicity of functionaries patterned after the officials of the Greek associations but keeping within the framework of Palestinian models. Jewry in Rome may be taken as representative inasmuch as there is more evidence from Rome and we have the benefit of the studies of J. B. Frey for the city.[91]

Each Jewish community at Rome was governed by a council of elders,[92] the *gerousia*, presided over by the *gerousiarch*. *Presbyteroi* do not appear to be mentioned in Rome,[93] so the idea has been presented that each member of the *gerousia* was called *archon*.[94] Frey, however, argues that *archons* were the executive committee of the *gerousia*.[95]

No installation ceremony is known for any officials of the Jewish communities. The only means of selection which is attested is that of Election

90. Krauss, *Synagogale Altertümer*, 114–30.

91. Frey, "Les communautea Juives a Rome," 136ff. We will follow this article in the references, but the same material is included in Frey's introduction to *CIL* 1:lxvii–cxi.

92. Frey, "Les communautea Juives a Rome," 136. There is no mention of a supreme *gerousia* at Rome. Frey, ibid., 161ff., answers the arguments that have been advanced for a central organization of Jewry at Rome such as Alexandria had.

93. However, Frey gives *presbyteros* in one restored reading, ibid., 138.

94. Easton, "Jewish and Early Christian Ordination," 317.

95. Frey, "Les communautés Juives a Rome," 139.

by the community. The Jewish *archons* were elected for a year by all the community in the month of September at the Feast of Tabernacles.[96]

The later patriarchs sought to maintain some control over Jewish communities through their apostles (*sheluchim*). Their introduction into discussions about the ministry of the church necessitate a word here.[97] There is no evidence for Jewish apostles of the patriarchs before the second century; neither is there evidence that they were ordained nor any reason to suppose they would be.[98] There was no place for a laying on of hands in the sending out of the *shaliach*.[99]

Functionaries in the Qumran Community

Although study is producing a fairly clear picture of the organization of the Qumran community,[100] only hints exist in regard to the subject under consideration. The emphasis on an orderly structure of the community may be seen in the following passages from the Manual of Discipline:

> This is the regulation for the session of the Many: each member (shall sit) in his definite seat. The priests shall sit in the first seats, the elders in the next seats, and the rest of all the people shall sit, each in his definite seat. (vi.8ff)

> They shall examine their spiritual qualities and their actions year after year, promoting one according to his insight and his perfect ways, and setting back another according to his perverseness. (v.23–24)[101]

96. Krauss, *Synagogale Altertümer*, 152.

97. The information about the *shaliach* is well summarized by Manson, *The Church's Ministry*, 47.

98. Easton, "Jewish and Early Christian Ordination," 319; Lohse, *Die Ordination*, 62–63.

99. The mischief that may come from the blind following of scholarly authority may be seen in the influence of Rengstorf's article "ἀπόστολος," 417. Rengstorf states that Jewish apostles received an Imposition of hands on the basis of Justin, *Dial.* 108:2, which speaks of them as "chosen and appointed (*cheirotonesantes*) men." There is no instance in the early centuries for *cheirotonein* meaning an imposition of hands—Siotis, "Die klassische und die christliche Cheirotonie in ihrem Verhältnis," 21 (1950) 251, 254 (althought Siotis too is awed by the authority of an article in *TDNT*). Rengstorf has been guilty of reading a medieval meaning into Justin's text.

100. Cross, *The Ancient Library of Qumran*, 173–76.

101. Translation by Wernberg-Møller, *The Manual of Discipline*.

These texts reflect in a new situation the same cycle of ideas about seating as the Mishnah *Sanhedrin* 4:4.

The idea of divine choice is strong in reference to the priests[102] and may have had a basis in the fact that the priests were the descendants of Aaron and thus divinely appointed. At any rate, the priests held a special position at Qumran simply by virtue of heredity. It is assumed that each priest was anointed.[103]

Despite the hierarchical structure there was a strong "democratic" element in the role played by the assembly in making decisions. The voice of the "Many" was especially heard in the selection of leaders. When judges (ten) were chosen for a special occasion, the whole congregation appears to have made the choice.[104] A common phrase, "the lot shall go out" (*ys' hgwrl*), was used figuratively for all decisions in which the whole body had a part.[105] In one passage it has definite reference to the selection of the leaders of the community, perhaps by an Election of the members.[106]

GLOSSARY

Capitalization indicates words given a special technical meaning in the paper. The use of the small case in the text indicates either a non-technical meaning or the action in a non-ordinal context. The capitalization is not extended to verb forms and derivative words, but as much as possible these other forms of the word are used only when referring to the technical action.

Acclamation—A spontaneous, unanimous Election or Ratification; in the cry, "*Axios*" (= *Dignus*), an Acclamation became part of the liturgy.

appointment—A general word covering selection and/or installation without reference to the manner in which accomplished.

Auspication—The divination or augury performed by the new Roman office-holder in order to determine the divine attitude toward his magistracy.

---

102. "God has chosen you," 1QSb v.22, in Barthelemy and Milik, eds., *Qumran Cave 1*.

103. See the note on 1QM ix.8–9 by Van der Ploeg, "La Regle de la Guerre," 409.

104. CD x.4–6. Rabin, *The Zadokite Documents*, 49.

105. 1QS v.2ff. Cf. Wernberg-Møller, *The Manual of Discipline*, 92.

106. 1QSa i.13–17. Barthelemy and Milik, eds., *Qumran Cave 1*, 112.

Benediction—The pronouncing of a personal blessing at an ordination with a view toward dedicating the person receiving the Benediction to the service of God.

Chrismation—Anointing with oil.

Co-option—Election by members of a collegiate body to replace vacancies in their numbers, thus providing for a self-perpetuating membership.

Designation—A selection for an office made or announced by a person in authority (preserving the meaning of *designatio*).

Divine Invocation—An appeal to the gods or God for favor in an enterprise, particularly an official undertaking.

Election—A selection made by voting, particularly by the whole assembly.

Enthronement—A special form of Solemn Seating, with the chair on a raised platform and containing the ornate trappings of royalty.

Episcopal Election—A choice made by one bishop, especially of a successor.

Formal Scrutiny—Examination of the qualifications of a candidate in public and according to a set form.

Imperial Nomination—Presentation of a candidate by the emperor for Election.

Imposition of hands—Laying of hands, or a hand, on the head of the ordinand, either with or without the exertion of pressure.

Inaugural Usurpation—Assuming an office by performing its duties for the first time.

Inauguration—An auspication performed by an auger in inducting a person into office (Latin *inauguratio*).

Inheritance—Qualifying for an office through birth.

Inspired Designation—Selection of a person for religious work by a spokesman of the divine will, especially a prophet.

installation—Induction into office, however performed.

Investiture—Putting on the garments pertaining to an office and worn in its exercise.

Lot-taking—Selection by chance.

Naming—Bestowing an office by giving the name of the office, or the title carried by its holder, in a verbal proclamation.

Nomination—Proposing a name for Election.

Oath-taking—A solemn promise, supported by an appeal to the divine, marking one's entrance into office.

ordination—A general word for selection and installation, but particularly the latter, ceremonially accomplished.

Ordination—The developed sacrament of orders in Catholic Churches.

Parochial Election—An Election by all the people of a Christian community.

Porrection—Bestowal of the instruments signifying an office and/or used in its performance.

Prayer—The ordination prayer.

Presbyteral Election—Election by the presbyters of a church.

Ratification—Approval by one party to the constitutive selection performed by another.

selection—A general word for choice without reference to the manner of choosing.

Solemn Seating—The taking a seat in the chair of office.

Synodal Election—An Election by a specially assembled synod of bishops.

5

Ordination in the Fourth Century
II: The Ceremony of Ordination

SOME ACCOUNTS OF THE CEREMONY OF ORDINATION

ONE OF THE FULLEST accounts of ordination in the ancient church is preserved in the *Apostolic Constitutions*, compiled in Syria toward the end of the fourth century. The instructions concerning the ordination of a bishop follow.

> As all of us have already commanded, a bishop to be ordained is to be irreproachable, being elected by all the people. When he has been designated and approved, the people come together, with the presbytery and the bishops who are present, on the Lord's Day. And the principal bishop is to ask the presbytery and the people if he is the one whom they have chosen as their ruler. After they give their consent, let him inquire further if all men testify that he is worthy of this great and glorious leadership: if he is truly religious toward God, has observed justice toward men, has ordered well his own household, is irreproachable in conduct. If all sincerely testify together that he is such a person, let them be asked again the third time, as in the presence of God, Christ, the Holy Spirit (who is also present), and all the

holy and ministering spirits, if he is truly worthy of the ministry, "that at the mouth of two or three witnesses every word may be established." If they agree the third time that he is worthy, they are to be asked for their consent, and giving it readily, let them be heard. When silence is made, one of the principal bishops standing with two others near the altar, while the rest of the bishops and presbyters pray silently and while the deacons hold the divine Gospels open upon the head of the one being ordained, is to pray to God . . .

After the prayer one of the bishops is to lift up the sacrifice upon the hands of the one who has been ordained. And early in the morning he is to be enthroned in a place set apart for him among the rest of the bishops, who give him the kiss in the Lord. After the reading of the Law, the Prophets, and our Epistles, Acts, and Gospels, the one who has been ordained is to salute the church, saying: "The grace of our Lord Jesus Christ, and the love of God the Father, and the fellowship of the Holy Spirit be with you." And all shall answer, "And with your spirit." And after these words he is to speak to the people words of exhortation.[1]

After a prior Election the ceremony of installation begins with a certification of the Election and a Formal Scrutiny of the worthiness of the candidate, acclaimed by the people. The ordination itself is a Prayer said while the book of the Gospels is held open over the ordinand's head, a feature still present in the ordinations of bishops in the Orthodox Church. After this point, he is spoken of as the "one who has been ordained." No Imposition of hands is mentioned, but in view of another passage (VIII. xlvi.9) this may be accidental. Following the Prayer the new bishop receives a symbol of his right to offer sacrifice (Porrection), is seated on his episcopal throne (Solemn Seating), delivers a sermon, and proceeds with the liturgy (Inaugural Usurpation).

The Prayer for a bishop is not quoted, because for all of its verbosity it adds no new information to that found in other Prayers which will be quoted.[2] The Prayer stresses God's appointment of rulers and priests for his people in all times. The priestly description of the bishop's work is quite prominent. There is a request that the bishop receive the "power" of the

---

1. *Apos. Const.* VIII.iv–v. Translated from the Greek text in Funk, *Didascalia et Constitutiones Apostolorurn*, vol. I. Translations are the author's unless otherwise noted.

2. The full quotation, along with the rescension of the Prayer in the *Constitutions through Hippolytus* (which is the same as the Prayer in the *Apostolic Tradition*), may be found in the ANF, vol. 7.

Holy Spirit, and then later that he may have the "communion" of the Holy Spirit. Aside from the priestly duty of sacrificing, the bishop is equipped by fellowship with the Spirit with power to remit sins, to "give lots," and to loose every bond.

The directions concerning a presbyter and deacon are briefer.

> When you ordain a presbyter, O bishop, lay your hand on his head, while the presbytery and the deacons are standing by you, and praying, say:[3]

> O Lord Almighty, our God,
>> who hast created all things by Christ,
>>> and in like manner takes care of the whole world by Him for He who had power to make different creatures, has also power to take care of them, according to their different natures;
>>> on which account, O God, Thou takest care of immortal beings by bare preservation,
>> but of those that are mortal by succession—
>> of the soul by the provision of laws,
>> of the body by the supply of its wants.
> Do Thou now also look down upon this Thy servant,
>> who is put into the presbytery by the vote and determination of the whole clergy;
> and do Thou replenish him with the Spirit of grace and counsel,
> to assist and govern Thy people with a pure heart,
> in the same manner as Thou didst look down upon Thy chosen people
>> and didst command Moses to choose elders
>> whom Thou didst fill with Thy Spirit.
> Do Thou also now, O Lord, grant this,
> and preserve in us the Spirit of Thy grace,
> that this person, being filled with the gifts of healing and the word of teaching,
> may in meekness instruct Thy people,
> and sincerely serve Thee with a pure mind and a willing soul,

---

3. In order to facilitate the comparison of these Prayers, I have attempted to make a division into clauses, returning to the margin for each principal clause, indenting for secondary ideas, and giving a double indentation for the completion of clauses.

The *Apostolic Constitutions*, the *Testament of Our Lord*, the *Constitutions through Hippolytus*, and the *Canons of Hippolytus* are indebted to the *Apostolic Tradition of Hippolytus* from the third century.

and may fully discharge the holy ministrations for Thy
people,
through Thy Christ, with whom glory, honour, and worship
be to Thee, and to the Holy Spirit for ever. Amen.
You shall appoint a deacon, O bishop, laying your hands
upon him, while the whole presbytery and the deacons stand
by you, and praying, you shall say:
O God Almighty, the true and faithful God,
who art rich unto all that call upon Thee in truth,
who art fearful in counsels,
and wise in understanding,
who art powerful and great,
hear our prayer, O Lord,
and let Thine ears receive our supplication,
and "cause the light of Thy countenance to shine upon
this Thy servant,"
who is being ordained for Thee to the office of a deacon;
and replenish him with Thy Holy Spirit, and with power,
as Thou didst replenish Stephen, who was Thy martyr,
and follower of the sufferings of Thy Christ.
Do Thou render him worthy to discharge acceptably the
ministration of a deacon,
steadily, unblameably, and without reproof,
that thereby he may attain a higher degree,
through the mediation of Thy only begotten Son, with
whom glory, honour, and worship be to Thee and the
Holy Spirit for ever. Amen.[4]

The *Testament of our Lord* represents another working up of the
traditional materials utilized in the *Apostolic Constitutions*. Although the
English editors[5] date the *Testament* in the 350s and give a preference to
Asia Minor, most students have dated it after the *Apostolic Constitutions*
and placed its origin in Syria.

Book I, chapter 20 contains the statement, "Let the bishop be appointed, being chosen by all the people according to the will of the Holy
Ghost." Qualifications are then given, following the Pastoral epistles.
Chapter 21 describes the "ordination"[6] on the first day of the week as including the assent to the appointment and the witness to his life by the

4. VIII.xvi–xvii.

5. Cooper and Maclean, *The Testament of Our Lord*, 41ff. Quotations are made
from this edition.

6. Literally, "the laying on of the hand," with the word being from the Semitic root
śim and so throughout the ritual.

people, the silent prayer by the presbyters, the laying on of the hands of the neighboring bishops while they pray,[7] and finally the laying on of hands by one bishop (commanded by the others) while he says the "calling of appointment." This Prayer belongs to the main stream of ordination liturgies but contains much flowery embellishment, especially in the address to God who is praised as the One who has always provided princes and priests for his sanctuary. The petitionary part may be quoted in order to give the atmosphere of the document. After petitioning for the Spirit to come to the Church the bishop prays as follows:

> Grant, O Lord, that this Thy servant may please Thee
>> for doxology, and for laud without ceasing, O God, for fitting hymns of praise, and for suitable times,
>> or acceptable prayers, for faithful asking, for an upright mind, for a meek heart, for the working of life and of meekness and of truth, for the knowledge of uprightness.
>
> O Father, who knowest the hearts,
> grant to this Thy servant whom Thou hast chosen for the episcopate,
> to feed Thy holy flock,
> and to stand at the head of the priesthood without fault,
> ministering to Thee day and night;
> grant that Thy face may be seen by him;
>> vouchsafe, O Lord, that he may offer to Thee the offering of Thy holy Church carefully and with all fear;
>> bestow upon him that he may have Thy powerful Spirit to loose all band,
>>> as Thou didst bestow Him on Thy apostles, to please Thee in meekness;
>> fill him full of love, knowledge, understanding, discipline, perfectness, strength, and a pure heart,
>> when he prayeth for the people,
>>> and when he mourneth for those who commit folly and draweth them to receive help;
>> when he offereth to Thee praises and thanksgivings and prayers for a sweet-smelling savour through Thy beloved Son, our Lord Jesus Christ,
>> by whom are given to Thee praise and honour and might,
>>> with the Holy Ghost, both before the worlds, and also now, and at all times, and for ever and ever without end.
>>> Amen.

7. This Prayer seems to be the work of the compiler and is without precedent or posterity in ordinations.

The people respond to the prayer by saying "Amen" and shouting three times, "He is worthy."[8]

The ceremony for the ordination of a presbyter in chapter 30 provides for the bishop to lay his hand on the ordinand while the presbyters touch him. The bishop's wordy prayer petitions for the Holy Spirit, apparently under the influence of the reference to the choosing of the elders by Moses in Numbers 11. The elders' duties are summarized as to "help and govern" the people, or elsewhere, "to shepherd."

According to chapter 33, "the deacon is appointed, chosen like the things which have before been spoken of," perhaps referring to the Election of the bishop. In chapter 38 the directions are given that the bishop alone lay a hand on the deacon, "because he is not appointed to the priesthood,[9] but for the service of attendance on the bishop and the Church." The bishop prays for God to "give the Spirit of grace and earnestness to this Thy servant," not the Holy Spirit. Both liturgical and benevolent activities are indicated for the deacon in the Prayer.

One of the most circumstantial accounts of ordination from the ancient church is found in the "Life of Polycarp," probably from the fourth century in the region of Asia Minor.[10] Unreliable for Polycarp's life, the work still has a capital importance for the climate of opinion in the author's own day. The author speaks of "those who are chosen by God as His ministers,"[11] and this popular conception of God's choice is embroidered at places by a touch of the miraculous. The description of Polycarp's ministerial career reflected the careers of others witnessed by the author.

> He (Bucolus) perceived therefore that he was worthy; and for the present, owing to his youthfulness, he enrolled him in the order of deacons with the approval of the whole Church. Blessed indeed was he in being permitted to cover such a head with his hand and to bless so noble a soul with his voice . . .
>
> As a deacon he approved himself among his own contemporaries, as Stephen did among those of the Apostles.[12]

---

8. This is the place where the acclamation, *Axios,* comes in the Orthodox liturgies today.

9. For a similar stress in the other church orders that the deacon is not a priest, Cooper and Maclean, *The Testament of Our Lord,* 191–92, 195.

10. Lightfoot, *The Apostolic Fathers,* 2:1011–12. Lightfoot's translation will be used.

11. Chap. x.

12. Chap. xi, xii.

Notice the stress on popular approval, the worthiness of the candidate, the recalling of the memory of Stephen, and the interpretation of the bishop's action as a Benediction.

An interesting picture of a presbyter emerges from the description of Polycarp's advancement to that position.

> Bucolus, therefore, seeing that Polycarp's age was adequate and that the propriety of his conduct throughout all his life was even more adequate than the number of his years, perceived that he was most excellent as a fellow-counsellor to him in questions relating to the Church and as a fellow-minister in teaching; while the Lord set His seal on and ratified his design; giving him commandment in a vision. Accordingly he appointed him to an office in the presbyterate, the whole Church with one accord welcoming him with great joy, although he himself shrunk from such an undertaking.[13]

The bishop Bucolus indicated a desire for Polycarp as his successor and then the people talked about their hope of getting such a man for their pastor (chap. xx). Then comes a fairly full account of the choice and installation of Polycarp as bishop.

> And without any delay, not many days after, gathering together bishops from the cities round about and making preparations for the reception of the visitors, they took measures for the appointment of a successor to preside over the Church. When they arrived, great crowds gathered from the cities and villages and fields, some knowing Polycarp, others desiring from what they had heard of him to behold him. So when they were assembled together and the church was filled, the glory of a heavenly light shone among them all, and certain brethren saw marvellous visions. One saw hovering over Polycarp a white dove encircled in light, Another beheld him, before he had sat down, as if already seated in his chair of office . . .
>
> And on the sabbath, when prayer had been made long time on bended knee, he, as was his custom, got up to read; and every eye was fixed upon him. Now the lesson was the Epistles of Paul to Timothy and to Titus, in which he says what manner of man a bishop ought to be. And he was so well fitted for the office that the hearers said one to another that he lacked none of those qualities which Paul requires in one who has the care of a Church. When then, after the reading and the instruction

13. Chap. xvii.

of the bishops and the discourses of the presbyters, the deacons were sent to the laity to enquire whom they would have, they said with one accord, "Let Polycarp be our pastor and teacher." The whole priesthood then having assented, they appointed him notwithstanding his earnest entreaties and his desire to decline.

Accordingly the deacons led him up for ordination (*cheirothesia*) by hands of the bishops according to custom. And being placed in his chair by them, he moistened and anointed with tears of piety and humility the place where in the Spirit he saw standing the feet of Christ who was present with him for the anointing to the priestly office. For where the ministers are—the priests and Levites—there in the midst is also the High-priest arrayed in the great flowing robe. Then the company present urged him, since this was the custom, to address them. For they said that this work of teaching was the most important part of the communion . . .

After this the others also having made the proper exhortations and appeals on the Sabbath and on the Lord's Day, and offerings and eucharists, rejoicing and partaking of food, returned each to his own home rejoicing greatly at having communicated with Polycarp, and glorifying Christ Jesus the Lord for it, to whom is the glory for ever. Amen.[14]

According to the vivid description given here the initiative in the Election belongs with the people. The Election as well as the installation takes place in a liturgical setting. The Imposition of hands is central, but the Enthronement occupies a prominent place in the mind of the people. There was eagerness for Polycarp to carry out the custom of delivering a sermon at this occasion. Most of the elements, therefore, found associated with the subject of ordination are brought together into a consistent whole in this narrative.

The ordination prayers contained in the Prayer-book of Serapion, fourth century bishop of Thmuis in the Egyptian Delta, have no literary connection with the other Prayers of the period but offer a valuable insight because they contain the same motifs. The titles in the manuscript, which serve as rubrics, for the Prayers at the ordination of a bishop, presbyter, and deacon, follow the same form: "Laying on of hands (*cheirothesia*) of the appointment (*katastasis*) of . . ." The word for the imposition of hands is used in other contexts in reference to catechumens, the laity, and penitents, in each case accompanying a prayer.

14. Chap. xxi–xxiii.

For a bishop:
Thou who didst send the Lord Jesus for the gain of all world,
thou who didst through him choose the apostles,
thou who generation by generation dost ordain holy Bishops,
O God of truth, make this Bishop also a living Bishop,
holy of the succession of the holy apostles,
and give to him grace and divine Spirit,
> that thou didst freely give to all thy own servants and proph-
> ets and patriarchs:

make him to be worthy to shepherd thy flock
and let him still continue unblameably and inoffensively in the
Bishopric
through thy only-begotten Jesus Christ,
> through whom to thee (is) the glory and the strength in holy
> Spirit both now and to all the ages of the ages. Amen.

For a Presbyter:
We stretch forth the hand,
O Lord God of the heavens, Father of thy only-begotten, upon
this man,
and Beseech thee that the Spirit of truth may dwell upon him.
Give him the grace of prudence and knowledge and a good
heart.
Let a divine Spirit come to be in him
that he may be able to be a steward of the people
and an ambassador of thy divine oracles,
and to reconcile thy people to thee the uncreated God,
> who didst give of the spirit of Moses upon the chosen ones,
> even holy Spirit.
> Give a portion of holy Spirit also to this man, and from the
> Spirit of thy only-begotten,

for the grace of wisdom and knowledge and right faith,
> that he may be able to serve thee in a clean conscience
> through thy only-begotten Jesus Christ,
> through whom to thee (is) the glory and the strength in holy
> Spirit both now and for all the ages of the ages. Amen.

For a Deacon:
Father of the only-begotten who didst send thy Son
and didst ordain the things on the earth,
> and hast given rules to the Church and orders for the profit
> and salvation of the flocks,
> who didst choose out Bishops, Presbyters, and Deacons for
> the Ministry of thy catholic Church,

who didst choose through thine only-begotten the seven
Deacons,

> and didst freely give to them holy Spirit,
> make also this man a Deacon of thy catholic Church,
> and give in him a spirit of knowledge and discernment,
>> that he may be able cleanly and unblameably to do service in
>> this ministry in the midst of the holy people,
> through thy only-begotten Jesus Christ,
> through whom to thee (is) the glory and the strength in holy
> Spirit both now and to all the ages of the ages. Amen.[15]

The ordination of Athanasius as bishop of Alexandria may be selected as a typical instance of fourth-century sentiment in Egypt. In answer to Arian charges of a clandestine and uncanonical Election of Athanasius, the Egyptian bishops wrote an encyclical letter that Athanasius incorporated into his *Apologia contra Arianos*. "Because all the multitude and all the laity of the catholic Church when they gathered together, shouting as if on one soul and one mouth, kept on crying out asking for Athanasius as bishop for the church . . . The majority of us ordained him under the eyes and with the acclamations of all."[16]

In Sulpicius Severus' "Life of St. Martin," who became bishop of Tours about 371, there is information which may be taken as typical of the popular conceptions in the West.

> An incredibly large number of people—not only from Tours but from nearby localities—had assembled to voice their vote. Among them there was one single will, one prayer, one judgment: Martin was the most worthy to be bishop; the church would be fortunate which had such as he for its head. Yet, there were a few men—among them some of the bishops who had been called together to ordain the future prelate—who set up an unscrupulous opposition . . . And the only course that lay open to them was to do what the populace, inspired by the Lord's will, thought best.[17]

The turning point came when the Scripture reading for the day seemed so appropriate as a judgment on the chief opponent to Martin that it was taken as an expression of the divine will.

15. The translation is by Wordsworth, *Bishop Serapion's Prayer-Book*, 72–74. The Greek text is given by Brightman, "The Sacramentary of Serapion of Thmuis," 266, 267.

16. *Apol. c. Arian.* vi. Cf. also, chap. xxx, and Gregory Nazianzen, *Or.* 21:8.

17. "Life of St. Martin," ix, from the translation of Peebles for FC 7.

IMPORTANT FEATURES OF THE PROCEDURE

From all regions the evidence converges to form a picture of nearly uniform practice, which may be summarized in the words of Priscillian of Spain about AD 380, "Even as the dedication of a bishop depends on the bishop, so the election depends on the petition by the people."[18]

Popular Election is prominent in the accounts cited above. The choice by the people was considered as expressing, or being influenced by, the divine will. In the narrative of the ordination of Ambrose as bishop of Milan in 374 the expectation of divine guidance was so strong that a childlike mistake was taken as an omen from God.

> When the people were about to revolt in seeking a bishop, Ambrose had the task of putting down the revolt . . . And when he was addressing the people, the voice of a child among the people is said to have called out suddenly: "Ambrose bishop." At the sound of this voice, the mouths of all the people joined in the cry: "Ambrose bishop." Thus, those who a while before were disagreeing most violently . . . suddenly agreed on this one with miraculous and unbelievable harmony.[19]

Ambrose himself later wrote to the church at Vercellae and gave the following interpretation of the Election of Eusebius, one of its early bishops:

> Justly did he turn out so great a man, whom the whole Church elected, justly was it believed that he whom all had demanded was elected by the judgment of God . . . Where the demand of all is unanimous, ought we to doubt that the Lord Jesus is there as the Author of that desire, and the Hearer of the petition, the Presider over the ordination, and the Giver of the Grace?[20]

The will of the people was often violently expressed and overcame strong opposition. The historian Socrates relates that at the Council of Constantinople in 381, "Nectarius was seized by the people and proposed for the episcopate."[21] In the oration on the death of his father Gregory

18. *Tract.* ii, in *CSEL* XVIII:40.

19. "Life of Ambrose" III.6 by Paulinus, quoted from the translation in Deferrari, trans., *Early Christian Biographies* in FC.

20. *Ep.* LXIII.2,3. *PL* 16:1240–41.

21. *H.E.* V.8. *PG* 67:577.

Nazianzen gives an account of the activities of the people of Caesarea that has all the fervor of a political campaign.[22]

Ratification by the Clergy of the Election by the people is to be expected. Their joint action with the people is noted in the sources. Theodoret relates that Eustathius was compelled to become bishop of Antioch (c. 324–331) "by the common vote of the bishops, priests, and Christ-loving laity."[23] The same historian speaks of Lucius, an Arian rival to the Alexandrian episcopate, in this way: "No synod of orthodox bishops had chosen him; no vote of genuine clergy; no laity had demanded him; as the laws of the church enjoin."[24] Roman practice is indicated by Siricius: "After the passage of time, he is appointed presbyter or bishop, if his election is proclaimed by the clergy and people."[25] Some of these passages may indicate clerical initiative and popular Ratification, for which see the next section.

The *Imposition of hands* by a bishop or bishops accompanying a *Prayer* was clearly the central element in the ceremony of installation. That only bishops were regarded as entitled to bestow an office is illustrated by Athanasius' quotation concerning Ischyras, "saying he was a presbyter when he is not a presbyter; for he was appointed by the presbyter Colluthus, who pretended to be a bishop."[26] The consecration of a bishop required three bishops.[27]

An *Inaugural Usurpatian* is prominent in the accounts of installation. A Solemn Seating in the chair of office was a regular feature, and the word "Enthronement," as the act was called in the fourth century, could stand for the whole ceremony. Synesius wrote to Theophilus of Alexandria an account of the appointment of Paul as bishop of Erythrum: "The bishops of the province said that in obedience to a letter received from you they proposed Paul to the people for bishop. These agreed to have him and the others proceeded to the enthronement."[28] Although of medieval derivation, the English word "install" represents etymologically this act. The demonstration of having assumed the office was given when the new bishop celebrated the Eucharist and delivered a sermon.

22. *Or.* XVIII.33.

23. *H.E.* I.vii.10. The second edition of his works in GCS.

24. Ibid., IV.xxiii.9.

25. *Ep.* I.10. *PL* 13:1143.

26. *Apol. c. Arian.* lxxv. *Apos. Const.* III.x, xi is emphatic in denying ordination to other than bishops.

27. Canon 4 of the Council of Nicaea, in Hefele and LeClercq, *Histoire des conciles,* 1:539.

28. *Ep.* LXVII (*PG* 66:1417).

NEW FEATURES

The importance of the clergy in the selection of officers is much more in evidence in the fourth century. The sixth canon of Theophilus of Alexandria outlines a procedure of clerical choice, popular Ratification, and then episcopal ordination for the orders below the bishop.[29]

A trend toward centralization is evident in the role assigned to the Metropolitan bishop and the synod of bishops in a province. Canon 4 of the Council of Nicaea decrees:

> It is by all means fitting that a bishop be appointed (*kathist-asthai*) by all the bishops in the eparchy. But if this should be difficult either on account of urgent necessity or of the great distance, at least three should meet together for this purpose, the absent bishops giving their favorable vote and communicating it in writing. Then perform the ordination (*cheirotonian*). But in every eparchy the ratification of what is done is given to the Metropolitan.[30]

A council at Antioch gave similar instructions:

> A bishop shall not be ordained without a synod and the presence of the metropolitan. When he is present, it is by all means better that all his fellow-ministers in the eparchy be with him, and it is proper that the metropolitan invite them by letter. And if all should meet, it is better. If this be difficult, it is necessary by all means that the majority be present or give their vote by letters, and thus the appointment shall take place with the presence or the vote of the majority.[31]

The ecclesiastical organization followed the civil. The Metropolitan had a preeminence not only because of the civil importance of his city, but also probably because his city was the first of the province to receive the Gospel. The other cities received the Gospel and their first ordinations from the capital city. What was initially necessity became custom and finally part of the constitutional structure of the Church.[32] Since these canons were written by and for bishops, they are silent on the role of other people.

---

29. *PG* 65:40.

30. Hefele and LeClercq, *Histoire des conciles*.

31. Translated from the Greek text of the canons of the council of Antioch in Lauchert, *Die Kanones der Wichtigsten Altkirchlichen Concilien*.

32. Hefele and LeClercq, *Histoire des conciles*, 1:540ff.

The approval of the neighboring bishops made the ordination representatively an act of the entire church.

Imperial interference had increasingly to be reckoned with in key bishoprics. Theodoret relates, for instance, that prior to the Election of Ambrose the emperor Valens had summoned the neighboring bishops and instructed them, "Now, therefore, seat a man of such character among the high priestly chairs."[33] The bishops and the emperor paid deference to each other: "After the emperor had spoken these things, the synod begged him as being a wise and religious ruler to make the choice. He said, 'The responsibility is too great for us. You who have been worthy of the divine grace and have received illumination from above will make a better choice.'"[34]

TERMINOLOGY

The fourth century terminology in regard to ordination is mirrored in the language of the *Apostolic Constitutions.*

Cheirotonein ("ordain") is used of any formal appointment or institution as well as technically of ordination in the church. It is used of the three major orders and of sub-deacons, but the compiler draws the line here on who receives *cheirotonia.* However, in some loose series the word covers the lesser orders as well. This word refers to the whole ceremony of installation in the *Apostolic Constitutions,* not to Election nor to Imposition of hands.

Procheirizein ("appoint," "select") occurs often and seems indistinguishable from the meanings of *cheirotonein* except for its reference to the appointment of lesser orders. *Kathistanai* ("appoint," "install") is also frequent and appears in the variety of senses noticeable in non-ecclesiastical Greek. It occurs both interchangeably with and in contrast to *cheirotonein.*

Cheirothesia ("imposition of hands") is used of confirmation, reconciliation of penitents, benediction on the faithful, and benediction on catechumens. The word is thus used of any benediction bestowed by an imposition of hands, but is distinguished from a benediction which did not include this act (*eulogia*). The word continues in the language of the Greek Church today to mean a benediction. *Cheirothesia* is contrasted to *cheirotonia;* the compiler here has introduced a distinction not found

33. Theodoret, *H.E.* IV.vi.7.
34. Theodoret, *H.E.,* IV.vii.1.

elsewhere in early church literature, for *cheirothesia* customarily refers to the laying on of hands in ordination.[35]

Epithesis cheiron ("imposition of hands"), except in New Testament quotations about healing and about the apostles conferring the Holy Spirit, is used exclusively of ordination. The phrase is not the equivalent of *cheirotonia* but expresses the visible part of which *cheirotonia* is the whole. The phrase is used of the appointment of deaconesses and readers, although these receive *procheirizein* and not *cheirotonein*. This usage suggests that the compiler's distinctions were largely verbal, or else these two were really considered as ordained.

Katastasis appears to have been, if not the technical, at least the normal word for installation in Egypt. In addition to Serapion's Prayer-Book, this conclusion is supported by the usage of Athanasius.[36]

Canon 10 of the Council of Ancyra in 314 uses *kathistanai* interchangeably with *cheirotonein*. At the end of the century Basil of Caesarea used *cheirotonein* for the formal installation into office by a bishop (e.g. *Ep.* 53); however, *kathistanai* could still be employed interchangeably with this word on occasion (*Ep.* 225).

The Council of Sardica in 343[37] has special interest due to the fact that it issued its canons in both Greek and Latin so that we have parallel Greek and Latin terminology from the same date and place. *Ordinatio* and *ordinare* are the technical terms in the Latin, translating a variety of terms still used in the Greek for the formal act of *installation—horizein* and *katastasis* in Canon 15 (19).

MEANING OF THE INSTALLATION CEREMONY

Earlier passages have shown that the selection was interpreted as a divine choice. Special attention must now be given to the significance of the installation ceremony.

With the exception of the unsuccessful effort of the *Apostolic Constitutions,* the literature surveyed made no distinction between the Imposition of hands (*cheirothesia*) in ordination and the same act in the bestowal of benedictions. That this circumstance was no accident of terminology

35. Turner, "Χειροτονία, Χειροθεσία, Ἐπίθεσις Χειρῶν," 496–97.

36. E.g. *Apol. c. Arian* xi, where *cheirotonein* also occurs but with the meaning "elect" in distinction to the *katastasis*; xii; lxxv; *ad. Dracon.* ii.

37. See the new study of Hess, *The Canons of the Council of Sardica.* The texts are in Hefele and LeClercq, *Histoire des conciles,* 1:797–98.

is demonstrated by two explicit interpretations of ordination, from an Eastern and a Western theologian. Chrysostom gave a definition which has become a classic in the Greek Church. In *Homily* xiv on Acts 6, after stating that the people chose the seven, Chrysostom continues his comment on Luke's narrative: "For he says not how, but simply that they were ordained by prayer; for this is the ordination. The hand of man is laid on, but God performs everything, and it is His hand which touches the head of the one being ordained, if he is truly ordained."[38] Imposition of hands is subordinated to the constitutive act of Prayer, in response to which God bestows a blessing. Jerome similarly makes Prayer the central element in his definition of ordination in his commentary on Isaiah, XVI.58: "*Cheirotonian*—that is, the ordination of the clergy which is accomplished not only at the verbal prayer but at the imposition of the hand (lest indeed in mockery someone be ordained ignorantly to the clergy by a secret prayer)."[39] Jerome defines the technical term as consisting of two parts, the Prayer of the voice and the Imposition of the hand. The latter he explains in a wholly practical way: with the sacramental associations being given to ordination (below) an outward sign was required. But it is to be noticed that the sacramental powers are not ascribed to the Imposition of hands; indeed the action had a wholly subordinate place and the manner of expression gives primary emphasis to the Prayer.

By the fourth century the blessing received in ordination was identified with the Holy Spirit. The doctrine of ordination for this period is set forth with unusual clarity about AD 360 in a work of Lucifer of Cagliari in Sardinia about Athanasius. "It was and is in God's hand to institute the one who was thought worthy by his people to be bishop through those manifestly his servants, namely the catholic bishops. For no one can be filled with the power of the Holy Spirit to govern the people of God except the one whom God has chosen and on whom a hand has been placed by Catholic bishops, just as when Moses was dead we find his successor Joshua the son of Nun full of the Holy Spirit."[40] Lucifer clearly makes ordination an act of God: if it is performed by him through bishops on those chosen by the people of God. The installation is accomplished through the Imposition of hands, the necessary precondition, although not necessarily the means, of the giving of the Holy Spirit. The sending of the Holy Spirit would be God's induction of the person into office.

38. *PG* 60:1, 16. The Greek text requires the punctuation given.
39. *PL* 24:591.
40. *De S. Athan.* 1,9 (*CSEL* XIV).

Gregory of Nyssa gives expression to a doctrine of a sacramental change worked in a person through ordination, the only statement of the kind to be found in this period.

> Although before the benediction they are of little value, after the sanctification bestowed by the Spirit each has its several operation. The same power of the word also makes the priest venerable, honorable, and separated by the benediction bestowed on him from the common mass. While yesterday he was one of the mass, one of the people, he is suddenly rendered a guide, a president, a teacher of righteousness, an instructor in mysteries. And he does these things without being at all changed in body or in form; but while continuing to be in all appearance the man he was before, by some unseen power and grace the unseen soul is transformed for the better.[41]

Observe that the change is attributed to the Benediction and not to an action.

Gregory Nazianzen seemingly connects the Spirit with the Imposition of hands in his oration in praise of Basil. "For when he was almost dead, and breathless and had lost the greater part of his powers, he grew stronger in his last words, so as to depart with the utterances of religion, and, by ordaining the most excellent of his attendants, bestowed upon them both his hand and the Spirit."[42]

Athanasius, writing to the monk Dracontius, gives expression to a belief in a special gift bestowed in ordination. In chapter two he speaks of the "grace of the episcopate" Dracontius received, and in chapter four he makes this gift parallel to the one received in baptism, citing 1 Timothy 4:14. Nowhere does he elaborate on the nature of the gift or how it is received.

Theodoret relates an outburst by the monk Moses against the Arian interloper at the see of Alexandria, Lucius: "God forbid that I should be ordained by your hand, for the grace of the Spirit answers not your calling."[43]

Although the fourth century gave a certain explicitness to the idea that the grace of the Holy Spirit is received at ordination, this gift was thought as coming in response to the Prayer so that a relation to the concept of Benediction was quite in evidence.

---

41. "On the Baptism of Christ," *PG* 46:581D.

42. *Or.* 43:78 (*PG* 36:600). The translation is from the NPNF 7:421.

43. *H.E.* IV.xxiii.

SOME THINGS ORDINATION DID NOT MEAN

The priestly interpretation of ordination occurs only in the Syriac church at this date. In the Edessene Canons, called "The Doctrine of the Apostles" by Cureton, as part of the introduction we read the following: "And at the time of the great morning our Lord lifted up his hands, and laid them upon the heads of the Eleven Disciples, and gave to them the gift of the Priesthood."[44] Later additions to the "Doctrine of Addai" and the "Martyrdom of Barsamya" speak of receiving "the hand of the priesthood."[45] The Syriac church appears to have had a more sharply focused concern to continue the priesthood of the Old Testament than did the church in other regions.

Ordination was not conceived as conferring an indelible character so that the rite could not be repeated. Canon 8 adopted by the Nicene Council dealt with the Cathari (Novatians).

> Concerning those who call themselves Cathari if they (who are clerics) come over to the catholic and apostolic church, it is decreed by the holy and great synod that upon receiving a laying on of hands (*cheirothetoumenous*) they are to continue in the clergy . . . But if some come over where there is a bishop or presbyter of the catholic church, it is evident that the bishop of the church has the rank of the episcopate; and the one named a bishop by those called Cathari has the honor of the presbytery . . . in order that he may be seen to be of the clergy, and that there may not be two bishops in the city.[46]

The central problem in the interpretation of the canon involves the significance to be attached to the Imposition of hands. Is this the usual act in receiving repentant schismatics or is this a new ordination? The earliest Greek writer to cite the canon, Theophilus of Alexandria at the close of the fourth century, understood it as enjoining a fresh ordination.[47] This

---

44. Translated by Cureton, *Ancient Syriac Documents*, 24–25.

45. Phillips, ed., *The Doctrine of Addai, the Apostle*, 38; and Cureton, *Ancient Syriac Documents*, 71. Ephraem Syrus, *Hymn contra Haereses* xxii.18ff., says God on Sinai extended his hand over Moses and the rite continued in the Old Testament through John to Jesus and through him to the apostles and the church.

46. Hefele and LeClercq, *Histoire des conciles*, 1:576. This work takes the laying on as referring to the reconciliation of penitents.

47. *PG* 65:44.

meaning seems demanded by the synodal letter in which similar instructions are given in regard to Meletian clergy on their return to the catholic church.

> Since the synod was disposed to act gently (for in strict justice he was worthy of no leniency), it was decreed that Meletius should remain in his own city and have no authority to make appointments or to lay on hands (*cheirotherein*) or to appear in any city or village for this purpose, but should possess the bare title of his rank. Those who have been appointed by him, after they have been confirmed by a more sacred ordination (*cheirotonia*), may on these conditions be fellowshipped and have their rank and officiate, but they shall be the inferiors of those enrolled in each parish and church who have been ordained by our most honorable colleague Alexander. These have no authority to make appointments of persons pleasing to them or to propose names or to do anything without the permission of the bishop of the catholic and apostolic church serving under Alexander.[48]

From this context *cheirothetein* would be to lay on hands in ordination, for the Meletian clergy are to receive a new ordination.

The use of *cheirothesia* for laying on of hands in ordination by the Nicene bishops is also illustrated by canon 19.

> Concerning the Paulicianists who have fled for refuge to the catholic Church, it has been decreed that they must by all means be rebaptized. If any of them who in time past were found in the clergy and if they appear to be blameless and without reproach, when they have been rebaptized they are to be ordained by the bishop of the catholic Church. But if the examination finds them unfit, they ought to be deposed. Likewise in the case of their deaconesses and generally concerning those enrolled in the canon, the same policy shall be observed. Weare mindful of deaconesses enrolled on the list (since they do not have any laying on of hands—*cheirothesian*) that they are numbered only among the laity.[49]

The last sentence has caused difficulties, but we propose the following solution. The council is saying that the same procedure is followed for minor orders as for major orders: the converts are to take up the same position, if worthy, they held among the Paulicianists, but they have to go through the

---

48. Translated from the Greek text preserved by Theodoret, *H.E.* I.ix.7ff.

49. Hefele and LeClercq, *Histoire des conciles*, 1:615. The interpretation of the canon given in this work is in error.

same process used in appointing the faithful to these positions. *Cheirotonia* has either the generalized sense of "appoint," or, if the sense of "ordain" as we have rendered it, is not intended to be included in the same policy later enjoined (the examination and the placing on the church's canon, that is, the assistance roll comprising clergy and benevolent cases). *Cheirothesia* certainly refers to the Imposition of hands in ordination. This act deaconesses did not receive; hence the council is at pains to specify that they are technically "laity," although among the enrolled persons of the church and probably regarded as clergy by the Paulicianists.

The baptism of schimatics such as the Novatians and Meletians was accepted, but the baptism of heretical Paulicianists was not. That the ordination of neither was recognized as binding shows that ordination had not attained the same sacramental status as baptism. Only out of the context of the Donatist controversy did a doctrine of the indelibility of orders emerge.

Ordination did not make one a "minister-at-large." Canons 15 and 16 from Nicaea legislate against the translation of clergymen from one parish to another, either with or without the people's consent. A person certainly had the rank of his office wherever he went (he did not lose the right to exercise his ministry, with the permission of the bishop of the church where he was visiting), and he was a minister of the whole church as well as of his local church. On the other hand, he was considered as wedded to the church where he was ordained. A minister was ordained in and for a given church; his work was for a particular people at a particular place. Canon 16 even seems to envision a new ordination for those translated to another church, but since this probably involved a promotion as well no special significance need be attached to the fact. In the known instances of translation of bishops (as that of Eustathius from Berroea in Syria to Antioch)[50] only an Election by clergy and people is mentioned. No evidence of a renewed Imposition of hands is forthcoming, but some ceremony, such as an Enthronement, would seem to have been demanded in order to indicate the assumption of the new see. The increasing practice of translation and emphasis on the universal nature of the church broke down the congregational concept of ministry.

---

50. Theodoret, *H.E.* I.vii.10.

6

Ordination in the Ancient Church
III: Ordination in the Second and Third Centuries

A FAIRLY UNIFORM PRACTICE IN ordination has been found to exist throughout the church in the fourth century. Can this practice be traced to an earlier period? The answer is, "Indeed, yes." Nevertheless, the second and third centuries show more variety than the fourth century.

ROME AND NORTH AFRICA

We may appropriately begin this unit by an examination of a document greatly influential on the later church orders, the *Apostolic Tradition* of Hippolytus, written in the early third century but designedly conservative in its contents. The doubts that have arisen about R. H. Connolly's thorough-going identification of the "Egyptian Church Order" as the *Apostolic Tradition*[1] have been successfully dispelled.[2] The best critical edition is by Gregory Dix.[3]

1. Connolly, *The So-called Egyptian Church Order and Derived Documents*.

2. Botte, "L'authenticite de la *Tradition Apostolique de saint Hippolyte*." Elfers, "Neue Untersuchungen über die Kirchenordnung Hippolyts von Rom."

3. Dix, *The Treatise on the Apostolic Tradition of Hippolytus of Rome*. Quotations will be made from this edition.

Concerning bishops Hippolytus provides for their Election by all the people, a formal Ratification of the Election, and consecration to office by Prayer and the Imposition of hands.

> Let the bishop be ordained[4] being in all things without fault chosen by all the people.
>
> And when he has been proposed (*nominatus*) and found acceptable to all,[5] the people being assembled on the Lord's Day together with the presbytery and such bishops as may attend, let *the choice* be generally approved;[6]
>
> Let the bishops lay hands on him and the presbytery stand by in silence,
>
> And all shall keep silence praying in their heart for the descent of the Spirit.
>
> After this one of the bishops present at the request of all, laying his hand on him who is ordained bishop,[7] shall pray thus, saying:
>
>> O God and Father of our Lord Jesus Christ,
>>> Father of Mercies and God of all comfort,
>> Who dwellest on high yet hast respect unto the lowly
>> Who knowest all things before they come to pass;
>>> Who didst give ordinances unto Thy church "by the Word of Thy grace";
>>>> Who didst foreordain from the beginning the race of the righteous from Abraham,
>> instituting princes and priests and leaving not Thy sanctuary without ministers;
>>> Who from the foundation of the world hast been pleased to be glorified in them whom Thou hast chosen;
>> And now pour forth that Power. which is from Thee,
>>> of the princely Spirit which Thou didst deliver to Thy Beloved Child Jesus Christ,
>> which He bestowed on Thy holy Apostles
>> who established the Church

4. The eastern versions indicate *cheirotonein* was the original word.

5. The effort apparently was to win unanimous approval. If the nominatus refers to the selection (Designation), the "found acceptable" may imply a Scrutiny of qualifications. If it refers to the nomination of a candidate (as in Dix's translation), then the latter phrase indicates the Election.

6. If we follow Dix's interpretation here, provision is made for the neighboring bishops to give their approval of the worthiness of the candidate.

7. The double prayer and laying on of hands may indicate that two practices have become fused in the ceremony: one a corporate action (by a presbytery?) and the other an individual action.

which hallows Thee in every place to the endless glory and
praise of Thy name.
Father who knowest the hearts of all
    grant upon this Thy servant whom Thou hast chosen for the
    episcopate
    to feed Thy holy flock
    and serve as Thine high priest,
        that he may minister blamelessly by night and day,
    that he way unceasingly behold and propitiate Thy countenance
            and offer to Thee the gifts of Thy holy Church,
        And that by the high priestly Spirit he may have authority to
        forgive sins according to Thy commandment,
To assign lots according to Thy bidding,
to loose every bond according to the authority Thou gavest to
the Apostles,
and that he may please Thee in meekness and a pure heart, offering to Thee a sweet-smelling savour,
through whom to Thee be glory, might and praise,
to the Father and to the Son with the Holy Spirit now and ever
and world without end. Amen.[8]

Observe that the descent of the Holy Spirit, which occupies a prominent place, is in response to Prayer and not by the Imposition of hands.
The authority of the bishop "to assign lots" has generally been taken as a
reference to appointing lesser clergy; on the other hand Schermann makes
a good case for interpreting this duty as the distribution of the offerings
brought to the altar for the bishop to give to the poor.[9] "To assign portions"
or "to make distributions" would then be the best rendering. The bishop's
ordination occurred in the setting of the Sunday worship. The new bishop
proceeded immediately to the celebration of the Eucharist.

The instructions concerning the ordination of a presbyter have been
the occasion of much confusion.

> And when a presbyter is ordained (*cheirotonein*) the bishop shall
> lay his hand upon his head, the presbyters also touching him.
> And he shall pray over him according to the aforementioned
> form which we gave before over the bishop, praying and saying:
> O God and Father of our Lord Jesus Christ,

8. Dix, *The Treatise on the Apostolic Tradition of St. Hippolytus of Rome*, 4–6. For
the Prayer the Greek text has been preserved in the *Constitutions through Hippolytus*.
Otherwise the early and literal Latin version is the best source, where it exists. It is
printed in Schermann, *Die allgemeine Kirchenordnung*.

9. Schermann, *Die allgemeine Kirchenordnung*, 85–97.

> Look upon this Thy servant
> and impart to him the spirit of grace and counsel,
> > that he may share in the presbyterate and govern Thy people
> > in a pure heart.
> > As Thou didst look upon the people of Thy choice
> > > and didst command Moses to choose presbyters
> > > whom Thou didst fill with the spirit
> > > which Thou hadst granted to Thy minister,
> > So now, O Lord, grant that there may be preserved among us
> > unceasingly the Spirit of Thy grace,
> > and make us worthy that in faith we may minister to Thee
> > praising Thee in singleness of heart,
> Through Thy Child Christ Jesus through Whom to Thee be glory, might, and praise, to the Father and to the Son with the Holy Spirit in the holy Church now and for ever and world without end. Amen.[10]

Most scholars have followed the suggestion of C. H. Turner to the effect that the first part of the bishop's Prayer was to be repeated (through the phrase "praise of Thy Name") and then followed by the special Prayer applicable to the presbyter.[11] Characteristically, the Biblical precedent to which appeal is made is the choice of the Seventy Elders in the time of Moses.[12]

The section on deacons gives the fullest discussion of the theory of the ministry.

> And a deacon when he is appointed *(kathistanai)* shall be chosen according to what has been said before,[13] the bishop alone laying hands on him in the same manner. Nevertheless we order that the bishop alone shall lay on hands at the ordaining of a deacon for this reason:
> > that he is not ordained *(cheirotonein)* for a priesthood, but for the service of the bishop that he may do only the things commanded by him.

10. Dix, *The Treatise on the Apostolic Tradition of St. Hippolytus of Rome*, 18–19.

11. Turner, "The Ordination Prayer for a Presbyter in the Church Order of Hippolytus."

12. The "spirit of grace and counsel" is simply grace and counsel. The Holy Spirit, especially in the first part from the bishop's Prayer, is the same Spirit given to the Apostles and puts presbyters as well as bishops in the "succession."

13. The Election of the bishop by the people seems to be the only possible previous action to which this could refer.

For he is not appointed to be the fellow-counsellor of the whole clergy but to take charge of property and to report to the bishop whatever is necessary.

He does not receive the Spirit which is common to all the presbyterate, in which the presbyters share, but that which is entrusted to him under the bishop's authority.

Wherefore the bishop alone shall make (*cheirotonein*) the deacon.

But upon the presbyter the other presbyters also lay their hands because of the similar Spirit which is common to all the clergy.

For the presbyter has authority only for this one thing, to receive. But he has no authority to give holy orders.

Wherefore he does not ordain (*kathistanai*) a man to orders but by laying on hands at the ordination of a presbyter he only blesses (lit. seals, *sphragizein*) while the bishop ordains (*cheirotonein*).

Over a deacon, then, let him say thus:

O God, who hast created all things and hast ordered them by the Word Father of our Lord Jesus Christ

whom Thou didst send to minister Thy will and reveal unto us Thy desire;

grant the Holy Spirit of grace and earnestness and diligence upon this Thy servant[14]

whom Thou hast chosen to minister to Thy church and to bring up in holiness to Thy holiness that which is offered to Thee by Thine ordained high priests to the glory of Thy name;

so that ministering blamelessly and in purity of heart

he may by Thy good will be found worthy of this high and exalted office,

praising Thee through Thy Child Jesus Christ our Lord

through whom to Thee with Him be glory, might and praise with the Holy Spirit in the holy Church now and ever and world without end. Amen.[15]

This passage is instructive, but some phrases are not as clear as might be desired. One receives the impression that Hippolytus protests too much. Are these relatively new ideas concerning a ministry of three grades?

14. On the basis of Hippolytus' statement that the deacon "does not receive the Spirit common to the presbyterate" and of the parallel phrase in the Prayer for a presbyter, this phrase should read "grant the spirit of grace. . ." (with the Ethiopic) and not "grant the Holy Spirit" as Dix reads following the Latin.

15. Dix, *The Treatise on the Apostolic Tradition of St. Hippolytus of Rome*, 15–17.

The Imposition of hands by presbyters in the ordination of another presbyter is interpreted as a Benediction, or an act of "sealing" what the bishop does. The bishop's Imposition of hands "ordains." But what content is to be put in the word *cheirotonein*? It cannot be the imparting of the Spirit, because in this passage the reason given for the presbyters' Imposition of hands is the "similar Spirit which is common to all the clergy." The fact that *cherotonein* in this section is used interchangeably with *kathistanai*, unlike the distinction made in the rest of the treatise, perhaps indicates that the bishop's action is nothing more than the constitutive act.

In both the deacon's and bishop's Prayers there is a statement that God has chosen the person to be his servant. The means of this choice was an Election by the people.

One important point emerges from the discussion of the lesser orders: *cheirotonia* and a laying on of hands are denied to all but the bishops, presbyters, and deacons. The reason given in the passage about widows is that the clergy offer the oblation and have a liturgical ministry (*leitourgia*). Other functionaries are "appointed" (*katastasis*) or "named" or given a symbol of their work (a book was handed to the Reader). The earliest use of *cheirotonein* in a restricted technical sense, referring to the bishop's action in the installation of church functionaries, thus occurs in the *Apostolic Tradition*.

A description of how the Election of bishops might be decided in actual practice and how the people viewed such occasions would supplement Hippolytus' formal directions. Such an insight is provided by Eusebius' account of the selection of Fabian as bishop of Rome in AD 236.

> It is said that Fabian, after the death of Anteros, came from the country along with others and stayed at Rome, where he came into the clergy in a most miraculous manner, according to the divine and heavenly grace. For when the brethren were all assembled for the election of the one who was going to succeed to the episcopate, many notable and distinguished men were in the thoughts of many. Fabian, who was there, came into no one's mind, but suddenly, they relate, a dove flew down from above and settled on his head in clear imitation of the descent of the Holy Spirit in the form of a dove upon the Saviour. Whereupon the whole people, as if moved by one divine spirit, with all eagerness and with one soul cried out, "Worthy," and immediately took him and placed him on the throne of the episcopate.[16]

16. *H.E.* VI.xxix. Greek text for Eusebius in GCS.

The psychology of early Christian Elections emerges clearly from this account. Nomination was not simply proposing a name in a casual way. The people expected some divine guidance as to the name that "came to mind"; a spontaneous recognition indicated the working of God's Spirit. Nomination was proposing a person who would have divine approval. The combination of Nomination, Acclamation, and Enthronement has a superficial resemblance to certain selections of emperors, but each item had ample roots in Christian practice.[17] The context, also, is specifically Christian—the omen of the dove became a substitute for the Inspired Designation of earlier times.

Cyprian's writings from the mid-third century bind together Rome and North Africa as having the same practice in ordination. Cyprian ascribed a definite role to the laity, the clergy of a city, and the bishops of neighboring churches. In his doctrinal interpretation he stresses that it is God who places the person into office.

The ordination of Cornelius as bishop of Rome and the subsequent schism by Novatian provided the occasion for some of Cyprian's most important pronouncements. One passage summarizes Cyprian's position: "Cornelius was made bishop by the judgment of God and his Christ, by the testimony of nearly all the clergy, by the vote of the people who were present, by the company of old priests and good men."[18]

Of the same import are numerous other passages.[19]

That ordination is God's action appears in many of Cyprian's statements.[20] Not only is the office the institution of God but individuals also fill the office according to God's will, knowledge, and assistance. A person is worthy because of the influence of God in his life, so it may be said that God's "decision" makes a bishop. The "judgment of God" is listed separately from the human actions. No *one* item in the process is made to correspond to the act of God. At the same time God is working through the laity in choosing a bishop and through the bishops in installing him into office, so that the parts of the process are united into one whole. The appointment from God is said to ensure worthy priests; on the other hand, one passage (*Ep.* LXVII.2) gives the reverse emphasis: the people are to choose those who are worthy so that God will accept their ministry.

17. Stommel, "Bischofstuhl und höher Thron," 66–72.

18. *Ep.* LV.9. For the Cyprian correspondence we follow the edition of Hartel for *CSEL*, vol. III.

19. *Epp.* LIX.5 and 6; XLIV.2 and 3; LXVIII.2.

20. In addition to previous references note *Epp.* XLVIII, 3; LV,9; LXI, 3; LXVI, 1 and 9.

In one place Cyprian seems to speak as if the only reason for the presence of the laity at Elections of bishops was to guarantee the choice of a worthy person (*Ep.* LXVII.4). Later in the passage the role of the laity is made more explicit as that of giving their vote. The same epistle stresses the obligation of the people to withdraw from unworthy clergymen (ibid., 3). *Suffragium* carries its full meaning of "vote" in Cyprian.

Although having a determinative role in the selection of episcopal candidates, the laity's suffrage may have been exercised only on a candidate given a prior Nomination by the clergy. This inherently probable procedure is indicated if (as seems likely) there is a deliberate sequence in the passage quoted above: the judgment of God, the testimony of the clergy, the vote of the people, the company of the priests (i.e. the assembly of neighboring bishops). In *Ep.* LXVIII.2 the local clergy share the *suffragium* of the people; whether a separate vote or participation in the general Election is not indicated. However, in the "Life of Cyprian," supposedly written by his deacon Pontius, the people had the initiative in the Election of Cyprian and presented him as their candidate to the clergy for Ratification. Some of the latter had their reservations, but the ordination proceeded with Cyprian being seated in the episcopal chair.[21]

The neighboring bishops were present to bestow the episcopate in a formal Imposition of hands (*Ep.* LXVII.5) . Otherwise, Cyprian has little to say about the Imposition of hands and the interpretation to be given to this act.

Other members of the clergy below the rank of bishop were filled by the bishop, but ordinarily with the approval of the rest of the clergy and of the people (which could be dispensed with in time of emergency.[22]

ASIA MINOR

The Greek East demonstrated its attachment to historic democratic processes in the prominence given to Parochial Election. The "Life" of the third century bishop Gregory Thaumaturgus by the fourth century Gregory of Nyssa gives striking details of the Election of a bishop. Although the later Gregory's language is that of his own time, there seems no reason to doubt the basic accuracy of the report of the events. The description accords well with the circumstances of the third century. The narrative is all

---

21. "Life of Cyprian," 5, 6. English translation in Deferrari, trans., *Early Christian Biographies*. The Latin text in *CSEL* Vol. III, Part III.

22. *Epp.* III.3; XXIX; XXXVIII.1 and 2; XXXIX.

the more remarkable because it records the institution of a new episcopal see. The people of Comana had invited the missionary Gregory to come and ordain a bishop for them.

> When the time came to accomplish their request and proclaim someone of the church their high priest, then the leading men busied themselves to put forward those considered conspicuous in eloquence, in ancestry, and in other things. Since these things were in the great Gregory, they considered it necessary that these things not be lacking in the one coming to this grace. Because the votes were divided and some preferred one and some another, Gregory awaited some counsel from God to come to him concerning one to be appointed . . . As the people presented their several candidates with commendations each in behalf of his choice, he recommended that they look among those of lower station of life (for it was possible that someone would be found among these more endowed with riches of the soul than those most conspicuous in life). One of those presiding at the vote felt pride and irony at such judgment of the great . . . and coming to him he said tauntingly: "If you recommend these things, to overlook such who have been chosen from the whole city and to take someone from the lowest ranks for elevation to the priesthood, it is time for you to call Alexander the charcoal-maker to the priesthood. If you say so, we, the whole city, transferring the votes to this one, will agree together." . . . It entered Gregory's mind that it was not without divine providence that Alexander came to the minds of the voters and was mentioned. And he said, "Who is this Alexander of whom you make mention?"

The man mentioned as occupying the lowliest position turned out to be a philosopher who had been converted to Christianity. He had taken up his trade in order to avoid observation and to follow his philosophical studies with greater privacy. Impressed, Gregory planned to win popular support for him as bishop. After accomplishing his purpose, Gregory gave a lecture on the dangers of superficial judgments. "After he said these things, he presents the man to God by consecration after the form prescribed for the impartation of grace."[23]

Presumably Gregory was the only bishop present to perform the ordination. The author's failure to speak of details in the ceremony of installation is more than compensated for by the full picture of the Election.

23. *Vita S. Greg. Thaum. PG* 46:933ff.

We see the full arrangements for Elections in Greek civil life, including Election-conducting officials, distinct from the visiting bishop. Nomination was important, and it was related to the expectation of divine guidance: God caused a given name to come to mind and be submitted to the people. There is abundant reference to the voting, the division of the populace so that no one had a clear majority, and the evident desire to secure unanimous support for a spiritually worthy candidate.

Asia Minor is also the locale which furnishes the earliest reference to the laying on of hands in an ordination setting outside the New Testament. In the *Acts of Peter* (The Vercelli Acts) from about the year 200 Peter is addressed: "If, therefore, you, on whom He imposed hands and whom He elected, did doubt, I, having this testimony, repent, and take refuge in your prayers."[24]

The reference is to the appointment of Peter as an apostle; apparently the act of Imposition of hands was so common in ordination that the author could not think of conferring an office in the church without it. The Imposition of hands must have already had a history in church life, a fact which would go far to fill the gap in our evidence in regard to ordination during the second century.[25]

PALESTINE AND SYRIA

The region of the first home of Christianity knew some anomalous practices. One of these, traces of which barely survive in the literature but which may not have been uncommon, was the appointment of a successor by a dying bishop. Theodoret records one definite instance of such in the late fourth century at Antioch:

> After him when Evagrius had occupied his see, hostility was still shown to the great Flavianus, notwithstanding the fact that the promotion of Evagrius was a violation of the law of the Church, for he had been promoted by Paulinus alone in disregard of many canons. For a dying bishop is not permitted to ordain another to take his place, and all the bishops of a province are ordered to be convened.[26]

24. *Act. Pet.* 10; Latin text in Vouaux, *Les Actes de Pierre*.
25. Behm, *Die Handauflegung im Urchristentum*, 73.
26. *H.E.* V.xxiii. Translation from NPNF.

Canon 23 of the Council of Antioch earlier in the century contains the prohibition:

> It shall not be lawful for a bishop to appoint another in his place as his successor, even if it happens at the end of his life. And if any such thing is done, the appointment shall be invalid.[27]

We may be reminded that what no one does no one prohibits. The canon is a confirmation of the practice of Episcopal Designation of a successor, presumably a practice which would reach back into the third century.

Alerted to the possibility, we may be able to see something in the earlier literature that otherwise would be missed. There is a set of passages in the Pseudo-Clementines giving a brief statement of the appointment of bishops at various places by Peter. At Tyre, "Peter established a church and installed (*kathistanai*) for them a bishop from one of the presbyters who were with him."[28] The same pattern was followed at Sidon, Beirut, and Laodicea.[29] A fuller statement of the same import is made of Peter's activities at Tripolis.[30] With Schmidt we would agree that the editor has the general standpoint of the catholic church of the third century that all bishops are of the same rank and have received their appointment from the apostles.[31] But is not even more indicated? The choice in each case is Designation by the Apostle. Puzzling is the fact that Peter makes the Designation out of Presbyters who traveled with him. A large entourage of traveling presbyters from whom local bishops are appointed is quite improbable. But another solution suggests itself. The compiler is reflecting practices from his own time—the bishop designated and ordained his successor from the circle of presbyters in his church.[32]

---

27. Lauchert, *Die Kanones der wichtigsten altkirchlichen Concilien*.

28. *Hom.* VII.v.3. The Greek text has been newly edited by Bernhard Rehm, *Die Pseudoklementinen*, for GCS. The latest study, and containing a review of previous research into the complicated literary history of the Pseudo-Clementines is Georg Strecker, *Das Judenchristentum in den Pseudoklementinen*. A brief survey in English of the critical positions is Fitzmyer, "The Qumran Scrolls, The Ebonites, and their Literature," 345–50.

29. *Hom.* VII.viii.3; xii.2; XX.xxiii.3.

30. *Hom.* XI.xxxvi.2.

31. Schmidt, *Studien zu den Pseudo-Clementinen*, 333–34.

32. More evidence of this practice will be forthcoming from the writings of Origen, but the Alexandrian stage will have to be set before considering his testimony.

The Pseudo-Clementines show a close affinity with Jewish Christianity. Another set of references presents in a Christian dress ideas which have been found in Rabbinic Judaism.

Jesus Christ is presented as the true prophet who, like Moses, hands down an authoritative tradition through a succession of teachers. In what has been called the "oldest document" of the Clementina,[33] the "Epistle of Peter to James," this idea is the dominant theme. Peter is pictured as warning James not to commit the books of his preachings to the Gentiles, or to any of "our own race" without examination. "But if any one who has been proved is found worthy, then to him commit them according to the traditional practice, even as Moses delivered his teaching to the seventy who succeeded to his chair."[34]

A Christian counterpart in the apostles and early disciples to the seventy elders of Numbers 11 and their role in Pharisaic tradition is evident from several passages.[35]

The taking over of the action and associations of Solemn Seating from the Jewish background is prominent even in those passages more in line with the orthodox tradition of the Church. The "Epistle of Clement to James" purports to be the announcement of the ordination of Clement as bishop of Rome. Now instead of a Jewish-Christian under the mask of Peter, a Gentile Christian writes under the mask of Clement.[36] Although there is Imposition of hands in this ordination, the central conception is the Seating of the candidate on the *cathedra* of the teacher. Peter speaks:

> I ordain *(cheirotonein)* for you as bishop this Clement, to whom
> I entrust my chair of discourse.[37]
> Clement protested his unworthiness:
> While he was speaking, I knelt before him and entreated him,
> declining the honor and authority of the chair.[38]

33. Schmidt, *Studien zu den Pseudo-Clementinen*, 316.

34. *Ep. Pt. ad Jas.* 1:2.

35. Ibid., 2; *Hom.* II.xxxviii.1; *Recog.* I.xl. According to Schoeps, *Theologie und Geschichte des Judenchristentums*, 51–52, the latter two passages go back to a "Preachings of Peter," one of the two main documents drawn on by the "Source Document" which is the basis of the two recensions surviving as the "Homilies" and "Recognitions" of Clement. In the *Contestatio,* the latter part of the document containing the "Epistle of Peter to James," there is described the initiation of a scholar into the Christian Rabbinic Academy, a ceremony without parallel in Christian or Jewish sources.

36. Schmidt, *Studien zu den Pseudo-Clementinen*, 328–29.

37. *Clem. ad Jac.* 2 :2.

38. Ibid., 3:1.

Peter replied as follows:
This chair has no need of a presumptuous man who loves the position.[39]

After a charge to Clement which gives first importance to teaching ahead of judging and an extensive discussion of the organization of the church Peter gives a charge to the people. "You also, my beloved brethren and fellow-servants, be subject to the president of the truth in all things, knowing this, that the one who grieves him has not received Christ, with whose chair he has been entrusted."[40]

The ordination of Clement was performed according to the following description: "Having said these things and laid his hands on me in the presence of all, he compelled me to be installed in his own chair."[41]

A similar account in some detail is given of Peter's ordination of Zacchaeus as bishop of Caesarea in the third *Homily*. Peter states the following:

> Since therefore it is necessary to set apart someone instead of me to fill my place, let us all pray to God with one accord, in order that he might make known who among us is the best, that having been installed in the chair of Christ he may administer his church piously.[42]

After a discourse on the value of monarchy, the narrative continues: "After he said this, he laid hold on Zacchaeus which was standing by and forced him to sit down in his own chair."[43]

Then *after* the Seating occurs the Imposition of a hand and the Prayer (which in this case bears no resemblance to any other that has been preserved).[44]

The word rendered "install" in these quotations is *kathistanai.* Its close association with the placing of the candidate in a chair in these accounts may have some relation to the prevalence of the word even at a later date.

The *Didascalia,* from Syria in the middle of the third century, has some references of importance for ordination. Concerning the "pastor who is appointed bishop and head among the presbytery in the Church" it

39. Ibid., 3:2.
40. Ibid., 17:1.
41. Ibid., 19:1.
42. *Hom* III.lx.1.
43. *Ibid.* lxiii.1.
44. *Ibid.* lxxii. Cf. *Recog.* III.65–66, for a briefer account in Latin.

is directed that he "be proved when he receives the imposition of hands to sit in the office of the bishopric."[45] In keeping with the general picture of the bishop as the center of the community, it is he who appoints the rest of the clergy, apparently without any intervention by the people.[46]

The region of Syria and Palestine definitely shows a greater prominence by the clergy and a more marked monarchial tendency than the rest of the Church at this period.

EGYPT, ESPECIALLY ALEXANDRIA

A series of relatively late but independent witnesses testify to something unusual in the ordination procedure of the church at Alexandria in the ante-Nicene period.

Jerome provides the earliest evidence in his letter to Evangelus.

> At Alexandria from the time of Mark the Evangelist until Heraclas and Dionysius the presbyters always named (*nominabant*) as bishop one elected out of their own number and placed on a higher rank, just as an army makes an emperor or deacons elect from themselves one whom they know to be diligent and call him arch-deacon. For what except ordination does a bishop do that a presbyter does not do?[47]

Jerome thus affirms that at Alexandria the presbyters both selected and installed their bishop. Although there was an Election and a placing in a higher rank (Solemn Seating?), the significant action was the Naming, bestowing the title "bishop."[48] The natural sense of the words indicates that the practice covered the episcopates of both Heraclas and Dionysius, but the manner of expression shows that Jerome did not know when it came to an end. Since these were the last two bishops known to Origen, Jerome's information may have come from Origen.[49]

45. *Didas.* 4. We quote the translation of Connolly, *Didascalia Apostolorum.* The Syriac word for "laying on" is from the root *śim.*

46. *Didas.* 9.

47. *Ep.* 146. *PL* 22:1194.

48. Müller, "Kleine Beiträge zur alten Kirchengeschichte," 278, points out that according to his parallels Jerome meant "called," not "nominate" by *nominabant.* The sentence structure also would be against "nominate."

49. Telfer, "Episcopal Succession in Egypt," 4.

The strongest independent support for Jerome comes from Severus Monophysite patriarch of Antioch in the early sixth century who was exiled to Alexandria. He offers the following testimony:

> The bishop also of the city, renowned for its orthodox faith, of the Alexandrines was in old times appointed by presbyters: but in modern times, in accordance with the canon which has prevailed everywhere, the solemn institution of their bishop is performed by bishops, and no one makes light of the accurate practice that prevails in the holy churches and recurs to the earlier condition of things, which has given way to the later clear and accurate, deliberate and spiritual injunctions.[50]

This tradition continued in the Alexandrian church and was preserved in the *Annals* of the tenth century Melkite patriarch of the city, Eutychius. Although Eutychius does not come off too well as a historian, his details and the agreement of his account with earlier testimony suggest that he was using good sources in the following passage:

> Mark the Evangelist appointed at the same time with the patriarch Hananias twelve presbyters who were to be with the patriarch, so that when there was a vacancy in the patriarchate they should elect one of the twelve presbyters and the remaining eleven laying their hands on his head should bless him and make him patriarch. Afterwards they should elect another eminent man who would be appointed in the place of the one made patriarch, that there might always be twelve. And this custom of the twelve presbyters of Alexandria appointing the patriarch out of themselves continued until the time of Alexander patriarch of Alexandria, who was one of the 318 (at Nicaea). He forbade the presbyters henceforth to appoint the patriarch. He decreed that on the death of a patriarch the bishops who would ordain a bishop should convene. He further decreed that on a vacancy in the patriarchate they should elect any excellent man of well-known worth, whether one of those twelve presbyters or any other, from the region and make him patriarch. And thus ceased that ancient custom by which the patriarch was made by the presbyters alone, and the power of making the patriarch came to belong in its place to the bishops . . . From Hananias, whom Mark the Evangelist appointed patriarch of Alexandria, to the time of Demetrius the patriarch (who was eleventh in the succession) there was no bishop in the provinces of Egypt,

50. Brooks, ed., *The Sixth Book of the Select Letters of Severus Patriarch of Antioch*, 2:213.

nor had the patriarchs before him appointed a bishop. When he was made patriarch he appointed three bishops, and he was the first patriarch of Alexandria who made bishops. On the death of Demetrius, Heraclas was elected patriarch of Alexandria, who appointed twenty bishops.[51]

Telfer has brought together the confirmations of Eutychius' statements and has shown the dependence of all of Egypt on Alexandria for its bishops.[52] Eutychius not only testifies to the custom of presbyters ordaining the bishop, but he also explains the reason. For a long time there were no other bishops in Egypt. Eutychius fixes the time of the change in the constitution of the Alexandrian church between the episcopates of Alexander and Athanasius.[53]

A younger contemporary of Eutychius, the Egyptian Monophysite bishop Severus, has been appealed to as preserving a more reliable Egyptian tradition. His accounts of the ordination of the patriarchs of Alexandria through the fourth century show considerable variety but within a pattern.[54] The early bishops were only names to the historian. In describing their appointment he stresses the selection by the people and generally mentions the presence of other bishops (but he gives incidental confirmation that Demetrius was the first bishop to appoint other bishops). These statements follow the same pattern as the formulas announcing the appointment of fourth-century patriarchs. The conclusion which presents itself is that Severus has made up the earlier accounts according to his knowledge of later practice.

Demetrius is the first bishop of whom Severus has historical knowledge, and this is through Eusebius. But it is to be noted that with Demetrius there begins a series of bishops of whom no details are supplied for their appointment. It hardly seems accidental that the first bishops for whom details of their lives are known are those for whom the least is recorded about their ordination. The first of the "historical" bishops details of whose appointment are given is Peter I; and with the addition of a selection of him by his predecessor the account corresponds exactly to the Jerome-Eutychius version of episcopal consecration at Alexandria.

51. A Latin translation is given in *PG* 111:982.

52. Telfer, "Episcopal Succession in Egypt," 2–4.

53. Perhaps Telfer (ibid., 12) is right in conjecturing that Alexander accepted the fourth canon of Nicaea requiring episcopal consecration of bishops in return for the extended jurisdiction granted Alexandria in the sixth canon.

54. Translated by B. Evetts in *History of the Patriarchs of the Coptic Church of Alexandria*, vol. 1, fasc. 2 and 4, 144–55, 175–211, 383–425.

Severus has apparently reproduced a source contrary to his own principles at this point.

The *Canons of Hippolytus* add a confirmatory testimony. Since the studies of R. H. Connolly, it is generally held that the *Canons of Hippolytus* are no earlier than the latter half of the fourth century.[55] Egypt would seem the most likely place of composition, both because the work survives only in Arabic and because the theory of the ministry would only have been stated by someone familiar with early Alexandrian history. Since the compiler of these canons was only revising the *Apostolic Tradition,* we need not quote from it at length. The person who imposes his hand and prays over the bishop-elect is said to be "one of the bishops and presbyters."[56] The regulations concerning the presbyter are most instructive:

> If now a presbyter is ordained, all things are done with him in the same way as with the bishop, except he is not seated in the chair.
>
> Also in the same way a prayer is prayed over him in all respects like that over a bishop, with the exception only of the name of the episcopate.
>
> The bishop in all things is equal to the presbyters except in the name of the chair and in ordination, which power of ordaining is not assigned to him.[57]

This is a theory of the ministry strikingly like that held by Jerome. The bishop differs from a presbyter only in the special seat given him and in the power of ordination. The similarity was enforced by directing that a similar Prayer be stated except for the name "bishop." The directions of the *Apostolic Tradition* apparently were misunderstood and its Prayer for a presbyter was simply omitted.[58] The obvious reason for the compiler taking this alternative and giving the directions which he did was that he had a theory of the ministry based on the recollection of an earlier state of affairs, when there was no great difference between presbyters and bishops and when ordination was restricted to the chief minister (who occupied the chair) for the sake of the order of the church.

55. Connolly, *The So-called Egyptian Church Order and Derived Documents,* 132–33.

56. *CH* II, 10. The Arabic has been translated into Latin by Haneburg and printed in Hans Achelis, "Die Canones Hippolyti," and into German by Riedel, *Die Kirchenrechtsquellen des Patriarchats Alexandrien,* 200–230.

57. *CH* IV, 30–32.

58. Turner, "The Ordination Prayer for a Presbyter in the Church Order of Hippolytus."

Origen, who himself received ordination to be a presbyter through the Imposition of the hands of Palestinian bishops,[59] is a key figure for Alexandrian practice. However, his interest was mainly theological, and his few statements of interest exist only in Latin translation.

In discussing Lev 8:4–5 Origen gives two reasons for the presence of the people at an ordination: to be witnesses to the person's character, and to prevent any refusal by the people to obey.[60] On another occasion Origen expresses the thought that a person who has the qualifications laid down by Paul is a bishop in God's sight even if he does not receive ordination by men.[61] Again, Origen stressed the selection of the man God would choose, appealing to the practice of the Apostles in selecting a successor to Judas by praying and committing the outcome "not to chance but . . . to a divine choice by providence."[62]

In commenting on the appointment of Joshua, Origen emphasizes that Moses did not select one of his sons or nephews but asked God to make the choice. He then applies a lesson to the practice of his own day.

> If therefore such a one as Moses gives not his judgment in elect-ing a leader of the people, in appointing a successor, what man would be he who dares to do so, either of the people who are always accustomed to be moved by shouts for favor or perhaps excited for money, or of those who may even be priests and judge themselves suitable for this task, except only him to whom through prayers and petitions it is revealed by God? You hear as God says to Moses: . . . (Num. 27:18–20). You hear obviously the ordination of a leader of the people clearly described, so that there is almost no need of exposition. Here there was held no ac-clamation of the people, no regard of kinship, no consideration of friendship . . . The Government of the people is delivered to him whom God elected.[63]

Origen's language in the whole context perhaps points to his knowl-edge of three different modes of selection: by the bishop himself (note that Moses does not appoint his own successor), by the clergy of the church or from neighboring churches (the "priests"), and the acclamation of the

59. Eusebius, *H.E.* VI.viii.4; xix.16; xxiii.4.

60. *Hom.* in Lev. VI.3. The text for Origen followed is that of Baehrens *Origenes Werke*, vol. 6.

61. *Comm. Mt.* Ser 12. Ibid., vol. 12 (cf. Clem. Alex., *Strom.* VI.xiii.106.)

62. *Hom.* in Joshua XXIII, 2. Ibid., vol. 7.

63. *Hom.* in Num. XXII, 4. Ibid.

people (who could be stirred by less than spiritual motives).[64] These procedures were characteristic of Palestine, Alexandria, and the Greek East, respectively. Against all of these methods Origen is advocating the committing or the choice to a spiritual man who through prayer knows the mind of God.

Egypt is the probable provenance of the *Apostolic Church Order,* which in its present form probably dates from the beginning of the fourth century. Harnack has identified two source documents dealing with the church order, which go back to the end of the second century, in the latter part of the work.[65] The instructions concerning the Election of a bishop belong to one of these sources. "If there are a few men and a congregation where there are not twelve men competent to vote at the election of a bishop, they are to write the neighboring churches where there is a settled one so that the selected men may come thence and examine carefully who is worthy."[66]

Election by the men of the congregation is presupposed, and there seems no necessity that the three men from neighboring churches be clergymen. The following chapter states, "He who has been appointed (*kathistanai*) bishop . . . shall appoint two presbyters whom he approves."[67] This provision is ascribed by Harnack to the last redaction of the church order. Accepting the analysis of Harnack, Hennecke has sought to place the document in the history of the Egyptian church by postulating an intermediate stage in its development, dating from c. 230, as part of the program of Demetrius and Heraclas for instituting bishops in the outlying churches from Alexandria.[68] Whether this be accepted, the primitive state of affairs could have prevailed almost anywhere, and thus we are prepared to turn to the earliest period of the church.

---

64. This interpretation accounts for different scholars finding in the passage what they want to find: Emil Goeller, "Die Bischofswahl bei Origenes," 611–13; Telfer, "Episcopal Succession in Egypt," 9; Müller, "Kleine Beiträge zur alten Kirchengeschichte," 283; Gore, *The Church and the Ministry,* 126–29; Kemp, "Bishops and Presbyters at Alexandria," 129–31.

65. Harnack, *Die Quellen der Sogenannten Apostolischen Kirchenordnung,* 6.

66. *ApCO* 16. The Greek text is printed by Schermann, *Die allgemeine Kirchenordnung.*

67. Ibid., 17.

68. Hennecke, "Zur Apostolischen Kirchenordnung," 246–48.

7

Ordination in the Ancient Church
IV: Ordination in the First Century

CONTINUING THE APPROACH OF bringing the evidence of the historical background and foreground to bear on the interpretation of the New Testament, we lead into the New Testament from the earliest non-canonical documents. Their testimony adds little new information but harmonizes with what the New Testament itself and the other evidence would lead one to expect.

THE APOSTOLIC FATHERS

The description of the ministry and the general tone of the *Didache* make it difficult to date this document much later than the opening years of the second century. There is one passage in the *Didache* of great significance for the constitutional development of the church. The document enjoins the following: "Elect (*cheirotonesate*) therefore for yourselves bishops and deacons worthy of the Lord—meek men, not lovers of money, truthful, and approved—for they minister also for you the ministry of the prophets and teachers" (*Did.* xv.1–12).[1]

The word *cheirotonein* still has the overtones of its classical meaning, regardless of how the community might actually proceed in selecting and

---

1. The Greek text edited by Kirsopp Lake is given in the LCL.

giving approval to its leaders.[2] The main point is that it is community action. The feature of worthiness (the kind of man God himself would choose) is confirmed by the man being "approved" (*dokimazein*, "scrutinized").

Although the Ignatian letters provide no information on the selection of the regular officers of the church, they do mention corporate congregational procedure in the choice of delegates to perform specific missions.[3] The word used for the church's action is *cheirotonein*. The church's choice serves "to commission" one for his task.[4]

The letter of the church at Rome to the church at Corinth, known as *1 Clement*, written at the close of the first century, includes a highly interesting passage.

> The Apostles received the Gospel for us from the Lord Jesus Christ, Jesus the Christ was sent from God. The Christ therefore is from God and the Apostles from the Christ . . . They preached from district to district, and from city to city, and they appointed their first converts, testing them by the Spirit, to be bishops and deacons of future believers . . .
>
> Our Apostles also knew through our Lord Jesus Christ that there would be strife for the title of bishop. For this cause, therefore, since they had received perfect foreknowledge, they appointed those who have been already mentioned, and afterwards added the codicil that if they should fall asleep, other approved men should succeed to their ministry. We consider therefore that it is not just to remove from their ministry those who were appointed by them, or later on by other eminent men, with the consent of the whole Church, and have ministered to the flock of Christ without blame.[5]

The "apostolic succession" of the first passage is not a perpetuation of the apostolate or its apostolic qualities. The bishops and deacons are successors of the apostles in the same way that the apostles are in succession from Christ.[6] Clement is leading up to the next section by showing that the offices of bishops and deacons are of apostolic appointment. The apostles

---

2. The compiler of the *Apostolic Constitutions*, for whom *cheirotonein* no longer meant "elect," when he reproduced the *Didache* substituted *procheirizein* in this passage (VII.xxxi).

3. "It is fitting that your church elect a divine ambassador"—*Smyr.* xi.2. Cf. *Philad.* xi.l. Lightfoot, *The Apostolic Fathers*, Part II, vol. II.

4. *Polyc.* vii.2.

5. *Clem.* xlii.1, 2, 4; xliv.1–3. Translation by Kirsopp Lake in LCL.

6. Cf. the comprehensive study of Gerke, *Die Stellung des Ersten Clemensbriefes.*

(the Twelve for Clement) appointed (*kathistanai*) men to office, having "proved them by the Spirit."

Clement speaks of a codicil or "second enactment" by the apostles. It must be granted that Dix has made a case on the basis of the grammar for this enactment referring to a succession of the apostles' function of appointing to office.[7] However, his reconstruction depends upon too many assumptions as to the meaning of words in the passage: the chief one being on the crucial point of limiting appointment to office to apostles and their successors and making this their distinctive "ministry." It is best, with Lightfoot,[8] to interpret chapter forty-four as describing a succession in the office of bishops. There was no strife over the succession to the apostolic function, and the introduction of this subject not only would have failed to clarify the situation at Corinth but also would be an intrusion into the context. The "approved men" refer to the same group, "bishops." The "eminent men," on the other hand, may refer to others than (or in addition to) "bishops," who appointed men to office (one thinks of Timothy and Titus).

The picture suggested by *1 Clement* involves community approval and an authoritative induction into office. The *kathistanai* more naturally refers to an induction into office, but the appointing officials may have had a larger function, inasmuch as the activity of the people in giving their consent implies that someone else has submitted names of nominees to them.

The occasion of the writing of *1 Clement* was the removal from office of a presbyter (or presbyters) by the majority at Corinth. This considerable exercise of congregational autonomy is not directly disputed by the Roman church, only the removal of worthy men. The removal of an unworthy presbyter is hinted at in Polycarp's letter to the Philippians, chapter eleven.

A very close parallel to Clement's language is to be found in a story about the apostle John passed on by the Alexandrian Clement. "For when the tyrant died, he passed from the island of Patmos to Ephesus, and he used to go also to the neighboring districts of the nations, when he was invited, in order to appoint bishops, or set in order whole churches, or place in the clergy some one of those pointed out by the Spirit."[9] Here is found Designation by the Spirit and an appointment (*kathistanai*) through human agency. In this narrative the apostle receives an invitation from

---

7. Dix, "The Ministry of the Early Church," 258–62.

8. Lightfoot, *The Apostolic Fathers*, Part I, Vol. II, 134–35.

9. *Quis dives salvetur* xlii.2. The Greek text is in the edition of GCS by Otto Stählin.

already established churches; he does not function as a missionary establishing a church and its ministry.

THE ACTS

According to the best supported text the choice of Matthias (Acts 1:23–26) followed a procedure without a parallel in the early history of the church. The prayer, however, finds echoes in the earliest ordination liturgies, particularly in the address to God as the "Knower of hearts." The "putting forward" assumes a general agreement by those present that the two men had the qualifications for apostleship and implies at least a formal Nomination if not an elective process.[10]

Two of the variants in the "Western" text as represented by Codex D produce a significantly different picture of the procedure. In v. 23 instead of the plural is found the singular so that Peter puts forward the candidates instead of the community. In v. 26 another slight variant gives the reading "they gave their lots (votes)" so as to indicate an Election by the community. Such a procedure of Nomination and Election occurred at a number of places in the early history of the church. An indication that the D text was in touch with early Palestinian terminology and an explanation of the use of "lots" to mean "votes" is supplied by the Qumran literature.[11]

Several considerations favor the genuineness of the best attested reading: The prayer presupposes some direct divine choice; the casting of lots accords with the doctrinal standpoint which would ascribe the choice of his apostles to the Lord himself; and the absence of this procedure anywhere in the church gave no reason for altering the text in this direction.

The most complete account of the selection of church functionaries in the New Testament, and one of the most influential, is the narrative of Acts 6:1–6. As the text stands the description closely parallels the form of Greek and Roman civil Elections. The apostles serve as Election-conducting officials; there is a laying down of qualifications, and the presentation before the apostles may indicate a veto-right by them (corresponding to a Scrutiny); the assembly does the choosing; and the procedure closes with

---

10. In Acts 6:6 the same word "put forward" (*estesan*) follows an Election.

11. See footnotes 105 and 106 to the first unit of this study. A Greek parallel to the accepted text is referred to in n. 19 of Part I. Origen's comment, based on the majority text, is significant: "Seeing that prayer precedes, the lot is not by chance but leads to a divine choice by providence" (*Hom. in Josh.* XXIII.2).

an induction into office, which includes a Prayer and the Jewish rite of Imposition of hands.

Once again there are textual variants which change the meaning significantly. The text of B in v. 3 gives the first person, "let us." This otherwise unsupported reading could be pressed to mean choice by the Twelve (but this contradicts v. 6) or may only mean "we Christians" and be intended to give the apostles a share in the choice. The text of D gives a more important variant at v. 6. Unless there is a somewhat clumsy change of subjects the majority text has the disciples laying hands on the Seven. If Luke had Numbers 8 in mind, this may very well have been the intended meaning. The practical problem of literal fulfillment of this action plus the ecclesiastical embarrassment of such a procedure may be considered motives behind the removing of any ambiguity in D and some of its allies. In D the verse would read, "These were placed before the apostles, who prayed and laid their hands on them." Congregational Election followed by Imposition of hands would have been acceptable in most places in the early church. Even in the better attested reading this may have been meant, but the manner of expression would indicate that the apostles functioned as congregational representatives and not as an independent party to the transaction.

Although the procedure conforms to Greek practice, the account is rooted in Old Testament texts.[12] Hence, the distinction between Acts 6 and Rabbinic ordination needs to be observed: Prayer has a central place in the texts pertaining to the Christian practice but is absent from Jewish descriptions; the Imposition of hands in Acts 6 is performed at least by a college of twelve; and the apostles did not have a master-disciple relationship to the Seven.

It is to be noted that the Seven were to be men "full of the Holy Spirit" prior to their designation. Behm seeks to escape the force of this fact in the interest of the theory that the laying on of hands meant the bestowal of the Holy Spirit.[13] Although possession of the Spirit might not exclude receiving an added gift, there is no evidence for such in the context. Such a gift would have to be assumed through a generalization from other passages. Acts 6 alone is a stumbling-block to the theory that the Imposition of hands signified the bestowal of the Holy Spirit, and particularly that it had this meaning in an ordination context.

---

12. Lohse, *Die Ordination*, 43; and Farrer, "Ministry in the New Testament," point out the resemblances to Numbers 27 and 11. The author's own interpretation of these resemblances is given in Ferguson, "Laying on of Hands in Acts 6:6 and 13:3."

13. Behm, *Die Handauflegung im Urchristentum*, 160ff.

We must now face the problem of the significance of the laying on of hands in the New Testament. This action appears in the New Testament in contexts of healing, benediction, setting apart to a function in the church, and bestowal of the Holy Spirit after baptism (later construed as confirmation). In the early church the imposition of hands was used in all these contexts and also in the reconciliation of penitents and heretics and in the exorcism of catechumens.[14] In view of the diversity of the situations in which this gesture seemed appropriate we are compelled to ask whether the theological meanings were equally diverse or whether a common principle undergirded them all.

David Daube has sought to classify the New Testament imposition of hands according to the Old Testament distinction between *samakh* (a leaning upon in order to create a deputy) and *śim* (a gentle touching in order to bless).[15] Daube is unconvincing, for Christian texts show no trace of the distinction either in terminology or circumstantial description. The church records preserve no memory of a laying on of hands involving the use of significant pressure. Moreover, if the distinction Daube makes had any real significance to Hellenistic Jews, some effort would have been made to show it in the Septuagint.[16] Nor is Daube's thesis supported by the Syriac translation of the New Testament. In every case where Daube would lead us to expect the Syriac equivalent of *samakh*, the word turns out to be the equivalent of the Hebrew *śim*. All of the Syriac texts from the early history of the church use *śim* for the laying on of hands, and in Neo-Syriac the technical words associated with ordination are developed from this root.[17]

The linguistic phenomena would indicate that in the divergent developments of ordination, the Jews adopted one complex of words (*samakh*)[18] and Christians another (*śim*). Was there a significance in this divergence? Yes. And this conclusion only grows in force if the distinction made by

14. See the previously cited works by Behm and Coppens.

15. Daube, *The New Testament and Rabbinic Judaism*, 234–45. Cf. our own observations in the first unit of the study. A further obstacle to Daube's view is the total absence of evidence for the action of "leaning upon" (or any Imposition of hands) in the creation of the exact kind of substitute he says the rite created, a *shaliach*.

16. The Greek version of the Old Testament translates both with a word corresponding to *śim*, *epitithenai*.

17. Smith, *Thesaurus Syriacus*, 2:2556–65.

18. Zeitlin, "The *Semikah* Controversy between the Zugoth," 499–500, traces the meaning of "ordination" to the sense of "relying upon an authority" and not to the sacrificial laying on of hands.

Daube continued to be felt (despite the evidence of the Septuagint) into New Testament times.[19] The affirmative answer is based on the fact that when theologically minded writers in the early church came to explain the symbolism of the imposition of hands, they did so in reference to prayer, more specifically, benediction.[20] When one applies this interpretation to the various circumstances of imposition of hands in the New Testament and the early church, he finds that, unlike the Old Testament usage, a common pattern emerges. Imposition of hands will serve in every context where it occurs as a symbolic expression of a blessing.

The imposition of hands appears to have been a familiar practice of Jesus in pronouncing a benediction (note especially Mark 10:13–16 and the parallel in Matt 19:13).[21] Not essentially different was the imposition of hands in healing.[22] In cases of healing there appears to have been some transfer of power or health (cf. Mark 5:30) and this may have been associated with the imposition of hands.[23] But this association should not be taken to the exclusion of the primary meaning, the bestowal of a blessing, in this case of a specific kind.

19. Even so some allowance must be made for a cross-fertilization of ideas due to the usage of the same term for all incidents in the Septuagint. On the Jewish side there is one instance of Rabbinic ordination interpreted as a blessing "through your hand" in the *Midrash Sifre Zuta* to Numbers 27.

20. Galtier, "Imposition des mains," 1339. He also calls attention to the fact that the imposition of hands in the practice of the early church was always accompanied by prayer, which specified the purpose and gave to the act its proper character, and thus was an essential trait of the act (1338).

The significant passages in regard to ordination have been cited. As an example of the same interpretation in other contexts note may be made of Tertullian, *de Bapt.* 8, where the imposition of hands following baptism is said to invoke and invite the Holy Spirit through benediction.

The word coined for the act of imposition of hands, *cheirotonia*, means a "blessing" in the Greek church.

21. The regarding of this gesture as characteristic of Jesus is not confined to the Gospels—cf. Rev 1:17.

In Luke 24:50 Jesus raises his hand in the act of blessing his disciples. This analogue to the procedure in the priestly blessing may differ from an imposition of hands only in its application to a group where the more personal form was impossible. If so, this verse may account for the tradition that Jesus had imposed hands on the apostles— *Act. Pet.* 10 (Chrysostom's *Hom.* xxxviii.4 in 1 Cor. is often cited, but incorrectly, in support of this tradition); and most clearly in the Edessene Canons (n. 44 of Part II).

22. So recognized by Daube, *The New Testament and Rabbinic Judaism*, 234.

23. Such is the common interpretation of the imposition of hands in healing—cf. Lohse, *Die Ordination*, 69.

Acts 8:14–24 (with which compare 19:6)[24] associates the laying on of hands with the communication of the Holy Spirit.[25] The implication of the passage is that only the apostles could bestow the Holy Spirit; one possessing the power of the Spirit could not thereby pass the power on. Even in this passage there is also a prayer that the Samaritans "might receive the Holy Spirit" (v. 15), but the actual means seems to be the laying on of hands (vv. 17–19). With Adler we would emphasize the distinctiveness of this episode from other New Testament impositions of hands.[26] However, we would go further and emphasize its distinctiveness (along with that of 19:6) from later rites in the church. The plan of Acts, to which Adler himself calls attention,[27] associates a distinctive outpouring of the Holy Spirit with each significant advance in the preaching of the Gospel—Pentecost in Acts 2, the Samaritans in Acts 8, Gentiles in Acts 10, the superiority of Christian baptism over that of John in Acts 19. The significance intended, therefore, can hardly be the rite of confirmation, which would be intended for all Christians.[28] Contrary to Adler, and in accord with several ancient commentators,[29] we would take Acts 8 (and 19:6) as a bestowal of charismata of the Spirit. Adler's arguments against this interpretation miss the point: what is meant by this interpretation is not an identification of the Holy Spirit and charisma, but the Holy Spirit manifesting himself through certain "gifts." This incident is not justification for concluding that every imposition of hands was a communication of the Holy Spirit.[30] This was one specific kind of blessing which might be bestowed through this means.

The preceding examination of imposition of hands in the New Testament offers a suggestion of the immediate origin of the Christian practice. In the first unit reasons were set forth for doubting that the laying on of hands with pressure in Rabbinic ordination originated before AD 70. Jesus, on the other hand, appears to have used the gesture of placing his hand upon one to be blessed with considerable frequency. It is unnecessary to look further than the practice of their Master to account for the frequency

24. Heb 6:2 does not permit a conclusion as to a specific purpose intended.

25. The most complete study of this incident is Adler, *Taufe und Handauflegung*.

26. Ibid., 68ff.

27. Ibid., 109ff.

28. Adler too denies such an explicit purpose by Luke, although adopting the "theological" interpretation in reference to confirmation (ibid., 111).

29. Noted by Adler, ibid., 13, 15 (cf. 81); his own position is developed on 81–90.

30. Ibid., 69.

with which the early disciples laid on hands. Moreover, the probability is that they used the action with the same significance as he did.

As Acts 6 marked the beginning of local organization, Acts 13 marks the beginning of planned full-time missionary work.[31] By its very difficulties for the traditional ecclesiastical doctrine of ordination, Acts 13:1–3 offers important evidence for the real significance.

The form and terminology of Ordination are present in Acts 13, but the usual meaning of Ordination is wholly absent. The previous activities of Barnabas and Paul's declaration in Galatians 1 indicate that this was not an Ordination.[32] Certainly there was nothing the other prophets and teachers could give to Barnabas and Paul except their benediction and a prayer to God for his favor upon the missionary endeavor.[33]

In Acts 13 there is a selection of missionaries by the Holy Spirit speaking through inspired spokesmen (Inspired Designation). Acts 20:28 similarly speaks of bishops made by the Holy Spirit. Because of the Spirit's initiative, the community's function was not "to send forth" but "to set apart." The language picks up the terminology of the consecration of the Levites in Numbers 8.[34] The setting apart of men called to the service of God and his Church fits all the circumstances of ordination in the New Testament. But a bestowing of the Holy Spirit or any special grace of office does not cover the events of Acts 13. Yet this passage can be excluded from discussions of ordination only on the doctrinal presupposition that ordination is something other than what is involved here.

The setting apart is performed by the other prophets and teachers in a ceremony of fasting, prayer, and Imposition of hands.

Acts 14:23 tells of the appointment of elders in the churches of Asia Minor. The key word of the passage, "appoint" (*cheirotonein*), may be taken in one of two ways. The Greek permits an interpretation identifying the "appointing" with the praying (accompanied by fasting). In this case the praying would either be the means of the *cheirotonein* or a central act of the whole process described by *cheirotonein*. This interpretation coincides with the later development of the word *cheirotonein* as the term for ordination. The original also permits an interpretation distinguishing the *cheirotonein* from the praying. In this case the *cheirotonein* refers to a process

31. Best, "Acts XIII.1–3."

32. Cf. Lohse, *Die Ordination*, 73. Coppens' discussion, *L'imposition des mains*, 131–33, exhibits the difficulty of upholding the Catholic position that only bishops can ordain.

33. Such is the significance ascribed to the event in Acts 14:26.

34. Daube, *The New Testament and Rabbinic Judaism*, 239–41, and n. 12.

of selection either with the meaning "caused to be elected"[35] (although this is without parallel) or with the meaning that Paul and Barnabas did the selecting. This interpretation coincides with the Hellenistic development of the word, which must now be presented.

From the classical sense "to elect by show of hands" *cheirotonein* came to mean "elect," without reference to manner, and frequently "appoint," even if by one man.[36]

In Hellenistic Judaism there was a religious usage of *cheirotonein* which prepares for its later Christian usage. Although Philo, in glancing at Greek institutions, refers quite naturally to magistrates chosen "by election (*cheirotonia*) and by lot,"[37] and Josephus in historical contexts uses *cheirotonein* of elections by an assembly of people,[38] both Jewish writers commonly use the word in the sense of "appoint."[39] But distinctively Josephus and Philo also use *cheirotonein* in the religious context of the selection of religious functionaries by God himself.[40] A passage from Josephus brings together characteristic ideas associated with ordination by Christian writers.

35. Siotis, "Die klassische und christliche Cheirotonie," 21 (1950) 48.

36. See the still useful word studies of Edwin Hatch, "Ordination," 1501. Siotis, ibid., has given an exhaustive study to *cheirotonein*, its cognates, and related words, in classical antiquity and the first centuries of the church: for the Hellenistic and New Testament usage, see 21 (1950) 244–53.

37. *Quod Deus sit immutabilis* xxiv.112; *de Mut. Nom.* xxviii.151; *de Spec. Leg.* II.xl.231 (cf. IV.ii.9).

38. *Ant.* IV.297; VI.81 (cf. VI.60 and *B.J.* IV.592); *Vita* 341. Interesting as illustrating classical usage is *B.J.* IV.256 where in the same context *psephizein* is used for a vote to surrender and *cheirotonein* is used of the election of ambassadors to carry the message of surrender.

39. Philo, *de Post. Cain*, xvi.54; *de Jos.* 248; *Quod. Det. Potiori* 145; *de Op. Mundi* 84. Josephus, *Ant.* VI.83, and passages cited below.
This appointment may be performed by a single person—Philo, *Quod. Bet. Pot.* 66; *In Flacc.* 109; Josephus, *Ant.* XIII.45. For the appointment of cult officers in particular, see Philo, *de Agriculture* xxix.130; *de Vita Mos.* 11.141–43. (In the latter passage *hairethenai* is also used of the choosing, whereas *kathistanai* occurs in reference to installation.) Josephus, *B.J.* IV.147 (in the following section *kathistanai* is used, apparently interchangeably with *cheirotonein*).

40. Philo, *Quod. Det. Pot.* 39; *de Sac. Abel.* 9 (= *Quod. Det. Pot.* 161); *de Vita Mos.* 1.198; *de Virt.* x.64; *de Vita Mos.* 1.148. Not specifically religious appointments are God's appointment of Joseph to his position in Egypt (*de Mig. Abrah.* 22) and the recognition of Abraham as a King (*de Virt.* xxxix.218; cf. *de Somn.* II.xxxvi.243 where the appointment is ascribed to nature and not specifically to God). Josephus, *Ant.* IV.34, 54, 66. Because of three separate expressions of the divine will Aaron is said to be "thrice elected." Josephus especially makes the choice of kings an act of God—*Ant.* VII.53; IX.108; VI.312.

> But now God himself has judged Aaron worthy of this honor and has chosen him to be priest, knowing him to be the most deserving among us . . .
>
> Coming from a man of His own choosing, He cannot but accept them (his divine services) . . .
>
> The Hebrews were pleased with this speech and acquiesced in the divine election (*cheirotonia*).[41]

In this passage *cheirotonia* is a divine choosing, based on the worthiness of a person, and guaranteeing the acceptableness of the person's ministry. Philo also made a significant combination of the religious interpretation with Greek practice. "It was God who appointed (*cheirotonetheis*) him by the free judgment of his subjects, God who created in them the willinginess to choose him as their sovereign."[42]

The New Testament usage shows exclusively the religious context. In 2 Cor 8:19 Paul uses *cheirotonein* of the appointment by the churches of "money messengers" to accompany Paul. The meaning of an Election by the members cannot be far away in this usage of *cheirotonein*. Certainly the selective aspect of the word continues prominent.

Paul's usage in 2 Cor 8:19 belongs to a special group of passages, chiefly from the first and second centuries, in which the elective or appointive idea is supplemented by the connotation of an authorization to a commission. Siotis concludes that this meaning of "commissioning" must come from a Jewish background, since it is missing in purely Greek usage.[43] This connotation of "commissioning" is well illustrated by Justin, *Dialogue* 108.[44]

Acts records a similar instance of a church electing envoys to represent it in an important matter. In connection with the conference at Jerusalem on Gentile converts Acts 15:22 states that the whole brotherhood shared in the elective function of choosing official envoys (although the whole brotherhood apparently did not share in the debate or in framing the decree).[45]

---

41. Josephus, *Ant.* III.190–192.

42. *de Praemiis et Poenis* ix.54.

43. Siotis, "Die klassische und die christliche Cheirotonie," 21 (1950) 249, 251–52.

44. This passage is discussed in n. 99 of Part I.

45. Hayman, "The Position of the Laity in the Church," 501–3.

THE PASTORAL EPISTLES

A set of passages from the Pastorals which belong together—1 Tim 1:18; 4:14; and 2 Tim 1:6—provide an interesting parallel to Acts 13:1–3. Timothy's "ordination" described in these verses apparently refers to the opening verses of Acts 16 when Timothy was selected as a traveling companion for Paul.[46] This would accord with the missionary context of Acts 13 and perhaps explain the other points of contact between the two sets of references. Prophecies first pointed out Timothy. Behm's effort to distinguish the prophecies of 1:18 from 4:14 is unwarranted.[47] Thus the Spirit made his will known through inspired men. It would be tempting to follow the translation of the *Revised Standard Version*, "through prophecy" (4:14), and find in these inspired words (thus distinguished from the prophecies of 1:18) a reference to prayer as the means of bestowing the spiritual gift on Timothy.[48] However, the plural "prophecies" of 1:18 probably indicates that the *dia propheteias* of 4:14 is also plural, and therefore the gift was given Timothy "on account of prophecies."[49] There was again a corporate imposition of hands, this time by a college of presbyters, who recognized Timothy's worthiness and commissioned him in a solemn ceremony. Daube offers a distinctive interpretation of the phrase "laying on of the hands of the presbytery." He takes it as equivalent to the technical term *semikhath zeqenim*, which he understands as a leaning on of hands to make elders. The Rabbinic phrase, however, had primary reference to the imposition of the elders' hands on the communal sacrifice.[50] Moreover, Timothy's position appears quite different from that of the presbyters in the Pastorals.

The Timothy passages have a special interest because of their reference to a *charisma* ("gift"). In one instance it is given *dia* ("through") the laying on of Paul's hands; in the other *meta* ("with") the laying on of the elders' hands. The different viewpoint is best explained by the different character of the two letters: 1 Timothy more public and official and 2 Timothy more private and personal.[51] Dibelius cautions against pressing

---

46. Spicq, *Saint Paul: Les Epitres Pastorales*, 324.

47. Cf. Dibelius and Conzelmann, *Die Pastoralbriefe*, 56.

48. Spicq, *Saint Paul: Les Epitres Pastorales*, 323.

49. Lohse, *Die Ordination*, 81.

50. Daube's position, *The New Testament and Rabbinic Judaism*, 244–45. Cf. n. 50 in Part I for the basis for controverting his interpretation.

51. Dibelius and Conzelmann, *Die Pastoralbriefe*, 57.

the difference between the prepositions,[52] but there must be some reason for the change. *Dia* is the ordinary preposition for causality; *meta* is more natural for accompaniment or circumstance.[53] First Timothy 4:14 is illustrated by the use of *meta* with the genitive in 1 Tim 2:9 and 4:4 to express an accompanying circumstance. The association in each case is not an intimate one, but still the idea is accompaniment and not means. The Roman Catholic scholars rightly call attention to the *charisma* as coming only through Paul; they also seem right in understanding this gift as a divine gift.[54] On the other hand, the *charisma* is not necessarily a gift associated particularly with office. It may be placed in the same category with the imparting of the Spirit in Acts 8 and 19. Therefore, these verses have a double reference—to a prophetic Designation of Timothy followed by a setting apart to the work of evangelism by human representatives, and to an imparting of a spiritual gift by Paul at the same time (a special event).

Titus 1:5 may be taken as parallel to Acts 14:23. In these two passages, instead of an Inspired Designation of missionaries, the emphasis is upon the human action in appointing elders. Whereas Acts has *cheirotonein*, perhaps with a primary reference to a selection, Titus 1:5 has *kathistanai*, which looks more in the direction of an installation.

The method Titus was to employ in installing elders was probably the same as in 1 Tim. 5:22, Imposition of hands. This verse has been claimed both for ordination and for reconciling penitents.[55] Considerations which weigh heaviest in favor of ordination include the following: The immediate context seems to be dealing with Timothy's relation to the elders in general; disciplinary procedures were slower in formulation in the church; and the general usage of laying on of hands in the Pastorals favors ordination.

52. Ibid., 73.

53. Spicq, *Saint Paul: Les Epitres Pastorales*, 323.

54. Coppens, *L'imposition des mains*, 134–35, is representative. Cf. similarly also Lohse, *Die Ordination*, 83–84; and Schlier, "Die Ordnung der Kirche nach den Pastoralbriefen," 56–58.

55. The case for the reconciling of penitents has been most thoroughly put by Galtier, "Imposition des mains," 1306–13. On the other side see especially Coppens, *L'imposition des mains*, 125–31.

CONCLUSIONS

Historical Summary

The earliest attested action for installation into church office is the Imposition of hands. This action had its immediate origin in Christianity from the practice of Jesus. Although drawing on a common Hebraic background, Christian and Rabbinic ordination had an independent development. The variety of circumstances in which Christians employed the imposition of hands point nonetheless toward a common purpose: benediction. From the Old Testament were derived subordinate motifs of consecration to God (Numbers 8) and authorization (Numbers 27).

The imposition of hands was always an adjunct of prayer in the Church. Prayer was the distinctively Christian act in the ceremony of ordination. Three elements may be distinguished: praise to God, petition for divine favor (Divine Invocation), and a personal Benediction. Since the same outward action was used for several different ranks in the Church, emphasis must be placed on the Prayer as the significant event, because only the Prayer spelled out that for which one was ordained. When theologians such as Chrysostom and Jerome interpreted the meaning of ordination, they put the emphasis on the Prayer.

Already in the earliest church order, the *Apostolic Tradition*, the Prayer included a petition for the Holy Spirit. When in the fourth century Gregory of Nazianzen connected the bestowal of the Holy Spirit with the Imposition of hands, the movement from the word to the accompanying action was natural enough. The sacramental change would have first been connected with the Prayer (as still in Gregory of Nyssa). Certain factors favored the transfer of associations from the word to the act. The variety of instances where the imposition of hands was employed meant that the significance in one instance could be applied to another. As an example, the forgiveness of sins in the reconciliation of penitents was applied to ordination. The imposition of hands at baptism was thought to convey the gift of the Holy Spirit promised to Christians (an interpretation reinforced from Acts 8 and 19). There is evidence that baptismal imposition of hands did influence the interpretation of the same act in ordination. The *Apostolic Constitutions* uses *cheirothesia* for all impositions of hands (in each case accompanying a verbal benediction) except two. For the action of Peter and John in Acts 8 and for ordination *epithesis cheiron* is used, thus indicating that these two were placed in a separate category. Moreover, the contemporary Basil of Caesarea interpreted the principles of Cyprian, which denied validity to baptism administered by schismatics on the grounds that men separated from the Church could not give the Holy Spirit, to mean that schismatics could not impart the Holy Spirit through Imposition of hands at ordination. Through such a transfer of associations the rite used in the New Testament for benediction came to have at ordination the specific connotation of the communication of the Holy Spirit.

Older than Rabbinic ordination by Imposition of hands was the admission to the Sanhedrin by Solemn Seating. Although lacking confirmation from the earliest Christian documents, the evidence of the Pseudo-Clementines indicates the practice of Solemn Seating at an early date among Jewish Christians. From the Jewish background the functions of teaching and judging were indicated for the person who occupied the official chair of the community. The language of "seating" and the "chair" occur regularly from the second through the fourth century, so this ceremony was not confined to the Jewish wing of the church. Fourth-century writers customarily designated the "chair" (primarily of a bishop) a *thronos* instead of a *kathedra*. The change is significant, for the associations were now royal instead of doctoral, Hellenistic-Roman instead of Jewish.

The relationship between Imposition of hands and Solemn Seating in early Christian ordination is not clear. Although having separate roots in Jewish practice, the two rites may have already been united in Judaism. However, there was no close relationship between the two acts where they occur in Christianity, and in one place in the Pseudo-Clementines the Solemn Seating comes first, contrary to the procedure generally followed. The indication, therefore, is the taking over of two separate actions. The Solemn Seating maintained its character as an installation and became particularly the installation of a bishop on the throne of his church. Imposition of hands from its early association with benediction and consecration was free to develop sacramental associations.

Solemn Seating, Porrection, and Inaugural Usurpation all had a civil as well as a religious background. The significance of these acts was induction into office.

The understanding of the Imposition of hands in terms of a benediction and prayer accords well with the frequent declaration that God himself gives ministers to his church (cf. 1 Cor 12:28–30; Eph 4:7–14). The prevailing doctrinal interpretation of ordination in the ancient Church was the divine choice of ministers. In the earliest period this view was made concrete in choices by the Holy Spirit. An Inspired Designation was recognized by the community in a ceremony of setting apart to the work for which the Spirit had called a person. The activity of the Spirit then gave way to other means of selection. The transition is well illustrated by the change in emphasis apparent in the following phrases: "made by the Holy Spirit" (Acts 20:28); appointed men having "proved them by the Spirit" (*1 Clement*); "elect . . . men worthy of the Lord . . . approved" (*Didache*). The stress on worthiness, to be found in "scrutinized" men, becomes a regular feature as the human element comes to predominate. God's elective function became identified with the more normal modes of choice. The voice of God might still be recognized in an authoritative Designation, a Nomination, an answer of prayer, or the spontaneous Acclamation of the people. The choice of the people might be expressed in several ways, but their choice (especially in an Election) was commonly interpreted as the channel of God's selection. The words for Election—*cheirotonein, eklegesthai*—are those employed for what God does.

God's role at first was particularly identified with the selection; later, with the installation. Where the sense of a divine choice was strong, as in a prophetic declaration, the setting apart was the community's recognition of those divinely chosen (Acts 13). When the assembled People of God were the organ of divine selection (Acts 6), ordination was the authorization to serve the community. As the sense of direct divine activity grew weaker, all parts of the Church were taken as functioning for God. Cyprian is a good illustration of this stage in the development; the testimony of the clergy, the vote of the people, and ordination by bishops were all part of one process with divine sanction. At the end of the fourth century the divine role in ordination was increasingly identified with the action of God's ministers in setting apart others through Prayer and the Imposition of hands. The selection was not so important as the granting of the special powers now attached exclusively to the ordained. The emphasis now tended to be the reverse of that at the beginning: ordination was God's recognition and authorization of those humanly chosen for the ministry.

The most important development in terminology involved the word *cheirotonein*. No doubt *cheirotonein* was helped along as a technical word by its close association with the Election by the people, and the connotations of commissioning acquired in Jewish writers. This circumstance confirms the conclusion that originally the selection was the important and decisive event. Even as the center of emphasis gradually shifted to the installation, so *cheirotonein* came to refer to the whole process of selection and installation and finally to the installation alone. Philo and Josephus had given the word a religious usage, referring to the selection of cult functionaries by God himself. This association with divine appointment continued to be felt in Christian usage. The doctrinal association with divine choice doubtless was an important factor in giving *cheirotonein* the victory over its more colorless rivals, such as *kathistanai*. If the eastern versions faithfully preserve Hippolytus' usage, then *cheirotonein* was already a technical term for ordination in the Greek-speaking church at Rome in the early third century. This fact would account for *ordinare* being the equivalent term in the West. Without such an early appearance of *cheirotonein* in a technical sense it would be hard to account for the Latin use, as an equivalent, of a term lacking any association with Election. Moreover, the usage of Hellenistic Jews shows that the terminological basis for such an application was already available. On the other hand, *cheirotonein* did not win its way in the Greek East (where the classical meaning was still felt) until the fourth century.

Ordination provides a specific illustration of the Church functioning as the body of Christ, his instrument in the world. God gives ministers, but the Church is the medium for their selection and setting apart. The constitutional structure is shown to be that of an organic unity of unequal parts working together.

A prevailing interpretation of the ministry will naturally find expression in the ceremony of ordination. Since there is often a time-lag, the absence of a certain rite is not conclusive evidence against the existence of the interpretation indicated by the rite. Nevertheless, there is a connection. For example, when the priestly interpretation of the ministry became the predominant one, the Old Testament practice of Chrismation and the bestowal of the power to offer sacrifice became a part of the liturgy of ordination. During the first four centuries priesthood was one interpretation among several. The ceremonies of ordination, if they do not permit an exact dating of the priestly interpretation, do show a relative chronology. The church orders are at pains to specify that the deacon is not ordained to the priesthood. That the main features of the rite are the same for the deacon as for the presbyter shows clearly that the Imposition of hands and the ceremony of ordination are older than the priestly interpretation. The Syriac church gave priestly connotations to the Imposition of hands, but generally the priestly interpretation was shown through the addition of other elements to the ceremony.

What does the ceremony tell about the conception of the offices? The Solemn Seating of the bishop points to his function of judging and teaching. When this act acquired royal association, the idea of judging was still present, but the main emphasis was on administration. Teaching was not suggested by a throne. The symbolism of teaching, lost through Enthronement, was recovered in the late fourth century in the opening of the Scriptures over the head of the ordinand and in the inaugural action of delivering a sermon.

Porrection is one of the most obvious ways of making the nature of an office clear, hence its presence in the installation of the lesser orders helps to supplement the scanty information about many of them. The same value applies to Inaugural Usurpation. The first appearance of this motif in Christian ordination, in the consecration of a bishop in the *Apostolic Tradition*, indicates that the fundamental function of the bishop (and perhaps thereby the origin of the episcopal office) was as the chief liturgical celebrant of the church.

Modern scholars trace the origin of the Christian presbyterate in the elders of Jewish communities. The study of ordination confirms this conclusion. The Prayers made specific appeal to the Seventy Elders appointed by Moses. The reference might be considered a generalized appeal to Biblical authority except for the fact that the Pseudo-Clementines place the Christian ministry in direct succession from the elders of Moses' time. The early church appears to have preserved a genuine recollection of the Jewish origin of the eldership.

Stephen and the Seven of Acts 6 are the precedent appealed to in the Prayers for deacons. That no effort was made to trace the diaconate to Old Testament times points to the New Testament origin of this office.

In the Prayers for bishops there is no specific biblical image called forth, only a generalized reference to God having always provided religious leaders for his people. Is not this circumstance an indication of the post-Biblical origin of the monarchial episcopate?

Contemporary Observations

There was an ordination (properly understood) in the New Testament church. Given the historical setting, the references in the New Testament can mean nothing else. There was a certain amount of variety (and in the early church outside the New Testament there was more) but it falls within a basic framework.

Selections were made through inspired prophets, by apostles and evangelists, or by the whole local community. One principle runs through the whole process, regardless of whose action was considered constitutive: the whole church acts and concurs (when an emphasis grew on the "universal church" the principle was expanded to accommodate the emphasis). The whole community either had a voice in the selection or ratified the choice.

The historical testimony shows that early Christians considered God to be the one choosing, no matter what the medium of the choice. The contemporary church would profit from a recovery of this consciousness of being the organ of divine selection. There is a responsibility imposed to choose the man God would choose.

Of all the modes of installation available and which later came into use, the New Testament mentions only Prayer accompanied by the Imposition of hands. Whatever other actions may have seemed appropriate were secondary to this central rite. Divested of its sacramental accretions and association with bestowing the Holy Spirit, the Imposition of hands becomes a spiritual symbol of great power and significant purpose. Moreover, Christians can hardly be conceived as undertaking any serious action without engaging in prayer.

It is correct that the Imposition of hands was a custom of the day and cultural customs must be taken into consideration in hermeneutics. But customs may be endowed with a spiritual significance that transcends culture (as for example the breaking of bread at the Last Supper). The apostles attached the Imposition of hands to an activity which has a permanent necessity to the Church, the setting apart of its functionaries to their duties.

The purpose of this series of articles has been to gather historical evidence and present it in a meaningful pattern. If the historian has done his task well, others presumably are as well qualified as he to apply the relevance of the material to other circumstances. Nevertheless, this writer feels compelled to conclude: we do have an example. My application would be: Since some method of "ordination" must be employed, it would seem that people interested in "doing Bible things in Bible ways" are ill-advised to seek excuses for not continuing biblical precedent.

8

Selection and Installation to Office in Roman, Greek, Jewish, and Christian Antiquity

IF THE CULTURAL MILIEU of early Christianity were described by concentric circles, one would move inward from the Roman to the Greek to the Jewish. The degree of influence in the formative years is in inverse ratio to the size of the circle. Later the relationship tends to be reversed.

This article takes a narrow slice through the series of rings—an aspect of the constitutional procedure. In so doing, our attention will be alert for underlying motifs which may indicate a close correlation. The study attempts to establish a *typology for modes* of selection and installation to office.[1] Capitalization is employed for terms given a technical sense for the type of method indicated.

MODES OF SELECTION

A characteristic expression of the practice of Co-option may be seen in the procedure for filling Roman priestly colleges and sodalities.[2] The pure

---

1. This article is based on the material assembled in the author's doctoral dissertation "Ordination in the Ancient Church" (Harvard University, 1959).

2. The references are given by Wissowa, *Religion and Kultus der Römer*, 487. Livy

form of Co-option was employed under the early Republic whereby the members selected replacements to fill vacancies in their number, thus providing for a self-perpetuating membership. Later the colleges made nominations to a special assembly (and still later to the Senate) and then went through the form of co-opting those selected.[3]

Co-option is the term which best describes the method of filling vacancies in the great Sanhedrin (and presumably the lesser Sanhedrins) of the Jews.[4] Here there was the further refinement of a subordinate body of scholars who according to their rank were advanced to fill vacancies in the Council.

Co-option is natural to an aristocratic society or to a body which is the custodian of traditional knowledge or practice. Its existence in the Christian church would seem to result from cultural influences, in this case probably Jewish. Quite controversial is the evidence of Jerome, Severus of Antioch, and Eutychius to the practice of Co-option in the church of Alexandria in pre-Nicene times.[5] According to the composite picture provided by their testimony the twelve presbyters of the Alexandrian church selected and installed one out of their own number as bishop and then appointed to his place on the presbytery another person in order to complete the number twelve. Greatly to be desired as a background for this testimony is information on the selecting of the members of the ruling Council of Alexandrian Jewry.[6]

In keeping with the meaning of "designation," the term *Designation* is used for a selection to an office made or announced by a person in authority. Rome had a long history of the exercise of such authoritative Designations to office. The Designation of a *rex* by the *interrex* or of a dictator by the consul was followed by an immediate assumption of duties. Even in the

xl.42.6ff. may be singled out because of his evidence for the Co-option of *pontifices, augures,* and *epulones.*

3. Wissowa, *Religion and Kultus der Römer,* 487. For Co-option in the senates of *municipia* in the second century AD, see Cary, *A History of Rome,* 634–36.

4. *m. Sanhedrin* iv.3, 4; cf. *b. Sanhedrin* 17b. See further below, 118 (280 in orig. article.

5. Jerome, *Ep.* 146 (partially quoted below at n. 114); Brooks, ed., *The Sixth Book of the Select Letters of Severus Patriarch of Antioch,* 2:213; Eutychius in *PG* 111:982. The case in support of unusual procedures at Alexandria is argued by Telfer, "Episcopal Succession in Egypt." An answer is given by Lécuyer, "Le problème des consécrations épiscopales dans l'Eglise d'Alexandrie"; and Lécuyer, "La succession des evêques d'Alexandrie aux premiers siècles."

6. For the meager evidence, see Tcherikover and Fuks, eds., *Corpus papyrorum Judaicarum,* 1:10, 57, 101.

Election of magistrates an essential feature of the elective process was the proclamation of the outcome of the Election by the presiding consul (who was spoken of as formally creating those elected in their office), whereby the successful candidate became *designatus* until the day of assumption of office.[7] The imperial *commendatio* and *nominatio* so infringed on the elective process that these expressions of the emperor's desires may be seen as later expressions of Designation, even where the forms of election were maintained.

The *pontifex maximus* in Roman religion designated the *rex sacrorum*, *flamines*, and Vestal Virgins.[8]

Designation occurred in the Hellenic world within the clubs and associations for the appointment of lesser functionaries by a higher officer.[9] Similarly a civic ruler had about himself a row of under-officers who were installed by the ruler himself.[10]

The selection of rabbis among the Jews may appropriately be classified as a Designation. At first each rabbi selected one of his students for ordination and raised him to a status equal with himself.[11] Later this prerogative was centralized in the Nasi (or patriarch), and then a further modification required the joint approval of both the Nasi and the Beth Din (council) for the ordination of a rabbi.[12]

The nearest approach in Christianity to the rabbinic choice of a student to succeed to the teaching function was the practice of a bishop selecting and ordaining his own successor. This practice lies buried under the later ecclesiastical proscriptions, but must have been fairly prevalent in Palestine and Syria.[13]

The New Testament era saw frequent manifestations of a type of Designation which is justly regarded as distinct from other expressions of this mode of selection—a choice made by a prophet as the inspired spokesman of the divine will.[14] Old Testament prophets functioned in this way

---

7. Mommsen, *Römisches Staatsrecht*, 1:578.

8. Wissowa, *Religion and Kultus der Römer*, 487.

9. Poland, *Geschichte des griechischen Vereinswesens*, 416.

10. Siotis, "Die klassische and die christliche Cheirotonie," 20 (1949) 331.

11. Ehrhardt, "Jewish and Christian Ordination," 135–36; Newman, *Semikhah*, 19–20.

12. Newman, *Semikhah*, 19–20.

13. Theodoret, *Hist. eccl.* V.23; IV.20; Council of Antioch, *Can.* 23; Socrates, *PG* 67:192.

14. Acts 13:1–3; 1 Tim 1:10 and 4:14; cf. Acts 20:28.

in pointing out objects of divine choice.[15] Inspired Designations ceased with the cessation of an awareness of direct activity by the Holy Spirit in the church.

The most frequent occurrences of Designation in the church are found in the appointment of the lesser clergy by the bishop.[16]

Sometimes a Nomination, ordinarily to be thought of as subordinate to the elective process, assumed such proportions as to have been the equivalent of a Designation. Candidates for Roman magistracies might make a voluntary announcement of their candidacy or be proposed through a public posting of their names by the election-director.[17] The candidates for Greek magistracies were supplied either by nominations from friends or by announcement.[18] As civic responsibility became burdensome under the Empire the enforced assumption of public office became increasingly common. Voting was a formality where the number of candidates did not exceed the positions to be filled or the names of the candidates had to be supplied by the election-director.[19]

A striking influence of the imperial system on the church is apparent in imperial Nominations to key bishoprics.[20] It would have taken special courage to regard such a Nomination as no different from that made by another party.

Members of the Christian clergy proposed names for Election or gave their approval to candidates through a "testimonium."[21] In ordinary circumstances this action must have carried a decisive weight, so that the popular Election amounted only to a ratification.

Republican Rome and the Romanized towns under the early Empire appointed their magistrates by *Election*. There was first an ascertainment of the candidates, followed by a written vote of the assembly of citizens wherein a majority of a voting division determined the vote of that division, and concluded by a proclamation of the outcome.[22] The procedure

---

15. 1 Kgs 11:20ff.; 19:15, 16.

16. *Didasc.* 9; Cyprian, *Ep.* XXXVIII.1, 2.

17. Mommsen, *Die Stadtrechte*, 423.

18. Busolt, *Griechische Staatskunde*, 1:1071.

19. Mommsen, *Die Stadtrechte*, 423.

20. Theodoret, *H.E.* IV.vii.1; V.ix.14ff.

21. Cyprian, *Ep.* LV.9; cf. *Apost. Trad.* ii.2.

22. Mommsen, *Römisches Staatsrecht*, 1:578ff.; Mommsen, *Die Stadtrechte*, 421–28.

for the Election of Grecian magistrates was similar except that the voting was by a show of hands and the basic voting unit was the individual.[23]

Democratic procedures prevailed in both Greek and Roman associations where the common method of choosing officers was Election.[24] Some civic priesthoods in Greece were filled by Election,[25] and the modification to include Election in filling Roman priesthoods has been noted above.

Hellenistic Judaism appears to have followed Hellenic precedents in electing their community officers.[26] Notable is the evidence that Election by the community was practiced by the sectaries at Qumran. When judges (ten) were chosen for a special occasion, the whole congregation appears to have made the choice.[27] The Old Testament phrase ys' hgwrl ("the lot shall go out") appears figuratively as a set expression for the making of any decision by the congregation, regardless of how arrived at.[28] In one passage the phrase has reference to the selection of leaders of the community.[29]

The prevalence of Election in the ancient world finds its counterpart in the prevailing practice of the ancient church. From the New Testament forward there is abundant reference to this method.[30] Our knowledge of the details is meager, but what evidence there is shows a close similarity to Greek election procedures.[31]

A special type of Election was the Acclamation. This might be a spontaneous response to a person's name or to an omen.[32] Or, it might be the manner in which approbation was given to a person submitted to the

---

23. Busolt, *Griechische Staatskunde*, 1:1071; Siotis, "Die klassische and die christliche Cheirotonie," 20 (1949) 524–29; Staveley, *Greek and Roman Voting and Elections*.

24. Poland, *Geschichte des griechischen Vereinswesens*, 417; Liebenam, *Zur Geschichte und Organisation des römischen Vereinswesen*, 199.

25. Stengel, *Die griechischen Kultusaltertümer*, 44–46.

26. The evidence is chiefly late: Krauss, *Synagogale Altertümer*, 152.

27. CD x.4–6; Rabin, *The Zadokite Documents*, 49.

28. 1QS v.2ff.; vi.16–21; CD xiii.2–4; Ferguson, "Qumran and Codex D," 75–80.

29. 1QSa i.13–17. Cf. Josephus, *B.J.* 11.8.123. Interpreting this passage as a selection by the community, in accord with the other usages of the phrase for a community action, provides forceful support for the parallels between Qumran and the Greek clubs drawn by Bardtke, "Die Rechtstellung der Qumran-Gemeinde," 94–104, even though he takes the references to the lot literally. See also B. W. Dombrowski, "*Ha-Yaḥ ad* in IQS and *to koinón.*"

30. Acts 6:1–6; *Did.* 15.1; *1 Clem.* 44; lgn., *Phil.* x.1 and *Smyrn.* xi.2; Hippolytus, *Apost. Trad.* ii.2: Cyprian, *Ep.* LV.9; LIX.5,6; LXVIII.2; LXVII.3,4.

31. *Vita Polycarpi* xxii; Gregory of Nyssa, *Vita S. Greg. Thaum.* in *PG* 46:933ff. Cf. Siotis, "Die klassische and die christliche Cheirotonie," 21 (1950) 612ff.

32. Paulinus, *Vita S. Amb.* 111.6; Eusebius, *H.E.* VI.xxix.

people for approval.[33] Acclamations became part of the ritual of ordination in the church orders.[34] The Elections were frequently voice votes and led to the abuse that results were decided in favor of the faction which could make the most noise. Such unruliness encouraged the clergy to keep a tight hold on the selective process.[35]

Nominations in established churches generally came from the bishop or clergy.[36] Even from an early period there are indications that the clergy made the constitutive choice which was then submitted to the people for their ratification of the action already taken.[37] When the people elected, the clergy were expected to ratify the choice.[38]

Lots were familiar in the ancient world, but the Greeks alone of the peoples under review made extensive use of *Lot-taking* in filling important positions. Both civil magistracies and priesthoods were filled in this way.[39] Democracy to the Greeks meant an equal opportunity to serve as well as an equal right to choose.

The belief that chance left the decision to deity[40] made Lot-taking appropriate for determining the divine will. As such the procedure is found in the Old Testament for the selection of Israel's first king.[41] Lots were employed in the New Testament for the choice of a successor to Judas in the apostolate, apparently because apostles were supposed to have their appointment directly from the Lord.[42] The practice, however, gained no currency in the early church.[43]

---

33. Athanasius, *Apol. c. Arian.* vi; Theodoret, *Hist. eccl.* IV.xx and xxi; Theophilus of Alexandria, *Can.* 6.

34. *Test. Dom.* I.xxi.

35. Laodicea, *Can.* 13, instead of a denial of election by the laity, may be a restriction of election to the faithful in exclusion of the "mob." See Siotis, "Die klassische and die christliche Cheirotonie," 22 (1951) 111.

36. Cyp. *Ep.* LV.8,9; LXVII.4; Theophilus, *Can.* 6.

37. This may be the procedure in *1 Clem.* 44 and *Didasc.* 4.

38. Sulpicius Severus, *Vita S. Mart.* ix; Gregory of Nazianzen, *Or.* XVIII.33; Hippolytus, *Apost. Trad.* ii.2; *Vita Polycarpi* xxii.

39. Ehrenberg, "Losung," col. 1476; Stengel, *Die griechischen Kultusaltertümer,* 44–46.

40. Ehrenberg, "Losung," col. 1462ff.: Plato, *Laws* 759C; *Inscr.Gr.* X11.3, 178.

41. 1 Sam 10:20–24.

42. Acts 1:15–26, especially v. 24.

43. Codex D changes Acts 1:23, 26 from a Lot-taking to a nomination by Peter and election by the community so that the selection of Judas is made to conform to later church practice; Ferguson, "Qumran and Codex D," 75–80 (see chap. 10 below).

Hereditary priesthoods were common among the Greeks,[44] and the Jewish priesthood was a matter of heredity.[45] The Christian Church, by way of contrast, has always opposed recognizing any right of *Inheritance* to its sacred functions. Although no office was filled on the basis of inheritance, protests had to be raised from an early time against preference being given by men in authority to their kinsmen.[46]

MODES OF INSTALLATION

On the solemn occasion of assuming official responsibilities it is natural to expect that the event would be brought into relation to the deity and the religious sentiments of the people involved. The specific manner of Divine Invocation varied with the genius of the religion involved.

Roman magistrates took the "auspices" on the morning of their first day in office. The purpose of Auspication was to receive a favorable sign from the gods for the assumption of the office, but the very performance of the Auspication was an indication that the person had entered upon his functions.[47] Among Roman cult functionaries, the *rex sacrorum, augures,* and *flamines* received an Inauguration by an augur.[48] Inauguration in this limited technical sense differed from Auspication only in that the signs were taken by another than the person entering office.[49] The ceremony of Inauguration meant the declaration of the assent of the deity to the accomplished Election or Designation.

Another form of Divine Invocation at one's installation to an office was oath-taking. The oath was universal in Greek and Roman life.[50] Roman magistrates had to lay an oath in the hands of the quaestors within five days of assuming office that they would observe the laws. A new mag-

44. Stengel, *Die griechischen Kultusaltertümer*, 44–46.

45. Priesthoods became hereditary among the Greeks when a family was regarded as descended from the god, when the family introduced a cult into the state or was honored for particular acts of piety. The Old Testament assigns the priesthood to the tribe of Levi by virtue of divine election.

46. Origen, *Homily in Numbers* XXII.4.

47. Mommsen, *Römisches Staatsrecht*, 615–16. In the civil context the decisive moment in a change in office was provided by the calendar, not by any act of installation.

48. Wissowa, *Religion and Kultus der Römer*, 490.

49. Oldenberg, "De inauguratione sacerdotum Romanorum," 161. Livy i.18 describes an inauguration.

50. In general see Ziebarth, "Eid," 2075–83; and for Roman public life Steinwenter, "Ius iurandum," col. 1256–57; Mommsen, *Römisches Staatsrecht*, 1:619–22.

istrate was limited in his duties until this was done.[51] This "oath of office" was distinct from the vow to Jupiter to offer certain sacrifices, which was apparently a regular feature of the activities of the day of entrance into offices.[52] Oath-taking, in the form of swearing by the statutes of the association, is the only ceremony attested for the induction into office in Roman associations.[53] Greek officers too at their entrance into their functions had to take an oath of office to rule according to the best of their ability and according to the laws.[54] The installation of officers of Greek associations was spoken of in wholly general phrases in the great majority of cases, but an oath was apparently taken on entrance into office, as it was on entrance into the association itself.[55]

Oaths appear to have played no part in the installation activities of Jews and the mainstream of the church in the early centuries. Exceptional is the requirement in the "Contestatio" concerning admission of a scholar into the Jewish Christian equivalent of the rabbinic academy. After being proved for a period of six years the new teacher took an oath of secrecy and faithfulness,[56] partook of bread and salt (a covenant meal) with his instructor, and was entrusted with the books of the sect's teaching.[57]

Sacrifices to the deity were a frequent act accompanying entrance into office in the ancient world. Such was a part of a Roman magistrate's activities on his first day in office.[58] Greek sources mention "entrance sacrifices" (*eisitēria*) brought by members of the Council and all magistrates at their entrance into office.[59] Some Attic inscriptions mention entrance

51. Pliny, *Paneg.* 64; Livy xxxi.50.8. The formula in Republican times was "by Jove and the gods of the household"—Cicero, *Acad.* 11.20.65. The oath in imperial times was taken on January 1: Dio xlvii.18.

52. Livy iv.27.1; xxxvi.2.3–5. For the vow to Jupiter that he had offered sacrifice: Cicero, *De leg.* ii.34.93; Dio xlv.17.

53. Liebenam, *Zur Geschichte und Organisation des römischen Vereinswesen,* 202. For one such statute, see *CIL* VI.10298, studied by Rudorff in *Zeitschrift für geschichtliche Rechtswissenschaft* 15 (1850) 232–40.

54. Busolt, *Griechische Staatskunde,* 472; Ziebarth, "Eid," col. 2079: Aristotle, *Ath. Pol.* 55.

55. Poland, *Geschichte des griechischen Vereinswesens,* 418, 499.

56. The explanation given in the document that the candidate does not swear an oath (which is unlawful), but only calls heaven and earth to witness his declaration seems to be largely a verbal distinction, so that this act may justly be classed as an Oath-taking.

57. *Ep. Pet. ad Jac.* in the Pseudo-Clementines.

58. See Livy's description of what was done on taking office in xxi.63.5–10.

59. Busolt, *Griechische Staatskunde,* 517–18. The clearest statement comes from

sacrifices offered by priests, presumably at the moment of entering on their charge (as was the case with magistrates).[60] The same term occurs in reference to an association,[61] and presumably sacrifices accompanied entrance into office in associations, at least in some cases.

Priests in the Old Testament performed certain sacrifices at their installation. The account of the installation of Aaron and his sons to the priesthood in Exodus 29 and Leviticus 8 gives the fullest description of installation to the priestly office in Israel. The seven-day ceremony, in the presence of the people, included sacrifices which were accompanied by the placing of blood on the right ear, thumb, and great toe and by the sprinkling of blood and oil on the person and garments of the new priest.

The Christian renunciation of material sacrifice meant that divine invocation took exclusively the form of prayer. Prayer was the constitutive part of Christian ordination.[62] It occurs already in the appointments to church office in the New Testament.[63] It is a uniform feature of the ordination rituals from the ancient church.[64] When church writers reflected on the significance of ordination, they defined the rite in terms of the prayer.[65] Three elements may de distinguished in the ordination prayers: praise to God who appoints leaders for his people; petition for divine favor in undertaking the task (Divine Invocation), and a personal benediction of the ordinand by the participants. The first two elements appear in the ordination prayer proper. The latter feature is present in the joint imposition of hands and silent prayers. The prayer spelled out that for which one was ordained, so there was a separate prayer for each new grade in the ministry. The prayer and Imposition of hands (considered below) indicate

---

Demosthenes, XIX.190; cf. XXI.114 and Thucydides viii.70. Attic inscriptions give *eisitēria*: *Inscr.Gr.* 112, 1011, and 1315. *Eisitēria* is mentioned at the yearly feast of Artemis in Magnesia: W. Dittenberger, Syll.³, No. 695. Dio uses *eisitēria* for the public sacrifices by which the Roman magistrates began the new year. The Greek entrance sacrifices were offered to Zeus Soter and Athena Soteira "on behalf of the Council and people": *Inscr.Gr.* 112, 689, and 1011.

60. *Inscr.Gr.* 112689; 690; 1315.

61. Ibid., 1315. See Poland, *Geschichte des griechischen Vereinswesens*, 253.

62. Acts 6:6; 13:3; 14:23.

63. Ferguson, "Jewish and Christian Ordination," 15, for the absence of prayer in Jewish ordination in contrast to its centrality in Christian ordination.

64. See the collection in Porter, *Ordination Prayers*. To his prayers may be added from the East those in documents derived from the *Apostolic Tradition* (*Apost. Const.*; *Const. per Hipp.*; *Test. Dom.*) and independently in Serapion's Prayer Book.

65. Jerome, *In Isa.* XVI,58 (*PL* 24:591); John Chrysostom, *Hom.* XIV in Acts 6 (*PG* 60:116); Gregory of Nyssa, "On the Baptism of Christ" (*PG* 46:581D).

that the character of the ordination was setting apart to divine service by a petition for divine grace and a personal benediction.

Demonstrating accession to office by the first performance of the duties of the office, implying *Inaugural Usurpation*, is widespread and natural. The type of office determined the function exercised in the Usurpation. A great amount of ceremony marked the entrance into office in ancient Rome. The office was not obtained by these ceremonies but rather was by them for the first time exercised (*usurpatio iuris*).[66] Among the opening day activities for a new consul was holding a session of the senate.[67] The praetors assumed judicial functions by hearing a case.[68] Installation by Usurpation was perhaps the most characteristic feature of Roman induction into office.

The sacrifices performed by Aaron and his sons on their installation (Exodus 29 and Leviticus 8 above) may be seen as exemplifying the category of Usurpation. The newly ordained rabbi in later Judaism gave a public discourse.[69]

Inaugural Usurpation was also a feature of early Christian ordination. The ordination occurred in the setting of the Sunday worship, and the new bishop proceeded immediately to the celebration of the eucharist.[70] Fourth century sources also indicate the preaching of a sermon by the newly ordained bishop.[71] These two acts together indicate the chief functions of the bishop—liturgical president and authoritative teacher of the community.

Teaching was associated with occupying the chair.[72] In Judaism and Christianity, where teaching was an important aspect of the religious life, a significant act of installation was Solemn Seating.[73] This was a feature of Roman civic life, where praetors, aediles, and quaestors showed their en-

---

66. Mommsen, *Römisches Staatsrecht*, 1:615–18.

67. Cf. Livy xxvi.26,5; xxvi.1.1; xxx.27.1; xxxii.8.1 and passim.

68. Mommsen, *Römisches Staatsrecht*, 1:618. Mommsen here only refers to Ovid, *Fast.* i.165ff., and Juvenal xvi.42 which are evidence for the hearing of law cases on the first of January.

69. Newman, *Semikhah*, 122–23.

70. Lengeling, "Der Bischof als Hauptzelebrant der Messe seiner Ordination."

71. *Apost. Const.* VIII.v.9ff.; *Vita Polycarpi* xxiii.

72. Cf. Irenaeus, *Demonstr.* 2: "The seat is a symbol of teaching."

73. Ferguson, "Jewish and Christian Ordination," 16–19. I have used Enthronement interchangeably with Solemn Seating for the formal occupying of the chair of office. *Thronos* was used of the teacher's chair and no distinction from *kathedra* can be maintained simply on the basis of these words.

trance into office by taking their seat.[74] Emperors under the later Empire, following an acclamation by the troops, were proclaimed and enthroned.[75] There may have been an "enthronement" in the initiation of certain Greek priests.[76]

All of the earliest descriptions of rabbinic ordination make the key feature the Seating of the ordinand in the teaching chair.[77] According to the Mishnah, three rows of disciples sat before the Sanhedrin. A vacancy in the Sanhedrin was filled by moving a man from the first row up to a seat on the Council, advancing a man from the second and third rows each, and choosing a man from the congregation to occupy the vacant place in the third row.[78] Taking the appropriate seat, therefore, represented one's admission to the Sanhedrin.

Solemn Seating remained a significant concept among Jewish Christians. "Even as Moses delivered his teaching to the seventy who succeeded to his chair" was the pattern for committing Peter's teaching to seventy chosen men who would carry on the tradition.[79] The Pseudo-Clementine Epistle to James, although referring to an imposition of hands, gives primary importance in its account of ordination to the Seating in the teacher's chair.[80] The similar account of an ordination in Homily III. 60–72 places the Seating before the Imposition of hands and prayer, which are tacked on somewhat incongruously after the ordinand has already taken his position. It would appear that in Jewish Christian circles being seated in the chair of the church was the key act in ordination.[81]

74. Mommsen, *Römisches Staatsrecht*, 1:618.

75. Instinsky, *Bischofsstuhl und Kaiserthron*, 32ff., finds the earliest instance with Pertinax. A thorough criticism of Instinsky's hypothesis that this event became a pattern for Christian appointment of bishops (and in particular that imperial enthronement was the basis of Solemn Seating as practiced by Christians) is given by Stommel, "Bischofsstuhl und hoher Thron."

76. Legrand, "Sacerdos. Grece," 938.

77. Ehrhardt, "Jewish and Christian Ordination"; review by Ferguson, "Jewish and Christian Ordination." The references include the Sifre to Numbers 27; Sifrè on Deuteronomy, cited in Lohse, *Die Ordination im Spätjudentum und im Neuen Testament*, 33; *p. Bikkurum* 3, 65d (quoted in Newman, *Semikhah*, 103). Cf. the account of Moses' ordaining of Joshua in *Assumption of Moses* xii.2: "raised him into the seat before him."

78. *m. Sanhedrin* iv.3,4. Similar information indicates that the same procedure was employed for the lesser sanhedrins, or councils of judges, in Palestine—*b. Sanhedrin* 17b.

79. *Ep. Pet. ad Jac.* 1.2; cf. also 3.1.

80. *Ep. Clem. ad Jac.* 2.2; 3.1,2; 17.1; 19.1.

81. Further evidence in Ferguson, "Jewish and Christian Ordination" (see chap. 9

Enthronement continued in the church mainly in the installation of a bishop into the chair of his church.[82] Enthronement language could stand for the whole process of induction into office.[83]

Divine Invocation and Inaugural Usurpation were common Roman and Greek practices, but the Christian applications of these motifs were so distinctive as to indicate an independent development.

Bestowal of the instruments signifying an office or used in its performance is called *Porrection*, and is a fairly obvious means of installation. The bishop's teaching role, indicated by the chair, was also expressed by the ceremony of holding the open Gospels upon the head of the bishop-elect during the ordination prayer.[84]

Porrection was known in Rome under the Empire. A sword was given to the prefect to indicate his appointment.[85] Greek priests would have received any insignia of their office at their installation.[86] The same applies to Israelite priests. The accounts of Exodus 29 and Leviticus 8 referred to above use words from the root "to fill" in connection with the installation of Aaron and his sons. The full form of the expression "to fill the hand" occurs in Judg 17:5, 12. The expression lost its specific sense in Hebrew, and in most Old Testament texts means only "appoint" or "ordain." What were the hands of the priest filled with? One view is that there was a handing over of sacrificial portions to the new priest, empowering him to lay these pieces on the altar, or, as the case may be, to receive them as perquisites from the sacrifice.[87] An alternative interpretation, based on the view that originally Semitic priests were diviners and not in charge of sacrifice, is that the hands were filled with the sacred lots.[88] The Jewish Christian Pseudo-Clementines provide, in addition to the oath, the committing of the secret books of the community to the newly ordained.[89]

---

below); Ferguson, "Eusebius and Ordination," 139–40 (see chap. 12 below).

82. *Apost. Const.* VIII.v.9–10; *Vita Polycarpi* xxiii; Theodoret, *H.E.* IV.20, 21. *Didasc.* 4 says: "He receives the imposition of hands to sit in the office of the bishopric."

83. Eusebius, *H.E.* VI.29; Gregory of Nazianzen, *Or.* XVIII.33; XXI.8; Synesius, *Ep.* LXVII. To hold office was to sit in the chair: Ircnaeus, *Adv. haer.* IV.xli.1 (xxvi.3–4); Muratorian Fragment.

84. First attested in the *Apost. Const.* VIII.iv.2ff.; cf. Ps. Chrysostom, *De leg.* (PG 56:404).

85. Dio lxviii.16.

86. Legrand, "Sacerdos. Grece."

87. Baudissin, "Priests and Levites," 70.

88. Arnold, *Ephod and Ark*, 134.

89. "Contestatio," in *Ep. Pet. ad Jac.*

Episcopal ordination in the Apostolic Constitutions included not only the opening of the Gospels upon the new bishop's head, but following the prayer, one of the attending bishops "lifted up the sacrifice upon the hands of the one who has been ordained," a symbol of his right to offer sacrifice.[90] Generally it was in regard to the lower orders that Porrection was used. This is attested already in the *Apostolic Tradition* where the reader was appointed by the bishop's handing him a book.[91] The spurious canons of the Fourth Council of Carthage, compiled at Arles in the fifth century, provide that at the appointment of a subdeacon the bishop hand him an empty patten and chalice and the archdeacon a ewer and towel. An acolyte received a candlestick and taper and the doorkeeper a key.[92]

Distinctive garments might pertain to an office as well as or instead of particular instruments, and installation by *Investiture* would be marked by donning the clothing pertaining to the office or worn in its exercise.

The ceremonial of ordination for the Israelite high priest in Exodus 29 and Leviticus 8 includes ceremonial washing, Investiture with the garments of the priesthood, and Chrismation (see below). There are several indications that the Investiture and the Chrismation were the basic elements in the appointment.[93] It would appear that in the latter days of the temple the high priest was no longer (or not always) anointed, for the Mishnah knows of high priests introduced to their office through Investiture,[94] and Josephus, *Ant.* XX. 1, would indicate that Investiture was constitutive in making the high priest.

Later rabbinic ordination included an Investiture. The candidate wore a special garment at his ordination and was thereafter distinguished by his clothing. The garment of honor meant much, and priestly garments came to be taken as an example of how rabbis should dress. The Nasi also was installed by Naming and Investiture.[95]

Anointing with oil or *Chrismation* had a widespread and distinctive role in the Old Testament. Chrismation was used in designating kings

---

90. *Apost. Const.* VIII.v.9ff.

91. *Apost. Trad.* xii.

92. Davies, "Deacons, Deaconnesses and the Minor Orders in the Patristic Period"; Arnold, *Ephod and Ark*, 134.

93. Exod 29:9, 29; 40:14–15; Num 20:26–28.

94. Such is the understanding of *m. Horaioth* iii.4 by Schürer, *Geschichte des jüdischen Volkes*, 2:284. *b. Yoma* 12a,b discusses only Investiture and Usurpation in the installation of a new high priest.

95. Newman, *Semikhah*, 117–20.

in Israel. This is a prominent feature in the stories of Saul[96] and David.[97] Thereafter, anointing seems only to be mentioned in connection with cases of disputed succession,[98] but perhaps it is only the irregular circumstances that call forth the explicit reference. The king, actual or ideal, was thought of as "anointed."[99]

Oil applied to priests and to the items they used in the service of God imparted a holy character—fit for divine service and removed from the circle of the profane.[100] The close association of Chrismation with divine service gave to the word *māshach* a metaphorical sense of any one chosen by God.[101] Chrismation is associated with endowment with the Spirit of God in some passages.[102]

One strand of priestly materials in the Old Testament suggests that all priests were anointed.[103] On the other hand, the term "the anointed priest" seems to have been a special designation of the high priest (but this interpretation is not necessarily demanded in Leviticus 4), and anointing is given as the mark of Aaron's successor in Lev 6:22.[104] Apparently at some point in Old Testament history all priests could be spoken of as "anointed," but "the anointed priest" par excellence was the high priest. Exodus 29 and Leviticus 8 do in fact make a distinction in the manner of the application of the anointing oil. It was only sprinkled on Aaron's sons (also on Aaron himself), whereas it was also poured on Aaron's head.[105] The virtual silence of sources outside the Old Testament leaves the question of what ceremony was in use for the installation of a high priest in later times uncertain. The continuation of Chrismation into Hellenistic times is indicated by Dan 9:26 and 2 Macc 1:10. Any cessation of Chrismation would have come in Herodian times.[106]

96. 1 Sam 10:1.

97. 1 Sam 16:13–14; 2 Sam 2:4; 5:3.

98. Macalister, "Anointings."

99. Lam 4:20; Ps 2:2; Zech 4:14 (apparently alongside the priest).

100. See especially Exod 30:22–33. For the various anointings in the Old Testament, see S. Szikszai, "Anoint," 139.

101. Ps 105:15; Isa 45:1.

102. 1 Sam 10:1, 6; 16:13–14; Isa 61:1.

103. Exod 28:40–41; 30:30; 40:14–15 (but do these passages refer to the sons of Aaron as successors in the high priesthood?); Exod 29:29–30; Lev 7:36; 10:7; Num 3:3.

104. For an analysis of the problem see Baudissin, "Priests and Levites," 83.

105. See further Lev 21:10, 12; Ps 133:2.

106. So Schürer, *Geschichte des jüdischen Volkes*, 2:284. 1QM ix.8–9, assumes each priest was anointed.

Early Christianity's break with the priestly conceptions of the Old Testament is indicated by the absence of Investiture and Chrismation in ordination until well into the Middle Ages. The first evidence of Chrismation in ordination is in the eighth century.[107]

Designation as a method of selection has its counterpart among acts of installation in *Naming*, a formal verbal proclamation of the name of the office or the title carried by its holder. The formal completion of Co-option to Roman priestly colleges came when the president *ad sacra vocabat* the newly designated member—a constitutive Naming.[108]

Verbal Naming came to replace Imposition of hands in rabbinic ordination. The Palestinian Talmud quotes the opinion that "elders are ordained by a verbal declaration," and adds that "one does not need to lay his hands on the ordained."[109] Billerbeck found the earliest evidence for Imposition of hands being obsolete in an event dated about AD 280,[110] but there is good reason to date the change in the second century when ordination ceased to be the action of a single rabbi in ordaining a successor and became the prerogative of the Patriarch on behalf of the community.[111] The new circumstances and the new ceremony gave the name *minnūy* to ordination in Palestine; the older term *semīkāh* continued in use among Babylonian Jews. The essential part of the Naming was the giving of the title "Rabbi" to the ordained.[112]

Naming occurs in Christianity in reference to certain lower orders; thus the *Apostolic Tradition* has the subdeacon appointed by being "named" to the function by the bishop and the widow "appointed by word only."[113]

Perhaps the most interesting use of this practice in Christianity is in the church at Alexandria, according to the testimony of Jerome. He declares that "at Alexandria from the time of Mark the Evangelist until Heraclas and Dionysius the presbyters always named ("nominabant") bishop one elected out of their own number and placed in a higher rank."[114] The

---

107. Ellard, *Ordination Anointings*, 7–13, 104. There was chrismation early at baptism, and Tertullian, *De bapt.* 7, connected this ceremony with admission to the Christian priesthood.

108. Toutain, "Sacerdos. Rome," 945.

109. *p. Megilloth* 1, 72b (also *p. Yoma* 1, 38d).

110. Billerbeck, *Kommentar zum Neuen Testament*, 2:655.

111. Newman, *Semikhah*, 103–10; cf. Lauterbach, "Ordination," 429.

112. *b. Sanhedrin* 13b.

113. *Apost. Trad.* xiv. and xi.

114. *Ep.* 146 (*PL* 22:1194). Müller, "Kleine Beiträge zur alten Kirchengeschichte,"

significant action, although there was an Election by the presbyters and a Solemn Seating, was the Naming, the bestowing of the title "bishop." The *Canons of Hippolytus* makes the same points as does Jerome, distinguishing the bishop from the presbyter in the "name of the episcopate" and by being "seated in the chair."[115] Since both sources affirm that the bishop can ordain but presbyters cannot, presumably the setting a part of a bishop did not entail a new ordination.

Imposition of Hands became the universal Christian rite of ordination for the offices of bishop, presbyter, and deacon. It was known already in the Roman world in an inaugural context,[116] but the background of Christian practice was clearly Jewish.

The laying on of hands was represented in Hebrew by two different words. *Sāmakh* ("to lean upon") was the more frequent term, employed in the following circumstances: witnesses laying their hands on the blasphemer who is to be stoned,[117] the person who brings an animal for sacrifice leaning upon it,[118] the people consecrating the Levites (which is assimilated to the form of a sacrifice),[119] and Moses appointing Joshua as his successor.[120] *Śīm* ("to touch") was used in connection with pronouncing a benediction.[121] The Moses–Joshua episode became an important model for rabbinic ordination, and *sĕmīkāh* (from *sāmakh*) became the technical term for ordination. The Imposition of hands was the essential part of the rite in early rabbinic ordination when a scholar ordained one or two of his pupils to carry on his teaching.[122] It has commonly been accepted that rabbinic ordination with its transfer of authority provided the background of Christian ordination practice.[123]

278, points out that according to his parallels Jerome means "called" and not "nominate." The sentence structure would also make "nominate" a difficult reading.

115. *Can. Hippol.* IV, 30–32. See Achelis, *Die Canones Hippolyti*; Riedel, *Die Kirchenrechtsquellen des Patriarchats Alexandrien*, 200–230; Coquin, "Les Canons d'Hippolyte." English translation by Bebawi in Bradshaw, ed., *The Canons of Hippolytus*.

116. Livy I.xviii.6–10.

117. Lev 24:14. This practice probably lies behind the judicial act in Susannah 34.

118. Leviticus passim; 2 Chron 29:23; Josephus, *Ant.* ix.13.3.

119. Num 8:10.

120. Num 27:15ff.; Deut 34:9.

121. Gen 48:14ff.

122. *p. Sanhedrin* 1.19a, 43. On rabbinic ordination see Newman, *Semikhah*; and K. Hruby, "La notion d'ordination dans la tradition juive."

123. Daube, *New Testament and Rabbinic Judaism*, 224–46; Lohse, *Die Ordination*, 33.

Laying on of hands occurred in Christianity for simple benedictions, healings, at baptism, reconciliation of penitents and schismatics, imparting the Holy Spirit, as well as in appointment to office.[124] The common theme in all of these occasions is the bestowal of a blessing; therefore, it may be argued that the Christian gesture is rooted in the benedictions of Jewish life, rather than in rabbinic ordination.[125] The fact that prayer consistently accompanied the Christian act, as it did *śīm*, but not the Jewish ordination (nor any instance of *sāmakh*) supports this distinction.[126] Laying on of hands as an accompaniment to prayer brings this study back to the divine Invocation with which this section began.

CONCLUSION

Typological studies have the value of sharpening points of agreement and difference. Similarities in the types of methods employed in selection and installation to office are in part due to the limited number of options available through which to carry out these functions. Christianity was a part of the ancient world and shows the influence of its surrounding cultures. At its beginning the *Jewish* influence was the strongest; in the course of time *Greek* and then *Roman influence* became more noticeable. Nevertheless,

---

124. Exhaustive references in Coopens, *L'imposition des mains*; Behm, *Die Handauflegung im Urchristentum*; Elderenbosch, *De Oplegging der Handen*. The use of Imposition of hands in ordination was so common that the second-century *Acts of Peter* 10 could even refer to the appointment of Peter as an apostle as being done by the Imposition of the Lord's hands; cf. also the *Edessene Canons* (Cureton, *Ancient Syriac Documents*, 24). There is some confusion whether one of both hands were ordinarily employed in the rite. In the case of sacrificial animals where the subject is singular the singular "hand" is always used except in Lev 16:21 (where the consonantal text is singular but the context demands the plural). The rabbis, however, always spoke of the action in the plural, "hands." Philo, *Spec.leg.* i.203, in speaking of a person's sacrifices says that he lays on "hands." The LXX, although generally following the number of the Hebrew, sometimes changes the singular to the plural (as in Lev 3:2, 8, 13). The evidence is more confused where persons are concerned. God tells Moses in Numbers 27 to impose his hand on Joshua; Moses then imposed his "hands" on him. The New Testament uses the plural in the great majority of cases. The plural is the common form in Greek Christian writers, but the singular is more often utilized in Latin: Galtier, "Imposition des mains," col. 1335–36.

125. Ferguson, "Jewish and Christian Ordination," 15 (see chap. 9 below). The blessing idea could be used in Judaism to interpret the meaning of ordination—*Sifré Zuta*, cited in Newman, *Semikhah*, 105.

126. The context of the gesture in early Christian art also favors this interpretation: DeBruyne, "L'imposition des mains," although going beyond the evidence in making some claims for the laying on of hands.

Christianity showed a *distinctive* development of motifs shared in common with its environment and so demonstrated its own genius. Comparative study of the selection and installation practices sharpens the theological significance of those practices and the offices involved.

9

Jewish and Christian Ordination
Some Observations

A FEW YEARS AGO ARNOLD Ehrhardt wrote an erudite and stimulating article[1] as a criticism and development of Eduard Lohse's *Die Ordination*.[2] A few observations in regard both to the laying on of hands in the Jewish background and to the seating of a candidate in the chair of office will serve to carry the discussion a step further.

LAYING ON OF HANDS

The discussion of this action must now be conducted in the light of David Daube's significant contribution distinguishing between *samakh* as involving significant pressure and *śim* as being a gentle touch to bestow a blessing.[3] Without agreeing with the psychological interpretation of *samakh* as signifying the pouring of one's personality into a substitute,[4] we may yet accept the basic distinction between the actions as well grounded.

1. Ehrhardt, "Jewish and Christian Ordination."

2. Lohse, *Die Ordination*. For other treatments of Jewish ordination note Mantel, "Ordination and Appointment in the Period of the Temple," giving a different perspective from mine; Hruby, "La notion d'ordination dans la tradition Juive"; Hoffman, "Jewish Ordination on the Eve of Christianity."

3. Daube, *The New Testament and Rabbinic Judaism*, 224–46.

4. Ibid., 226ff. The case of the witnesses (Lev 24:14) does not fit this frame of

Undaunted by the fact that the LXX recognizes no difference between *samakh* and *śim*, Daube proceeds to classify the New Testament impositions of hands as instances of either *samakh* or *śim*. Ordination is placed in the former category, where Rabbinic ordination also belongs. On the other hand, Christian texts show no trace of the distinction either in terminology or circumstantial description. The church records, early and late, preserve no memory of an imposition of hands involving the use of significant pressure. A decisive argument is supplied by the terminology of the Syriac church. In the Syriac version of the New Testament (unfortunately the Peshitta is our earliest text for the Acts and the Epistles) the equivalent of the Hebrew *śim* is uniformly used for the laying on of hands. *Samakh*, in contrast, occurs in the Syriac Bible chiefly for reclining at a table. All of the Syriac texts from the early history of the church use *śim* for the laying on of hands,[5] and in Neo-Syriac the technical words associated with ordination are developed from this root.[6]

Ehrhardt's article has brought forth another significant consideration: private ordination of a Rabbi by his teacher by imposition of hands did not originate, or at least did not come into prominence, until the troubled years between AD 70 and 135. *Samakh* as a technical term, "to ordain," in Rabbinic literature, therefore, may be derived from its sense of relying upon an authority rather than from its usage of leaning upon with the hands.[7] Apart from the word, the evidence is still convincing that imposition of hands was employed in Rabbinic ordination.[8]

---

thinking. Moreover, an animal represented the offerer in only one particular aspect (his sins or his feeling of gratitude); therefore the distinction from *śim* breaks down, for this word is said to indicate the transference of something other than or less than the whole personality. Moreover, in the healings, which Daube says carried no notion of conveying personality, some positive quality must have been thought of as imparted and this is hardly less than is said for the peace offerings.

5. As examples of ordination passages may be cited *Didas.* 4; *Testament of Our Lord* I.21, 30, 33; Edessene Canons, Int.; *Doct. of Addai* (ed. Phillips, 50).

6. R. Payne Smith, *Thesaurus Syriacus*, 2:2556–65.

7. Zeitlin, "The *Semikah* Controversy between the Zugoth," 499–500. Ehrhardt, "Jewish and Christian Ordination," suggests the meaning "support."

8. Strack and Billerbeck, *Kommentar zum Neuen Testament*, 2:654. To their arguments we may add the consideration that the Rabbis connected ordination with the imposition of hands in sacrifice—*b. Sanhedrin* 13b; *p. Sanhedrin* 19a; *t. Sanhedrin* I,I. The phrase *semikah zeqenim* in these passages is interpreted by Strack-Billerbeck (*Kommentar zum Neuen Testament*, 653) and Daube (*The New Testament and Rabbinic Judaism*, 244–45) as meaning "ordination to be elders." Lohse (*Die Ordination*, 28) and Newman (*Semikhah*, 3–4) dissent, and with their dissent we must agree. In *m. Sanhedrin* 1.3 the context makes clear that the expression means the "laying on of the elders'

Finding the arguments connecting the laying on of hands in Christian ordination with *samakh* unconvincing, and accepting Ehrhardt's conclusions concerning the date of Rabbinic ordination by imposition of hands, we are left with the question of the origin of Christian practice.

The laying on of hands appears to have been a familiar practice by Jesus in pronouncing a benediction and in performing acts of healing,[9] two circumstances placed by Daube within the associations gathered around *śim*.[10] The immediate origin of the practice by Christians was probably the familiar gesture by their Master.

The early Christians used the act as a symbol of a blessing. All of the circumstances in which the laying on of hands seemed appropriate in the church permit the rite to be interpreted as bestowing a blessing of one kind or another—the Holy Spirit, the fellowship of Christians, forgiveness or reconciliation.

A confirmation that Christian ordination is rooted in *śim* and not in *samakh* is the fact that laying on of hands in the church occurs only as an accompaniment to prayer.[11] There is no indication that prayer was a part of Jewish ordinations.[12] Prayer is appropriate to an act of benediction but is unnecessary in creating a "substitute." This circumstance is in harmony with the earliest theological interpretations of ordination, which place the emphasis on the prayer and indeed call it a benediction.[13] The imposition of hands was the outward symbol of the prayer—a personal benediction on the candidate and a petition for divine blessing upon him.[14]

---

hands" as is the biblical usage. With the precedent of the Bible and the Mishnah before them it does not seem possible that the Talmudists reversed the usage. Verbal naming replaced imposition of hands in Rabbinic ordination during the reorganization under Hadrian (Newman, *Semikhah*, 104–10).

9. Note especially Mark 10:13–16; 5:23; 6:5; 8:23, 25.

10. Daube, *The New Testament and Rabbinic Judaism*, 234.

11. Galtier, "Imposition des mains," 1338. Note that the word coined for the laying on of hands, *cheirothesia*, means "benediction" in the Greek Church today.

12. Lohse, *Die Ordination*, 77–79.

13. Jerome, *In Isa.* XVI, 58 (*PL* 24:591); Chrysostom, *Hom.* XIV in Acts 6 (*PG* 60:116) ; Gregory Nyssa, "On the Baptism of Christ" (*PG* 46:581D) ; Leo, *Ep.* IX; *Stat. Eccl. Ant.* 90–92. Cf. *Vita Polyc.* xi, "cover such a head with his hand and to bless . . . with his voice." In a non-ordination context Tertullian interprets the laying on of hands as a benediction and relates this rite in the church to Jacob blessing the sons of Joseph (Genesis 48)—*de Bapt.* 8.

14. Cf. the church orders: *Ap. Trad.* (ed. Dix, *The Treatise on the Apostolic Tradition of St. Hippolytus of Rome*, 4–6, 13, 15–17); *Ap. Const.* VIII.iv.2ff.; *Testament of Our Lord* I, 21, 30.

This understanding of the nature of ordinal imposition of hands breaks any necessary connection between the gesture and the bestowal of the Holy Spirit.[15] Ehrhardt is wrong in concluding that the transference of the Spirit was connected with the laying on of hands in pre-Rabbinic Judaism.[16]

Ehrhardt has already argued the differences in purpose between Rabbinic and Christian ordination: Rabbinic ordination conferred an equal status and had a legal rather than spiritual significance in that it conferred judicial functions.[17] That these features were absent or not prominent in Christian ordination further supports a separation of the Christian rite from a background in *samakh*.

SOLEMN SEATING

Ehrhardt has called attention to the abundance of evidence which indicates that ordination in Judaism was originally performed through the formal seating of the candidate in the chair of office and signified admission to the Sanhedrin.[18] The Mishnah provides as follows: "Before them [Sanhedrin] sat three rows of disciples of the Sages, and each knew his proper place. If they needed to appoint (*samakh*) another as judge, they

---

15. The Holy Spirit was one blessing which might be given in this way—Acts 8—but even here there is also an accompanying prayer, v. 15.

16. Not even Philo, *de Gigantibus* 24–25, is an exception to this, although it is the main passage to which Ehrhardt appeals, in spite of his skepticism about Philo's value for views held by Palestinian Jews ("Jewish and Christian Ordination," 131). Justin, *Dial.* 49, combines Num 21:27 with Num 27:18 and Deut 34:9 in a way not found in Jewish sources. Nevertheless, even in Justin's treatment the transfer of Moses' spirit to Joshua is not ascribed in the imposition of hands but to a separate act by God. The only Rabbinic passage this writer has found which would connect the imposition of hands with the giving of the spirit is the quite late *Midrash Rabbah, Numbers*, xv.25, which seems to connect the honor bestowed on Joshua with the spirit given to the elders in Numbers 11.

The following statement accords with the available evidence: "It is precarious also to assume that Rabbinic ordination by the laying on of hands in the first century was meant to signify the transmission of the Holy Spirit." Davies, *Paul and Rabbinic Judaism*, 212–13.

17. Ehrhardt, "Jewish and Christian Ordination," 125, 134–36. In the Pseudo-Clementine account of Peter's ordination of Clement (*Clem. ad Jac.* 5:3,4) the bishop's teaching function is stressed to the disparagement of the responsibility of judging. Perhaps this is a deliberate contrast between Christian and Jewish ordination.

18. Ibid., 229ff. Lauterbach, "Ordination," 428, has anticipated Ehrhardt in connecting the original practice of ordination with admission to the Sanhedrin, although he does not argue the case.

appointed him from the first row, and one from the second row came into the first, and one from the third row came into the second; and they chose yet another from the congregation and set him in the third row."[19]

There is definite evidence that the same procedure of taking the appropriate seat represented one's admission to the lesser Sanhedrins, or councils of judges, in Palestine. In the Babylonian Talmud (*Sanhedrin* 17b) the number one hundred twenty is given as the minimum population of a city in order that it may qualify for a Sanhedrin. In arriving at this number the commentator first counts the twenty-three members of a minor Sanhedrin, and then lists three rows of twenty-three who must sit before the council. There is no need to carry the arithmetic further; this much shows that the major Sanhedrin was the pattern for the lesser ones and presumably vacancies would be filled by both in the same way as outlined in the Mishnah.

Ehrhardt cautiously suggests that originally "elder" (*zaqen*) was the status conferred in ordination.[20] The evidence supports Lauterbach's bolder assertion.[21] The Talmudic statements which link the laying on of the hands of the elders in a communal sacrifice with ordination imply that "elders" are involved in both cases.[22] The comments on Numbers 11 make the transition from the "elders" of the text to ordained teachers directly.[23] One of the texts denying ordination "outside the Land" speaks of it as ordination of elders.[24] Two passages referring to the later ordination by naming speak of this as "appointment to be elders."[25] The term would appear to have been an early title for the ordained that enjoyed a revival in later times. The term "rabbi" is first used as a title in reference to the disciples of Johanan ben Zakkai.[26] The Gospels show "rabbi" as a respectful form of address to a teacher, but are an evidence against its usage at that time for ordained teachers. "Rabbi" apparently acquired official connotations only at the time we also hear of the first ordinations performed by individual

19. *Sanhedrin* 4:4 following Danby's translation. I think it more reasonable to take the passage for what it purports to be—a description of the Sanhedrin prior to the destruction of 70—rather than a description of the time of centralization in the second century as Lohse (*Die Ordination*, 30–31) suggests.

20. Ehrhardt, "Jewish and Christian Ordination," 131.

21. Lauterbach, "Ordination."

22. See the references cited in n. 8.

23. *Sifrè Numbers* 11:16.

24. *p. Bikkurim* 3.

25. *p. Megilloth* 1, 72b and *p. Hagigah* 76c.

26. Moore, *Judaism*, 3:15.

teachers (c. AD 70); therefore an added confirmation is given to Ehrhardt's thesis concerning the beginning time of Rabbinic ordination.

Solemn seating was a feature of ordination as performed by Jewish Christians. In the Pseudo-Clementine "Epistle of Clement to James" the central conception is the seating of the candidate on the *kathedra* of the teacher.[27] A similar account in some detail is given in the third Homily. In this account, however, the seating occurs first and is then followed by the imposition of hands and prayer. This striking reversal of the usual procedure in the church indicates a circle where the seating was the constitutive act.[28]

Independent corroboration of the importance which the Pseudo-Clementines would indicate solemn seating had for Jewish Christians may be obtained from Eusebius. Ten times Eusebius in his formulas of succession to episcopal office speaks of occupying the "throne."[29] Eight of these statements refer to the church at Jerusalem, and four of these eight to James. Most of Eusebius' information about Jerusalem, on his own statements, comes from Hegesippus, an orthodox Jewish Christian. Irenaeus, who also builds on Hegesippus, developed the theory of apostolic succession from one holder of the teaching chair to the next.[30] Now Ehrhardt has elsewhere traced the origin of the doctrine of apostolic succession to Jerusalem and has shown the place of Hegesippus in the formation of this doctrine.[31] Eusebius' usage of "throne" shows the logical connection between an ordination by "seating" to this doctrine, and further indicates that for Hegesippus (and doubtless other Jewish Christians) seating was the most important part of the ordination.

27. *Clem. ad Jac.* 2:2; 3:1,2; 17:1; 19:1.

28. *Hom.* III.lx–lxxii. Strecker, *Das Judenchristentum in den Pseudoklementinen*, 101–3, has argued that the accounts of ordination in the Clementines are derived by the editor from one source, a document containing an ordination ritual. I incline to the view that the editor has taken a Jewish Christian account in which seating was the key act and adapted this account to later practice.

29. *H.E.* II.i.2; xxiii.1; III.v.2; xi; xxxv; IV.xxiii.1; VI.xxxix.4; VII.xiv; xxxii.29; xix. In addition Eusebius twice refers to the thrones for the "presidents" in the new church at Tyre (X.iv.44; iv.66), quotes the disparaging report of the exalted throne Paul of Samosata prepared for himself (VII.xxx.9), and refers to "Heraclas now seated in the presbytery of the Alexandrians" (VI.xix.13).

30. Molland, "Irenaeus of Lugdunum and the Apostolic Succession." For Irenaeus, to be a presbyter was to hold a "chief seat" (*Adv. Haer.* IV.xli.1). Cf. "the seat is a symbol of teaching" (*Demons.* 2).

31. Ehrhardt, *The Apostolic Succession*, 65, 82.

By the fourth century the judicial-doctoral chair of the Jewish background became the throne of Hellenistic-Roman rulers.[32] If it is the latter which is in mind, then Ehrhardt is being anachronistic when he speaks of "enthronement" in the Jewish and early Christian context.[33]

Inadequate attention has been given to seating in Christian ordination. In fourth century accounts this act is especially associated with episcopal consecration.[34] In some instances enthronement stands for the whole process of induction into office.[35]

The relationship between imposition of hands and solemn seating in early Christian ordination needs to be studied further. Meanwhile we offer a few preliminary remarks. There seems to be no close connection between the two rites where they occur together in Christianity. In the two passages in the Pseudo-Clementines where they occur together the one account has the reverse order to the other. The indication, therefore, is that the two rites have two completely separate roots, as this study has suggested, brought together for the first time in Christian practice. Imposition of hands became the more important action because it was tied to the prayer which was the center of the ordination ceremony. From its early associations with blessings it was free to develop sacramental associations. The solemn seating maintained its character as an installation and became particularly the installation of a bishop on the throne of his church.

32. Instinsky, *Bischofsstuhl und Kaiserthron*, 13–34, and the even more significant review article by Stommel, "Bischofstuhl und höher Thron."

33. Ferguson, "Jewish and Christian Ordination," 330 and passim.

34. *Apos. Const.* VIII.v.9–10; *Vita Polyc.* xxiii; Theodoret, *H.E.* IV.xx, xxi. A third-century testimony is supplied by *Didasc.* 4.

35. Gregory Nazianzen, *Or.* 18:33; 21:8; Synesius, *Ep.* LXVII.

10

Qumran and Codex D

B O REICKE HAS SHOWN that the organization of the Qumran community exhibits elements of monarchic, oligarchic, and democratic structures, and he has used this "mixed constitution" at Qumran to shed light on what the Acts of the Apostles indicates concerning the organizational structures of the early church.[1] What is especially confusing about the Qumran material is that all three elements are juxtaposed in one document.[2]

Of special interest for this paper is the extent of participation by the assembly of the Many in the decisions of the community. The whole membership of the community was involved in decisions concerning the

1. Reicke, "The Constitution of the Primitive Church." See now Schmidt, "Election et triage au sort."

2. The *mebaqqer* or *paqid* presided over the sessions of the Many, served as financial agent, directed labor, and examined candidates for membership, according to Cross, *The Ancient Library of Qumran*, 177. Priests had charge of cultic affairs and were the principal religious teachers: *Rule of the Community* IX.7 also gives the priests control "over judgment and property." If it is legitimate to extend the thought of Lindars ("Qumran and the Christian Ministry") that the organization was an anticipation of the eschatological polity, then one might conclude that the presiding priest and the *mebaqqer* were counterparts to the Priest and the Messiah of Israel in the eschatological age (*Supplement to the Rule of the Community* II.11ff.). As an example of an "oligarchic" element it may be noted that the *Rule of the Community* VIII provides for a council of twelve men and three priests. For the "democratic" element, see the next three notes.

admission and readmission of members.[3] The assembly acted in conjunction with the priests in deciding the norm of the community.[4] The members elected the ten judges for special occasions.[5]

"THE LOT GOES OUT"

In this connection note should be taken of the phrase יצא הגורל (translated "the fixed measure of the lot shall go out" by Wernberg-Møller[6] and "the decisive edict," i.e., "the decision of the lot" by Leaney),[7] which occurs in five passages in the documents for which a concordance is available.[8] The phrase has its origin in the practice of drawing or casting lots and refers literally to the divining stones or lots coming out of the box or container in which they were held.[9] Thus the phrase is fairly common in the Old Testament for the result of taking lots—Num 33:54; Josh 16:1; 19:1, 17, 24, 32, 40; 21:4; 1 Chr 24:7; 25:9; 26:14 (in every case passages associated with the priestly tradition in the Old Testament).[10] It is interesting that the priestly oriented Qumran sect uses the same expression. The Septuagint translates these passages literally ἐξῆλθεν ὁ κλῆρος except in Josh 16:1 where a different phrase occurs.

The word "lot" acquired various metaphorical meanings in Hebrew and was especially used for any divine decision.[11] This prepares us for the extensive figurative use of the term "lot" in the Qumran documents. The phrase יצא הגורל in particular appears to have been used figuratively at

3. *Rule of the Community* VI.18–20; VII.21. In the *Damascus Document* XV.11 the *paqid* alone makes the decision.

4. *Rule of the Community* V.2ff.

5. *Damascus Document* X.4–6 (Rabin, *The Zadokite Documents*, 48, makes reference to the *m. Sanhedrin* 3:1).

6. Wernberg-Møller, *The Manual of Discipline*, 92.

7. Leaney, *The Rule of Qumran and Its Meaning*, 166.

8. Kuhn, *Konkordanz zu den Qumrantexten*; and Kuhn, "Nachträge zur Konkordanz zu den Qumrantexten." Cf. the indexes in *Discoveries in the Judaean Desert* (Oxford, 1955 and following).

9. The Latin *evenio*, literally "go out," seems to have derived its common meaning "happen" or "befall" from such a practice.

10. On the subject as a whole in the Old Testament, see Lindblom, "Lot-casting in the Old Testament."

11. Beardslee, "The Casting of Lots at Qumran and in the Book of Acts." Leaney, *The Rule of Qumran and Its Meaning*, 166–67.

Qumran for all decisions especially those in which the whole community participated.[12]

(1) *Rule of the Community* V.3: "according to them [members of the community] the lot shall go out [= the norm shall be decided] about everything concerning Torah study, property, submission of response."

(2) *Rule of the Community* VI.16: "as the lot goes out following the counsel of the Many"; 18–19 and 21–22 "if the lot goes out" [= if decision is made] to admit the candidate to the community.

(3) *Rule of the Community* IX.7: "The sons of Aaron alone shall have control over judgment and property. According to them the lot shall go out [=decision shall be made] concerning every norm [literally: rank (or seat)] of the men of the community."

(4) *Damascus Document* XIII.4: "The decision to go out or to come in for all who enter the camp shall be made according to his direction," understanding the phrase about the lot to refer to decisions made by the Levite after his appointment rather than to his selection itself.[13]

(5) *Supplement to the Rule of the Community* I.13–17—"At the age of thirty" he assumes responsibilities "in obedience to the priests, sons of Aaron, and to all the heads of the elders of the congregation who have been chosen [literally: for whom the lot has gone out] to hold office and to go and come before the congregation."[14]

In the last passage we are not told whether the assembly of the Many functioned as they did in the admission of new members (example 2), but the general pattern would give them a voice in the selection of leaders even if there was not a democratic election.[15] How the members expressed their will is not said. But it is clear that "the going out of the lot" has become a set metaphorical expression for the making of any decision by the community, including the selection of its leaders.

---

12. Wernberg-Møller, *The Manual of Discipline*, 92.

13. The translation is from Burrows, *The Dead Sea Scrolls*, 362, which brings out the meaning better than Rabin does. Wernberg-Møller, *The Manual of Discipline*, 93, understands a reference to the selection of the Levite.

14. Two passages referring to the appointment of priests give no indication of method: *Damascus Document* XIV.6–7 is perhaps simply "the priest who oversees the many," and *War Scroll* XV.6–8 the "designated priest," in allusion to Deut 20:2.

15. Josephus, *B.J.* II.viii.123, states that the overseers of the Essenes were elected (χειροτονητοί) by all.

THE WESTERN TEXT OF ACTS 1:15–26

Scholars have noted contacts of Acts 1:15–26 with Qumran. Schmidt has pointed to a similarity of terminology between Acts 1:15–26 and Qumran and has suggested possible patterns for the procedure in Acts based on a Jewish context. He notes the use of "lot" in the sense of "rank" and the role of the community.[16] William Beardslee has connected the casting of lots of Qumran with the selection of Matthias in Acts 1:15–26.[17] He made no use, however, of the *Supplement to the Rule of the Community* quoted above, which has to do with the selection of leaders and is therefore the most appropriate text for comparison with Acts 1. Moreover, he did not consider the readings of the "Western" text, notably Codex Bezae (= Cantabrigiensis), which would have put the matter in a new perspective.

The majority of the manuscripts of Acts gives us what appears to be a straightforward narrative: the community proposes two names of men who meet the qualifications laid down by Peter for an apostle. After prayer, lots are taken, and the lot falls on Matthias, who is then numbered among the apostles. The Lord made the choice, and lots are cast with a view to disclosing the identity of the one chosen.[18] This assumes that ἔδωκαν κλήρους αυτοῖς means "they [the apostles] gave lots for them" [i.e., the candidates]. It is true that "give" with "lots" is not the normal expression, but it does occur in the Greek version of 1 Sam 14:41. The meaning is not greatly altered if one follows Haenchen's suggestion that the candidates gave their lots to the apostles who then cast them until Matthias' came out.[19] On the other hand, if Black is correct in suggesting that this may be an ethical dative,[20] the genitive of Codex Cantabrigiensis (="D") would be better Greek.

This is one of two small variants in Codex "D" which radically alter the description of what took place. Acts 1:23 has the singular ἔστησεν, so Peter makes the nominations instead of the community of one hundred and twenty.[21] Acts 1:26 by the change from the dative to the genitive (αὐτῶν) indicates an election or choice by the community: "They gave

16. Schmidt, "L'organisation de l'église primitive et Qumrân," 224–25.

17. Beardslee, "The Casting of Lots at Qumran and in the Book of Acts."

18. Thornton, "The Choice of Matthias." For the theological significance of the narrative see further Gaechter, "Die Wahl des Matthias (Apg. 1, 15–26)"; and Menoud, "Les additions au groupe des Douze Apôtres d'après le livre des Actes."

19. Haenchen, *Die Apostelgeschichte*, 127.

20. Black, *An Aramaic Approach to the Gospels and Acts*, 104.

21. Cf. *m. Sanhedrin* 1:6 for the significance of the number one hundred and twenty.

their lots (or votes?)." Perhaps the Western readings represent a revision of the text to conform to procedures in the church at a later time when nomination by a leading figure was followed by congregational election or approval.[22]

Another possibility, however, presents itself. Even on the basis of the majority reading and before the discovery of the Dead Sea Scrolls, Lake and Cadbury had proposed an election interpretation of the passage.[23] This seems unlikely for the text represented by the majority of the manuscripts,[24] but hardly any other meaning fits so well for "D."

The problem has been that the use of the word "lots" in the required sense of a vote or decision was without analogy. Lots certainly were widely employed in the Hellenistic world for filling magistracies.[25] And the lots were understood as a means of making the divine will known.[26] But "lot" had not acquired this particular connotation of a decision. Now the non-Hellenistic use of "lots" to mean "votes" has, as we have seen, a counterpart at Qumran where the "going out of the lot" was a figurative expression for making a decision. Thus, even if the person responsible for the "D" text was thinking of later church practice, it would seem that he was in touch with a terminology known to us only from Qumran and which led him to interpret the procedure in Acts 1:15–26 in the way he did. We should understand "D" as saying: "The community gave their decision and the decision fell on (went out for) Matthias."[27]

The metaphorical use of "lots" in connection with appointment to an office continued in the church. The same phrase as Acts 1:26, "to give lots," occurs in a list of a bishop's duties in Hippolytus, *Apostolic Tradition* III.5, where the meaning, if not the general "make decisions," is "assign to the clergy." This usage would be a development from the circle of ideas we have been considering, either directly from the Jewish sources or under the influence of the Western Text.

---

22. *1 Clement* 44; Hippolytus, *Apostolic Tradition* II,1–2; Cyprian, *Ep.* LV.8–9; LXVIII.2; Eusebius, *H.E.* VI,xxix; Gregory of Nyssa, *Life of Saint Gregory the Wonder-worker* (*PG* 46:933ff.).

23. In Jackson and Lake, ed., *The Beginnings of Christianity*, vol. 4, 15.

24. See the criticisms by Haenchen, *Apostelgeschichte*, 127; and Thornton, "The Choice of Matthias."

25. Aristotle, *Constitution of Athens* XLIII.1; Aristotle, *Politics* IV,12 (1299 A); Demosthenes, *Oration* LVII.46 (1313); Cicero, *Against Verres* 2.2.126.

26. Plato, *Laws* 759C; *Inscriptiones Graecae* XII:3, 178.

27. The Septuagint uses ἔπεσεν with the "lot" in 1 Chr 26:14; Esth 3:7; Ezek 24:6; and Jonah 1:7, in dependence on the Hebrew.

CONCLUSION

This study points to a connection between the "D" text and Semitic, Palestinian terminology, which the majority text with its literal casting of lots does not share. Codex "D" at Acts 1:26 is supported by the Harclean Syriac. Since this version gives Western readings, it is not necessarily support for a special Semitic meaning at this point. It is of interest that the Peshitta sought to remove ambiguity between the dative and genitive by omitting the pronoun altogether. The result of this study agrees with those studies which have found that Codex "D" reveals a greater Semitic influence than its rivals.[28] If one is convinced by Epp's arguments for an anti-Judaic bias, then one might expect a locality in proximity to Judaism.[29]

The result of this study does not argue that "D" reflects the original reading, only that its reading arose with someone who knew the Qumran meaning of "lots." The context would favor the originality of the "B" text: the prayer presupposes a divine choice, better expressed by lots than by a community choice; and the theology of an apostle as chosen by the Lord better accords with the casting of lots. Moreover, the "D" text is generally regarded as secondary.[30] If that is so, Beardslee must be revised. The "D" text stands as an argument against Luke having recast the story; rather "D" has understood the words according to the figurative usage with which its editor was familiar.

If this parallel between Qumran and "D" should stand examination, someone should pursue Qumran contacts with "D" further.[31]

---

28. Black, *An Aramaic Approach to the Gospels and Acts*, 277–78; Torrey, *Documents of the Primitive Church*, 112–48; Wilcox, *The Semitisms of Acts*, 180, 185. Some authors have even ventured to locate the place of origin of the "D" text in Palestine or Syria, specifically Antioch: Ropes, *The Text of Acts*, ccxlii–ccxlv; Chase, *The Old Syriac Element in the Text of Codex Bezae*, 115–49; Klijn, *A Survey of the Research into the Western Text of the Gospels and Acts. Part Two, 1949–1969*, 68. Yoder cautions against generalizations from the Semitisms: "Semitisms in Codex Bezae"; and see the next note.

29. Epp, *The Theological Tendency of Codex Bezae Cantabrigiensis in Acts*. Hanson's review of Epp ("The Ideology of Codex Bezae in Acts") has argued against any special interest in Judaism on the part of the editor of the Western text. Hanson himself has located the "interpolator" in Rome: "The Provenance of the Interpolator in the 'Western' Text of Acts and of Acts Itself." Certainly anti-Judaic tendencies need not imply a Palestinian origin.

30. Zuntz, "A Textual Criticism of Some Passages of the Acts of the Apostles"; plus the works cited in n. 28.

31. Wilcox, *The Semitisms of Acts*, 185.

11

Origen and the Election of Bishops

ORIGEN'S FULLEST STATEMENT ON the selection of church officers occurs in his *Homily in Numbers* 13.4. The following is a fairly literal translation of the passage:

At the end of his life he prayed to God that He would provide a leader for the people. What are you doing, O Moses? Are not Gersom and Eleazar your sons? Or if you distrust any one of these, are not the sons of your brother great and distinguished men? Why do you not pray to God for them so that He might appoint them leaders of the people? But the leaders in office of the churches should learn not to designate by testimony nor to deliver the leadership of the churches as an inheritance to those who are related to them by blood or are associated with them by fleshly closeness, but to submit to the choice of God and not to choose that one whom human affection commends but to grant entirely to the judgment of God the choice of a successor. Was not Moses able to choose a ruler for the people by a true judgment and to make choice by a correct and just sentence, to whom God had said, "Choose elders for the people, whom you know to be the elders," and he chose such in whom immediately God's "spirit rested, and they all prophesied." Who therefore is able to choose a leader of the people unless Moses was able? But he did not do it, did not choose, did not dare it. Why did he not dare? That he would not leave to posterity an example of presumption. But listen to what he says, "Let the Lord, the

God of spirits and all flesh, provide a man over this congregation, who shall go out and come in before them and who shall lead them forth and lead them back." If therefore such a one as Moses gives not his judgment in choosing a leader of the people, in appointing a successor, what man would be he who dares to do so, whether of the people who are always accustomed to be moved by shouts for favor or perhaps excited for money, or of the priests themselves who will there be who would judge himself equal to this task, except only him to whom through prayers and petitions it is revealed by God? And just as God says to Moses, "Take to yourself Joshua the son of Nun, a man who has the spirit in him, and lay your hands upon him; and stand him before Eleazar the priest, and command him in the presence of the whole congregation and commission him from yourself before them; and give your honor to him that the children of Israel may hear him." You hear obviously the ordination of a leader of the people clearly described, so that there is almost no need of exposition. Here there was held no acclamation of the people, no regard of kinship, no consideration of friendship . . . The government of the people is delivered to him whom God chose.[1]

The writings of Origen have been claimed as evidence for election of bishops by the people,[2] choice by presbyters,[3] or joint participation by the community, the clergy and bishops.[4] Both Gore, in order to refute the contention of an unusual situation at Alexandria,[5] and Telfer, in order to support such a claim,[6] have appealed to Origen. Kemp has cast uncertainty on such appeals, inasmuch as Origen's language is a homiletic contrast between various possibilities and the more spiritual approach which he advocates.[7]

I suggest that Origen's language, however homiletical it might be, reflects different modes of selection to church office actually practiced in different regions in the third century.

---

1. The text used is that of Baehrens in *Origenes Werke 7* (GCS).

2. Göller, "Die Bischofswahl bei Origenes." Göller recognizes that in practice the influence of the clergy at elections was strong enough that their relatives were often chosen. Origen's information on the clergy has been assembled by von Harnack, "Der Kirchengeschichtliche Ertag der Exegetischen Arbeiten des Origenes."

3. Telfer, "Episcopal Succession in Egypt," 5.

4. Müller, "Kleine Beiträge zur alten Kirchengeschichte," 283.

5. Gore, *The Church and the Ministry*, 126–29.

6. Telfer, "Episcopal Succession in Egypt," 5.

7. Kemp, "Bishops and Presbyters at Alexandria," 129–31.

The *principes* ("leaders") appear to be bishops, and Origen speaks of their delivering the *principatus* ("leadership") of the churches to those whom, out of human affection, they have chosen. From the fourth century there comes definite evidence of bishops choosing and ordaining their own successors. Theodoret records that at Alexandria itself Athanasius chose Peter II as his successor: "First, his blessed predecessor had selected (*psēphizō*) him, then both the priests and worthy men gave their concurrence. All the laity demonstrated their pleasure by acclamations . . . The neighboring bishops came together." He further records an instance of actual ordination in the late fourth century at Antioch:

> After him when Evagrius had occupied his see, hostility was still shown to the great Flavianus, nothwithstanding the fact that the promotion of Evagrius was a violation of the law of the church, for he had been promoted by Paulinus alone in disregard of many canons. For a dying bishop is not permitted to ordain (*cheirotonein*) another to take his place, and all the bishops of a province are ordered to be convened.[8]

Canon 23 of the Council of Antioch earlier in the century by its prohibition attests the currency of the practice which its decree failed to eliminate: "It shall not be lawful for a bishop to appoint (*kathistan*) another in his place as his successor, even if it happens at the end of his life. And if any such thing is done, the appointment shall be invalid."[9] The historian Socrates relates that in the 330s Alexander, Bishop of Constantinople, died, without having ordained (*cheirotonēsas*) a successor.[10]

In the light of these passages Origen's language seems explicit enough to confirm the practice for the third century. It may be possible to adduce further evidence and to locate the origin of the practice in the region of Syria and Palestine when we recall that two of the fourth-century texts were associated with Antioch.

---

8. Theodoret, *H.E.* 4.20 and 5.23. I follow the Greek text of the second edition of Theodoret in GCS. Cf. Pseudo-Ignatius, *ad Hero* 7–8.

9. Translated from the Greek text of Lanchert, *Die Kanones der wichtigsten alt-kirchlichen Concilien*. This practice may be the occasion for the positive canon requiring the presence of other bishops at ordination (can. 19).

10. *PG* 67:192–93. *Cheirotonein* may have the generalized sense of "appoint" (choose to be a successor), but this seems precluded by the fact that Alexander had named two possibilities. Later in the context the word is used once to mean "elect" and twice to mean "ordain." For the terminology see Ferguson, "Eusebius and Ordination," (chap. 12 below).

A set of passages in the Pseudo-Clementines gives a brief statement of the appointment of bishops at various places by Peter. At Tyre "Peter established a church and installed (*katastēsas*) for them a bishop from one of the presbyters who were with him."[11] The same pattern was followed at Sidon, Beirut, and Laodicea.[12] The choice of a bishop in each instance was a designation by the apostle. Peter was not appointing successors to himself but "apostolic vicars," as it were, and so made the selection from his personal associates. Puzzling is the fact that these travelling companions are called presbyters. The unlikely circumstance of presbyters travelling with Peter may be explained if the compiler (or his source) is accommodating his narrative to practices with which he was familiar—a bishop choosing and ordaining his successor from the circle of presbyters in his church.

A Jewish background for episcopal ordination of a successor may be found in rabbinic ordination, which would further point to the same geographical region. Rabbinic ordination raised one to an equal status, and customarily only one or two are mentioned as ordained by one rabbi, indicating that the rite was meant to designate the successor to the master's teaching.[13] There was the difference between a rabbi and a bishop in that the former had a general power of jurisdiction but a bishop was the officer of a given congregation, and it was not for centuries that he could be transferred to another diocese without objection.[14] Still the idea of designating one's own successor provides a close parallel in the two circumstances.

Belonging to a different category, but perhaps included in Origen's language, was the practice of a bishop selecting and appointing (*constituere*) the presbyters and lesser clergy of his church. The *Didascalia Apostolorum* from Syria attests this practice, apparently without any participation by the people,[15] contrary to the pattern which generally prevailed.[16]

---

11. *Hom.* 7.5.3. Translated from the Greek text edited by Rehm for GCS.

12. Ibid., 8.3; 12.2; 20.23.3. These passages all seem to come from a late stage in the reduction of the *Homilies*. Contrast *1 Clem.* 44.2 where the apostles appointed bishops from the firstfruits of their converts at the locality concerned; see Eusebius *H.E.* 3.37. Origen, *Hom. in Num.* 11.4 refers to the missionary himself becoming the bishop.

13. Strack and Billerbeck, *Kommentar sum Neuen Testament*, 2:647ff.; Newman, *Semikah*, 109ff.; and Ferguson, "Jewish and Christian Ordination," chap. 9 above..

14. Ferguson, "Attitudes to Schism at the Council of Nicaea," 62.

15. *Didas.* 9 in Connolly, *Didascalia Apostolorum*, 96. Chapter 4 (p. 30) does provide for the congregation "to give testimony that he is worthy" in the election of a bishop.

16. Cyprian notes that his practice was to fill positions in the clergy with the approval of the rest of the clergy and of the people, an approval which could be dispensed with in times of emergency (*Ep.* 38.1, 2). The ordination prayer of a presbyter in the

The theme of Origen's discussion is the choice of a church leader (as seen in the frequency of the term *eligere*). Where the bishop did not actually "deliver the leadership" to a successor, he might make his wishes known through a "testimony."[17] A *testimonium* to the worthiness of a person was the clergy's means of proposing a name for election,"[18] or of ratifying a previous choice by the people.[19]

The second method of episcopal selection with which Origen shows an acquaintance is that which has been best recognized in the study of the ancient church—an election or acclamation by the people. Origen speaks of "the people who are always accustomed to be moved by shouts for favor or perhaps excited for money" choosing a leader.

Although approval by the people was required even when the selection was made by someone else, direct election by the people themselves was especially characteristic of the Greek East. One of the most graphic accounts is to be found in the *Life* of the third-century Gregory Thaumaturgus by the fourth-century Gregory of Nyssa.[20] According to the narrative the people of Comana invited the missionary Gregory to come and ordain a bishop for them:

> When the time came to accomplish their request and proclaim someone of the church their high priest, then the leading men busied themselves to put forward those considered conspicuous in eloquence, in ancestry, and in other things . . . Because the votes were divided and some preferred one and some another, Gregory awaited some counsel from God to come to him concerning one to be appointed . . . As the people presented their several candidates with commendations each in behalf of his choice, he recommended that they look among those of lower station in life . . . One of those presiding at the vote felt pride and irony at such judgment of the great . . . "If you recommend

Apos. Const. 8.16 describes the ordinand as "put into the presbytery by the vote and determination of the whole clergy." The sixth canon of Theophilus of Alexandria calls for clerical choice and popular ratification in orders below the bishop.

17. In the circumstance cited by Socrates (and referred to at n. 10 above), Bishop Alexander of Constantinople, although he had not ordained a successor, "had enjoined the proper persons to select one of the two whom he nominated."

18. Note the sequence in Cyprian's statement, "Cornelius was made bishop by the judgment of God and His Christ, by the testimony (*testimonio*) of nearly all the clergy, by the vote of the people who were present, by the company of old priests and good men (the neighboring bishops)" (*Ep.* 55.9).

19. See *Apos. Trad.* 2.2.

20. *Vita S. Greg. Thaum.* in PG 46:933ff.

these things, to overlook such who have been chosen from the whole city and to take someone from the lowest ranks for elevation to the priesthood, it is time for you to call Alexander the charcoal-maker to the priesthood. If you say so, we, the whole city, transferring the votes to this one, will agree together."

Learning that Alexander was really a philosopher who had been converted to Christianity and had taken a lowly occupation in order to secure privacy for his studies, Gregory planned a means of winning popular support for him as bishop. We see here the full arrangements for elections in Greek civil life, including nominations, election-conducting officials, and voting by the people.[21] Voting in the Greek city-states was performed by a show of hands, but we do not know the method in the early church.[22]

Although popular election had its deepest roots in the ancient world in Greek civic and club life,[23] the practice was observed by Jewish communities of the Diaspora in the selection of their archons,[24] and apparently by the Qumran community in selecting certain officials.[25] Election by the Christian community was widespread in the third century, including Rome and North Africa.[26]

When one remembers that the bishop had charge of distributing the charity of the community, it is no surprise that the populace could become "excited for money" at the selection of a bishop. The method of acclamation lent itself to a popular tumult. One of the most vivid pictures of unruliness is that given by Gregory Nazianzen in the oration on the death of his father. The divided populace of Cappadocian Caesarea finally agreed on an unbaptized person and "not in the best of order but with all sincerity" (as Gregory mildly puts it) secured the aid of a band of soldiers and with violence brought their candidate before the bishops for ordination.[27]

21. Busolt, *Griechische Staatskunde*, 1:1071. In the *Vita Polyc.* 22, the deacons are sent to the assembled laity to inquire concerning their vote, very much as the herald called for a show of hands in Greek elections.

22. The term *psēphos* is used for vote in the above passage, but the words in this family had long since come to mean "vote" without reference to mode, Siotis, "Die klassische und die christliche Cheirotonie," 20 (1949) 725ff. and 21 (1950) 459.

23. Busolt, *Griechische Staatskunde*, 1000, 1071; Poland, *Geschichte des Griechischen Vereinswesens*, 38:417.

24. Krauss, *Synagogale Altertümer*, 152–54.

25. Ferguson, "Qumran and Codex D," 77; see chap. 10 above.

26. *Apos. Trad.* 2.1; Cyprian, *Ep*, 55.9; 59.5, 6; 68.2; 67.3; 4; for later sources see Optatus, *De schism. Donat.* 1:18; *Gesta apud Zenophilum* 10; Possidius, *Vita S. Augus*, 4.

27. *Or.* 18.33. See "Nectarius was seized by the people and proposed for the episcopate of Constantinople," Socrates, *H.E.* 5.8.

Sulpicius Severus' Life of St. Martin of Tours describes a stormy scene in which the majority laughed down opposition by bishops and some others to the ordination of Martin as bishop.[28] There was a popular demand at Alexandria for Athanasius as bishop, and the ordination was performed "with the acclamations of all."[29] Sometimes the election was unanimous and such was taken as an indication of divine choice.[30] The choice of the people, sensitive to indications of the divine will, was frequently determined by omens. A child's mistaken cry, "Ambrose bishop," set up a popular clamor,[31] and a dove settling on the head of Fabian caused the people to acclaim him "Worthy!" of the bishopric of Rome.[32]

Origen, in discussing Lev 8:4ff., gives two reasons for the presence of the people at an ordination: to be witnesses to the person's character and to prevent any refusal by the people to obey.[33] This would serve as a ratification by the people even if the constitutive choice should have been made by others.

Origen considers, as a third factor, priests who judge themselves the appropriate ones to select a bishop. Here we must face the question of presbyterial election of bishops at Alexandria. The testimony of Jerome, Severus of Antioch and Eutychius of Alexandria to the effect that prior to the fourth century the presbyters of Alexandria elected and ordained a bishop out of their own number contains mutual contradictions but in its substance has not been overthrown.[34]

---

28. *Vita S. Mart.* 9.

29. Athanasius, *Apol. c. Arian* 6. For popular acclamations at Alexandria see also Theodoret, *H.E.* 4.20.

30. Ambrose, *Ep.* 63.2, "Justly was it believed that he whom all had demanded was elected by the judgment of God."

31. Paulinus, *Vita. S. Antb.* 3.6.

32. Eusebuis, *H.E.* 6.29.

33. *Hom. in Lev.* 6.3. Origen 's language is very similar to that used by Cyprian, *Ep.* 67.4. The sixth canon of Theophilus of Alexandria forbids secret ordinations. The ordination liturgy of the *Apostolic Constitutions* prescribes a public examination of the candidate in which the people are called upon three times to testify to his worthiness before the ordination can proceed (8.4.2ff.). In the *Testament of Our Lord* this is stylized into a formal cry of *Axios* following the ordination prayer.

34. Jerome, *Ep.* 146; Brooks, *The Sixth Book of the Select Letters of Severus Patriarch of Antioch*, 2:213; Eutychius in *PG* 111:982. The latest statement of the case and with some new results is by Telfer, "Episcopal Succession in Egypt." Lecuyer has shown the inconsistencies in the three sources in "Le problème"; he has also undertaken a point by point refutation of Telfer in "La succession." He puts too much reliance on *Vita Saturn.* 8 in the *Historia Augusta* for bishops in Egypt at an early date, but more importantly he does not overthrow the main point or offer conclusive evidence against

Jerome's testimony is as follows:

> At Alexandria from the time of Mark the Evangelist until Hera-
> clas and Dionysius the presbyters always named (*nominabant*)
> as bishop one elected out of their own number and placed in a
> higher rank, just as an army makes an emperor or deacons elect
> from themselves one whom they know to be diligent and call
> him archdeacon. For what except ordination does a bishop do
> that a presbyter does not do?

Both the sentence structure and Jerome's parallels make it clear that
nominate means "called" and not "nominate."[35] Thus the presbyters not
only elected the bishop but also installed him by seating him in a higher
chair and bestowing on him the name "bishop." No separate imposition of
hands seems to be indicated.[36]

With the addition of providing for an election by the people, the
Canons of Hippolytus makes the same points as Jerome in regard to bishops (a higher rank, the name and the power of ordaining).

> If now a presbyter is ordained, all things are done with him in
> the same way as with the bishop, except he is not seated in the
> chair.
>
> Also in the same way a prayer is prayed over him in all
> respects like that over a bishop, with the exception only of the
> name of episcopate.
>
> The bishop in all things is equal to the presbyter except in the
> name of the chair and in ordination, which power of ordaining
> is not assigned to the latter.[37]

---

it. His four arguments to challenge the testimony of Jerome are: (1) the silence of Ambrosiaster; (2) the evidence of Origen which we are considering; (3) the possibility that
the *Apostolic Tradition* derives from Egypt; and (4) the later idea that it was a heresy to
identify presbyters with bishops.

35. Müller, "Kleine Beiträge zur alten Kirchengeschichte," 278.

36. For the importance of seating in the chair, see Ferguson "Jewish and Christian
Ordination," 16–19 (see chap. 9 above). Eutychius's account is different: the twelve
presbyters elect one of their number and "laying their hands on his head bless him
and make him patriarch" and then elect a replacement to keep the number at twelve.
Lêcuyer, "La succession," 92, suggests that the Arabic may refer to election, not imposition of hands, as in the Latin translation (which I have rendered); but if so, there is a
redundant second reference to election in the sentence. Severus simply says that the
bishop of Alexandria "was in old times appointed by presbyters" but after Nicaea his
institution was performed by bishops.

37. Translated from the Latin version of Haneburg printed by Achelis, "Die Canones Hippolyti." Riedel, *Die Kirchenrechtsquellen des Patriarchata Alexandrien*, 203,
gives a briefer rendering of the Arabic into German: "If a presbyter is ordained, the

C. H. Turner has explained the instruction to use the same prayer as for a bishop as the result of a misinterpretation of the *Apostolic Tradition*, which calls for a prayer like that used for a presbyter and then proceeds to give a prayer to be used.[38] The apparent contradiction was solved by the *Canons of Hippolytus* in the simplest way by omitting the prayer altogether. By going one step further, I would raise the question why the compiler chose this alternative. He had a theory of the identity of the two orders save for the power of ordaining, a power which to him was not given through ordination. The development of the parish system could have suggested this theory to him, as it did to Jerome (for whom it was reinforced by study of scripture). But a more immediate basis may have been a recollection of the earlier situation of the Egyptian church. The *Canons of Hippolytus*, therefore, may also be adduced for support of Jerome's testimony.

The Egyptian Monophysite bishop Severus has been appealed to as preserving a more reliable Egyptian tradition than his older contemporary Eutychius.[39] Certain conclusions, however, will emerge from his accounts of the ordination of the patriarchs of Alexandria.[40] The early bishops were only names to the later historian. In describing their appointments he stresses the selection by the people and generally mentions the presence of other bishops (but he gives incidental confirmation that Demetrius was the first bishop of Alexandria to appoint other bishops).[41] These statements follow the same pattern as the formulas announcing the appointment of fourth-century patriarchs. The conclusion which presents itself is that Severus made up the earlier accounts according to his knowledge of later practice. Demetrius was the first bishop of whom Severus had historical knowledge, and this is through Eusebius. But it is to be noted that with Demetrius there is a series of bishops for whom no details are supplied for their appointment. It hardly seems accidental that the first bishops for whom details of their lives are known are

same things are done as with a bishop, with the exception of the word 'bishop.' The bishop is in every relationship like the presbyter, except for the throne and ordination, for no power to ordain is given to the presbyter." A French version is given by Coquin, *Les Canons d'Hippolyte*.

38. Turner, "The Ordination Prayer for a Presbyter in the Church Order of Hippolytus." Turner's solution is rejected by Barlea, *Die Weihe der Bishöfe, Presbyter, und Diakone in Vornicänischer Zeit*, 229.

39. Gore, *The Church and the Ministry*, 37: Lecuyer, "La probleme"; and Lecuyer, "La succession," 83.

40. English translation by Evetts in *History of the Patriarchs of the Coptic Church of Alexandria*, I/2, 4.

41. Ibid., 153.

those for whom the least is recorded about their ordination. The first of the "historical" bishops details of whose appointment are given is Peter I; and with the addition of a selection by his predecessor the account corresponds exactly to the Jerome–Eutychius version of episcopal consecration at Alexandria.[42] Severus has apparently reproduced a source contrary to his own principles at this point.

Telfer's reconstruction of the ceremony by which the Alexandrian bishops entered office ascribes a central place to the action of the bishop-elect in lifting the hand of the dead predecessor and placing it on his head.[43] The principal evidence for this comes from Liberatus in describing the rivalry of Theodosius and Gaianus to succeed the Monophysite Timothy III in 536. He relates that nothing appeared so decisive to either rival as the touch of the dead man's hand and the transfer of the pallium of St. Mark.[44] A connection may be observed between this and the language of the Egyptian Severus. From the bishops at the end of the third century forward Severus makes a point of recording the dying bishop's choice of a successor. Is the touch of the dead man's hand in Liberatus' account meant to take the place of such a choice?

A problem in Origen's passage remains: does "priest" mean "presbyter" here? The translator uses *sacerdos*, which in third-century Latin (so in Cyprian) normally means bishop. On the other hand, Origen speaks of the presbyters as priests,[45] and his translator elsewhere uses *pontifex* where the bishop is meant.[46] Understanding Origen's priests in our text passage as presbyters fits his testimony neatly into the picture drawn by the later evidence.

There is a parallel to this Alexandrian Christian practice in the priestly colleges and sodalities of Rome which filled their ranks by cooption and elected from their membership *magistri* to preside over their functions.[47]

---

42. "When Abbe Theonas, the patriarch, went to his rest, the clergy of Alexandria assembled with the people and laid their hands upon Peter the priest, his son and disciple, and seated him upon the episcopal throne of Alexandria" (ibid., 383). Even Eutychius' number twelve for the presbyters at Alexandria may reflect an old tradition. Clement of Alexandria, *Strom.* 6.13.107, understands the twenty-four elders of the Apocalypse as representing twelve Jewish and twelve gentile (Christian?) elders; and see the twelve elders of the Pseudo-Clementine *Hom.* 11.36.2.

43. Telfer, "Episcopal Succession in Egypt," 10.

44. *PL* 68:1036–37.

45. *Hom. Jer.* 12:3: *en toutois tois hiereusi (dieknumi de tous presbyteriou emas).*

46. *Hom. in Lev.* 6.3.

47. Wissowa, *Religion und Kultus der Römer,* 487, 495.

Nearer to hand, the Great Sanhedrin, and presumably the lesser sanhedrins of the Jews, practiced cooption.[48] The gerousiarch of Jewish inscriptions at Rome may have been selected by his fellow elders to his position as president of the *gerousia* or council.[49] Much to be desired would be information relative to the selection of members of the ruling council of Alexandrian Jewry.[50] It would be reasonable to suppose that the Christian community there followed the precedents of the ruling body of the Jews.

Whatever method of selection is employed—by the bishop, by the people, by the presbyters—Origen advocates that divine guidance be sought in prayer. He prefers choice to be made by a spiritual man to whom the will of God has been revealed in answer to prayer.[51] It is to be God's judgment or decision.[52] Origen thus picks up the theme of inspired or prophetic designations which occur in the New Testament.[53] He further enunciates the principal doctrinal interpretation of ordination in the ancient church, namely that the selection of a bishop is God's action.[54]

48. *m. Sanhedrin* 4.3, 4; *b. Sanhedrin* 17b.

49. Frey, "Les communautés Juives a Rome," 136.

50. The meager evidence is in Tcherikover and Fuks, eds., *Corpus Papyrorum Judaicarum*, 1:10, 57, 101.

51. *Hom. in Josh.* 23.2 comments about the selection of a successor to Judas: "Seeing that prayer precedes, the lot is not by chance but leads to a divine choice by providence."

52. Origen's word *iudicium* is also Cyprian's in the passage cited in n. 18; see also *Ep.* 59.5 and 68.2 and Ambrose in the passage cited in note 30.

53. Acts 13:1–3; 1 Tim 1:18; 4:14. See Clement of Alexandria, *Quis dives* 42.

54. Cyprian, *Ep.* 48.3; 55.9; 61.3; *Vita S. Mart.* 9; Eusebius, *H.E.* 6.29; Theodoret, *H.E.* 4.7.4.

12

Eusebius and Ordination

THE *ECCLESIASTICAL HISTORY* OF Eusebius employs a variety of expressions in describing the episcopal successions of the important churches. Some of these are theologically colorless, as the forms of λαμβάνειν to declare that one has "received" the episcopate, or often the "ministry" (λειτουργία), of a given church. Other formulae are related to the most important motifs associated with ordination in the ancient Church.

Eusebius most often speaks of changes in those presiding over the churches in terms of a succession (διαδέχεσθαι, διαδοχή).[1] The non-technical nature of Eusebius's terminology is indicated by his using the same words in regard to emperors,[2] heretics,[3] prophets,[4] and teachers in catechetical schools.[5]

On the other hand, one recalls that Irenaeus developed the theory of apostolic succession, not from ordainer to ordained, but from one holder

1. A sampling of the numerous instances may be given: *H.E.* II.xxiv; III.xiv; xxxv; xxxvi.1, 15; xxxvii.4; IV.i; v.5; xix; xx; V.pref.; V.v.8–9; v.12. Ehrhardt (*Apostolic Succession*, 35–61) finds the pattern for Christian episcopal lists in Jewish succession lists of high priests. Cf. also C. H. Turner's note on "succession" language in non-Christian and early Christian writers—*Essays on the Early History of the Church and the Ministry*, 197ff.

2. *H.E.* II.viii.1; III.xii.1; xx.8; xxi; IV. iii.1; and frequently.

3. *H.E.* III.xxvi.1.

4. *H.E.* V.xvii.4.

5. *H.E.* VI.vi.

of the teaching chair (καθέδρα) to the next.[6] Significant for Eusebius's "succession" language, therefore, may be his usage of θρόνος. At least ten times Eusebius speaks of someone occupying the θρόνος of an episcopal see.[7] In addition he twice refers to the thrones for the "presidents" in the new church at Tyre, dedicated in 317.[8] The extension of "enthronement" language to presbyters is also seen in the reference to "Heraclas now seated in the presbytery of the Alexandrians."[9] Eusebius also quotes the disparaging report of the exalted throne which Paul of Samosata prepared for himself.[10]

An examination of the ten instances where θρόνος occurs in the formulae of succession reveals that eight of these refer to the church at Jerusalem. Of these eight, four have reference to James. Most of Eusebius's information about Jerusalem, on his own statements, comes from Hegesippus. Irenaeus, who connected apostolic succession with the teaching chairs, also built on Hegesippus. Occupying the "seat" or "chair," therefore, seems to have had a special significance to the circle of Jewish Christians of whom Hegesippus is representative.

A "solemn seating" was part of the ritual of admission to the Sanhedrin in pre-Christian times.[11] The "chair" was thus closely associated with the judges or elders of Jewish community life. Occupying the καθέδρα takes a prominent place in the ordinations recorded in the *Pseudo-Clementines*,[12] even in one place preceding the imposition of hands.[13] If Eusebius reflects a pattern of thought drawn from Hegesippus, there is good reason for tracing an act of "solemn seating" in Christian ordination to Jewish believers at an early period of the Church.[14]

6. Molland, "Irenaeus of Lugdunum and the Apostolic Succession." Cf. the statement of the *Demonstration of the Apostolic Preaching*, 2: "The seat is a symbol of teaching." *Adv. Haer.* IV.xli.i (IV.xxvi.3–4) identifies being a presbyter with holding a seat.

7. *H.E.* II.i.2; xxiii.1; III.v.2; xi; xxxv; IV.xxiii.1; VI.xxix.4; VII.xiv; xxxii.29; xix. The references have been compiled with the aid of the index in the edition of Eusebius by Eduard Schwartz for *Die griechischen christlichen Schriftsteller*.

8. *H.E.* X. iv. 44; iv. 66.

9. *H.E.* VI. xix. 13, using καθεζόμενον.

10. *H.E.* VII. xxx. 9.

11. Ehrhardt, "Jewish and Christian Ordination."

12. *Clem. ad Jac.* ii.2; iii.1, 2; v.3, 4; xvii.1; xix.1.

13. *Hom.* III.lx–lxxii.

14. Instinsky (*Bischofsstuhl und Kaiserthron*, 11–34) traces the origin of enthronement from the practice of eastern kings to the Roman emperor and thence to Christian bishops. Stommel ("Bischofsstuhl und höher Thron") reviews Instinsky and concludes that a high throne was used by other officials than the emperor and that solemn seating in the ante-Nicene Church began from Jewish roots.

The word θρόνος is, from Plato onwards, specifically the chair in which someone sits to teach.[15] However, Christian literature uniformly uses καθέδρα prior to the fourth century, at which time θρόνος becomes the prevailing word. Eusebius uses καθέδρα in the *Ecclesiastical History* only in quotations (as in V.1.36).

The "enthronement" occurs primarily in accounts of episcopal ordination.[16] Enthronement language even in some instances stands for the whole process of induction into office.[17] Eusebius's terminology thus ties in with common language and with the ordination ritual.

Another motif of importance to Eusebius, and/or his sources, is indicated by the frequency with which an individual is said to have been counted worthy of a position among the clergy.[18] This expression looks not so much to the dignity of the office, occurring as it does more often in connection with presbyters than with bishops, as to the kind of worthiness that God would honor. Eusebius records instances where the motif of divine selection was strongly felt by the people,[19] and he indicates that this was a living conception for himself.[20] This feeling of divine choice is related to the worthiness of the candidate. The terminology of worthiness certainly implies some examination into a person's qualifications, perhaps even a formal scrutiny.[21] Eusebius's language may be an echo of the cry, Ἄξιος, by which the people recognized during the liturgy the divine qualities of the candidate.[22]

---

15. I am indebted to Prof. A. D. Nock of Harvard, invaluable tutor in many respects, for calling my attention to this relevant fact.

16. *Didasc.* 4; *Apos. Const.* VIII.v.9–10; *Vita Polyc.* xxiii; Theodoret, *H.E.* IV.xx, xxi.

17. Gregory Nazianzan, *Or.* xviii.33; xxi. 8; Synesius, *Ep.* lxvii.

18. Ἀξιοῦν—*H.E.* III.xi; VI.xliii.17; VII.vii.6, xxxii.30. Δοκιμάζειν ἄξιον—VI.viii. 4.

19. *H.E.* VI.xi.1; VII.xxx.57; VI.xxix. For other strong assertions of divine choice see Cyp., *Ep.* xlviii.3; lxvi.1, 9 (and frequently); Lucifer of Cagliari, *de S. Athan.* i.9; Ambrose, *Ep.* lxiii.2 and 3.

20. *H.E.* VII.xxxii.23; X.iv.23.

21. The δοκιμασία was a feature of entrance into office in Greek civil life: Aeschines, iii.15; Plato, *Laws* vi.763–65; and especially, Aristotle, *Ath. Pol.* 55. Indications of an examination of a candidate's worthiness for church office, particularly as it related to the approval of the people, are found in the following passages *Did.* xv.1; *1 Clement* xlii.4; *Ep. Pet. ad Jac.* i.2; *Didasc.* 4; Origen, *Hom. in Lev.* vi.3; Hippolytus, *Apos. Trad.* ii.2; Cyprian, *Ep.* lxvii.4; *Hist. Aug.* "Life of Severus Alexander," xlv.6–7; Nicaea Can. 9 (where an examination is supposed but not as a general practice).

22. *Testament of Our Lord* i.21, where the people three times cry, "He is worthy," after the ordination prayer, the place where the cry Ἄξιος occurs in the Orthodox Liturgy today. In the *Apos. Const.* VIII.iv.2 the bishops before proceeding with the ordination three times call upon the people to testify that the candidate is worthy. This

The theme of divine choice may also have been felt in the word κληροῦσθαι, for those "allotted" a ministry in the Church.[23] The lot had a religious origin and in classical antiquity kept the inner assumption of divine selection.[24] Although no longer indicating a mode of selection, the verb form in Eusebius still has an overtone of God making an assignment. Eusebius uses κλῆρος of the clergy, but in the formulae of appointment the middle form of the verb is completed by a noun indicating the sphere to which assignment is made. A position in the clergy does not inhere in κληροῦσθαι; that which is allotted must be supplied by another word.[25] The conception, therefore, is the charge given to a person, the responsibility which is apportioned.[26]

A similar thought, but lacking the special connotations of κληροῦσθαι, is expressed by the frequently occurring ἐγχειρίζειν.[27] The meaning is simply "entrusted," "given into the hand" of a person.

More important for the fourth century, but rarer in Eusebius, is προχειρίζεσθαι. Eusebius uses the word twice, both times for the selection of the Seven in Acts 6.[28] This inadequately studied word is a technical term for ordination in the present Eastern rite. One meaning of προχειρίζεσθαι in ecclesiastical Greek is "to propose a name for election."[29] Contrary to what has been accepted,[30] the evidence is against this being the dominant meaning in the fourth century.[31] In Hellenistic Greek the word means

---

testimony may have been given by the acclamation, Ἄξιος, which became stylized in the later liturgy. See Stendahl, "ΑΞΙΟΣ im Lichte der Texte der Qumran-Höhle."

23. *H.E.* III.2; iv.8; v.2; xxxvi.2; IV.i; V.vi.2.

24. Ehrenberg, "Losung." Cf. Plato, *Laws* 759C; and *IG* XII.3, 178.

25. The fact that in Eusebius's quotation of Irenaeus (*H.E.* V.vi.2) Clement is allotted the ἐπισκοπήν weakens the suggestion that κληροῦσθαι may have been taken as a technical term for Clement "inheriting" the function of Peter, a suggestion made in Ullmann's provocative article, "Significance of the *Epistola Clementis*," 297–98.

26. For κληροῦσθαι as an expression for the selection of Church officers, Siotis, "Die klassische und die christliche Cheirotonie," 21 (1950) 458. See Liddell, Scott, Jones, *Greek-English Lexicon* for Old Testament precedent and neutral meaning of the verb.

27. *H.E.* II.i.2; xvii.23; xxiii.1; III.xxxvii.3; IV.xi.6; xxiii.1, 3; V.ix; VI.xxi.2.

28. *H.E.* II.i.10; III.xxix.1.

29. *Vita Const.* III. 62; Socrates, *H.E.* II.6.

30. Hatch, "Ordination," 1501; Siotis, "Die klassische and die christliche Cheirotonie," 21 (1950) 459.

31. A case in point is the synodal letter of the council of Nicaea preserved in Theodoret, *H.E.* I.ix.7ff. and Socrates, *H.E.* I.9. The translators have taken προχειρίζεσθαι to mean "nominate." Its usage alongside both χειροθετεῖν and ʽυποβάλλειν ὄνομα would seem to exclude a reference to either ordination in the limited sense or proposing a name. Either "select" (with a view to someone else ordaining) or "appoint" to a minor

"select." It seems to have had a parallel development to χειροτονεῖν, from referring to the selective process to referring to ordination.[32] The two occurrences in Eusebius preserve a neutral meaning of "select" or "appoint." Although still in the fourth century a less technical term than χειροτονεῖν, προχειρίζεσθαι was moving into acceptance for "ordination."[33]

The *Ecclesiastical History* illustrates the range of meanings which χειροτονία had in reference to ordination for the early Church. In one passage it means election.[34] The installation alone is meant in some instances.[35] The whole process of selection and installation is included elsewhere.[36] A general sense of "appointment" is indicated in a passage quoted from Dionysius of Alexandria where χειροτονία and κατάστασις are apparently used synonymously (VII.ix.2). It is this latter word which Eusebius uses overwhelmingly[37] in preference to the later technical term χειροτονία. The meaning is simply "appointment."

The terminology for ordination did not crystallize as rapidly in the East as in the West and in the fourth century χειροτονία had not won the field as the usual word for ordination.[38] However, in the *Apostolic*

---

order would fit the linguistic history of the word and the context.

32. In the *Apostolic Constitutions* προχειρίζεσθαι occurs often and with the same range of usage as χειροτονεῖν. It covers any formal appointment or institution, especially by God: Paul (II.xxiv.4), a judge (II.xxxvi.9), the Christian priesthood (III.ix.2), rulers and priests in the Old Testament (VIII.v.4), Melchisedec (VIII.xii.23), Philip and Ananias (VIII.xlvi.17). In VII.xxxi.1, where the *Didache* has χειροτονεῖν (perhaps preserving the meaning "elect") the *Apostolic Constitutions'* compiler (to whom χειροτονεῖν had lost this sense) substitutes προχειρίζεσθαι. A similarly less technical reference to ordination is VI.xxii.5. Προχειρίζεσθαι refers to the installation into office in III.xvi.1 and VIII.xlvi.15—specifically mentioned are the bishop (II.iii.1), deacon (VIII.xxiii.2), and sub-deacon (VIII. xxi. 4), all of whom receive χειροτονία; προχειρίζεσθαι but not χειροτονεῖν is used of deaconnesses (VIII.xx.1) and readers (VIII.xxii.2), but these too receive a laying on of hands.

33. Canon 3 of Ancyra and Canon 10 of Nicaea (where προχειρίζεσθαι is the equivalent of the laying on of hands in Canon 9) use προχειρίζεσθαι for ordination.

34. *H.E.* VI.xxix.3. The continuation of the meaning "elect" into the fourth century may be illustrated by Athanasius, *Apol. c. Arian.* xi and Socrates, *H.E.* ii.6 (a passage which uses χειροτονεῖν in other senses also).

35. *H.E.* II.i and VI.xliii.10, 17, where χειροτονεῖν is accomplished by the laying on of hands and prayer; probably VI.x also.

36. *H.E.* VI.xix.16.

37. For example, *H.E.* III.iv.9; xxxvii.3; IV.xx; xxiii.3–4; VI.xi.4; xlvi.4; VII.xi.26; xiv.1; xxx.7; xxxii.1, 22.

38. Κατάστασις was the prevailing word in Egypt; see, e.g., Athanasius (*ad Dracon.* ii), Serapion's *Prayer Book, Apostolic Church Order*, 17. Note the Council of Sardica in the mid-fourth century which issued canons in both Latin and Greek. The Greek

Constitutions a certain narrowing of the word's usage occurs, so that it refers either to any formal appointment (especially by God) or to ordination in the Church (neither to election nor to the whole process but to the ceremony of installation).[39]

In Hellenistic Judaism there was a religious usage of χειροτονεῖν which prepared the word for its Christian development. Josephus and Philo, in addition to using χειροτονεῖν in the classical sense "to elect"[40] and the Hellenistic sense "to appoint,"[41] employ the word in the religious context of the selection of religious functionaries by God himself.[42] C. H. Turner has attributed the adoption of χειροτονία as the regular word for ordination to its earlier association with election and its close parallelism in form with χειροθεσία.[43] I would think a more potent influence was the connotation of divine appointment given to the word in Hellenistic Judaism. A passage in Josephus brings together characteristic ideas associated with ordination

---

generally has κατάστασις for the Latin *ordinatio*: e.g., Can. 10 (13); but once ὁρίζω renders *ordinare*, in Can. 15 (19). If the eastern versions faithfully preserve Hippolytus's usage in the *Apostolic Tradition*, then χειροτονεῖν was already a technical term for ordination in the Greek-speaking Church at Rome in the early third century and it is, perhaps, to this locality that we should look for the origin of what became the exclusive use of χειροτονεῖν.

39. In the former category belong VII.xvi.1 (God's appointment of kings), V.xx. (His ordaining of the Roman monarchy), II.xxvii.5 (His ordination of the high priest in the Old Testament), III.ix.3 (Gentiles' ordaining women priests), and II.xliii.3 (the Devil's ordination of wicked persons to be a reproach to the Church). In the latter category belong III.xx; II.ii.3; and frequent references in Book VIII where χειροτονία is used of the three major orders and sub-deacons and is specifically denied to confessors, virgins, widows, and exorcists.

40. Josephus, *Ant.* iv.297; vi.81 (cf. vi.60 and *B.J.* iv. 592); *Vita* 341; *B.J.* iv.256. Philo, *Deus* xxiv.112; *de Mut. Nom.* xxviii.151; *de Spec. Leg.* II.xl.231 (cf. iv.ii.9).

41. Josephus, *Ant.* vi.83, and passages cited below. Philo, *de Post. Cain.* xvi.54; *de Jos.* 248; *Quod. Det. Pot.* 145; *de Op. Mundi* 84. This appointment may be performed by a single person: Josephus, *Ant.* xiii. 45; Philo, *Quod Det. Pot.* 66; *In Flacc.* 109. For the appointment of cult officers in particular, see Philo, *de Agri.* xxix. 130; *de Vita Mos.* ii.141–143 (in the latter passage αἱρεθῆναι is also used of the choosing, whereas καθίστανται occurs in reference to installation); Josephus, *B.J.* iv.147 (in the following section καθίστανται is used, apparently interchangeably with χειροτονεῖν).

42. Josephus, *Ant.* iv. 34, 54, 66. Josephus especially makes the choice of kings an act of God: *Ant.* vii.53; ix.108; vi.312. Philo, *Quod Det. Pot.* 39; *de Sac. Abel.* 9 (= *Quod. Det. Pot.* 161); *de Vita Mos.* i.198; *de Virt.* x.64; *de Vita Mos.* i.148; Not specifically religious appointments are God's appointment of Joseph to his position in Egypt (*de Mig. Abrah.* 22) and the recognition of Abraham as a king (*de Virt.* xxxix. 218; cf. *de Somniis*, ix. xxxvi. 243 where the appointment is ascribed to nature and not specifically to God).

43. Turner, "Χειροτονία, Χειροθεσία, Ἐπίθεσις χειρῶν," 499.

in early Christian writers: a divine choosing, based on the worthiness of the person, and guaranteeing the acceptableness of the person's ministry:

> But now God himself has judged Aaron worthy of this honour and has chosen him to be priest, knowing him to be the most deserving among us . . .
>
> Coming from a man of His own choosing, He cannot but accept them [his divine services] . . .
>
> The Hebrews were pleased with this speech and acquiesced in the divine election (χειροτονία).[44]

Philo made a significant combination of the religious interpretation with Greek practice, which ties in with the common understanding of the selection of bishops as a divine choice: "It was God who appointed (χειροτονεῖν) him by the free judgment of his subjects, God who created in them the willingness to choose him as their sovereign."[45]

The doctrinal association with divine choice doubtless was an important factor in giving χειροτονεῖν the victory over its more colorless rivals, such as καθίσταναι.

Imposition of hands does not have a prominent place in Eusebius. Χειροθεσία occurs only in VI.xxiii. 4—with reference to Origen's ordination as a presbyter, which is described in VI.viii.4 by the equivalent phrase, τιθέναι χεῖρας.[46] Apart from quotations, the phrase "laying on of hands for the episcopate" is found (VII.xxxii.21), and the laying on of hands of the Seven in Acts vi is noted (II.i). This phrase occurs for healings (I.xiii.17; V.vii.4) and reconciliation of penitents (VII.ii.1). Eusebius, therefore, does not appear to make any distinction between χειροθεσία and τιθέναι χεῖρας.[47]

44. *Ant.* III.190–92.

45. *De Praemiis et Poenis* ix.54. Cf. Ambrose, *Ep.* lxiii.3: "Where the demand of all is unanimous, ought we to doubt that the Lord Jesus is there as the Author of that desire!"

46. Χειροθεσία in *Vita Const.* iv. 61 may refer either to admission to the catechumenate or to confirmation.

47. The *Apostolic Constitutions* makes a distinction, reserving the latter for ordination. This distinction is foreign to earlier writers: cf. Turner, "Χειροτονία, Χειροθεσία, Ἐπίθεσις χειρῶν," 496–97. The context shows χειροθεσία referring to ordination in Canon 19 of Nicaea and in its Synodal Letter (Theodoret, *H.E.* I.ix.7 ff.) and therefore probably in Canon 8.

13

Laying On of Hands
Its Significance in Ordination

D AVID DAUBE HAS ESTABLISHED a distinction in the Old Testament between *samakh*, "to lean upon" (to create a substitute), and *śim*, "to touch" (an act of benediction).[1] He argues that *samakh* kept its force in rabbinic literature and so in New Testament times. He classifies the New Testament benedictions and healings as representing *śim* and the instances of appointment to a function in the church and of imparting the Holy Spirit as representing *samakh*.

There are difficulties in maintaining the distinction for New Testament times. One of these Daube recognized: the Septuagint and Hellenistic Jewish authors translated both Hebrew terms by ἐπιτίθημι (τὰς χεῖρας). The New Testament too makes no distinction in terminology for laying on of hands. Daube's explanation is that the rite of leaning one's hands upon a being would have struck a Hellenistic public as very outlandish.[2] If the

1. Daube, *The New Testament and Rabbinic Judaism*, 224–46. After my present article was published, there appeared Coyle, "The Laying on of Hands as Conferral of the Spirit." There is now a book-length study of the gesture by Tipei, *The Laying on of Hands in the New Testament*; see my review in *Review of Biblical Literature* (posted online 15 Feb 2010).

2. The laying on of hands was known in the Greco-Roman world—Livy i.18.6–10. The National Museum in Copenhagen contains a votive relief from Cyzicus (first century BC) on which a seated Cybele has her right hand on an offering which is being presented to her. A krater in the museum, no. 4332, shows a male with his hand on

distinction, however, had any real significance to Hellenistic Jews, surely some effort would have been made to show it. The other difficulty is that the Dead Sea Scrolls have produced a passage where *samakh* is used in an account of Abraham healing Pharaoh by prayer and laying his hands on Pharaoh's head.[3] David Flusser notes that this gesture for healing is not found in the Old Testament nor rabbinic literature, but it is now known to have been practiced among pre-Christian Jews. He further concludes that laying on of hands in the New Testament translates *samakh* in its healing as well as its ordination passages.[4]

If the Hebrew concepts were kept distinct, there is still the question of the category to which Christian ordination belongs.[5] If the linguistic terms had become mixed, as it appears, the question of the conceptual background of Christian usage is in even more urgent need of clarification. On the surface there appears to be good reason to connect Christian usage with *samakh*. It was used for appointment to office in the Old Testament[6] and became the technical term for ordination in Judaism.[7] However much a cross-fertilization of ideas may have occurred, it will be argued here that the background of Christian usage is to be found in the associations with *śim*. The basic idea in early Christian ordination was not creating a substitute or transferring authority, but conferring a blessing and petitioning for the divine favor. Blessing, of course, in ancient thought was more than a kindly wish; it was thought of as imparting something very definite (as in the patriarchal blessings of the Old Testament). "Hand" in biblical usage was symbolic of power.[8] The laying-on of hands accompanied prayer in Christian usage. It was essentially an enacted prayer, and the prayer spelled out the grace which God was asked to bestow. As an act of blessing, it was considered to effect that for which the prayer was uttered.

the head of a smaller male who is offering a chest held in his hands. The emperor is depicted as granting freedom to a slave by laying his hand on him—Klausner, "Studien zur Entstehungsgeschichte der christlichen Kunst."

3. *Genesis Apocryphon* xx.22,29, ed. Avigad and Yadin. Cf. *Jubilees* 25.

4. Flusser, "Healing through the Laying-on of Hands in a Dead Sea Scroll," 107–8.

5. See my earlier effort to distinguish Christian and rabbinic ordination in Ferguson, "Jewish and Christian Ordination," chap. 9 above. A different view on questions of dating is given by Mantel, "Ordination and Appointment in the Period of the Temple."

6. Num 8:10; 27:15ff.; Deut 34:9.

7. Newman, *Semikhah*; Lohse, *Die Ordination*. For a recent survey of the evidence for Jewish ordination see Hruby, "La notion d'ordination dans la tradition juive."

8. Grayston, "The Significance of the Word 'Hand' in the New Testament." Thiselton, "The Supposed Power of Words," 293, cites some examples in contemporary language of words having a performative power.

A number of considerations in my early study had led me to this con-clusion, but the discovery which seemed to clinch the matter was Syriac Christian word usage. The Syriac church's use of the equivalent to *śim* rather than *samakh* for the laying on of hands in ordination confirms the idea of blessing as forming the conceptual background of early Christian usage. There are a number of different terms used for ordination in Syriac, of which the oldest is definitely the *śim* root plus *'ida*, hand.[9] Thus there is the phrase *sam 'ida* ("to ordain") in the *Doctrine of Addai* (Phillips, p. 52) and Ephrem, *Hymn. c. Haereses* xxii.18. The phrase *qabbel syamida* ("to re-ceive laying on of hands" or "ordination") occurs in Afrahat, *Dem.* xiv (*Pat. Syr.* col. 633).[10] As an indication of the technical status acquired by this terminology, *syamida* (plus *qabbel*) is the term still used in the Chaldean Pontifical (ed. Rome, 1957) to the exclusion of all other terminology. The Syrian Orthodox ordination service, however, employs the other terms available as well as *syamida*, including the Greek loan word *cheirotonia* which became common in Syriac writers from the fifth century onwards. The opening prayer begins, "Support (root *smk*), 'Lord, with thy mighty right hand . . . these thy servants' . . ." Otherwise, the root *smk* does not seem to occur in connection with ordination in Syriac, and this occur-rence is distinct from the ordination laying on of hands.

In the divergent developments of ordination the Jews adopted one complex of words (*samakh*) and Christians another (*śim*). Such may be paralleled in the distinctions which emerged between συναγωγή and ἐκκλησία, εὐλογία (*berakh*) and εὐχαριστία, βαπτισμός and βάπτισμα. It may not be possible to establish a continuity between primitive Aramaic speaking Christianity and the later Syriac church, but there is a linguistic affinity that makes this evidence pertinent. It points to the use of *śim* in the Old Testament as the proper background for Christian conceptions sur-rounding the laying on of hands. Here the important text is Gen 48:14ff., Jacob's blessing of his grandsons Ephraim and Manasseh. This episode permits a probe whether there is a conceptual as well as linguistic back-ground here to early Christian usage.

The inquiry into the influence of Genesis xlviii on the early church's conception of the laying on of hands may begin with Tertullian, *De bap-tismo* 8. After the immersion and anointing:

9. I gratefully acknowledge the assistance of Dr. S. P. Brock of Cambridge (later Oxford), whom I follow for the references in this paragraph.

10. Other early ordination passages employing the *śim* root include *Didasc.* 4; *Tes-tament of Our Lord* i.21, 30, 33; *Edessene Canons* (Cureton, *Ancient Syriac Documents*, 24, 33–34).

> Next follows the imposition of the hand in benediction, inviting
> and welcoming the Holy Spirit . . . But this too is involved in that
> ancient sacred act in which Jacob blessed his grandsons, Joseph's
> sons, Ephraim and Manasseh, by placing his hands interchanged
> upon their heads, turned transversely upon themselves in such a
> manner as to make the shape of Christ, and at that early date to
> prefigure the blessing that was to be in Christ.[11]

Here it is to be noted that the baptismal imposition of hands is under-stood as a benediction, in the form of a petition or invocation (*advocans*) for the Holy Spirit to come upon the person, and this is seen as prefigured in the Old Testament account of Jacob blessing Joseph's sons.

The crossing of the arms permits a ready identification of this scene in Christian art. To the two representations listed by L. DeBruyne[12] (a sarcophagus in the catacomb of St. Callixtus and a miniature in the Vienna Genesis—Folio XXIII, p. 45; cf. also XII, pp. 23–24) may now he added a picture in cubiculum B of the catacomb on the Via Latina.[13] Representations of the multiplication of the loaves and fish in Christian art depict Christ's prayer of blessing by showing him extending his arms to lay a hand on loaves on one side and a plate of fish on the other which are presented to him by two disciples. This is the most common form of showing one of "the most popular of Jesus' miracles in Christian art.[14] DeBruyne claims that the multiplication is the only scene in Christian art where an imposition of hands is applied to inanimate beings, but this must be extended somewhat, for he also notes imposition of hands in scenes with a more direct eucharistic setting.[15] DeBruyne understands the imposition of hands on the bread and fish as an act of benediction, which accords with the early Christian understanding of meal prayers and the eucharistic invocation as consecrating by a prayer of thanksgiving.[16] The verb "to bless" in the Gospels (Mark 6:41 and parallels; 8:7;

---

11. Evans, *Tertullian's Homily on Baptism*, 17, 19. Cf. *Barn.* 12.5–6 for another Old Testament figure of the blessing in Christ.

12. DeBruyne, "L'imposition des mains," 119–20.

13. Ferrua, *Le pitture della nuova catacomba di Via Latina*, plate 25. The scene is also found in the Dura synagogue.

14. DeBruyne, "L'imposition des mains," 196ff. On the multiplication of the loaves in Christian art see also Nilgen, "Brotvermehrung," 326–30; and Vloberg, *L'Eucharist dans l' art*, 28ff.

15. Ibid., 199ff. See Hippolytus, *Apos. Trad.* I.iv.2 for placing hands on the elements at the consecration.

16. Atchley, *On the Epiclesis of the Eucharistic Liturgy*; Cirlot, *The Early Eucharist*.

14:22 and parallels) was thus depicted by a laying on of hands, which says something about the action suggested by the word and about the signification of the act. The crossing of the arms can be explained as an example of the influence of Jacob's blessing on early Christian conceptions. The simple placing of a hand on the head is the way Isaac's blessing of Jacob is shown in a mosaic in Santa Maria Maggiore, incidentally an act not explicitly mentioned in Gen 27:23, 27 and thus significant for the way a blessing was depicted in art.[17]

More important for Christian usage than the Old Testament background was the practice of Jesus himself. Surely the employment of the imposition of hands in the early church derives from the example of Jesus. Mark makes frequent mention of this act in connection with Jesus' healings.[18] On one occasion he records a petition employed by Jesus in healing (Mark 7:32ff.). Again Jesus is said to have ascribed the casting out of certain demons to the power of prayer (Mark 9:29). There seems to have been some transfer of power or of health in the healings (cf. Mark 5:30), and this is the common interpretation of the laying on of hands in healing.[19] Yet the laying on of hands in healing may be interpreted as the bestowal of a blessing, in this case of a particular kind. Quite significant for this study is the way Jesus used the imposition of hands for bestowing a simple blessing. It seems to have been a familiar gesture by Jesus in pronouncing a benediction. Mark 10:13–16 relates that certain persons were bringing children to Jesus "in order that he might touch them." Jesus "took them in his arms and blessed them, laying his hands upon them." That is, the way he blessed them was by laying his hands on them. Matthew's version states "they were bringing children to him so that he might lay his hands on them and pray." Jesus' usage of the gesture thus was as an act of blessing.

"Hands" have frequent association with prayer. Lifting up the hands was the common gesture for prayer in the ancient world.[20] Raising the hand was employed in the priestly benediction[21] and was imitated by Jesus in his parting benediction on his disciples (Luke 24:50). This association of prayer with hands obtains especially in regard to the Christian act of imposition of hands. Often quoted is Augustine's statement in reference

---

17. Karpp, *Die frühchristlichen und mittelalterlichen Mosaiken in Santa Maria Maggiore zu Rom*, plate #42. Similarly the angel blesses Jacob by placing a hand on his head in the Vienna Genesis #24.

18. Mark 5:23; 6:5; 7:32; 8:23, 25; cf. 1:31, 41; 5:41; 9:27.

19. Cf. Lohse, *Die Ordination*, 69.

20. For a large collection of references, see Dölger, *Sol Salutis*, 301ff.

21. Lev 9:22; Sir 50:19–22.

to the laying on of hands in reconciliation of penitents, "What is it more than a prayer offered over a man?"[22] Lifting up the hands would naturally suggest praise and petition to God; the laying on of hands suggests from the identification of the object toward whom benediction is directed.

Nowhere is the association of hands with prayer clearer than in ordination.[23] In the New Testament the acts of "prayer and the laying on of hands" belong together, with prayer mentioned first.[24] The association of prayer and laying on of hands is a persistent feature of accounts of Christian ordination. Hippolytus, *Apos. Trad.* I.ii, gives the earliest full account of the ordination of a bishop: "With the agreement of all let the bishops lay hands on him and the presbytery stand by in silence. And all shall keep silence praying in their heart for the descent of the Spirit. After this one of the bishops present at the request of all, laying his hand on him who is ordained bishop, shall pray thus, saying . . ."[25]

The association of prayer with the laying on of hands may be seen in the usage of the word χειροθεσία. Made up from the phrase for laying on of hands, the word came to mean in the Greek church "benediction." It was mainly used in the early centuries, apart from the *Apostolic Constitutions*, for the laying on of hands in ordination.[26] It could be used of any rite in which the laying on of hands was employed, and only much later was it distinguished from χειροτονία and confined to non-ordination benedictions. Its early use shows that the laying on of hands in ordination was not distinct from the laying on of hands in other situations and had the content of a blessing.[27] The "Prayerbook" of Serapion demonstrates this point, for

22. *De bapt.* 3. 16. 21; cf. 5. 20. 28. Origen, In *Hom. in Lev.* ii.4 cites Jas 5:14 as "laying on hands" rather than praying; *P.L.* 13.611, fragment 7, a fourth-century Arian saying that uses the imposition of hands as equivalent of benediction.

23. Galtier, "Imposition des mains," 1338, makes the point strongly: Imposition of hands is accompanied by a prayer that specifies the purpose and gives to it its proper character. It is an essential trait of the act. More recently but in the same vein, Vogel affirms, "Imposition of hands acquired its signification only by the prayer which accompanied it and the cultic context in which it was inserted"—"L'imposition des mains," 57.

24. Acts 6:6; 13:1–3; cf. 14:23.

25. Dix, *The Treatise on the Apostolic Tradition of St. Hippolytus of Rome*, 3. The same conjunction of prayer and laying on of hands occurs in the ordination of presbyters and deacons—ibid. viii.1 and ix.1, 9.

26. Turner, "Χειροτονία, Χειροθεσία, Ἐπίθεσις Χειρῶν"; Vogel, "L'imposition des mains," 57–65.

27. Vogel, ibid., 58–59, states that before the third century χειροθονία and χειροτεσία were used only of "simples gestes de bénédiction polymorphes" and concludes that it is radically out of place to oppose these terms and draw theological conclusions from

χειροθεσία heads not only the ordination prayers for a bishop, presbyter, and deacon, but also the benedictions after the breaking of bread, after the blessing of the water and oil, and on catechumens, the laity, and sick persons.[28] The *Apostolic Constitutions* defines "the power of the χειροθεσία in each case" as the prayer (VII.xliv.3).[29]

The idea of blessing or benediction, especially in the sense of an efficacious sign, is the meaning which best explains all the varied occasions when the rite was employed in the ancient church. A transfer of personality or authority, creating a substitute, or other such explanations fail to cover the multiplicity of occasions where this gesture was felt appropriate. If there is any unifying conception it is in terms of a benediction. The kind of blessing would vary according to the occasion when used.

The New Testament attests the use of the act, in addition to its uses by Jesus noted above, in healings,[30] appointment to a work in the church,[31] and imparting of the Holy Spirit.[32] Since the bestowing of the Spirit is often taken as normative for the significance of the imposition of hands,[33] it is important to note that the Spirit is only one of the blessings that might be given in this way, and in the principal passage (Acts 8:15) there is also prayer, so there was no automatic transfer of the Spirit through touch.

When one moves to the post-New Testament literature, one finds the imposition of hands used on catechumens, in connection with baptism ("confirmation"), at the reconciliation of penitents and schismatics, at the eucharist, in healing, and at ordination.[34] DeBruyne classifies the occurrences of the gesture in art as follows: rites of simple benediction, healing, symbol of supernatural graces (multiplication of loaves, creation

the differentiation (65).

28. English translation by Wordsworth, *Bishop Sarapion's Prayer-Book*; and Greek text by Brightman, "The Sacramentary of Serapion of Thmuis." See now Johnson, *The Prayers of Sarapion of Thmuis*.

29. The passage is studied by Galtier, "Imposition des mains," 464–66.

30. Mark 16:18; Acts 9:12; 28:8; cf. 19:11.

31. Acts 6:6; 13:3; 1 Tim 4:14; 5:22 is possible.

32. Acts 8:17–19; 19:6; probably 2 Tim 1:6; Heb 6:2 is uncertain.

33. Behm, *Die Handauflegung im Urchristenium*, 160ff. On Acts 8 see Adler, *Taufe and Handauflegung*.

34. For references on each see Turner, "Χειροτονία, Χειροθεσία, Ἐπίθεσις Χειρῶν"; and more fully Coppens, *L'Imposition des mains*; Elderenbosch, *De Oplegging der Handen*; and Behm, *Die Handauflegung im Urchristenium*.

of man, symbol of the immortalized, etc.), rite of the Holy Spirit, and judiciary rite.[35]

The representation of a blessing or association with prayer is fairly evident in most of these instances, but some comments on certain of these occasions for imposition of hands will serve to sharpen the point. For one thing, Christian art always shows the gesture as a gentle imposition with no indication of pressure exerted (*śim* and not *samakh*). Furthermore, interpreters of the art generally emphasize the benediction idea.[36] Thus concerning the healing scenes DeBruyne concludes that the laying on of hands has the same efficacy as a simple touch or a word itself, but conveys more than they the benediction and divine condescension.[37] In the multiplication scenes "the gesture certainly has the sense of a benediction."[38] The placing of a hand on the sheep in the judgment scene of the sheep and goats reminds one that in Jesus' parable the sheep who are welcomed into the kingdom are described as 'blessed" (Matt 25:34).

At the same time, the benediction by laying on of hands is interpreted by DeBruyne as efficacious.[39] Accordingly he sees the baptismal imposition of hands as signifying the gift of the Holy Spirit.[40] Baptism is shown in early Christian art, with few exceptions, with the hand of the baptizer on the head of the baptizand. DeBruyne contends that the monuments are contrary to the thesis which considers the Spirit as the positive effect of baptism properly speaking; they do not connect the symbol of the Holy Spirit with the baptismal ablution but rather with the imposition of the hand.[41] One might very well draw the opposite conclusion. The uniting of the baptism with the imposition of the hand would seem to

35. DeBruyne, "L'imposition des mains." See also Cabrol, "Imposition des mains." There are no certain examples of ordination in early Christian art.

36. Wilpert, *Le pitture delle catacombe roman*, 110, says that the rite signifies primarily a benediction and this precedes all other significations. This view is endorsed by Cabrol, "Imposition des mains," 397.

37. DeBruyne, "L'imposition des mains," 173.

38. Ibid., 199; cf. p. 176 and *passim* in the following pages.

39. Ibid., 169, "In the imposition of hands a grace is conferred on the one on whom the hand is imposed and on no other one"; and 195, "Imposition of hands underlines especially the spiritual graces which descend on this one."

40. Wilpert, *Le pitture delle catacombs roman*, 222ff. He further says that the baptismal imposition of hands meant the communication of grace (246); cf. 230 that it signifies a special grace, a spiritual benefit on the recipient. I would not want to put it that strongly; rather it represents the petition for divine grace, which is assured by the promise of the gospel to the baptized.

41. Ibid., 246.

be against this contention. Moreover, since the dove also represents the Spirit, the presence of both in many pictures goes against his own canon that the tendency of Christian art was to simplify and not to duplicate symbolism.[42] Thus he has to import the later theological difference between baptism of water and the Spirit and post-baptismal gifts of the Spirit in confirmation to account for the two symbols of the Spirit. I find the art more straightforward. If the hand on the head has reference to the Holy Spirit, the pictures are a striking testimony to the unity of water and Spirit in Christian initiation.[43] Actually there were several moments in the baptismal ceremony when hands were laid on. The *Apostolic Tradition* specifies it in the pre-baptismal exorcism (xx.8), at the baptismal confession (xxi.12), in the actual immersing (xxi.14), and at the post-baptismal blessing (xxii.1) and anointing (xxii.2). The pre-baptismal renunciation of Satan, "when the presbyter takes hold of each one of those who are to be baptized" (xxi.9) perhaps should be added, for Tertullian says the renunciation was made "under the hand of the president."[44] It seems precarious to single out any one of these as alone depicted in the art, but since the Holy Spirit is sometimes depicted streaming from the beak of the dove upon the baptized, it seems unlikely that the post-baptismal anointing is being symbolized. The hand on the head could be understood, in an immersion, as purely functional. Better would be to see the act as both functional and a blessing.[45] In that case, the art depicts a composite scene, but it focuses on the confession (in answer to the baptismal interrogations) or perhaps the prayer at the completed immersion.[46] We are thus brought back to our earliest theological interpretation of the baptismal imposition of hands—as a benediction—by Tertullian, although in his description of

42. Ibid., 230–31. In this connection, note that Optatus finds the counterpart to the church's imposition of hands in baptism in the voice of God at Jesus' baptism—*C. Donat.* iv.7.

43. This unity is strongly argued in Lampe, *The Seal of the Spirit.*

44. *De cor.* 3. A papyrus fragment of the *Acts of Paul* (Schmidt, *Acta Pauli,* 32ff.) in the baptism of Artemilla by Paul has the sequence prayer, laying on of a hand, and going down into the water.

45. Personal communication from Professor Nikos A. Nissiotis. Cf. *Didasc.* ii.32 (Connolly, *Didascalia Apostolorum,* 93) for laying on hand in baptism equaling the blessing, "You are my son."

46. I would now more definitely connect the hand on the head in the depictions of baptism with the moment of the confession of faith; see Ferguson, *Baptism in the Early Church,* 125–26.

an invocation of the Holy Spirit he has made it an act separate from the baptism itself.[47]

The laying on of hands required of those who received schismatic baptism and then returned to the catholic church has been understood as a confirmation, completing an incomplete baptism by imparting the Spirit.[48] Many, however, would see the laying on of hands in such instances as parallel to the same rite in reconciling penitents.[49] The laying on of hands here was a sign of fellowship, an expression of favor and blessing. Prayer and the laying on of hands readmitted one to the communion of the church.[50]

As examples of the meaning of benediction attaching to the imposition of hands in the earliest non-canonical sources, we note the use of the gesture in *Ascension of Isaiah* 6.4 for Isaiah blessing the prophets. It serves as a closing benediction to a worship assembly in *Acts of John* 46: "After the discourse to the brethren, the prayer, and the eucharist, and the laying of hands upon every one of the congregation."[51] Clement of Alexandria's argument against wearing a wig makes a pertinent parallelism: "For on

47. Cyprian has followed him in *Ep.* 72.9 where we read, "The baptized obtain the Holy Spirit by our prayers and imposition of hands."

48. Such is the standpoint of the pseudo-Cyprian, *De rebaptismate*. Macdonald, "Imposition of Hands in the Letters of Innocent I," 49ff., argues that Innocent understood the laying of hands on heretics as a confirmation, but the passages seem susceptible of another interpretation, especially since *Ep.* 24 (*PL* 20:549–51) speaks of receiving converted Arian laity "under the symbol of penance."

49. References for the penitential imposition of hands are collected in Coppens, *L'imposition des mains*, chap. 5; see 389–90 for the judgment that the imposition of hands on returning heretics was for penance and not confirmation. So also Watkins, *A History of Penance*, 1:492. This was clearly Stephen's view, as cited by Cyprian, *Ep.* 73.1, "It is the tradition that hands are laid on them in penance."

50. Cyprian reflects a regular three-stage cycle leading to the reconciliation of penitents: acts of repentance, confession before the church, and restoration to communion by the laying on of the bishop's hands—*Epp.* 9; 10; 29. The *Didasc*, 10 (Connolly, *Didascalia Apostolorum*, 104) makes the parallel with baptism. "And afterwards, as each one of them repents and shows the fruits of repentance, receive him to prayer after the manner of a heathen. And as thou baptizest a heathen and then receivest him, so also lay hand upon this man, whilst all pray for him, and then bring him in and let him communicate with the Church. For the imposition of hand shall be to him in the place of baptism: for whether by the imposition of hand, or by baptism, they receive the communication of the Holy Spirit." Galtier, "Imposition des mains," 1398, sees the penitential imposition of hands as giving the Holy Spirit, but this interpretation seems to be a product of the rebaptism controversy in the third century.

51. Cf. Pseudo-Clement, *Hom.* xvi.21, where Peter "laid his hands on them and prayed" in dismissal.

whom does the presbyter lay his hand? Whom does he bless?"[52] The laying on of hands in blessing contexts appears in *Acts of Thomas* 10; 29; 49; 53; and 67.

This variety of occasions is, at least in part, the reason why prayer was always associated with the act. The prayer spelled out the kind of blessing intended. The laying on of hands was really an accompaniment to prayer. It was a sign of favor, a personalized marking out of the individual as the object of the benediction requested from God. The specific blessing might be health, the Holy Spirit, the forgiveness and fellowship of the church, God's favor in general, or an office in the church.

When theologians came to reflect on the theological meaning of ordination, they put the emphasis on the prayer and interpreted the rite in terms of a benediction. This may be seen already in Hippolytus' comments on the role of presbyters in ordaining other presbyters. Their imposition of hands is interpreted as a benediction, or an act of "sealing" what the bishop did. Their laying on of hands is described as "touching" in the Latin version.[53] Origen, *Hom. in Num.* 22.4,[54] at the beginning is evidence of prayer as the constitutive part of ordination. It is in fourth-century authors mainly where theological reflections on the meaning of ordination are found.

Gregory of Nyssa goes the farthest of any writer before Augustine in attributing to ordination the power to effect a sacramental change in a person, but he attributes this change to the benediction. He puts the change accomplished by ordination in the same category with that made in the elements used for baptism and the eucharist.

> Although before the benediction [εὐλογία] they are of little value, after the sanctification bestowed by the Spirit each has its several operation. The same power of the word also makes the priest venerable, honorable, and separated from the common mass by the benediction bestowed on him. While yesterday he was one of the mass, one of the people, he is suddenly rendered a guide, a president, a teacher of righteousness, an instructor in mysteries. And he does these things without being at all changed

52. *Paed.* iii.xi; cf. *Strom.* III.i.2.

53. *Apos. Trad.* viii.1 and ix.8; Barlêa, *Die Weihe*, 216–17, whose overall scheme I find unacceptable, yet makes the pertinent remark that the presbyters' laying on of hands was more than a cooption or confirmation of the election but served to seal the solidarity of the college of presbyters.

54. I study the passage in Ferguson, "Origen and the Election of Bishops," chap. 11 above.

in body or in form; but while continuing to be in all appearance the man he was before, by some unseen power and grace the unseen soul is transformed for the better.[55]

Jerome offered a definition of χειροτονία that ascribes a subordinate place to the laying on of hands (its necessity is wholly practical) and assigns the constitutive role to the prayer: "χειροτονία—that is, the ordination of the clergy which is accomplished not only at the verbal prayer but at the imposition of the hand (lest indeed in mockery someone be ordained ignorantly to the clergy by a secret prayer)."[56]

John Chrysostom's definition is similar. He gave central importance to the imposition of hands in ordination, but he understood this in relation to the prayer. Commenting on Acts 6:6 he says: "For Luke says not how, but simply that they were ordained by prayer: for this is the ordination. The hand of man is laid on, but God performs everything, and it is His hand which touches the head of the one being ordained, if he is truly ordained."[57]

Theodoret relates how the monk Moses was brought to Alexandria to receive episcopal consecration and there discovered that it was an Arian who was to perform the ceremony:

> When he arrived and saw Lucius attempting to lay the hand on him, he said. "God forbid that I should be ordained by your hand, for the grace of the Spirit answers not your calling."[58]

Finally note the *Vita Polyc.* xi, "to cover such a head with his hand and to bless so noble a soul with his voice."[59]

Because of the association of the hands with the prayer and the New Testament texts which connect the Holy Spirit with the imposition of hands, some fourth-century sources connect the imparting of the Holy Spirit at ordination with the imposition of hands. Gregory of Nazianzen speaks of the dying Basil "ordaining the most excellent of his attendants" and bestowing "upon them both his hand and the Spirit."[60] Lucifer of Cagliari declares as follows: "For no one can be filled with the power of the Holy Spirit to govern the people of God except the one whom God has

---

55. Gregory Nazianzen, *De bapt. Christi* (*P.G.* 46.581 D).

56. *In Isa.* xvi.58 (*P.L.* 24. 591).

57. *Hom.* xiv, *in Acts* (*P.G.* 60.116).

58. *H.E.* iv.xxiii.

59. Later references include Leo, *Ep.* ix.i and *Stat. Eccl. Ant.* 90–92.

60. *Or.* 43. 78 (*PG* 36:600).

chosen and on whom a hand has been placed by Catholic bishops." (And there follows a quotation of Deut 34:9.)[61]

Such appeals to Old Testament appointments by the laying on of hands are rare in early Christian texts and are absent from the ordination prayers of bishops. The Old Testament precedent cited for the ordination of presbyters is the elders appointed by Moses, who received the Spirit without an imposition of hands (Num 11:16ff.).[62] The bestowal of the Spirit was more commonly connected with the divine invocation, hence the importance of prayer.[63]

The Old Testament background (as indicated by Syriac terminology), Jesus' usage, the association with prayer, early Christian art, the variety of occasions when it was used, and the theological interpretation of fourth-century authors all converge in support of the contention that the laying on of hands in ordination signified a divine blessing.

The interpretation of the laying on of hands in ordination advanced here may justly claim to have been set forth by Luke in Acts 14:26, where he gives his own interpretation of the ceremony of prayer and the laying on of hands by which Paul and Barnabas had been sent forth on their mission to the Gentiles as recorded in Acts 13:1–3. "From there they sailed to Antioch, where they had been *commended to the grace of God* for the work which they had fulfilled."

61. *De S. Athan.* i. 9.

62. *Apos. Trad.* viii.3; *Apos. Const.* VIII.xvi; Serapion's *Prayerbook* (Brightman, "The Sacramentary of Serapion of Thmuis," 266–67).

63. See the petition for the Spirit in the ordination prayers—*Apos. Trad.* iii.3; *Apos. Const.* VIII.vi; Serapion's *Prayerhook* (Brightman, "The Sacramentary of Serapion of Thmuis," 267).

14

The Covenant Idea
in the Second Century

DELBERT HILLERS CONCLUDES HIS survey on *Covenant: The History of a Biblical Idea* with these words:

> The Essenes had a covenant, but it was not new; the Christians had something new but it was not a covenant. That is to say, to call what Jesus brought a covenant is like calling conversion circumcision, or like saying that one keeps the Passover with the unleavened bread of sincerity and truth. For Christians the coming of the substance made shadows out of a rich array of OT events, persons, and ideas, among them covenant . . . The reality brings the image to an end.[1]

The covenant was a central category in Israel's faith. There have been a number of important studies of the covenant idea in the Bible,[2] and there have been studies of the covenant as articulated in the Middle Ages and Reformation.[3] Thus far, however, I have found no monograph on this

---

1. Hillers, *Covenant*, 188.

2. Mendenhall, "Covenant"; McCarthy, *Treaty and Covenant*; McCarthy, *Old Testament Covenant*; Buchanan, *The Consequences of the Covenant*; Pohlmann, "Diatheke," includes *Barnabas*; Baltzer, *Das Bundesformular*, includes the Apostolic Fathers but does not deal with the question of this essay; Behm, *Der Begriff Diathēkē im Neuen Testament*, includes an appendix on Justin, 102–6; and relevant articles in *TDNT* and *TDOT*. Thompson, "The Covenant Concept in Judaism and Christianity."

3. E.g., Preus, *From Shadow to Promise*; Hagen, *A Theology of Testament in the*

important theological idea dealing with patristic literature.[4] Stuart Currie, demonstrating his mastery of second-century Christian literature, explored the use and significance of *koinōnia* in the early church and pointed out the close association of this term with the concept of covenant in Paul's writings and elsewhere.[5] Thus, it seems fitting in a volume dedicated to Stuart Currie to undertake a consideration of the way the concept of covenant functioned in the writings of second and early third-century authors.

My intention is to present as complete a set of texts bearing on this subject as possible and then draw some conclusions. The study is ordered by three developments related to the discussion of "covenant" in the early church. First, "covenant" was an important topic in the dialogue and debate between Christians and Jews. Second, questions concerning "covenant" were also kept alive in the controversies of the "orthodox" with "heretics" who rejected or disparaged the Jewish heritage of the church. Third, the establishment of a two-part Canon in the church extended theological reflection on the function of the "old covenant." As Hans von Campenhausen discussed the "pre-history of the New Testament canon,"[6] much of this material may be considered a pre-history of "Old and New Testaments" as a title of the Christian scriptures.

As preparation for this study, however, brief note must be taken of the biblical (particularly the New Testament) use of the term "covenant" as the background out of which the developments of the second and third centuries emerged.

The Hebrew word translated "covenant," *berith*, referred to a mutual relationship. It was used in a wide variety of human contracts and agreements and was chosen to describe the gracious relationships which God established with chosen individuals and the nation of Israel. The Greek translation of the Old Testament might have been expected to render *berith* by *synthēkē* ("treaty" or "compact"). The translators, however, presumably thought *synthēkē* implied too much of mutual agreement and thus chose instead *diathēkē* ("disposition" and "testament") in order to emphasize, it seems, God's initiative and superiority.

Young Luther; Emerson, "Calvin and Covenant Theology"; Trinterud, "The Origins of Puritanism."

4. There is now Gräbe, *Der Neue Bund in der frühchristlichen Literatur*, which includes the second-century fathers and the Syriac tradition.

5. Currie, *Koinonia in Christian Literature to 200 A.D.*

6. Von Campenhausen, *The Formation of the Christian Bible*, ch. 4; cf. 262–68, where the terminology of "old and new covenant" as a title for the two parts of the Christian Bible is discussed. See now Kinzig, "*Kainē diathēkē*."

The New Testament clearly used *diathēkē* in the Hellenistic sense of "last will" in Gal 3:15 and Heb 9:16. A larger number of the occurrences of the term are in quotations from or references to the covenants of the Old Testament (Luke 1:72; Acts 3:25; 7:8; Rom 9:4; Eph 2:12; Heb 9:4, 18–20; Rev 11:19). Otherwise the word *diathēkē* appears in three contexts.[7] (1) It occurs in the accounts of the Lord's supper (Matt 26:28; Mark 14:24; Luke 22:20; 1 Cor 11:25) in order to explain the significance of Jesus' death, viz., his blood sealing a new covenant (with allusion to Exod 24:5ff. and Jer 31:31ff.). (2) It was used by Paul in explaining the relationship between the Mosaic and Christian dispensations (2 Cor 3:6, 14) and between the fleshly and spiritual Israel as recipients of the promises to Abraham (Gal 3:17; 4:24). (3) It is especially frequent in the Epistle to the Hebrews which combines the themes of covenant blood and a new covenant people in order to demonstrate the superiority of the Christian dispensation over the Jewish because Jesus is the mediator of a better covenant offering better promises (Heb 7:22; 8:6; 9:15; 10:29; 12:24; 13:20) in fulfillment of Jer 31:31–34 (Heb 8:8–10; 10:16).

The earliest use of *diathēkē* in Christian literature outside the New Testament is in *1 Clement* when Clement used the word in two quotations from the Septuagint.[8] It is characteristic of Clement that in both passages the Old Testament was used for moral exhortation. Perhaps significantly both passages are about unfaithfulness to the covenant. While Clement used the texts as warnings to Christians, the texts could just as well be turned against Jews.[9]

The first extra-canonical Christian author for whom the covenant was an important category was Barnabas.[10] In chapter 4 Barnabas punctuated his eschatological message with this anti-Jewish polemic:

> Be not like some, heaping up your sins, by saying that the covenant is theirs and ours. It is ours. They lost it forever when

7. Colin Brown, ed., *NIDNT*, 365–76.

8. *1 Clem.* 15:4, citing Ps 77 [78]:36–37; and 35:7 citing Ps 49 [50]:16.

9. As was Psalm 49, quoted in its entirety by Justin, *Dial.* 22. Psalm 49 became a part of the anti-sacrificial polemic; Prigent and Kraft, *Epître de Barnabé*, 82–83. Psalm 77:36–37 is followed by the declaration of forgiveness and so was not so suitable for the anti-Judaic argument.

10. Giversen, "The Covenant—Theirs or Ours?," took *Barnabas* as the theme for introducing the conference from which came the papers of the book this essay originally appeared in. For *Barnabas* in general, see Hvalvik, *The Struggle for Scripture and Covenant*, 156–66, on covenant. Horbury, "Jewish-Christian Relations in Barnabas and Justin Martyr."

> Moses had barely received it. For Scripture says: "Moses was
> on the mountain fasting forty days and forty nights, and he re-
> ceived the covenant from the Lord, stone tablets written by the
> finger of the hand of the Lord." But they turned to idols and lost
> it. For the Lord says, "Moses, Moses, Go down quickly, because
> your people whom you brought out of Egypt broke the law." And
> Moses understood and threw the two tablets from his hands.
> And their covenant was broken in order that the covenant of
> Jesus the Beloved might be sealed in our heart by the hope of his
> faith. (*Barn.* 4:6–8; trans. mine)

This passage reflects the language of an actual intramural discussion among Christians (Jewish Christians?) about their heritage. The passage, based on Deut 9:12–17 (cf. Exod 24:18; 31:18; 34:28; and 32:7, 9),[11] about Moses breaking the tablets containing the ten commandments was important to Barnabas, for he returned to it in his major discussion of the covenant in chapter 14. In the latter passage he included, apparently as if part of the biblical text, the statement, "And the tablets of the covenant of the Lord were broken" (14:3). Since the breaking of the stone tablets symbolized for Barnabas the breaking of the covenant, the text provided scriptural proof that the Jews had lost their right to the covenant from the beginning.

While discussing things characteristic of Judaism—after sacrifices, circumcision, food laws, washings, and before the sabbath and the temple—Barnabas raised the question of the covenant in 13:1: "Let us see if this people [i.e., Christians] or the first people receive the inheritance, and if the covenant is ours or theirs." Barnabas then introduced two narratives from the Old Testament where a younger son was favored over an older: Jacob over Esau (Gen 25:21–23) and Ephraim over Manasseh (Gen 48:9–19). Concerning the latter, he concluded, "You see whom he has appointed [the younger son] to be the first [people] and the heir of the covenant" (13:6). Not only did Isaac and Jacob (who bestowed the blessings) have knowledge (*gnōsis*) of who would be God's people, but so also did Abraham, to whom God promised that he would be the father of the nations [Gentiles] who believed in God (14:7). That made all three patriarchs witnesses to the claim that a later people (Gentile Christians) would have the favor of God.

---

11. The author of *1 Clem.* 53 also quoted from this episode but for an entirely different purpose. He included the sequel where Moses prayed for the forgiveness of the people and commended the willingness to be blotted out for the sake of the people.

Barnabas then considered in chapter 14 whether the covenant which God swore to the fathers ever was given to the older [first] people.[12] It was given, Barnabas admitted, but they were not worthy to receive it (14:1). In this context came the proof from Moses referred to above (14:1–3) followed by the important corollary:

> Moses received it, but they were not worthy. How do we receive it? Learn. Moses as a servant received it, but the Lord himself has given it to us to be the people of the inheritance, because he suffered on our behalf . . . We receive it through the one who inherits the covenant, the Lord Jesus. He was prepared for this very purpose in order that when he appeared and ransomed us out of darkness . . . he might establish in us a covenant by his word. (14:4–5; trans. mine)

That Christ should ransom and prepare a holy people for himself was a matter of prophecy. Isaiah 42:6–7 was quoted as if addressed to Christ: "I gave you for a covenant of the people, for a light of the nations" (14:7). Barnabas' other quotations (Isa 49:6–7; 61:1–2) share the universalism of salvation found in 42:6–7 and are so used by later Christian authors.

The concern with the identity of the people of the covenant was shown also in Barnabas' conclusion to the discussion of the eschatological promises: "If then this does not happen at present, he has told us the time when it will: when we ourselves are perfected to be the heirs of the covenant of the Lord" (6:19). The sign of the Jewish covenant, circumcision, prompted Barnabas to recall other peoples who were circumcised—Syrians, Arabs, and Egyptians—and to comment sarcastically, "They therefore are of their covenant" (9:6).

To summarize, for Barnabas Jesus was both the giver of the covenant and the covenant itself. The covenant of Jesus and the covenant of Moses are essentially identical in their meaning. Barnabas did not speak of a new covenant, but of a new people (5:7). The covenant had not changed, but the recipients were different.[13] "Whose is the covenant?" was another way of asking "Who are God's people?"[14] *Diathēkē*, therefore, carried the Old Testament meaning of a relationship. This understanding of covenant

12. Studied by Prigent, *L'epître de Barnabé I–XVI et ses sources*, 60–65.

13. Pohlmann, "Diatheke," 987–90.

14. See Simon, *Verus Israel*, 102–5, for the relation of the new people to the new covenant. Barnabas would indicate that the question of people was prior. He gave one answer—different people but the same covenant—but later thinkers decided that a new people required a new covenant. Cf. Simon, ibid., 203–8, on the rejection of Israel in Christian authors.

accounts for the full appropriation of the Jewish scriptural heritage by Barnabas, yet at the same time his full rejection of Jewish religious practices and institutions. This Old Testament understanding of relationship with a people was not lost in the second century but it was altered subtly by the Hellenistic idea of "testament" as may be seen in the repeated association of "inheritance" with "covenant."

One further topic deserves comment: the prevailing scholarly view that Barnabas viewed the covenant as timeless. For example, "*Diathēkē* is for Barnabas simply the expression of the same divine saving will from the beginning and for all time."[15] Without entering into a serious debate with such a statement,[16] I consider it important to point out some signs of historical consciousness in Barnabas. For instance, he did not deny that the Jewish ritual was actually in operation for a long time. He also recognized the historical fact of Moses but contrasted the servant Moses' giving the covenant with the Lord Jesus' giving the covenant. Finally, Barnabas clearly had an eschatological frame of reference, hardly a "timeless" notion. Nevertheless, Barnabas' approach left too many unresolved questions for him to be copied exactly by later thinkers.

With Justin Martyr, Barnabas' intramural contest was moved into the arena of the church's actual combat with Judaism.[17] The understanding of the covenant was crucial in this competition. Justin's view of salvation-history was in the tradition of Paul and Luke, although without explicit use of their writing.[18] For Justin the covenant was an important category for interpreting God's saving plan as it related to Jews and Christians.

The importance of covenant for Justin is seen in his discussion of circumcision. Justin's Jewish opponent, Trypho, identified the covenant

---

15. Pohlmann, "Diatheke," 989; cf. Wengst, *Tradition und Theologie des Barnabas Briefes*, 75ff.

16. In relation to the later Alexandrian reading of the Old Testament one might liken Barnabas to an advance scout who goes well beyond the ground occupied by the main party.

17. Simon, *Verus Israel*, 166ff., opposed Harnack's view that the *Dialogue with Trypho* was a literary exercise, and without going to the extreme of Williams, *Adversus Judaeos*, saw a real contact between Jews and Christians. He pointed out that even when used for other purposes the arguments arose initially in an anti-Jewish context. He added that in general the writings "Against the Jews" are by themselves insufficient to determine whether real Jewish-Christian relations were being addressed, for certain themes and methods of argument remained constant.

18. Luneau, *L'Histoire de salut chez les Pères de l'Église*, 89–92; von Campenhausen, *The Formation of the Christian Bible*, 169 and 178; Stylianopoulos, *Justin Martyr and the Mosaic Law*, 104ff. and 116ff.

with circumcision, its seal (Gen 17:7, 13). Trypho reproached Christians for not observing various Jewish practices. Concerning circumcision he said, "But you, rashly despising this covenant, do not care for the consequent duties" (*Dialogue with Trypho* 10:4). Justin's reply begins in chapter 11, which introduces the doctrinal debate proper, thus showing the importance of the covenant concept. Justin employed several arguments based on the Old Testament itself for the invalidity of the Mosaic law: the prophecies of a new covenant point to the cessation of the law through the coming of Christ; the prophets declared that God did not really desire observance of the ritual law but a spiritual obedience; worthies such as Noah, Job, Abraham and other patriarchs were justified without keeping the law. Justin affirmed in *Dialogue* 11 that Christians trusted in "no other God" than the one "who led your fathers out of Egypt," perhaps with his eye on the Gnostics and Marcion.[19] But Christians did not trust "through Moses or through the law." "I have read," Justin wrote, "that there shall be a final law, and a covenant, the best of all." He continued,

> For the law given on Horeb is already old and is yours alone; but this one is for all universally. Now, law placed against law has put an end to that which is before it, and a covenant which comes after in like manner has annulled the previous one; and an eternal and final law—namely, Christ—has been given to us, and the covenant is trustworthy. [trans. mine]

This new covenant was a matter of prophecy; Justin cited Isa 51:4–5 and Jer 31:31—32:17a. God had "proclaimed a new covenant" and "this for a light to the nations" (cf. Isa 42:6; 49:6).[20] Jesus Christ "is the new law and the new covenant," and the "true spiritual Israel . . . are we who have been led to God through this crucified Christ." In chapter 12 Justin continued by quoting Isa 55:3ff. about "an eternal covenant" and charging, "This same law you have despised, and his holy covenant you have slighted."

In Justin, unlike Barnabas, was used the explicit language of an old and new covenant.[21] This, moreover, was discussed in terms of the law embodying the covenant, so that the content of the covenant (again unlike

---

19. Von Campenhausen, *The Formation of the Christian Bible*, 94–95, sees *Dial.* 10–29 originally as a self-contained treatise directed against Gnostics and Marcion. In this view he follows Prigent, *Justin et l'ancien testament*, 235–85 which studies *Dial.* 10–29 in relation to primitive Christian testimonia. Stylianopoulos, *Justin Martyr and the Mosaic Law*, 31, 75, 157ff., sees Justin's historical periodization as first arrived at in opposition to Marcion and Gnostics and then applied to the anti-Judaic polemic.

20. Skarsaune, *The Proof from Prophecy.*

21. Cf. Mark 14:24; 1 Cor 11:25; 2 Cor 3:6, 14; Heb 8:6–10; 9:15; cf. Gal 4:24.

Barnabas) comes to the fore. The combination of "law" and "covenant" was frequent in the *Dialogue*. Christ established "a new law and a new covenant" (34:1).[22] "There is now another covenant and another law has gone forth from Zion" (24:1—see excursus at the end on Isa 2:1–4). After his initial consideration of the proper understanding of the covenant, Justin discussed (with numerous digressions) washings, fasting, circumcision, food laws, sabbath, and sacrifice. The Christian had no need of these things, for their spiritual counterparts have been established (here we are in the perspective of Barnabas except that Justin did not reject the literal meaning as historically valid for a time): circumcision of heart, "perpetual sabbath," "sacrifices of praise and thanksgiving," baptism accompanied with "the Holy Spirit," etc. These spiritual interpretations were found by Justin in the Old Testament scriptures themselves. Although the old covenant was rejected, the scriptures were not. These words "are contained in your scriptures, or rather not yours but ours" (29:2).[23] Since he held that God gave something which was temporary, Justin was obligated to give a reason for these abrogated rituals. His explanation was that they were imposed because of the transgressions and hardness of heart of the Jews (18:2; cf. 27:2). The laws were to keep them from idolatry (67:8) and by their very number to keep God ever before them (46:5).[24] A somewhat more positive statement of purpose is found in 44:2:

> Some commandments were laid down in reference to the worship of God and practice of righteousness; but some commandments and actions were likewise mentioned either in reference to the mystery of Christ, or on account of the hardness of your people's heart. (trans. mine)

This statement approximates the threefold classification of law as moral, ceremonial, and judicial.[25]

The old covenant, therefore, was limited to the Jews and temporary:

22. Cf. "new law of our Lord Jesus Christ," *Barn.* 2; "we have a law," Athenagoras, *Plea* 32. The new covenant as a new law finds full expression in Tertullian. On the idea see Simon, *Verus Israel*, 100–105.

23. Origen acknowledged that the scriptures were common to Jews and Christians (*C. Cels.* II.lviii) but claimed that Christians understood them better (II.lxxvi).

24. The purpose of particular regulations are given in different places: circumcision (16:2), food laws (20:1); sacrifices (22:11); sabbath (21:1).

25. Stylianopoulos, *Justin Martyr and the Mosaic Law*, 51–68 described Justin's classification as ethics, prophecy, and historical dispensation.

> As, then, circumcision began from Abraham, and the sabbath and sacrifices and offerings and feasts from Moses, and it has been proved that they were enjoined on account of the hardness of your people's heart, so it was necessary in accordance with the Father's will that they should cease in . . . Christ the Son of God, who was proclaimed to all the world as about to come as the eternal law and the new covenant. (43:1)

Justin sketched a fourfold periodization: before the law, under the law, under Christ, and eschatological glory at Christ's second coming.[26] The covenant (as Barnabas too had said) and the new law was Christ. "The new covenant which God formerly announced was then present, Christ himself" (51:3).[27] Therefore, this covenant was considered eternal (final) and universal. "God promised that there would be another covenant, not like that commandment and without fear, trembling, and lightnings . . . and showing that God knows the command and work that is eternal and suited to every race" (67:10; trans. mine).

"Through the wonderful foreknowledge of God . . . that we might be found more understanding and God-fearing than you through the calling of the new and eternal covenant, that is of Christ" (118:3). The prophecies about a "covenant . . . and light to the nations" (Isa 42:6) referred not to proselytes but to Christ and all those enlightened by him (122:3). "What is the inheritance of Christ? Is it not the Gentiles? What is the covenant of God? Is it not Christ?" (122:6). And he is not to be limited to one race:

> If the law were able to enlighten the nations and those who possess it, what need is there of a new covenant? But since God announced beforehand that he would send a new covenant and an eternal law and commandment, we will not understand this of the old law and its proselytes but of Christ and his proselytes, namely us Gentiles whom he has enlightened. (122:5; trans. mine)

These passages show that "people" and "relationships" were still important aspects of the covenant for Justin despite his frequent identification of covenant with law. The covenant which was Christ was for the "true spiritual Israel" (11:5). This association of covenant with Christ also implied the continued association of covenant with God's promises.

---

26. Luneau, *L'Histoire de salut chez les Pères de l'Église*, 34, 45ff., 95ff.; cf. von Campenhausen, *The Formation of the Christian Bible*, 97.

27. For Jesus as himself the covenant, cf. Daniélou, *The Theology of Jewish Christianity*, 163–66.

When the surviving literature of the Gnostics and the Jewish Christian groups is examined, it appears that the covenant was not a significant category for them. In the Gnostic *Gospel of Truth* Jesus was presented as the revealer of "the living Book of the Living" (the *Gospel of Truth* itself? a metaphor for salvation?) and that Book compared to a testament before and after being opened. Then the author wrote, "This is why Jesus appeared: he opened that Book. He was nailed to a tree, he fastened the testamentary disposition from the Father to the Cross. O such magnanimity!" (19:35—20:28).[28] The language was influenced by Col 2 14, but instead of nailing to the cross what was "against us" Jesus nailed a testament that was for believers and so validated the wonderful gift of life.

Without using the word "covenant," Ptolemy, the Valentinian, in his *Letter to Flora*, did a piece of source criticism on the Pentateuch. A part, he concluded, came from God, a part from Moses, and a part from the elders. That part which came from God himself was further subdivided into three parts: the pure law of God, free from evil (the decalogue), which Christ came to perfect and fulfill; laws concerning retribution for wrongdoing (an eye for an eye), which Christ took away completely; and the "typical" ceremonies (sacrifice, circumcision, sabbath, fasting, etc.) which the Savior transformed from physical into spiritual realities. The God who gave the law was the Creator. Ptolemy offered this view as a middle ground between the view that the law came from the Perfect Father (which he thought impossible) and the view that it was given by the devil (perhaps held by later Marcionites and a view which Ptolemy considered not "just" to hold).[29] Ptolemy gave a theoretical basis for what the church did in practice, but this did not make it any more acceptable (in fact less so). His separation of the Creator God from the Father of the Savior ruined anything he had to say in the eyes of the orthodox.

The orthodox Christian position, as the orthodox Jewish position, maintained against the Gnostics the unity and wholeness of scripture. Gnostics, however, were not the only ones to make a theoretical as well as a practical distinction in the contents of the old law. Certain Jewish Christians did the same. In this way it was possible to maintain a loyalty to the Mosaic covenant and yet treat its documents in their existing form as less

28. Grobel, *The Gospel of Truth*, 58–67.

29. Epiphanius, *Adv. haer.* XXXIII.3–7 in Grant, *Second-century Christianity*, 30–37 (2nd ed., 63–68).

than sacrosanct. The Ebionites formulated a theory of "false pericopes" introduced into the scriptures.[30]

> For the scriptures have had joined to them many falsehoods against God on this account. The prophet Moses having by the order of God delivered the law, with the explanations, to certain chosen men, some seventy in number, in order that they also might instruct such of the people as chose, after a little the written law had added to it certain falsehoods contrary to the law of God . . . (Pseudo-Clement, *Hom*. II.xxxviii)[31]

> If, therefore, some of the scriptures are true and some false, with good reason our Master said, "Be good money-changers," inasmuch as in the scriptures there are some true sayings and some spurious. (II.li; this was not a doctrine to be proclaimed in public lest it perplex the unlearned multitude. Cf. II.xxxix)

The false sayings could be identified, according to the Ebionites, by those passages which had an inferior view of God or attributed sins to the Old Testament fathers. One feature of the law in particular that was rejected by the Ebionites was the entire sacrificial cultus (*Hom*. III.xlv; *Recogn*. I.xxxvi–xxxix). Moses and Christ really taught the same doctrine: "For, there being one teaching by both, God accepts him who has believed either of these. But believing a teacher is for the sake of doing the things spoken by God" (*Hom*. VIII.vi).

> Neither, therefore, are the Hebrews condemned on account of their ignorance of Jesus . . . if doing the things commanded by Moses, they do not hate him whom they do not know. Neither are those from among the Gentiles condemned, who know not Moses . . . provided that these also, doing the things spoken by Jesus, do not hate him whom they do not know. (*Hom*. VIII.vii)

There seems to be a view of a covenant for the Jew through Moses and a covenant for the Gentiles through Jesus, parallel but essentially the same in content. Although the word covenant was not used, the idea is another variation on the covenant theme.

A radical distinction within the contents of the Old Testament, but without assigning any of it to a source other than God, could also be made

---

30. Schoeps, *Theologie and Geschichte des Judenchristentums*, 147ff.

31. Trans. from the Pseudo-Clementines in Smith, ed. and trans., *Ante-Nicene Fathers*, 8:236; cf. *Hom*. XVIII.xix–xx on the "false pericopes" as in scripture to test us.

within orthodox circles. The third-century Syriac *Didascalia* warned constantly about the dangers of the Deuterosis (the second legislation):[32]

> For the first Law is that which the Lord God spoke before the people had made the calf and served idols, which consists of the Ten Words and the Judgements. But after they had served idols [the golden calf episode], he justly laid upon them the bonds, as they were worthy. But do not thou therefore lay them upon thee; for our Saviour came for no other cause but to fulfill the Law, and to set us loose from the bonds of the Second Legislation.[33]

There is an extended discussion of this concern in chapter XXVI. "The Law therefore is indissoluble; the Second Legislation is temporary, and is dissoluble."[34] Among those things abolished were the distinctions of meats, sacrifices, circumcisions, washings. These were a burden imposed because of idolatry and making the calf. "[Christ] came, that he might affirm the Law and abolish the Second Legislation."[35] Although the sabbath was included in the Ten Words, the *Didascalia* treated it as part of the Second Legislation superseded by the Lord's day.[36] So, such efforts at making distinctions within the Old Testament were troubled by a lack of consistency.

A different approach to the problems posed by Gnostic and Jewish Christianity that did not accept the premises of either was needed. The anti-Gnostic fathers achieved this. Where the sense of proximity or alienation with reference to the Old Testament was strongest, covenant was not an important word. Covenant became important when Christians wanted to maintain both a significant continuity and a significant discontinuity.

Against the attacks of Marcion and the Gnostics,[37] the only hope of salvaging the old Bible was to acknowledge different eras.[38] The covenant scheme of the interpretation of holy history became the foundation of Irenaeus'

32. Simon, *Verus Israel*, 111–18.

33. *Didasc.* II (Connolly, *Didascalia Apostolorum*, 14).

34. Connolly, ibid., 218.

35. Ibid., 224.

36. Ibid., 236–38.

37. See Ptolemy's criticism discussed above and compare Irenaeus' description of Marcion as "the only one who has dared openly to mutilate the scriptures" (*Adv. haer.* I.xxvii.2).

38. Von Campenhausen, *The Formation of the Christian Bible*, 166.

theological method. He employed it not in anti-Jewish polemic but in anti-Gnostic polemic. He used the covenant not to explain why Christians did not keep the law but to affirm that the law was from the same God as the gospel. God gave the law as a stage in his preparation and education for Christ. According to Justin, Christianity replaced, not just fulfilled, Judaism; the law disappeared as darkness before light. According to Irenaeus, the law retired as a pedagogue was effaced before the teacher.[39]

The letter of introduction from Irenaeus' home church of Lyons described him as "zealous for the covenant of Christ" (Eusebius, *H.E.* V.iv.2). Irenaeus was a "covenant" theologian.[40] He held the divine dispensations together in continuity because they came from "one and the same God."

Irenaeus made an understanding of the covenants part of the foundation scheme of the faith which learned teachers imparted: "they reveal why several covenants came to mankind and teach what is the character of each of the covenants" (*Against Heresies* 1.x.3).[41] He himself laid out "four general covenants given to mankind" (III.xi.8). Unfortunately the old Latin version and the later Greek texts of Irenaeus differ as to what these covenants were. According to the Greek: "One was from the flood of Noah with the rainbow; the second was from Abraham with the sign of circumcision; the third was the giving of the law by Moses; the fourth was the covenant of the Gospel through our Lord Jesus Christ" [trans. mine].

According to the Latin, "One was before the flood, under Adam; the second, then, after the flood, under Noah; the third, the law, under Moses; and the fourth, then, that which renews man and sums up all things in itself by means of the Gospel" (trans. mine).

The Greek has in its favor that the Bible uses the word covenant in connection with the four named (see below from Irenaeus's *Proof of the Apostolic Preaching*). The Latin translates *diathēkē* by *testamentum*, the usual translation in the western languages, a fact which has given a legal and formal cast to the understanding of the covenant. Such an understanding does not seem appropriate to Irenaeus, who rather maintained the interpretation of the covenant found in Justin.

---

39. See Luneau, *L'Histoire de salut chez les Pères de l'Église*, 90.

40. Lawson, *The Biblical Theology of St. Irenaeus*, 235–38, treats the relation of Old and New Testaments but not particularly of the covenants as such. Benoit, *Saint Irénée*, 74–102 more adequately looks at Irenaeus' relation to the Old Testament but without reference to the covenant idea.

41. I employ the numbering in Massuet (and the Sources chrétiennes edition) followed in the Ante-Nicene Fathers.

More commonly Irenaeus wrote of two covenants, for that of Moses and that of Christ were the major concern for his polemical situation. Interpreting Matt 13:52, Irenaeus gave to the two covenants the designations law and gospel, so familiar to us: "Now those things new and old which are brought forth from his treasure certainly mean two covenants. The old would be that previous giving of the law; and the new points out that manner of life according to the gospel" [(IV.ix.1); trans. mine].

Irenaeus then cited Old Testament passages about a new song and a new covenant and New Testament passages about the greatness of Christ and his legislation. He continued: "For the new covenant has been known and preached by the prophets . . . that men by believing in Christ might always make progress and grow to the attainment of salvation through the covenants. For there is one salvation and one God" (IV.ix.3; trans. mine).

This passage summarizes some of the characteristic emphases of Irenaeus: two successive covenants, one for Jews and the other for all; the old law replaced by the gospel of liberty; the different covenants suited to the stage of human development contributing to human maturity; the whole sequence, as the prophecies demonstrated, presided over by one God.

That there would be two covenants, Irenaeus held, was foreshadowed in Abraham. He was the forerunner of Christian faith, having received justification before circumcision by means of a faith which sprang up once more among humankind through the coming of the Lord. "Circumcision and the law of works obtained during the intermediate time." Of this too Abraham was the source, for he received the covenant of circumcision (IV. xxv.1).

The contrast which Irenaeus saw between the old and the new was that between bondage (law) and liberty (gospel), based perhaps on Gal 4:21ff. "The new covenant of liberty" was a favorite description—III.xii.14; IV.xxxiii.14; IV.xxxiv.3; IV.xvi.5—contrasting with "laws of bondage." The gospel was not just a new law for Irenaeus but a new spiritual relation of humanity to God.[42] The old covenant was superseded. In one passage Irenaeus wrote that the law ended with John the Baptist, for Jerusalem had an end of legislation when the new covenant was manifested (IV.iv.2). In the *Proof of the Apostolic Preaching*, Irenaeus made more of the termination of the old covenant, treating the history of salvation and referring to the covenants with Noah (ch. 22), Abraham (ch. 24), David (ch. 64), and Jeremiah's prophecy of a new covenant (ch. 90). "These promises were to be inherited by the calling from the Gentiles, in whom also the new covenant

42. Hitchcock, *Irenaeus of Lugdunum*, ch. 11.

was opened" (ch. 91).[43] The heirs of the new covenant supplant Israel and have no need of the law (93–96; cf. 87 and 89). The descent of the Spirit at Pentecost in Acts 2 was the "opening of the new covenant" (III.xvii.2; cf. *Proof* 8 and 91).

Nevertheless, "both the Mosaic law and the grace of the new covenant were adapted to the times and given for the benefit of the human race by one and the same God" (III.xii.11).[44] So, Irenaeus promised to discuss "the cause of the differences in the covenants and their unity and harmony" (III.xii.12). The necessity for dealing differently with humanity in an earlier era was because humanity was in its childhood (IV.xxxviii.1). So the laws of Moses were "for the instruction or for the punishment" of the people (IV.xvi.5). To a people prone to idolatry God called them "by secondary things to what is primary, by types to the reality, by temporal things to what is eternal, by carnal things to the spiritual, by earthly things to the heavenly . . . By means of types they learned to fear God and to persevere in his service" (IV.xiv.3).

Whereas Justin had emphasized the hardness of heart of the Jews, Irenaeus (without omitting the punitive aspect) emphasized the immaturity of mankind and so the educative aspect of typology.[45]

There were two covenants and two people, but only one God.[46] As the old covenant came from the same God, Irenaeus could argue that it contained in its fundamentals the same laws as the new.

> In the law therefore and in the gospel the first and greatest commandment is to love God with the whole heart, and then like to it, to love one's neighbor as oneself. So is shown one and the same author of the law and the gospel. The precepts of the best life, since they are the same in both covenants, demonstrate the same God. He has prescribed particular laws which are adapted to each covenant, but the highest and best laws, without which there is no salvation, he has exhorted us to the same in both covenants. (IV.xii.3)

43. Irenaeus, *Proof of the Apostolic Preaching*, 103. Cf. ch. 8, "opened the testament of the adoption of sons" (52).

44. See Luneau, *L'Histoire de salut chez les Pères de l'Église*, 96–101, on the "Divine Pedagogy" in Irenaeus.

45. *Adv. haer.* IV.xiv.3; IV.xvi.1 and 5; IV.xxvi.1. Paul's solution in Gal 3:24 has had a long history in Christian theology; Clement of Alexandria picked up the word pedagogue—Simon, *Verus Israel*, 96–99,

46. Hitchcock, *Irenaeus of Lugdunum*, ch. 11.

This argument was of obvious importance against the Gnostic separation of Jesus from the Creator. Irenaeus' terminology of law and gospel seems still to refer to covenants of which these were the chief characteristics, but his language closely approximates the identification of these terms with the books containing each.

Irenaeus' major connected treatment of the covenant idea is found in IV.xxxii–xxxiv where he claimed to present the reasoning of a certain "old man, disciple of the apostles, showing that the two testaments were both from one and the same God." The one God is the creator God. If the scriptures are read in company with the presbyters of the church, Irenaeus argued, it will be seen that every word is consistent. "For all the apostles taught that there were two covenants for the two peoples but one and the same God who ordered both for the good of the man to whom the covenants were given" (IV.xxxii.2). The former covenant was not given without purpose: "It subdues those to whom it was given to the service of God for their good . . . exhibited a type of heavenly things . . . prefigured the things which are now in the church . . . and contained a prophecy of future things" [trans. mine].

This valuable statement of the purposes of the old covenant anticipated later classifications of the levels of interpretation of the Old Testament. Chapter xxxiii then showed how this understanding refuted various heresies. There was an extensive appeal to the prophets, including reference to those who spoke "of a new covenant to be given by God to men, not like that given to the fathers on mount Horeb." This "new covenant of liberty" would be for God's chosen people acquired through Christ to show forth God's praise (IV.xxxiii.14). Christ by his advent fulfilled the new covenant foretold by the law. The prophets would not have had the power to predict all of the things concerning Christ, including the new covenant, if they had received their inspiration from another than the God revealed by Christ. This line of argument demonstrates a major apologetical reason why the church could not give up the Old Testament: the argument from prophecy. Such an argument could work two ways: not only proving Christ (as in Justin), but (as used by Irenaeus here) also proving that the Old Testament scriptures belonged to the one God. With Irenaeus the various covenants were integrated as progressive and ordered phases in a total, organic history of salvation.[47]

---

47. Luneau, *L'Histoire de salut chez les Pères de l'Église*, 103. Bacq, *De l'ancienne à la nouvelle alliance selon S. Irénée.*

The word "covenant" has thus far been found mainly in Christian works dealing with Judaism and Gnosticism. Tertullian also used it principally in his *Against the Jews* and *Against Marcion*. The former treatise began with the Christian interpretation of the two peoples. Then Tertullian developed the idea (ch. 2–3) of a general and primordial unwritten law from Adam to Moses. Moses' law was viewed as a change and intended to be temporary,[48] as shown by the prophecy of a new covenant (Jer 31:31–32) and a new law (Isa 2:2–3).[49] Tertullian considered especially circumcision, sabbath, and sacrifice (as well as the law) as being superseded. The word "covenant" is not prominent but is included in the summary passage in chapter 6:

> First we must inquire whether there be expected a giver of the new law, and an heir of the new testament, and a priest of the new sacrifices, and a purger of the new circumcision, and an observer of the eternal sabbath, to suppress the old law, and institute the new testament, and offer the new sacrifices, and repress the ancient ceremonies, and suppress the old circumcision together with its own sabbath, and announce the new kingdom which is not corruptible.[50]

The new covenant as a new law has been encountered already, and Tertullian's balancing of old law and new testament in this quotation is a reminder that the concept of a new law was completely at home with Tertullian.[51] The legal understanding of *testamentum* (a last will)[52] perhaps facilitated this. Tertullian's preference seems to have been to express *diathēkē* by *instrumentum* (an authorization, hence a legal document), but he recognized that more usual usage was to call it *testamentum* (*Adv. Marc.* IV.i below).[53] Tertullian often wrote, moreover, of two dispensations, old and

---

48. Cf. his "disciple" Cyprian, *Test.* III:99, who quoted Rom 2:12 to distinguish a time before the law of Moses and after the law.

49. Daniélou, *The Origins of Latin Christianity*, 267–68, points to Justin's influence on Tertullian here.

50. Translation by Thelwall in ANF, 3:157.

51. Cf. *Adv. Iud.* 9, "Two testaments of the old law and the new law," and *Adv. Marc.* IV.1, "new law of the gospel." See the list of references in Quasten, *Patrology*, 2:322.

52. The meaning of covenant or agreement is present in *De pud.* XI. 3, "For Christian discipline dates from the renewing of the testament and . . . from the Lord's passion," and in XII.10 about the conditions of the "latest testament."

53. *Instrumentum* is used of the scriptures in *Apol.* XXI.1; *Res. carn.* XXI.1; XXXIII.1; XXXIX.8; XL.1; *Adv. Herm.* XIX; XX; *Adv. Marc.* IV.vi.7; *De praesc. haer.* XXXVIII. 8. On Tertullian's usage, see Braun, *Deus Christianorum*, 463–73.

new, in order to express the covenant idea.[54] Repeatedly he emphasized that the law was temporary, ending with John the Baptist (Luke 16:16).[55]

Tertullian followed the path marked by his predecessors in his polemic against Marcion. His own standpoint was succinctly stated when he summarized the nature of Paul's controversy with his opponents: "The whole essence of the discussion was that while the same God, the God of the law, was being preached in Christ, his law was under criticism" (*Adv. Marc.* I.xxi).[56] This view was set over against Marcion's *Antitheses* which "strained into making such a division between the Law and the Gospel as thereby to make two separate gods, opposite to each other, one belonging to one instrument (or, as it is more usual to say, testament), one to the other" (IV.i; cf. IV.vi and *Prescription of Heretics* 30). Books IV and V of *Against Marcion*, devoted to a refutation of Marcion's interpretation of the scriptures as set forth in his *Antitheses*, demonstrate Tertullian's use of covenant. The gospel did not indicate that a new God was being revealed, for the Old Testament prophesied a new covenant (Jer 31:31ff.). "Thus he indicates that the original testament was temporary, since he declares it changeable, at the same time as he promises an eternal testament for the future" (Isa 55:3). So the prophet, according to Tertullian, was declaring that "other laws and other words and new ordainings of testaments would come from the Creator" (IV.i; cf. IV.xxii). Therefore, Marcion derived no advantage from the supposed diversity between the law and the gospel, since the Creator predicted this "by that promise of a new law and a new word and a new testament" (IV.ix). Tertullian proposed a figurative interpretation whereby the law signified spiritual truths by material ordinances.[57] He developed an Irenaeus-like relationship between the covenants in IV.xi: "We admit this separation, by way of reformation, of enlargement, of progress, as fruit is separated from seed, since fruit comes out of seed. So also the gospel is separated from the law, because it is an advance from out of the law, another thing than the law, though not an alien thing, different, though not opposed."

---

54. *Apol.* XXI; *Adv. Marc.* III.20; V.4; IV.1 and 6; *Virg. vel.* 1.

55. *Adv Mar* IV. 33; *De pud* VI; *Adv Prax* 31; cf. *Adv. Iud.* 2–3; 6–7; 8; *De or.* 1 (a "new covenant" with changes from the past); *Ad ux.* 1.2; *De monog.* 7; 14; *Adv. Marc.* I. 19ff.; IV.1; IV.11; V.2; 4; 13.

56. Cf. V.ii. Quotations from *Against Marcion* are based on Evans, *Tertullian Adversus Marcionem*.

57. *Adv. Marc.* II.19; V.11. Other uses for the law suggested by Tertullian were these: to cause the people to think about God at all times (*Adv. Marc.* II.xix); to fit the needs of the time (II.xviii); and to give an advance announcement of Christ (III.ii).

The word "covenant" (testament) occurs in Book V in quotations from Paul's epistles with "dispensation" coming to the fore as Tertullian's own term. On Gal 4:24 Tertullian argued that he need only to prove that the Creator intended to break down the law in order to show that Paul's words were not in opposition to the Creator (V.iv). On 2 Cor 3:6ff. he affirmed that "if . . . the brightness of the New Testament, which remains in glory, is greater than the glory of the Old Testament, which was to be done away, this too is in agreement with my faith, which sets the gospel above the law." On the other hand, "the giving of superiority is possible only where there has existed something to give superiority over" (V.xi), proving the two were connected.

Tertullian also used the covenant idea in intramural polemics, but this was only occasional and mainly because "covenant" was becoming a title for scripture.[58] It was a logical step for Tertullian to use "covenant" as a designation for the documents[59] which contained and witnessed to the covenant. Since Marcion's *Antitheses* purposely arrayed passages from the "New" over against the "Old" Testament, Tertullian in *Against Marcion* IV.i appears to have referred to the respective bodies of writing as "testament." This understanding is made explicit later in the chapter: "I do not deny a difference in records [*documenta*] of things spoken [in the two dispensations (*dispositiones*)]." Book IV.vi also may be compared: the *Antitheses* have "the one purpose of setting up opposition between the Old Testament and the New." This terminology was Tertullian's but may it not have been a reality for Marcion? Von Campenhausen has argued strongly that the two-part Bible was a creation of the later second century in reaction to Marcion. Though the actual text of the *Antitheses* has been lost, its methodology as reflected by Tertullian's refutation seems to presuppose something very much on its way to a two-part Bible. Tertullian, to be sure, used the terminology of his day, namely, "covenant," to refer to the books of the New Testament. "The documents of the gospel [*evangelicum instrumentum*] have the apostles for authors" (*Adv. Marc.* IV.ii). "For the new testament[60] is made very concise, and is disentangled from the intricate burdens of the law" (IV.i).

58. *Adv. Prax.* 15 and *De Ieiun.* 14. *De praesc. haer.* 37 is the regular legal use of *testamentum.*

59. Van Unnik, "*Hē Kainē Diathēkē*—A Problem in the Early History of the Canon"; von Campenhausen, *The Formation of the Christian Bible,* 264–68; Kinzig, "*Kainē diathēkē.*"

60. Evans did not capitalize the term here, as he did when he understood Tertullian to refer to the scriptures of the New Testament. The decision does not appear to me to

The use, however, of "covenant" as a title for the books of the two parts of the Christian Bible appears relatively recent in Tertullian's time (ca. 160–225). Melito of Sardis (d. ca. 190) reported that he went to Palestine to "learn accurately the books of the old covenant" (Eusebius, *H.E.* IV.xxvi.14). An anonymous anti-Montanist writer (ca. 192) wrote of "the word of the new covenant of the gospel" (*H.E.* V.xvi.3). That the author had in mind the total message and not only a collection of books, however, is evident later in the passage, because his list of prophets of the old covenant and the new included persons of the early second century not mentioned in the New Testament books. He apparently had an era in mind (V.xvii.2–3). Irenaeus' *Against Heresies* is the first surviving Christian document to construct a "formal proof from Scripture"[61] using the New Testament as the Old Testament had previously been used. There is no clear indication, however, that he knew the name "New Covenant" as a collective designation of the new Christian Canon.

Clement of Alexandria, Irenaeus' near contemporary, did seem to use the terms of old and new covenants as designations of the canonical books. "Covenant" meant or referred to written documents in *Miscellanies* V.vi.38, "In both covenants mention is made of the righteous," and V.xiii.85, "It is preached and spoken by the old and new covenant." Moses was described as laying down the law in the old covenant (III.vi.54; cf. IV.xxi.134), and Matt 5:27, 28 was quoted as "the voice of the Lord in the new covenant" (III.xi.71). Clement in *Excerpts from Theodotus* 24 wrote that the "holy Spirit worked continuously according to the old covenant." For Origen "old and new covenants" were designations for two parts of the Bible, although somewhat strange as book titles to his philological training: "the divine scriptures of the so-called old and new covenant" (*De princ.* IV.i.1; the same qualification in *Comm. Joh.* V.8 and for Old Testament in *De or.* XXII.1; "so called covenants" in *Mart.* 12).

"Law" and "Gospel" were both designations of written documents as well as descriptions of an unwritten reality. The rather constant association of these terms with the old and new covenant respectively[62] prepared for the acceptance of the latter terminology as the designations of the two parts of the Bible, a usage established by the beginning of the third century.

---

be clearcut. *Testamentum* is a title for Scripture in *De pud.* I.5 and VI.5; *Adv. Prax.* 15 ("old scripture and new testament").

61. Von Campenhausen, *The Formation of the Christian Bible*, 185.

62. Cf. Tertullian, *Adv. Marc.* III.14, "Two testaments of law and gospel."

The theology with its development of covenant themes attained in the struggle with Jews and heretics was used for the edification and spiritual development of the community and the individual Christian. Melito of Sardis, as his predecessors generally, did not employ the word "covenant" in writings directed to the church. His homily *On the Passover*, however, offered an original illustration to explain the relationship between the Jewish scriptures and Christian faith and practice. This illustration certainly places him in the tradition of the covenant interpretation of salvation-history found in Justin and Irenaeus (cf. Eusebius, *H.E.* IV.xxvi.14 cited above). Melito had much to say about the law as old, temporal, and a type, and about the gospel as new, eternal, and grace (ch. 3, 4, 7, 58). The law issued in the gospel. Their relationship was more fully worked out in chapters 34–45 in the comparison of a model to a finished product. Material or earthly things require a pattern or model, whether of wax, clay, or wood. The reality surpasses its model; the model had its place for a time, but after the thing itself comes into existence the model has no more value. The Lord's salvation and truth were prefigured among the Jews in this way. "The people, therefore, became the model for the church, and the law a parabolic sketch. But the gospel became the explanation of the law and its fulfillment." The type had value prior to its realization. "The law was fulfilled when the gospel was brought to light, and the people lost their significance when the church came on the scene, and the type was destroyed when the Lord appeared."[63]

The writer of the Pseudo-Cyprian sermon *Adversus Iudaeos* used the traditional themes associated with the covenant in Christian thought with the intention of "de-Judaizing" the church.[64] The sermon declared its theme as the transfer under the new covenant of the inheritance (the fusion of the testamentary with the relational idea of covenant) to the Gentiles. The heirs of Christ are able to understand the spiritual nature of his covenant. The old people have been disinherited because of their crimes, and God has written a new covenant (testament), witnessed by heaven and earth. The new covenant invites the Gentiles to enter the eternal inheritance which Israel rejected. "Christ tore up your old covenant and wrote a new one by which he called Gentiles to the possession of your privileges" (ch. 31). Chapter 43 refers to the new covenant on the mount

63. The translation is that of Hawthorne, "A New English Translation of Melito's Paschal *Homily*," 158–59.

64. Van Damme, *Pseudo-Cyprian Adversus Iudaeos*, 21–24, 27–30.

of transfiguration to be revealed after the resurrection. The appeal is to a spiritual understanding.

Spiritual understanding is also the hallmark of Clement of Alexandria's writings, albeit of a different type from that of the Latin author of the *Adversus Iudaeos*. The term "covenant" entered Clement's vocabulary fully apart from a polemical context. The occurrences of the word are too numerous to treat exhaustively here. Clement's writings present a many-sided theology of the relationship of the covenants.

The language of the "old and new covenant" came naturally to Clement. The covenants were among the good things of which God was the cause (*Strom.* I.v.28). Corollary with the idea of the two covenants was the idea of two peoples: "Formerly the older people had an old covenant, and the law disciplined the people with fear . . . but to the fresh and new people has also been given a new covenant" (*Paed.* I.vii.59).[65] Since the same Word was the instructor in both, one can find many of the teachings of the "new covenant written in the old letter" (*Paed* I.vii.59). Clement believed there were pious men before the giving of the law (*Strom.* I.ix.44; cf. VI.vi.47, "those who lived rightly before the law").[66] Thus Clement posited a periodization: before the law, under the law, and under Christ (*Strom.* I.xxi.135; II.xix.100).[67] He associated covenants with five figures: Adam, Noah, Abraham, Moses, Christ (*Ecl.* 51–52).[68] So thoroughly was Clement embued with the idea of covenant that he even described philosophy as "given to the Greeks as a covenant peculiar to them" (*Strom.* VI.viii.67).[69]

The new covenant brought by Christ in fulfillment of Jer 31:31ff. made both the Jewish law and Greek philosophy old:

> He made a new covenant with us; for what belonged to the Greeks and Jews is old. But we who worship Him in a new way, in the third form, are Christians. For clearly, as I think, he showed that the one and only God was known by the Greeks in

65. Translations from Clement follow the ANF, vol. 2.

66. For the pious before the law, a kind of "Christianity before Christ," a view most fully formulated by Eusebius, see Simon, *Verus Israel*, 105–11.

67. Luneau, *L'Histoire de salut chez les Pères de l'Église*, 112. Christians are not under the law—*Paed.* I.vi.

68. The same in Origen, *Comm. Matt.* 15:32 on the parable of the workers in the vineyard, called at five different times (Matthew 20). Aphrahat, *Hom.* XI.11, has the same five. See Jacob Neusner, *Aphrahat and Judaism*. Cf. Pseudo-Cyprian, *Adv. Iudaeos* and the discussion of Irenaeus above.

69. But note *Ecl.* 43 as recognizing there was no proper covenant with the heathen.

a Gentile way, by the Jews Judaically, and in a new and spiritual way by us.

And further, that the same God that furnished both the Covenants was the giver of Greek philosophy to the Greeks. . . (*Strom.* VI.v.41–42)[70]

Since the different covenants came from the same Lord, they were in harmony: "The ecclesiastical rule is the concord and harmony of the law and the prophets in the covenant delivered at the coming of the Lord" (*Strom.* VI.xv.125). Similar terms occur in the two covenants (*Strom.* I.ix.44.3). Thus, Clement summed up the results of the anti-heretical polemic: "'The just shall live by faith' which is according to the covenant and the commandments. Since these—the old and the new—are two in name and time, given by economy in accordance with the degree of development and advancement, but are one in power, they are administered through the Son by one God" (*Strom.* II.vi.29; trans. mine). Here is Irenaeus' distinction in time under one God of covenants adapted to the state of mankind's maturity. Christ is the real mediator of all the covenants, for "the covenant of salvation, reaching down to us from the foundation of the world, through different generations and times, is one, though conceived as different in respect of gift. For it follows that there is one unchangeable gift of salvation given by one God, through one Lord, benefitting in many ways" (*Strom.* VI.xiii.106).

Indeed, on the basis of Gen 17:4 Clement claimed that the Lord was himself the covenant (*Strom.* I.xxix.182). Clement went further than his immediate predecessors in affirming that the different covenants were in reality one: the universal church collects the righteous "into the unity of the one faith, which results from the distinctive covenants, or rather the one covenant in different times by the will of the one God through one Lord" (*Strom.* VII.xvii.107). This viewpoint prepared for the distinctive Alexandrian way of using the Old Testament as a Christian book. Accordingly, the "gnostic" Christian "advances in the gospel, using the law not only as a step but comprehending it as the Lord who gave the covenants delivered it to the apostles" (*Strom.* IV.xxi.130; cf. later in the chapter: "Faith in Christ and the knowledge of the gospel is the exegesis and fulfilling of the law . . . ," 134).

---

70. The first two sentences may be part of Clement's quotation from the early second-century apologetic work, *The Preaching of Peter*, but I have assumed that the quotation stops earlier. The quotation from *The Preaching of Peter* includes a quotation of Jer 31:31–32 about a new covenant. Cf. *Q.d.s.* 37.

Clement offered some of the fullest and most varied statements on the purposes which the law served. It was a preparatory discipline (*Strom.* II.viii.37) which by fear taught the beginning of wisdom, enjoined human beings to avoid bad things, showed what sin was, taught what was salutary, and trained in the good (*Strom.* II.vii.32–35). Clement's theology resembles some Reformation theology in its description of the uses of the law: it "trains in piety, prescribes what is to be done, and restrains each one from sins, imposing penalties even on lesser sins" (*Strom.* I.xxvii.171). In *Miscellanies* II.xviii he discussed the reason for a number of Old Testament regulations under the theme "teaching wisdom by abstinence from sensible images and by inviting to the Maker and Father of the universe" (78). In addition to this educative aspect there were also typical and prophetic purposes: "The sense of the law is to be taken in three ways—either as exhibiting a symbol, or laying down a precept for right conduct, or as uttering a prophecy" (*Strom.* I.xxviii.179). The symbols in the Old Testament had three purposes: to arouse curiosity so people would study in order to discover words of salvation; to hide the true meaning from those who were not worthy; and to make it possible to speak of the incomprehensible God (*Strom* VI.xv.126ff).

Origen is an appropriate figure with whom to close this essay. There is no attempt to offer a complete review of Origen, but only to note how some of the themes already uncovered relate to his writings. As mentioned above, Origen qualified "covenant" as a title of the scriptures by "so-called." He did this even for the general use of the word: "We must also realize that we have received the so-called covenants of God on conditions, set forth in the agreements which we have made with him" (*Exh. ad mart.* 12). This passage keeps the biblical sense of "covenant" as "an agreement." Origen seemed to lack the testamentary emphasis frequently encountered in other writings from this period. The beginning of the law was in the time of Moses, "while the beginning of our legislation and second covenant" was in the time of Jesus (*C. Cels.* II.lxxv).[71] From Origen's lofty standpoint the old burning issue of the relation of the Christian writings to the Jewish scriptures was on the same level with other discrepancies within the various books of each collection. "There is too a third peacemaker, the man who shows that what to others seems the discord of the Scriptures is no discord, and who makes their harmony and peace evident, be it of the old with the New; or the Law with the Prophets, or of one passage from the

---

71. Cf. *In Ex hom.* 11.2, "Christ on the cross caused the fountains of the new covenant to flow."

Gospel with another; or of the Gospels with the Apostolic writings; or of one Apostolic writing with another."[72]

Origen invoked Paul's authority for the spiritual exegesis of the Old Testament; Paul taught the Galatians how to allegorize lest the church "run risk in using a strange covenant."[73] So Christians when they read the Old Testament do not become disciples of the Jews. A controlling idea in Origen's *Commentary on John* was the unity of scripture. There was no difference between the Old and New Testament for exegetical purposes (I.119ff.). In fact, in Book II Origen seems to debate with ecclesiastical typologists. He denied that historical events were the primary means of revelation. The prophets spoke by the Logos of direct spiritual reality. Moses' breaking the tablets of stone "signifies that the power of the law resides not in its letter but in its spirit" (*Comm. Rom.* II.14). With the allegorical method of discovering new meanings in the old writings, temporal distinctions disappear: "I do not call this law an Old Testament if I understand it spiritually. The law becomes an Old Testament only for those who want to understand it carnally" (*In Num hom* IX.4).[74] From one direction Origen sounds like Barnabas; from another he approaches the view of Augustine, which has improved in translation: "In the Old Testament the New is concealed; in the New the Old is revealed."[75]

These brief comments concerning Origen bring this review to its end. Several conclusions seem justified on the basis of this study:

(1) Covenant was part of the Old Testament-Jewish heritage of the church. Like other Old Testament categories it was subsumed in Jesus Christ (the Covenant), becoming less important as a category in itself to second-century Christians.

(2) The covenant idea had its significance in structuring holy history against Jewish claims for and the Gnostic repudiation of the law. The polemical and theological setting of the remarks of these early

72. Tollinton, *Selections from the Commentaries and Homilies of Origen*, 48, citing *Comm. Matt.* 2 (= *Philocalia* 6).

73. Tollinton, ibid., 72, citing *In Ex hom.* V.I.

74. "When one begins to understand the law spiritually then he passes from Old Testament to new"—*In Ex hom.* 7.3.

75. *Quaest in Hept.* 2, q. 73; cf. *C. adv leg et proph.* 1.17.35 and *Enarr in Ps* 56.9 (57.7 in NPNF).

Christian authors slants the material as it relates to the Old Testament scriptures. A study of the respective authors' actual use of the Old Testament would perhaps modify some of the statements above. Nevertheless, a covenantal, "dispensational," "history of salvation" view was one of the fundamental hermeneutical principles employed by many early Christian writers. Although I have not attempted to do so, I think that we could find this covenant scheme fundamental in catechesis and liturgy.[76]

(3) This covenantal structure may fairly be claimed to be rooted in the early kerygma and to be based on the first developments of it by Paul and Luke.

(4) The covenant concept is closely related to the theme of "God's people."

(5) Both Hebraic (relationship) and Hellenistic (testament) components persisted in early Christian texts about *diathēkē*.

(6) The association with "law" and "gospel" prepared for the adoption of the term "covenant" as a title for the scriptures.

EXCURSUS ON ISAIAH 2:2–4 [=MIC 4:1–4][77]

Isaiah 2:2–4 has served as an important Old Testament prophecy for the beginning of the church and proclamation of the new covenant on Pentecost in Acts 2, this in spite of the absence of a direct quote of the text in the New Testament (with the possible exception of an allusion in John 4:22, which does not bear on this particular point).

Origen indicated that the text was familiar to all Christians: "For who of all believers does not know the words of Isaiah?" quoting 2:2–4 and Mic 4:1–3.[78] He used it himself in his treatise *Against Celsus* (V.xxxiii), giving a sort of homily on the phrases, from which are these excerpts:

> For the law came forth from the dwellers in Zion and settled among us as a spiritual law. Moreover, the word of the Lord

76. For catechesis, Irenaeus, *Proof of the Apostolic Preaching*; and see Musurillo, "History and Symbol"; for liturgy, see Melito's sermon and the eucharistic prayer in *Ap. Const.* VIII.xii.

77. See the interesting suggestions about the use of this text in early Christian authors by Daniélou, *Primitive Christian Symbols*, 89–101.

78. Origen, *Ep. to Africanus* 15. Cyprian, *Test.* I:10 quoted both passages along with Matt 17:5 under the heading, "That a new law was to be given." He quoted it again in II.18.

came forth from that very Jerusalem that it might be disseminated through all places and might judge in the midst of the heathen . . . We have become children of peace for the sake of Jesus, who is our leader, instead of those whom our fathers followed, among whom we were as strangers to the covenant.[79]

Clement of Alexandria quoted "For out of Zion shall go forth the law, and the word of the Lord from Jerusalem" in his *Exhortation* chapter 1, but made no interpretation or application of it. Melito alluded to the text in a declaration based on the contrast of the two covenants: "For indeed the law issued in the gospel [*logos*]—the old in the new, both coming forth together from Zion and Jerusalem; and the commandment issued in grace, and the type in the finished product [the truth]."[80]

Justin and Irenaeus both explicitly connected the text with the new covenant. Justin alluded to it in *Dialogue* 24, "There is now another covenant, and another law has gone forth from Zion." In his *First Apology* (39), he quoted the text and declared it fulfilled in the fact that from Jerusalem there went out into the world twelve men who preached the word of God. Justin emphasized also the aspect of peace in the passage, calling attention to the peaceful ways of Christians. Justin quoted the Micah version of the prophecy in full with reference to the conversion of the Gentiles in *Dialogue* 109 (so presumably the allusion in 110 is to this quotation). Irenaeus included an extended discussion of Isaiah 2 in *Against Heresies* IV.xxxiv.4. In refutation of the Jewish claim that the new covenant consisted in the rebuilding of the temple after the Exile, Irenaeus declared that no new covenant was given but the people lived under the Mosaic law until the coming of the Lord. "But from the Lord's advent, the new covenant which brings peace, and the law which gives life, has gone forth," and he then quoted Isa 2:3–4. "The law of liberty, that is the word of God, preached by the apostles (who went forth from Jerusalem) throughout all the earth" brought in a reign of peace among the Gentiles. He too stressed that Christians did not fight but turned the other cheek. Irenaeus again quoted Isa 2:3 in *Proof of the Apostolic Preaching* 86 to confirm the universality of the word of God ("which is also for us [Gentiles] the law") preached by the apostles. The use of "law of the Lord" in Isaiah seems to be a contributing factor in the frequent conjunction of law and covenant in the authors examined.

---

79. Trans. in *Ante-Nicene Fathers*, 4:558.

80. *On the Passover* 7 (Hawthorne, "A New English Translation of Melito's Paschal Homily," 151).

Tertullian made very extensive use of the text. His *Against the Jews* 3 quoted the entire text of Isa 2:2–4 as referring to the fulfillment of the new covenant prophecy of Jer 31:31–32. The "house of Jacob" was the new people, and the word of the Lord that judged among the nations applied to the Gentile church.[81] Those who no more learn to fight are Christians, who instead of taking vengeance practice clemency and instead of war take up peaceful pursuits. The passage was quoted three times in *Against Marcion*. In III.xxi the "house of God" is "Christ, the universal temple of God." "The gospel" is "the way of the new law and new word in Christ, no longer in Moses." Once more there is emphasis on pursuing peace. In IV.1 Tertullian declared that it was not the Jewish race alone but the Gentiles "who by the new law of the gospel and the new word of the apostles are being judged." Because of this the dispositions of those once cruel and fierce become productive of good fruit. Finally in V.4 there is a briefer allusion to Isa 2:3 as indicating that "old things might pass away and new things might arise."

81. Cf. *De Anima* 50:4; cf. Pseudo-Cyprian, *Adv. Iudaeos* 3 and 9; and Pseudo-Cyprian, *De mont Sina et Sion* 4. The relation of Tertullian's writings and other passages dealing with the text from Isaiah are discussed in Daniélou, *Origins of Latin Christianity*, 47–49.

15

Justin Martyr on Jews, Christians, and the Covenant[1]

RECENT YEARS HAVE BROUGHT a large number of studies on relations between Jews and Christians in the early centuries of the Common Era.[2] Some of these have dealt with Justin Martyr, a crucial figure in the transition from the intra-faith debates of New Testament times to the anti-Judaism of Gentile Christianity.[3] And some recent studies have noted the importance of the covenant to the discussions between

1. An earlier form of this paper was presented as "Some Patristic Views" at the Israel Colloquium on the topic "Continuity and Change: Jews, Christians, and the Covenant," held at Georgetown University, Washington, DC, on November 19, 1986.

2. Blanchetière, "Aux sources de l'anti-judaïsme chrétien"; Bokser, "Justin Martyr and the Jews"; Gager, *Origins of Anti-Semitism*; Wilson, ed., *Anti-Judaism in Early Christianity*, vol. 2, *Separation and Polemic*; Segal, *Rebecca's Children*, who suggestively invokes the comparison of sibling rivalry for relations between Judaism and Christianity in the early period; the idea is picked up in the title of Perelmuter, *Siblings: Rabbinic Judaism and Early Christianity at their Beginnings*; Rokéah, "The Church Fathers and the Jews"; MacLennan, *Early Christian Texts on Jews and Judaism*. Two major recent works are Skarsaune and Hvalvik, eds., *Jewish Believers in Jesus*; and Sandgren, *Vines Intertwined*.

3. Remus, "Justin Martyr's Argument with Judaism"; and MacLennan, *Early Christian Texts*, ch. 2; note the observations by Strecker, "On the Problem of Jewish Christianity," 275–79, on the difference between Justin Martyr and Irenaeus with regard to Jewish Christianity; Horner, *Listening to Trypho*; Rokéah, *Justin Martyr and the Jews*.

Jews and Christians.[4] Justin Martyr's views on the covenant, however, seem not to have received special attention.

The article on *berith* in the *Theological Dictionary of the Old Testament* distinguishes two semantic fields associated with covenant in the Hebrew Bible.[5] The primary association of *berith* is with imposition, obligation, and commandment. Derived from this is the association with commitment, fellowship, and love, from which association comes the idea of agreement. The translation of the Bible into Greek introduced a third semantic field of association. The Greek διαθήκη preserved the idea of disposition but added the special Hellenic use of the word for a will or testament. That meaning was already employed in the Christian scriptures to explicate the Christian understanding. Paul in Gal 3:15–18 appealed to the unchangeable nature of a duly ratified will in order to argue that the promise to Abraham (a covenant or will) was not changed by the giving of the law through Moses 430 years later. The Epistle to the Hebrews 9:16f. used the principle that there must be the death of the testator before his will takes effect in order to show the necessity of the death of Jesus for his will or covenant to come into force.[6] However, the Hebrew idea of the divine initiative and the resulting relationship were not lost in the Christian understanding.

Justin Martyr offers a good point of departure for consideration of early Gentile Christian views on the covenant. Justin was born and grew up a pagan in the Roman colony of Flavia Neapolis, the modern Nablus, near ancient Shechem, where perhaps he had the opportunity to learn something about Samaritan and Jewish religion. He undertook the study of philosophy, and he was converted to Christianity while later resident in Ephesus or Corinth. The following factors entered into his conversion: the biblical prophecies, the steadfastness of the martyrs, and the answer which Christianity offered to his intellectual question. He sealed his faith by his own martyrdom in Rome, c. 165. Justin's writings belong to the mid- second century. He was knowledgeable in Middle Platonic philosophy; he

---

4. Segal, *Rebecca's Children*, describes the covenant as the root metaphor underlying Hebrew society. For the larger issue of covenant in Jewish and Christian relations see D'Costa, "One Covenant or Many Covenants?"; Lohfink, *The Covenant Never Revoked*.

5. Weinfeld, "*berith*"; cf. Morrice, "New Wine in Old Wine-Skins: XI. Covenant." The literature in recent years on the background to and biblical concept of covenant is enormous, but these issues are not directly relevant to the thrust of this paper.

6. Some have argued that even in these passages the translation should be "covenant," not "will." See Hughes, "Hebrews 9:15ff. and Galatians 3:15ff."

knew Christianity at several of its geographical centers; and of special significance for this study, he was reasonably well informed about Judaism, both in Palestine and in the Greek diaspora.

Justin's longest writing is the *Dialogue with Trypho*, a Jew. In this work Justin draws a picture of a fair-minded and inquisitive Jewish teacher who had fled Palestine as a result of the rebellion led by Bar Kokhba against Rome. Indeed, Trypho appears more courteous and open-minded than Justin himself in Justin's own account of their discussions.[7] This portrait plus the very form of the account itself show that meaningful discussion of real issues could still take place between Christians and Jews who shared the same Hellenistic education. Justin shows himself acquainted with Jewish views and Jewish interpretations of the scriptures. On the other hand, there are limitations to Justin's presentation in the *Dialogue*. He uses exclusively the Greek version of the scriptures, the Septuagint. Where it differs from the Hebrew text, he rejects the latter as corrupted by the Jews in order to avoid the Christian argument: hardly a good basis on which to build the Christian case. Moreover, Justin speaks bitterly against the Jews, impugning motives with little justification, but bitterness in religious debate has not been confined to Christian-Jewish polemic.

Justin Martyr is a good object of study, furthermore, because his frequent references to the covenant express the viewpoint that came to prevail in Christianity. The second century was a formative period in Christian thought and in the Christian-Jewish debate. Various attitudes toward the Jewish Bible and the Jewish heritage of the church were expressed. After looking at Justin's views on the covenant in some detail, we will present some of the competing views that were present in order to sharpen the perception of Justin's position.

Justin understood covenant as "disposition." For him God delivered the covenant and remained sovereign over the covenant, able to revoke it and establish a different one. He did not make much of the Greek legal concept of a "testament" or "will," except for the idea of a later will replacing an earlier one and the association of covenant with inheritance. And here his real concern, as with many of the early Christian writers who discussed the covenant, was the "people": Who are God's people? Who are those in covenant relationship with God?

Justin's understanding and emphases in regard to the covenant are shown by the words that he associated with covenant. Thus, "law" and

---

7. The significance of this is treated by Trakatellis, "Justin Martyr's Trypho."

"covenant" are repeatedly combined.[8] Another word frequently combined with "covenant" is the adjective "new."[9] This usage reinforced Justin's, history-of-salvation view, according to which the covenant with Israel at Sinai was replaced with another covenant inaugurated by Jesus, the Christ of Christian faith. This new covenant is the final and ultimate covenant, as shown by the phrase "eternal covenant."[10] The adjectives are combined, "new and eternal covenant"[11] or with the variation, "new covenant and eternal law."[12] Better than by such summary statements, his thought can be seen by an analysis of some passages.

The *Dialogue with Trypho* has a major discussion of covenant set right at the beginning of the debate, in chapters 10–11, after the preliminaries have set the stage for the discussion of differences between the Jew Trypho and his companions and Justin, the Christian. Here Justin enunciates the themes to which he will return throughout the *Dialogue.*

Trypho expressed amazement that the Christians, although professing to be pious, to fear God, and to be better than others, did not separate themselves from the nations by observing the festivals, sabbaths, and circumcision. If Christians claim the Jewish Bible as theirs, why do they not live by its prescriptions? As did other Jews, Trypho identified the covenant with circumcision.[13] The passage, with Justin's reply, reads as follows:

> (Trypho:) "Have you not read, that soul shall be cut off from his people who shall not have been circumcised on the eighth day? And this has been ordained for strangers and for slaves equally. But you, despising this covenant rashly, reject the consequent duties, and attempt to persuade yourselves that you know God, when, however, you perform none of those things which they do who fear God . . ."

> (Justin:) "There will be no other God, Trypho, nor was there from eternity any other existing but he who made and disposed all this universe. Nor do we think that there is one God for us, another for you, but that he alone is God who led your fathers out from Egypt with a strong hand and high arm. Nor have we trusted in any other (for there is no other), but in him in whom

8. *Dial.* 11; 24; 34; 43; 118; 122.

9. *Dial.* 11; 34; 51; 67; 118; 122.

10. *Dial.* 43; 118; 122.

11. *Dial.* 118.

12. *Dial.* 122.

13. Segal, "Covenant in Rabbinic Writings," 57–58.

you also have trusted, the God of Abraham, and of Isaac, and of Jacob. But we do not trust through Moses or through the law; for then we would do the same as yourselves. But now—for I have read that there shall be a final law, and a covenant, the chiefest of all, which it is now incumbent on all men to observe, as many as are seeking after the inheritance of God. For the law promulgated on Horeb is now old, and belongs to yourselves alone; but this is for all universally. Now, law placed against law has abrogated that which is before it, and a covenant which comes after in like manner has put an end to the previous one; and an eternal and final law—namely, Christ— has been given to us, and the covenant is trustworthy, after which there shall be no law, no commandment, no ordinance. (There follow quotations of Isa 51:4–5 and Jer 31:31ff.). If, therefore, God proclaimed a new covenant which was to be instituted, and this for a light of the nations, we see and are persuaded that men approach God, leaving their idols and other unrighteousness, through the name of him who was crucified, Jesus Christ, and abide by their confession even unto death, and maintain piety. Moreover, by the works and by the attendant miracles, it is possible for all to understand that he is the new law, and the new covenant, and the expectation of those who out of every people wait for the good things of God. For the true spiritual Israel, and descendants of Judah, Jacob, Isaac, and Abraham . . . are we who have been led to God through this crucified Christ." (*Dial.* 10–11)[14]

Justin's reply is notable on several points. He affirms the one God, saying that Christians trust in the same "God of Abraham, Isaac, and Jacob" who led Israel out of Egypt. However, Christians, he said, do not trust in Moses or his law. "The law promulgated on Horeb is now old." There is a final law and covenant that is for all persons universally, not for one race. The Christ is this new law and new covenant, and "the true spiritual Israel . . . are we who have been led to God through this crucified Christ." This new covenant accomplished the purpose of the old in leading the nations to abandon idols. Justin quotes according to the Septuagint from Isa 51:4–5 ("a law shall go forth from Me"), Jer 31:31–32 ("I will make a new covenant with the house of Israel and with the house of Judah"), and Isa 55:3 ("I will make an everlasting covenant with you, even the sure mercies of David"), and makes allusion to Isa 43:6 ("a light to the nations"), as the basis for his terminology and claims.

14. Translations from Justin follow the ANF, vol. 1.

This passage sets forth all the themes relative to the covenant that we have identified from Justin's repeated terminology and that will recur throughout the *Dialogue.* The law and the covenant belong together. The law delivered at Sinai, valid for the Jewish people for a period of time, has been annulled and replaced by a new covenant. This new covenant is in Christ, or more strongly stated, Christ is this covenant. It is universal in scope and eternal in duration.

The association of law and covenant is shown by the allusion to Isa 2:2–4 in chapter 24 of the *Dialogue,* where Justin says, "There is now another covenant, and another law has gone forth from Zion."[15] Justin also applies the language of a "new covenant" from Jer 31:31 to the law, as in the statement, "God declared that he would establish a new law and a new covenant" (*Dial.* 34). Justin does not repeat the quotation from Jer 31:31ff., but he continues to allude to it, as in *Dialogue* 51, "the new covenant which God formerly announced."[16] This new covenant was made necessary because Israel broke the covenant, language taken from Deut 31:16–18.[17]

The association of Christ and the covenant occurs frequently: "As, then, circumcision began with Abraham, and the sabbath and sacrifices and offerings and feasts with Moses, . . . it was necessary . . . that they should have an end . . . in Christ the Son of God, (who is) the everlasting law and the everlasting covenant" (*Dial.* 43).

The new covenant is identified with Christ on the basis of Isa 42:6–7, "I have given you for a covenant of the people, for a light of the Gentiles," cited three times.[18] The first of these quotations (*Dial.* 26) follows on a reference to Jewish persecution of Christ and his followers. Justin contrasts the conduct with the Gentiles who have believed on Christ, and have repented of the sins which they have committed; they shall receive the inheritance along with the patriarchs and the prophets and the just men who are descended from Jacob, even though they neither keep the sabbath nor are circumcised nor observe the feasts.

According to Justin, God "promised to dispense a new covenant" designed to be universal in place of the covenant given to one people at Horeb. That old covenant came with "fear, trembling, and lightnings."[19]

15. Cf. *Apology* I.39 and the quotation of the parallel from Mic 4:1–4 in *Dial.* 109–10.

16. His usage is similar to that in Hebrews 8 and may have been influenced by it; cf. *Dial.* 67.

17. *Dial.* 74.

18. *Dial.* 26; 65; and 122. The last passage cites also Isa 49:8 to this effect.

19. *Dial.* 67; cf. Heb 12:18–19.

The new covenant is unlike that one. It contains "commands and deeds God knows to be eternal and suited to every nation" (*Dial.* 67). There is the implied contrast with the institutions of the Mosaic law, which are criticized throughout the *Dialogue.* They were particular to one nation and in Justin's mind unsuited to a world-wide religion. The new covenant is for all (chap. 11), so it is universal in application.

The new covenant is, likewise, everlasting. Affirmations of the eternal covenant occur especially in contexts identifying the covenant with Christ. The declaration, "He is the chosen priest and eternal King, the Christ, inasmuch as he is the Son of God" is followed by the result that "We (Christians), through the calling of the new and eternal covenant, that is, of Christ, might be found more understanding and God-fearing than yourselves, who are considered to be lovers of God and men of understanding but are not" (*Dial.* 118).

Here, as often, the contrast comes down to a contrast of peoples.

One of Justin's statements about Christ as the new covenant occurs in a passage that sets forth what might be termed Justin's *Kerygma*, or proclamation of the gospel:

> John came first, calling on men to repent, and Christ, while John still sat by the river Jordan, having come, put an end to his prophesying and baptizing, and preached also himself, saying the Kingdom of heaven is at hand, and that he must suffer many things from the scribes and Pharisees, and be crucified, and on the third day rise again, and would appear again in Jerusalem, and would eat and drink again with his disciples; and foretold that in the interval between his advents . . . priests and false prophets would arise in his name, which things do actually appear . . . Moreover, he referred to the fact that there would be no longer in your nation any prophet, and to the fact that men recognized how that the new covenant which God formerly announced . . . was then present, i.e., Christ himself. (*Dial.* 51)

Justin argued that the many Gentiles who had come to believe in Jesus were evidence that he was the Christ and the fulfillment of such passages as Isa 49:6, which says, "I have appointed you for a light to the Gentiles that you may be their salvation to the earth." Trypho understood the light as the law and those enlightened as proselytes (*Dial.* 121–22). Justin, on the other hand, referred the prophecies to "us who have been illumined by Jesus" (122). His reasoning was this:

> Since if the law was able to enlighten the nations and those who
> possess it, what need is there of a new covenant? But since God
> announced beforehand that he would send a new covenant, and
> an everlasting law and commandment, we will not understand
> this of the old law and its proselytes but of Christ and his pros-
> elytes, namely us Gentiles, whom he has illumined, (followed by
> a quotation of Isa 49:8). What, is the covenant of God? Is it not
> Christ? (*Dial.* 122)

The growth of the church primarily among Gentiles and not among the Jews, among whom she began, became an argument for Christianity instead of against it. The rejection of Jesus by the great majority of Jews might be taken as a failure, and it certainly was a puzzling phenomenon, for which various explanations were offered, most of them unflattering to the Jewish people. On the other hand, the church was seen as fulfilling the passages of the Bible about the Gentiles. Justin continues by arguing that the proselytes to Judaism did not need a new covenant, since all who were circumcised were incorporated into the Jewish people and became subject to the same covenant with them (*Dial.* 123; cf. *b. Yeb.* 62a). Rather, it is the case that Gentile Christians are Israel and the true sons of God. Justin says, "As therefore from the one man Jacob, who was surnamed Israel, all your nation has been called Jacob and Israel; so we from Christ, who begat us unto God, . . . are called and are the true sons of God" (*Dial.* 123).

Justin Martyr's views may he sharpened by being set alongside those of Christians in the second century who differed from him and then by seeing how his views were elaborated by Irenaeus at the end of the century.[20]

The author of the document know as the *Epistle of Barnabas*, an Alexandrian teacher earlier in the second century, had a distinctive approach to the Jewish Bible.[21] There is implied in his statements a difference between the covenant and the law: the covenant is still binding but belongs not to the Jews but to the Christians, who understand the laws properly, i.e., spiritually and not literally. *Barnabas* does not speak of a new covenant. For him there was only one covenant. The question was, "Whose is the

20. I have written for a popular audience a survey of early Christian attitudes toward the Jewish Bible in "Christian Use of the Old Testament," and for an academic audience a more detailed treatment in "The Covenant Idea in the Second Century," 170–97, the preceding entry in this collection.

21. To the literature cited in my articles in n. 20, add Lowy, "The Confutation of Judaism in the Epistle of Barnabas"; O'Hagan, "Early Christian Exegesis Exemplified from the Epistle of Barnabas"; see now MacLennan, *Early Christian Texts*, chap. 1; and Paget, "The Epistle of Barnabas and the Covenant of the Lord."

covenant?" Or, in *Barnabas*'s words, "Let us see if this people (Christians) or the first people (Jews) receive the inheritance, and if the covenant is for us or for them" (13.1). His answer is a resounding "It is ours." God offered the covenant to Israel by Moses at Sinai. But twice the author tells the story of the sin of the golden calf and Moses coming down the mountain and breaking the tablets of stone that contained the Ten Commandments (4 and 14). His interpretation of the incident is that when Moses threw down the tablets, "their covenant was broken, in order that the covenant of Jesus the Beloved might be sealed in our heart" (4.8). Moses had received the covenant and offered it to the people, but they were not worthy.

Barnabas reasons that the Jews mistakenly understood the sacrifices, circumcision, food laws, washings, sabbath, and temple literally. God intended them spiritually, so it is Christians who really keep the law through the Christian counterpart of these activities. On the subject of the covenant, however, the author does not take the same approach. For him the covenant is essentially one and the same, but it was transferred to a people who will understand it properly. The Lord has now given the covenant to a new people to receive the inheritance. The frequent association of covenant with inheritance shows the Hellenistic meaning of "testament" (6.19). *Barnabas*, nevertheless, certainly included the idea of relationships, for his principal concern was with the question, "Who are God's people?" He may not have spoken of a new covenant, but he did refer to a new people (5.7). The idea of supersession is definitely present, even though the sense of identity with the Jewish covenant is different from Justin's approach.

Barnabas has other similarities with Justin in spite of their differences. For *Barnabas*, as for Justin, Christ is both the giver of the covenant and the covenant itself. And the two writers invoke some of the same prophecies (Isa 42:6–7; 49:6–7) in support of the claim that Christ is the covenant and salvation that belong to all peoples.

Almost the exact opposite of Barnabas was Marcion, excommunicated at Rome in 144 and one of those against whom Justin wrote.[22] Whereas *Barnabas* appropriated the Jewish Bible as the Christian scriptures and tried to read the whole Christian message out of it, Marcion totally rejected the Jewish heritage of the church. The Jewish Bible remained for him a Jewish book that should be left to the Jews. It came from a God, the

---

22. For balanced treatment of Marcion in the light of recent studies, see Balás, "Marcion Revisited"; May, "Marcion in Contemporary Views." A new perspective on Marcion in Moll, *The Arch-Heretic Marcion*.

creator and judge, different from the God who is Father of Jesus Christ and Redeemer. Marcion's opponent Tertullian characterized his position as follows: "Marcion's special and principal work is the separation of the law and the gospel . . . These are Marcion's *Antitheses*, or contradictory proposition, which aim at committing the gospel to a variance with the law, in order that from the diversity of the two documents which contain them, they may contend for a diversity of gods also" (*Against Marcion* 1.19; cf. 4.6).[23]

Marcion "devised different dispensations for two Gods" (ibid. 3.15). His Christ came not to fulfill but to destroy the law. For Marcion the Jews had read the Bible correctly; their scriptures prophesied the coming of a military Messiah. Christians should dissociate themselves from all such understandings. Let the Jews have their covenant.

The "all or nothing at all" approaches of *Barnabas* and Marcion were not the only other options in the second century. Some teachers made distinctions, but not between historical covenants, as Justin had done, but within the Jewish Bible itself. The Gnostics in general shared Marcion's negative view of the literal message of the Hebrew scriptures, but having received them as a sacred book, they sought to interpret them according to their systems of thought.

One Gnostic teacher, Ptolemy, a somewhat younger contemporary of Justin, did, for his time, a rather sophisticated piece of source criticism on the Pentateuch. Without expressly using the word covenant, he took a position relevant to our subject. According to Ptolemy, the New Testament attributes part of the Pentateuch to God, part to Moses, and part to the elders. The legislation which came from Moses and the elders is without lasting significance. That part which came from God can be further subdivided into three parts. (1) The pure legislation of God, free from evil, is the Ten Commandments and has been perfected by Jesus. (2) The laws concerning wrongdoing and retribution ("an eye for eye and a tooth for a tooth") were abolished by the Savior as foreign to his nature. (3) Typical or symbolical ceremonies (such as sabbath, fasting, circumcision, sacrifice) were transformed by the Savior from material and bodily ordinances into spiritual realities (abstaining from evil, circumcising the heart, praise and thanksgiving).[24] Ptolemy's approach provided a theoretical basis for what the church was in practice doing. Part of the law was still valid, part had been abolished, and part had been spiritually transformed. Ptolemy's solu-

---

23. Translation from ANF, vol. 3.
24. Preserved in Epiphanius, *Heresies* 33.3–7.

tion, however, did not commend itself to the great church. The fact that Ptolemy was a Gnostic and made a distinction between the Creator God and the Father of the Savior prejudiced the church against any proposal he offered.

Many Jewish Christians, considering the law still binding, held to a rather opposite evaluation of much of the ritual law to that of Gnostics. Those known as Ebionites impressed Gentile members of the church with their adherence to the law. Irenaeus says of them: "They use the Gospel according to Matthew only, and repudiate the apostle Paul, maintaining that he was an apostate from the law. As to the prophetic writings, they endeavor to expound them in a peculiar manner. They practice circumcision, persevere in the observance of those customs that are enjoined by the law, and are so Judaic in their style of life, that they even adore Jerusalem as if it were the house of God."[25]

The Ebionites sought to bind the law on Gentile converts and themselves attempted to be both Jews and Christians. Eusebius says of them, "Like the Jews they used to observe the sabbath and the rest of the Jewish ceremonial, but on Sundays they celebrated rites like ours in commemoration of the Savior's resurrection."[26] Eusebius's language represents the attitude of most Gentile Christians that the Ebionites were "they," not part of "us."

The Ebionites made distinctions in the biblical documents that had come down to them. They advanced the theory that "false pericopes" had been introduced into the scriptures.[27] They claimed the following: "The scriptures have had joined to them many falsehoods against God on this account. The prophet Moses having by the order of God delivered the law, with the explanations, to certain chosen men, some seventy in number, in order that they also might instruct such of the people as chose, after a little the written law had added to it certain falsehoods contrary to the law of God."[28]

By this position they could maintain their loyalty to the Mosaic covenant and yet reject large parts of the law. Jesus as the True Prophet,

25. Irenaeus, *Against Heresies* 1.26.2.

26. *H.E.* 3.27.5.

27. This is a feature of the *Kerygmata Petrou*, one of the sources of the *Grundschrift* behind the Pseudo-Clementine writings; see Schoeps, *Theologie und Geschichte des Judenchristentums*, 147ff.; and Strecker, *Das Judenchristentum in den Pseudo-Klementinen*, 226. Strecker identifies Pseudo-Clement, *Homilies* 3.39, 43–56, dealing with the false pericopes, as belonging to this source, which he dates c. 200.

28. Pseudo-Clement, *Homilies* 2.38; cf. 3.47–48. Translation from ANF, vol. 8.

according to the Ebionites, had restored the true law of God, rejecting the sacrifices, the monarchy, and false prophecy.[29] Jesus' mission had been especially to annul the sacrifical system.[30] Forgiveness was now obtained through daily immersion baths.[31]

Moses and Jesus really taught the same things, according to these Jewish Christians: "For there being one teaching by both, God accepts him who has believed either of these. But believing a teacher is for the sake of doing the things spoken by God."[32] And again:

> Neither, therefore, are the Hebrews condemned on account of their ignorance of Jesus . . . if doing the things commanded by Moses, they do not hate him whom they do not know. Neither are those from among the Gentiles condemned, who know not Moses . . . provided that these also, doing the things spoken by Jesus, do not hate him whom they do not know.[33]

Some of the Ebionites, therefore, seem to have approximated the view that there is one covenant through Moses for Jews and another through Jesus for Gentiles. Both are essentially similar in content with regard to moral duties, the doing of which is the important consideration. Such speculation has been picked up again in the ecumenical twentieth century,[34] but in the early centuries of the Common Era did not have an opportunity to flourish.

Not only Ptolemy and the Ebionites, from their quite opposite premises, wanted to make distinctions in the law. Within the mainstream of Christian orthodoxy the Syriac *Didascalia* in the third century also was concerned with what parts of the Pentateuch were applicable to Christians. The author addressed a community in close contact with Jews and was perhaps himself of Jewish background. His approach drew on earlier Christian interpretations but with an original result. The moral law (the Ten Commandments) is eternal, but the ceremonial law (the "Deuterosis" or second law) was temporary (chap. 26). "For the first Law is that which the Lord God spoke before the people had made the calf and served idols, which consists of the Ten Words and the Judgements. But after they had

29. Pseudo-Clement, *Homilies* 3.52.

30. Pseudo-Clement, *Recognitions* 1.35ff.

31. Cf. *Barnabas* 11.

32. Pseudo-Clement, *Homilies* 8.6.

33. Ibid., 8.7.

34. See Schoeps, *Theologie und Geschichte*; Schoeps, *Jewish Christianity*; and works cited in notes 2 and 4.

served idols, He justly laid upon them the bonds, as they were worthy. But do not thou therefore lay them upon thee (the Christian); for our Savior came for no other cause but to fulfill the Law, and to set us loose from the bonds of the Second Legislation" (chap. 2).[35]

Among the things abolished were the sacrifices, distinctions of meat, washings, and circumcision. Although the sabbath was part of the Ten Commandments, it too was treated as part of the Second Legislation that had been replaced, so the author did not carry through his distinction with full consistency.

The views surveyed above are interesting but did not make much use of the word covenant. Where the sense of proximity to Judaism was strong, as with the Ebionites, or where the sense of alienation was strong, as with Marcion and the Gnostics, covenant was not an important word: in the former case probably because it was assumed and in the latter case because it was part of an alien tradition. Covenant was an important concept where Christians wanted to maintain both a significant continuity and a significant discontinuity with their Jewish heritage. The view which came to prevail in Christianity, although with significantly different nuances in different thinkers at different times and places, was in terms of an old and a new covenant.

Irenaeus, bishop of Lyon in Gaul at the latter part of the second century, elaborated the thinking of Justin concerning successive covenants. Irenaeus combated the Gnostic distinction between the creator God and the redeemer God by insisting that it was one and the same God who had administered his saving plan through successive covenants. He did not have the same anti-Jewish concerns as Justin, but he built on Justin's distinction between dispensations of God's dealing with human beings to explain the differences between the old and the new. These covenants were historical and valid in their own time, but God's dispensations now found their consummation in the covenant mediated through Jesus Christ. There were similarities in emphasis and content between the covenants because the same God was at work in both.

Irenaeus recognized that the Bible spoke of several covenants initiated by God,[36] but his common scheme of interpretation worked with two covenants, one of Moses and one of Jesus. He made the association, now familiar to Christians, of the Mosaic covenant with law and the covenant

---

35. Trans. by Connolly, *Didascalia Apostolorum*, 14. The view that the ceremonial law was imposed on the Jews as a punishment is found also in Justin, *Dial.* 18.2; 27.2; cf. 67.8 for the connection with idolatry.

36. *Against Heresies* 1.10.3; 3.11.8.

of Jesus with gospel: "Now those things new and old which are brought forth from his treasure certainly mean two covenants. The old would be the previous giving of the law; and the new points out that manner of life according to the gospel."[37]

Irenaeus's principal discussion of the covenants comes in *Against Heresies* 4.32–34, where he appeals to the teaching of a presbyter before him. This presbyter said, "All the apostles taught that there were two covenants for the two peoples but one and the same God."[38] The former testament served the following purposes: "It subdues those to whom it was given to the service of God for their good . . . exhibited a type of heavenly things . . . prefigured the things which are now in the church . . . and contained a prophecy of future things."[39]

Among those prophecies in the former covenant, accompanied by a new heart and new spirit and the bringing of liberty.[40] Those who examine the Prophets and the Gospels, he affirms, will find a correspondence. Irenaeus used the illustration of messengers announcing beforehand the coming of a King who does exactly what the messengers said he would do. "When the King has actually come, and those who are his subjects have been filled with that joy which was proclaimed beforehand, and have obtained that liberty which he gives, have shared in the sight of him, have listened to his words, and have enjoyed the gifts that he bestows, the question will not then be asked by any of good sense what new thing the King brought beyond what was proclaimed by those who announced his coming. For he has brought himself."[41]

Irenaeus emphasized that the new covenant is a "covenant of liberty,"[42] a characteristic theme with him. Irenaeus responded to the interpretation that the new covenant had to do with the restoration of Israel from Babylonian captivity under Zerubbabel by saying that the Mosaic law continued to be observed, but only after the coming of Jesus and the sending of his apostles did a new law of liberty go forth and bring in a reign of peace among the Gentiles who accepted it.[43]

37. Ibid., 4.9.1.

38. Ibid., 4.32.2.

39. Ibid.

40. Ibid., 4.33.14.

41. Ibid., 4.34.1.

42. Ibid., 4.34.3.

43. Ibid., 4.34.4.

In summary, Irenaeus thought primarily in terms of two successive covenants, one for Jews and one adapted to all people. Both were foreshadowed in Abraham, who received the covenant of circumcision but who was also justified by faith before he was circumcised.[44] The Gentiles who accept the new covenant have no need of the law,[45] which ended with the preaching of John. Both covenants were adapted to the level of human maturity at the time,[46] yet in their highest and best laws they are in agreement, namely that one should love God and love one's neighbor.[47]

To return to Justin Martyr: he wrote at a time when the church had become predominantly Gentile in membership. Nevertheless, there was a sizable number of Christian Jews, especially in the land of Israel and surrounding regions. Some Jewish converts to Christianity had given up their Jewish identity and accommodated themselves to a Gentile church. The many who did not take this course of action occupied an ambivalent position in relation to the two faiths. Those called later the Ebionites, who simply added faith in Jesus to their Jewish style of life, were treated as heretics by the Gentile Christians (so Irenaeus). On the other side, the Jews excluded from the synagogues and treated as apostates those of their people who confessed Jesus as the Messsiah. Justin was more sensitive to the dilemma of Jewish Christians than most, and he allowed for a middle ground, soon to be lost as both sides asked for all or nothing at all. Justin noted, perhaps with some exaggeration, that "daily some (Jews) are becoming disciples in the name of Christ."[48] This may be what provoked the Jews, as he states, to "curse in your synagogues all those who are called . . . Christians"[49] and to send messengers throughout the world to warn against teachings about Jesus.[50] Yet Justin was magnanimous enough to say, "You are our brethren,"[51] and to affirm that Christians pray for God to have mercy on the Jews.[52]

It is especially interesting, I think, to note what Justin says about the two kinds of Jewish believers in Jesus and the two attitudes taken by

44. Ibid., 4.25.1.

45. Ibid., 4.4.2; *Proof* 93–96.

46. *Against Heresies* 3.12.11; 4.38.1.

47. Ibid., 4.13.3.

48. *Dial.* 39.

49. Ibid., 96.

50. Ibid., 108.

51. Ibid., 96.

52. Ibid., 96; 108.

Gentile believers toward Jews.[53] (1) There were Jewish Christians who insisted on converted Gentiles keeping the law, and (2) there were Jewish Christians who themselves kept the law but did not insist on Gentiles doing so. On the other side, (1) there were Gentile Christians who insisted that Jewish believers give up the law, and (2) there were Gentile Christians who said to let Jewish Christians continue to keep the law. Justin identified himself with this attitude. This important passage should be read in its context in the *Dialogue*.

> And Trypho again inquired, "But if someone, knowing that this is so, after he recognizes that this man is Christ, and has believed in and obeys him, wishes, however, to observe these ordinances, will he be saved?"
>
> I said, "In my opinion, Trypho, such a one will be saved, if he does not strive in every way to persuade other men—I mean those Gentiles who have been circumcised from error by Christ—to observe the same things as himself, telling them that they will not be saved unless they do . . ."
>
> Then (Trypho) replied, "Why then have you said, 'In my opinion, such a one will be saved,' unless there are some who affirm that such will not be saved?"
>
> "There are such people, Trypho," I answered; "and these do not venture to have any intercourse with or to extend hospitality to such persons; but I do not agree with them. But if some, through weak-mindedness, wish to observe such institutions as were given by Moses, from which they expect some virtue, . . . yet choose to live with the Christians and the faithful, as I said before, not inducing them either to be circumcised like themselves, or to keep the sabbath, or to observe any other such ceremonies, then I hold that we ought to join ourselves to such, and associate with them in all things as kinsmen and brethren. But if, Trypho," I continued, "some of your race, who say they believe in this Christ, compel those Gentiles who believe in this Christ to live in all respects according to the law given by Moses, or choose not to associate so intimately with them, I in like manner do not approve of them. But I believe that even those, who have been persuaded by them to observe the legal dispensation along with their confession of God in Christ, shall probably be saved. And I hold, further, that such as have confessed and known this man to be Christ, yet who have gone back from some cause to the legal dispensation, and have

53. Cf. the slightly different analysis of attitudes by Strecker "On the Problem of Jewish Christianity," 273–74.

denied that this man is Christ, and have not repented before death, shall by no means be saved. Further, I hold that those of the seed of Abraham who live according to the law, and do not believe in this Christ before death, shall likewise not be saved, and especially those who have anathematized this very Christ in the synagogues." (*Dial.* 47)

Justin does not state his view very kindly, but it was a view which would have allowed for a bridge between Jews and Christians. That bridge or middle ground, to my knowledge, has seldom existed, and almost never been tolerated. Justin's view was, I suspect, a minority view even when expressed.

Christian Jews feel themselves rejected on both sides: when they believe in Jesus, they are not accepted any more by Jews; when they live as Jews, they are not accepted by Gentile believers. Yet their very existence would encourage dialogue and perhaps promote mutual understanding. As a noticeable number of such Christian Jews emerge in our own time, they are in need of a special measure of understanding and encouragement, for a special responsibility rests on them. Perhaps they can help us all to a better understanding of what is involved in the covenant and in being a covenantal people.

16

Canon Muratori
Date and Provenance

A LBERT C. SUNDBERG JR. used the Third International Congress on New Testament Studies at Oxford in 1965 to offer a "Revised History of the New Testament Canon."[1] Subsequently he published a major attack on the early date of the *Canon Muratori* in the *Harvard Theological Review*.[2] The scholarly community can be grateful for his collection of evidence, from which, however, it is possible to draw a conclusion quite different from Sundberg's conclusions. The following examination follows the arguments of the article in the *Harvard Theological Review*.

I wish, first, to make a general observation: Even if the argument for a fourth-century date and eastern (Palestinian or Syrian) provenance for the *Canon Muratori* should be sustained, a major revision of the understanding of the history of the canon would not be required. The evidence for the church having a collection of books (although with the limits not precisely defined) by the end of the second century does not depend on this document and is well established from the writings of Irenaeus, Tertullian, and

1. Sundberg, "Revised History."

2. Sundberg, "Canon Muratori." Page numbers in the text refer to this article. Major support for the fourth-century date in the east comes from Hahneman, *The Muratorian Fragment and the Development of the Canon*; my review in *JTS* is the next item in this collection, 223–30. Rejections of Hahneman's position by Henne, "La Datation du Canon de Muratori"; Hill, "The Debate over the Muratorian Fragment and the Development of the Canon"; and Verheyden, "The Canon Muratori."

others apart from its existence.[3] What would be lacking is evidence that someone had attempted to reduce that collection to a list.

I agree that the *Canon Muratori* was not written from Rome (p. 6), but the language about Rome (*ll.* 74–76) does suggest a place where Rome was important and the situation there well known and thus a place with close connections with Rome. When the author says, "we receive" (*ll.* 72, 82), he purports to speak for "the catholic church," not one community.

Sundberg argues that "very recently in our own times" (*l.* 74) in reference to the date of the *Shepherd* of Hermas may be translated "most recently in our time" (that is in the church's time and not in apostolic time) (p. 11). The author of the *Canon*, therefore, contrasted "our times" with "apostolic times" in order to show that the *Shepherd* was late and not authoritative. Sundberg claims this only as a possible interpretation in order to open up the consideration of a later date for the composition of the work. It must be granted that this may be a correct understanding, but this meaning is still compatible with a second-century as well as with a later date. Even if the possibility is granted, this is not the most natural meaning of the author's statement.

When Irenaeus spoke of the Apocalypse, which was seen "almost in our own generation," he said something more specific, his own lifetime.[4] Irenaeus says "almost"; his point was to bring it near his own lifetime and not to deny it to apostolic times, as a contrast between apostolic times and subsequent times would demand. He was not trying to make a point about the lateness of the Apocalypse. If the words "our times" and "our generation" are indeed parallel, then the Irenaeus passage argues against Sundberg by unequivocally putting Hermas in the lifetime of the author of the *Canon*. Indeed, that is the natural way to take the fragment: it would normally be understood as "our generation," not "our Christian times." Christians certainly distinguished apostolic from post-apostolic times, but "our times" was not the usual way to speak of post-apostolic times. Although the author of the *Canon* does not make the charge of heresy, his terminology is parallel to the point Tertullian (and others) repeatedly made that lateness was sufficient basis for rejecting a teaching which purported to be apostolic but was not.[5]

---

3. Von Campenhausen, *Formation of the Christian Bible*.

4. ἐπὶ τῆς ἡμετέρας—Irenaeus, *Adv. Haer.* V.30.3 (=Eusebius, *H.E.* V.8.6); the same in *1 Clement* 5. Eusebius, *H.E.* III.32.8 confirms the meaning "lifetime"; the Anonymous Anti-Montanist in *H.E.* V.16.22 uses "in our times" to mean lifetime.

5. *Praesc.* 30–31; *Adv. Marc.* IV.5.

These are preliminary considerations. Sundberg's other arguments are the substantive case, but they are no more conclusive and by-pass serious obstacles to his proposal. In general it may be said that if the *Canon Muratori* was written early, there still is no surprise that it agrees with views found in the fourth century, for there was much continuity. To turn his observations on pages 11f. around: What must be done is to show that the document agrees with views which could only have arisen in the fourth century. Absence of earlier evidence is not conclusive by itself. Although the case is not definitive, the affinities are stronger with the west about 200 than they are with the east about 350.

Arguments from the language employed in the Muratorian Fragment have limited value. Since the *Canon Muratori* is generally recognized to be translated from a Greek original,[6] considerations based on the Latin can take us back only to the date of the translation. The examples cited by Sundberg from Donaldson (p. 12) are unfortunate for his case. *Disciplina* in the sense of "rule of life" in the church is common in Tertullian.[7] The same purpose behind the writing of the pastoral epistles stated by the Muratorian canon ("for the ordering of ecclesiastical discipline"—*ll.* 62–63) is also expressed by Tertullian (*Adv. Marc.* V.21).[8] The reference to the bishop's chair (*ll.* 75–76) finds a counterpart in Irenaeus' conception of the office: "the chair is the symbol of teaching" (*Demonstration* 2).

The statement about the *Shepherd* of Hermas by the author of the Muratorian canon is important for determining the date of both, but the date of the *Shepherd* is not a concern here.[9] The approval which Irenaeus gave to the work and Clement of Alexandria's regard for it as inspired (pp. 12–13) could be the very use against which the *Canon Muratori* was

---

6. Exceptions are von Harnack, "Über den Verfasser und den literarischen Charakter des Muratorischen Fragments," 1–2; and Ehrhardt, "The Gospels in the Muratorian Fragment," 1–2. If the original was Latin, the provenance is already determined; but I accept a Greek original. If the date is late, then the document originated in the east; but if it was early, Greek was possible in either the east or west.

7. *Praesc.* 36; 44; *Or.* passim; cf. *Virg. vel.* 16.

8. This description of the Pastorals seems characteristic of the west—Zahn, *Geschichte des Neutestamentlichen Kanons*, II.1:77 cites Ambrosiaster and the prologues in Codex Amiatinus.

9. A late document, even polemically inspired, could contain correct information about Hermas, and an early writing could be mistaken. The solution to the problem of dating posed by the *Shepherd* seems to be that it is a composite of material over the career of the prophet Hermas or that it was compiled from material over a period of time. Multiple authorship is advocated by Giet, *Hermas et les pasteurs*; and W. Coleborne, "The Shepherd of Hermas"; but it is rejected by Joly, "Hermas et le pasteur."

protesting, or alternatively the very kind of private use which the author approved (*ll.* 73–80). At any rate, the attitude toward the Shepherd is not anomalous for the time around 200. Tertullian at first accepted the *Shepherd* (*Or.* 16) and then rejected it (*De pud.* 10, 20). Although Tertullian's sympathies with Montanism accounts for his change of attitude toward the *Shepherd*, anti-Montanism has little bearing on the attitude of the *Canon Muratori*, for it distinctly approves of Hermas' orthodoxy. Moreover, controversialists do not reject everything their opponents say or accept every position of their allies. There were councils on the provincial level in the later part of the second century, so there is no need to reject out of hand Tertullian's statement that councils of the orthodox rejected the *Shepherd* (*De pud.* 10). That may be the very basis on which *Canon Muratori* says, "It cannot to the end of time be read publicly in the church to the people" (*ll.* 77–80).

Eusebius was not the turning point in regard to the *Shepherd*'s acceptance in the church. His statements are in a historical context[10]; he was reporting a situation which we know goes back at least to the time of Tertullian. The *Canon Muratori* represents the view of those whom Eusebius reports as rejecting (the public reading of?) the *Shepherd* but finding it valuable for elementary instruction. It is notable that the support for the *Shepherd* was mainly in the east (p. 13 n. 39): it was contained in the Codex Sinaiticus, and such was Jerome's testimony (p. 14 n. 46). The opposition was mainly in the west (Tertullian, Jerome), and it was in the west where the *Shepherd* was put in the Old Testament apocrypha (p. 15 n. 48).

The position of the Wisdom of Solomon in the *Canon Muratori* is sufficiently anomalous to be problematic for any view. One of Sundberg's stronger points is calling attention to Epiphanius' inclusion of Wisdom in his New Testament and Eusebius' mention of Irenaeus' quotations of the book in discussing his New Testament (pp. 17–18). Although Sundberg claims that the Jamnia list of the Old Testament canon[11] was not a live issue in the east until the time of Athanasius, the similarity of that Jewish canon to the one reported by Melito shows it was known in the east (pp. 16f.) from the second century, and the debate between Origen and Julius Africanus in the third century over the apocrypha may reflect such an issue a century before Athanasius.[12] If Eusebius' report (*H.E.* V.8.1–8) on

10. *H.E.* III.3.6f.; III.25.4; V.8.7.

11. If there was such a thing—see Lewis, "What Do We Mean by Jabneh?"

12. Julius Africanus, *Ep. ad Or.* 1 affirms, "All the books of the Old Testament have been translated from Hebrew into Greek." Origen, *Ep. ad Af.* 1–5 defends what was in the Greek but not in the Hebrew; cf. 13 on Tobit and Judith not used by the Jews.

Irenaeus carries any weight and is not accidental in its positioning, then the New Testament canon of the Muratorian fragment has a parallel in the west before 200. Although Wisdom had its greatest popularity in the east, specifically Alexandria,[13] it was known and used in the west quite early— Hebrews 1:3; *1 Clement* 3:4; 7:5; 27:5. Tertullian quotes it as Solomon's (*Praesc.*7; *Adv. Val.* 2) and so presumably as authoritative, but we cannot tell whether he would have put it in his Old or his New Testament.

Sundberg next devotes much attention to the status of the Apocalypse of John (pp. 18–26). He concludes that the Apocalypse was on the fringe of the Muratorian canon, because it is joined to the *Apocalypse of Peter* as the last of the accepted books. This is not persuasive at all. In a list something has to be last, and being last does not imply doubt or lateness of acceptance. The apocalypses are put together (*ll.* 71–73), and it may have seemed fitting to conclude with them. That some did not want the *Apocalypse of Peter* read in church (*ll.* 72, 73) says nothing about the Apocalypse of John. Since the serious questioning of the Apocalypse was in the east, it is important to Sundberg's case to throw doubt on the canonical status of the Apocalypse in the Muratorian fragment. In this he is unsuccessful. That the Apocalypse is on a level with Paul is incontrovertible (*ll.* 48–50, 55–58). Outside of Gaius of Rome, the western acceptance of the Apocalypse was complete. Of course, not everyone in the east rejected the Apocalypse, so the attitude toward this book is not sufficient by itself to place the Canon Muratori, but its treatment of the Apocalypse agrees better with the attitudes of the west than with those of the east. This is pointedly shown in the declaration that writing to seven churches meant speaking to all the churches (*ll.* 57–58). Tertullian has the same statement (*Adv. Marc.* V.17). All of Sundberg's references to this idea (p. 19 n. 60) are western (after Tertullian, there were Cyprian, Victorinus, and Jerome).

The *Apolcalypse of Peter* was better known in the east, so the case for an eastern origin of the *Canon Muratori* is helped by its reference to this work. Nevertheless, the work was known in the west, and its attestation in general is so meagre that it does not afford a strong argument one way or the other. Eusebius is supposed to provide the closest parallel (pp. 28–29) to the situation reflected in the *Canon Muratori,* yet he comes down on the negative side of this question whereas the Canon comes down on the positive side.

The lack of other lists of the New Testament writings before the fourth century is the strongest argument against an earlier date for the

---

13. Grant, "The Book of Wisdom at Alexandria."

Canon Muratori. Nevertheless, that remains an argument from silence. Something had to be first, and this may be it. There is no inherent reason why a list could not have been drawn up around 200. As noted above, the evidence for the concept of a collection of New Testament books by the end on the second century is quite firm. There is no reason why someone should not have undertaken to summarize the situation in list form. Sundberg sees Eusebius as the critical figure (pp. 34–35), and he may have had some influence on the flurry of lists which began to appear in the fourth century, if he was not simply reflecting a general concern. But it should be noted that Eusebius essentially repeats the views which he attributes to Origen. There seems to be no great development in the situation on the canon from c. 200 until the fourth century; the only difference is that Eusebius sought to reduce Origen's data to list form.

If Eusebius is the closest parallel to the *Canon Muratori*, that circumstance itself would throw us back to the time of Origen for the contents and attitudes of the *Canon Muratori*. And so we once more confront the matter of a list as the only thing which distinguishes the *Canon Muratori* from the situation at the beginning of the third century. Each person must decide how much of a novelty a list was[14] and how much weight to put on the absence of lists before the fourth century.

Not only are the arguments for a fourth-centruy eastern setting so tenuous as to fail to carry conviction, but other considerations point strongly to an earlier western setting. The major consideration arguing for a western provenance is the absence of Hebrews from the canon. Sundberg's discussion of the preservation of eastern lists in western manuscripts (pp. 38–41) is a clever by-pass of the problem for his theory posed by the fact that the west early rejected Hebrews whereas the east (Clement of Alexandria, Origen, etc.) accepted it.[15] The theory that the list originated in the east and was copied in the west in order to resist pressure to include Hebrews in the New Testament still does not account for the silence on Hebrews in an eastern list; indeed the later the date the more problematical the very silence becomes. Is there anything comparable in an eastern list of the fourth century?

It may have been observed how many parallels have already been noted between the Canon Muratori and early western authors. Several incidental features fit the second century and the west. The heresies mentioned are those of the second century: Marcion, Gnostics (Basilides and

---

14. Marcion's "canon" probably was not a list but a collection of documents.

15. Cf. Westcott, *A General Survey*, 367–68, 376, 380.

Valentinus), and Montanists (*ll.* 63–67, 81–85). The name Cataphrygians for the Montanists is first attested in Pseudo-Tertullian, *Haereses* 7 (21). Its introduction here may be due to the Latin translator. The earliest Greek sources employ "Phrygians."[16] "Kataphrygians" appears first in surviving Greek sources in Cyril of Jerusalem (*Catecheses* XVI.8). The composition of summaries of the apostolic message (*ll.* 20–25)—canon of truth or rule of faith—was characteristic of the second century.[17] The two advents, the first in humility and the second in royal power (*ll.* 24–25), is a feature of the second century.[18] Varying but similar accounts of the occasion for the writing of the Fourth Gospel (*ll.* 9–10) arose in the second century, perhaps in response to the challenge from the Alogi.[19]

The classification of the two categories of reading in the church as "prophets" and "apostles" has its counterpart in Justin's account of a Christian assembly in Rome (*Apol.* I.67). The association of Luke with Paul was commonly expanded to include a connection of the Gospel of Luke with Paul's authority (*ll.* 3–6).[20] The reference to a Marcionite "Epistle to the Laodiceans" (*l.* 64), if a mistake for the Marcionite Ephesians (Tertullian, *Adv. Marc.* V.17), is an argument for an early date, since later this usage would more readily be known. If the author mistook it for the Latin Epistle to the Laodiceans,[21] then there is another argument for a western origin of the *Canon Muratori*, although the Latin Laodiceans is usually given a much later date.[22]

---

16. Clement of Alexandria, *Strom.* IV.3; VII.17; Hippolytus, *Ref.* X.25; Anonymous in Eusebius, *H.E.* V.16.22. "Cataphrygians" in Latin derives from an earlier Greek phrase, "the heresy according to the Phrygians."

17. Ignatius, *Trall.* 9; Justin, *Apol.* 1, 31.7; Aristides, *Apol.* 2 (Syriac); Irenaeus, *Adv. Haer.* I.10; Hippolytus, *C. Noet.* 1; *Apos. Trad.* xxi; Tertullian, *Praesc.* 13; *Virg. vel.* 1; *Adv. Prax.* 2, Cf. A. Ehrhardt, "The Gospels in the Muratorian Fragment," 25, for the comment that this passage follows the Roman *regula fidei*.

18. Justin, *Dial.* 32–33; 52; 110–11; cf. Tertullian, *Apol.* 21; *Adv. Iud.* 24.

19. Clement of Alexandria in Eusebius, *H.E.* VI.14; the Anti-Marcionite Gospel Prologues; cf. Victorinus, *Comm. in Apoc.* 11:1; Jerome, *Vir. ill.* 9; *Praef. Comm. in Mt.*

20. Tertullian, *Adv. Marc.* IV.5; cf. Irenaeus, *Adv. Haer.* III.1.1; 14:1; 10.1; Ambrosiaster on Col. 4:4; Jerome, *Vir. ill.* 7; John Chrysostom on 2 Tim 4:11.

21. As Zahn thought, *Geschichte des Neutestamentlichen Kanons*, 85–88.

22. It survives only in Latin and derivative western vernaculars. The earliest unambiguous external attestation is Ps.-Augustine, *De divinis scripturis* (fifth or sixth century), and the earliest manuscript is sixth century. But the work could have been composed from the second to fourth century—Hennecke, *New Testament Apocrypha*, vol. 2 (1965) 128–31, (1992) 42–46.

There is much that remains unclear and little that is conclusive, but the evidence is such that in the present state of knowledge there is little to support and much to call into question regarding Sundberg's proposed revision in dating the Canon Muratori.[23]

23. A recent study by Armstrong, "Victorinus of Pettau as the Author of the Canon Muratori," argues for authorship by Victorinus in the third century.

17

The Muratorian Fragment and the Canon

A Review of Hahneman

G. M. Hahneman provides the most thorough study of the Muratorian Fragment available.[1] Barring unlikely new discoveries, we have before us an examination of everything relevant to the study of the Muratorian Fragment. Apart from the dispute over the date and provenance of the Fragment, his book will be the standard point of reference for future studies because of the valuable collection of source material.

A better case is made for the fourth-century eastern provenance of the Muratorian Canon than was made by A. C. Sundberg. My response to him anticipated most of the concerns.[2] In part because of the fullness of the study, but also because of the plausible argumentation, the number of converts to the later dating will no doubt grow. Nevertheless, some cautions are still in order. The reader is put on guard on page 1, where the traditional history of the canon is said to be based on the Peshitta and the Muratorian Fragment, and reference is made to B. F. Westcott, *A General Survey of the History of the Canon of the New Testament*. Westcott, in fact,

1. Hahneman, *The Muratorian Fragment and the Development of the Canon*.
2. Ferguson, "Canon Muratori: Date and Provenance," chap. 16 above.

treated the Latin version as the western counterpart of the Peshitta[3] and says of the Muratorian Fragment that it "adds but little to what has already obtained in detail from separate sources."[4]

There are occasional inconsistencies in the argument and, by the nature of the evidence, the case is circumstantial and not conclusive. In order to move beyond circumstantial evidence to proof there must be in the contents of the Fragment something only possible in the fourth century or something impossible in the second century. Despite Hahneman's effort, neither has been shown to be the case.

The first chapter deals with the manuscript itself and preliminary matters of provenance and authorship. The orthography need not prove, but the vocabulary conceivably would, a late fourth-century origin for the Latin. The dates of the other works in the codex are an argument only for the Latin version. If the Fragment is a translation from Greek, there is nothing conclusive here about the date of the original.

The second chapter gets into the heart of the argument by dealing with the statements about Hermas' *Shepherd*. Hahneman's contention is that all the information about Hermas is mistaken or garbled. The net result would be that a fourth-century author has posed as a near contemporary in order to discredit the *Shepherd*. Yet this is the only place that the implied pseudonymity occurs. Since the author approves of the private use of the *Shepherd*, the issue does not seem so crucial as to justify a pseudonymous posture here but nowhere else. The pseudonymity would seem to be of doubtful value in a polemic against the *Shepherd* in the fourth century. Hahneman does not deal with the difficulty of accounting for the posture of pseudonymity.

The problems Hahneman raises about the date posited by the Fragment for the *Shepherd* are easily explained. Monepiscopacy was not attained everywhere at the same time; a long career by Hermas is possible. The *Shepherd* gives many indications of being a composite work, if not of composite authorship; the date of the materials is not necessarily the date of final writing, editing, or redacting. The reference in Hippolytus to a *Book of Elchasai* (p. 38) is to that, not to the *Shepherd*. A knowledge of the Greek of Romans 15 was indeed "likely" (contra p. 49) in the West at the end of the second century. The spelling *Spania* occurs before Paul in Diodore of Sicily 5.37.2 and 1 Macc 8:3, and is the spelling in the *Acts of Peter* (Vercelli Acts) 1 and 6. Tertullian, who knew Greek, quotes Romans

---

3. Wescott, *A General Survey*, 239.

4. Ibid., 215.

15:24 as from Paul (*Fuga* 9.1). If the *Shepherd* was "almost unknown in the West" in the fourth century (Jerome, p. 68), this was more likely due to an earlier pronouncement (such as in the Muratorian Fragment) than to the Catholic Church accepting the Montanist protest against it. The work was certainly highly regarded earlier, as the early Latin version (as well as Tertullian's statements) attests. That situation provides a much more plausible context for the Fragment's polemic than a fourth-century date. Would an argument from Hermas' connection with Pius of Rome have any force in fourth-century Palestine? If the information is incorrect, as Hahneman argues, the implied pseudonymity ("most recently in our own times") becomes even more unintelligible. The pseudonymity could be invented as well as the relationship to Pius. Of course even an early work could be mistaken.

A broader question than the dating of the Muratorian Fragment is the history of the development of the canon (chapter 3). There are several problems here, beginning straight away with the claim that it was the "third century and later" (p. 1) before Christians struggled with establishing their own canon of Jewish writings. That flies in the face of the evidence from Melito. Moreover, recent study (some probably not available at the time of writing the original thesis) puts the establishing of the Jewish canon prior to the Church's separation from the synagogue.[5] If the early church began with a relatively fixed (not to make a stronger claim) Bible (Old Testament), then the climate for delimiting their own scriptures was there early.

Sundberg and Hahneman do not go far enough in making distinctions. Between "scripture" and "closed canon" another stage needs to be inserted, "open canon." "Scripture" implies "canon," and "canon" implies "closed canon," but they are not the same. When the scripture principle is accepted, there will be a concern to identify which writings are authoritative. Commenting on, collecting, or even cataloguing does not necessarily imply that no other can be recognized. There is the stage, at least theoretically, when one acknowledges certain writings but does not rule out that there might be others not yet brought to one's attention or still under consideration. This intermediate stage of "open canon" may be reflected in the Muratiorian Fragment.

---

5. Beckwith, *The Old Testament Canon of the New Testament Church*; Ellis, *The Old Testament in Early Christianity*; earlier—Leiman, *The Canonization of Hebrew Scripture*; Freedman, "Canon of the Old Testament."

The references on p. 74 to the Old Testament show precisely the situation of a canon, but not a closed canon to which nothing else could be added. Hahneman's own statements about disputes among Jews (p. 76) show that there can be in principle a "closed canon" while the exact contents are disputed. Can one seriously claim that disputes among the Amoraim mean that the Jews did not have a closed canon in the age of the Talmud? Yet this is the kind of evidence being adduced for the absence of a Christian canon in the fourth century. That there was discussion in the fourth century does not mean that the Church "began fixing" (p. 83) an Old Testament canon only then. The reasoning applied to the Muratorian Fragment, if applied to the Old Testament, would mean that it was not "established" even in the fourth century.

Even a "catalogue" (p. 89) can be theoretically "open," especially when it includes names of works in dispute. Indeed, if "closed canon" is defined as rigidly as Hahneman does (p. 73), then one would not have to mention the rejection of other works, for everything else would be by definition automatically excluded. Thus, the mentioning of rejected works hardly indicates that the Muratorian Fragment is a "closed" canon. Rather, mentioning such works shows that there was still discussion, and some writings were being promoted or (more likely) there was the possibility of some confusion.

Hahneman takes as his point of departure for the study of the formation of the canon the work of Westcott at the end of the last century. He does not interact with more recent studies of the canon: Metzger makes the bibliography but was too late to be taken into account in the writing, and Bruce does not make the bibliography. Von Campenhausen, Farkas-falvy and Farmer, and Gamble were available and cannot be dismissed as representing a conservative bias on the history of the canon. Von Campen-hausen, on strictly critical principles, shows how the two-part Bible is the premise of Christian thought for Hippolytus, Tertullian, Clement, and Origen. Although the Muratorian Fragment plays an important part in his reconstruction, the case does not depend on it, for the evidence points to the time of Irenaeus when the general contours of the Christian Bible were drawn, although the limits were not yet sharply drawn (pp. 209, 232, 242). The same conclusion is reached by Metzger (p. 75) and Bruce (p. 177).

Hahneman tries to break the evidence on which other scholars have reached their conclusions by an atomizing approach. Let us follow him.

It is curious reasoning that other gospels would not have been composed if a Fourfold Gospel canon was established (p. 94). Their production did not stop in the fourth century. Irenaeus' remarks may be read in different ways, but it seems to me that the analogies he appeals to are not arguments for an innovation but are introduced because he has Four Gospels (if he had had more or less, he would have found some other fitting symbolism). That Marcion did not know other Gospels than Luke is an inference from silence, no more plausible than that he rejected other Gospels—in fact less so, given his claim that Paul was called to be an apostle because the others Judaized. Marcion may in fact be an indirect witness to an early formation of a Gospel collection (if not a Gospel canon). He includes Luke but not Acts. If he did not break the two volumes apart himself, then they were already separated, and this must have been early. I know of no external evidence of Luke and Acts transmitted together. Why and how were Luke and Acts separated if not to form a canon of Gospels?

Again, the reasoning that changes in the text indicate an absence of absolute authority is a modern assumption that does not match the early history of the transmission of authoritative texts (pagan, Jewish, or Christian). One could even say that because texts are authoritative, they can be handled freely (compare the New Testament use of the Old Testament). One could assume the knowledge of well known texts and play with the actual wording.

In order to break the testimony of Irenaeus to the Fourfold Gospel canon the author appeals to quotations by Origen and others to apocryphal gospels (pp. 100ff.), even against these writers' explicit testimony to the Fourfold Gospel canon (Origen in Eusebius, *H.E.* 6.25.3–4), as evidence that the Gospel canon was still open. Yet he disallows such quotations (comments are not collections, which are not catalogues, pp. 87ff.) of the Four as evidence of their canonical status. If comments do not indicate canonical status, how do they call in question the Fourfold Gospel canon? He cannot have it both ways. Indeed, why is it inconsistent with the Fourfold Gospel canon to use other gospels? To have a "canon" does not mean one stops reading anything else.

The same considerations apply to the reasoning about Paul. Later apocrypha are not an argument against an established Pauline canon. Was it not the authority of Paul's letters that provoked the attempts? Clement of Rome, Ignatius, and Polycarp already knew a Pauline collection, and for Polycarp that included the Pastorals (contra p. 117). It is a tremendous leap from one papyrus (P^{46}) to the conclusion "the Pastorals . . . were only added in the third century" (p. 115). Hahneman seems to think that a closed canon means an invariable order (p. 124). That strikes me as a novel idea. Rearranging the order does not affect canonicity or limits of the canon. (For instance, if we posit a Greek original for the Muratorian Fragment, the order of the Gospels in Clement, Origen, and Irenaeus once is not anomalous pp. 186–87.)

The information of the Catholic Epistles in the present condition of the Muratorian Fragment is an anomaly for any time and place, not only for the traditional date, but certainly is more plausible then than later.

The firm acceptance of Revelation by the Muratorian Fragment (p. 23 on its early acceptance in the East and "thoroughgoing rejection" in the late fourth century) ill accords with the proposed date and provenance.

What Hahneman (p. 129) calls "canon forming" in the fourth century (p. 129) I would call "canon settling." If Christians at the beginning of the fourth century did not know they had a canon, Diocletian thought they did. The Church did not have to wait until the fourth century to try to limit and combat writings used by heretics (p. 170). Indeed, the arguments used against a "canon" in some sense in the late second century, if consistently applied, would mean that there was not one in the fourth century. The situation Hahneman describes after the fourth century is not essentially different from that at Origen's time. The agreement of Eusebius with Origen shows that the position represented by Eusebius goes back a century earlier (the systematizing by categories may be due to Eusebius, but the result is the same as that reflected by Origen). One could as well take the evidence of "occasional continuing dispute" and "occasional appearance in a manuscript of an apocryphal writing" (p. 129) as evidence that the canon was not "closed" until the fifth century or later. If that seems implausible, by reversing the reasoning we have a canon at the end of the second century. The evidence of the anti-heretical or old Catholic Fathers (and the Letter of the Churches of Vienne and Lyons, not taken into account by Hahneman) to a "core" canon of the Four Gospels, the Pauline Epistles, Acts, varying Catholic Epistles, and either Hebrews or Revelation at the end of the second century still seems an accurate description of the data.

That brings us to Hahneman's discussion in chapter 4 of catalogues. He places the Muratorian Fragment firmly in the group of fourth-century Eastern catalogues. But to the great embarrassment of the argument, the principal characteristics identified for the fourth-century Eastern catalogues prove to be untrue for the Muratorian Fragment. The author attempts to account for the differences (pp. 180–82), but the fact of the matter is that, as the Fragment now stands, none of the characteristics applies: (a) the fourth-century lists associate a New Testament catalogue with the Old Testament; (b) the Gospels are numbered and often not named (only true for some lists); (c) Hebrews is nearly always included in the Corpus Paulinum. Pages 118ff. have the evidence ignored on pp. 25–26 for the early Western hesitancy about Hebrews that continued to the fourth century. The speculation on pp. 124–25 does not explain the anomaly of the omission of Hebrews on his hypothesis nor does the appeal to the fragmentary condition of the document escape the problem that the affinities are Western and the contents at home c. 200.

There is another crucial matter. Despite the claim "the Muratorian Fragment does not differ in form from the undisputed catalogues of the fourth century" (p. 180), it does not fit comfortably into these catalogues. There is a great difference. The catalogues of the fourth century are bare "lists." In spite of the author playing down the narrative element (p. 131), the Muratorian Fragment is considerably more than a list. It contains the kind of information on many of the works that one finds in the prologues to the Gospels and Epistles of Paul. In form it is not comparable to the fourth-century catalogues.

Moreover, the peculiarities of the Fragment (chapter 5)—including the *Apocalypse of Peter* and the Wisdom of Solomon, which General Epistles are included and which omitted, and which heretical books are condemned—are not exactly paralleled in the fourth century. The anomalies are so extensive as better to be explained by an earlier than a later date.

The name "canon" for lists of scriptures appears in the fourth century and is appropriate for the fourth-century catalogues, which are lists. There was an earlier name for the Christian scriptures. The title "New Covenant" was already established at the end of the second century (Clement, *Strom.* 5.6.38; 5.13.85; Tertullian, *Marc.* 4.1,6; *Prax.* 15; Origen, *Princ.* 4.1.0). These writers must have had a precise idea of what they meant when they gave a name to a collection of writings.

The affinities of the Muratorian Fragment with the late second-century West have not been explained away. Besides the substantive matters already noted, there are incidentals. (1) Only second- century heretics are mentioned. The fourth- and fifth-century anti-heretical writers, as Epiphanius and Theodoret, assuredly include second-century heretics (p. 29), but they continue their listing to their own time. Is there a late fourth-century listing of heretics that names only second-century figures? (2) The similarity to the Roman *regula fidei* fits the second-century West. [Ph. Henne argues that this biographical summary of Christ is unlike the dogmatic summaries.] Would any fourth-century Eastern source be content with such a simple summary of the career of Christ? (3) Luke's relation to Paul is described by a technical Latin term, *iuris studiosum*. This fact led Arnold Ehrhardt to contend for a Latin original for the document. (4) The designation of the two parts of scripture as the prophets and apostles is comparable to Justin, *1 Apology* 67.3.

We are all indebted to the author for his collection of material and earnest argumentation. The issue, however, is not clear cut, and the evidence is finely balanced. There needs to be caution exercised, moreover, about the framework in which this material is put.

18

Pseudepigraphy
Post-Canonical Letters

Given the frequency of pseudonymity in Greek and Jewish literature there is no reason a priori to exclude the possibility of pseudonymous writings in the New Testament canon. Especially is this so since recent studies make pseudepigraphy a broader category than forgery and identify many occasions, motives, and purposes, other than deliberate deception.[1] These studies, however, also remove the justification for pseudonymity based on the (inaccurate) claim that antiquity did not have a concept of intellectual property so pseudonymity would not be judged in the same way as in our times when copyright laws seek to protect literary ownership. The Greeks did have the concept of intellectual property and passed that concept on to Romans and Jews. Some forms of pseudonymity were acceptable, but some forms were not.[2]

1. Note the distinction by Wolfgang Speyer: Pseudepigraphon is a literary work which does not derive from the author to which the title, content, or transmission attributes it. Only where the writer's intention is to deceive is there forgery. *Die literarische Fälschung*, 13–14. Cf. the review by Brox, "Zum Problemstand in der Erforschung der altchristlichen Pseudepigraphie"; and his own book, *Falsche Verfasserangaben*, 81–99; Metzger, "Literary Forgeries and Canonical Pseudepigrapha"; Wilder, *Pseudonymity, the New Testament, and Deception*.

2. Note Brox's comment that in early Christianity literary falsification was neither self-evidently acceptable nor was it treated as a moral disaster, *Falsche Verfasserangaben*, 65, and his treatment on 65–79; Speyer, *Die literarische Fälschung*, 5–7, 111–51, 175.

This essay probes the practice of pseudonymity in non-canonical Christian letters of the second century. Here, as a historian and student of non-canonical literature, I have problems with claims of extensive pseudonymity in the New Testament. Before surveying the surviving Christian literature, the Greek and Jewish context needs to be considered.

Pseudonymity was widespread in the Greek world, especially in philosophical circles.[3] Notable even in antiquity was the Pythagorean pseudepigrapha, for the Neopythagoreans considered it proper to publish their treatises in the name of their founder rather than to take credit to themselves for the ideas they had learned.[4]

The period after 100 BC was a time of many pseudonymous letter collections; between Cicero and Hadrian was the flourishing time of pseudonymous letters.[5] We may take special note of *The Cynic Epistles*[6] including the *Epistles of Heraclitus*.[7] Most of these belong to the early empire,[8] but the "Epistles of Crates" may be second century, the "Epistles of Diogenes" 30–40 are probably second century, and one group of the Socratic epistles may be from around 200 or later.[9] Any pseudonymous letters in the collection ascribed to Apollonius of Tyana would belong to the second century, between the death of Apollonius at the end of the first century and the writing of his life by Philostratus, who used his letters, at the beginning of the third.[10] Outside philosophy are the 148 letters supposedly written by Phalaris (sixth century BC) but exposed by Richard Bentley as the work of a sophist, probably in the second century. There is sufficient indication, therefore, that the Greek convention of pseudonymous letters continued beyond its flourishing period throughout the period of interest for this paper. Moreover, even as rhetorical education included composition of fictitious speeches (what would so and so have said under certain circumstances),[11] so rhetoricians produced handbooks

---

3. Brox, *Falsche Verfasserangaben*, 46, observes that many forgeries occurred in the philosophical schools where it was important to show identity of doctrine with the sayings of the founder. The greatest extension of forgery was in letters, but not all were deceptions and fictions, since many were harmless school exercises in style.

4. Ibid., 73; Theslef, *An Introduction to the Pythagorean Writings*.

5. Sykutris, "Epistolographie," 212, 218.

6. Malherbe, *The Cynic Epistles*.

7. Attridge, *First-Century Cynicism*.

8. Ibid., 6, 12; Malherbe, *The Cynic Epistles*, 2.

9. Malherbe, ibid., 10, 16, 28–29.

10. New edition and commentary by Penella, *The Letters of Apollonius of Tyana*.

11. Marrou, *A History of Education in Antiquity*, 267–81; Clark, *Rhetoric in*

for the writing of different kinds of letters; and these continued to be written until the fourth century and later.[12]

Jewish literature presents a different situation. Very little survives between Josephus and the Mishnah. Pseudonymity found expression among Jews mainly in the production of apocalypses. At least two of these were nearly contemporary with Josephus—*2 Baruch* and *4 Ezra*[13]—and represent a different reaction to the destruction of the temple. Some of the legal rulings of the Mishnah and Tannaitic Midrash are formally pseudonymous, but other factors may be involved in the tradition than deliberate falsification. The letter form was not popular as a literary vehicle among Jews: the *Epistle of Jeremiah* and *Epistle of Aristeas* are earlier than our period of concern here. Until recently we had no Jewish letters, pseudonymous or otherwise, from the first and second centuries for comparison. We now have the Bar Kokhba letters, but they are genuine letters and had no literary pretensions.[14]

Since the letter was not a popular literary form in Judaism for religious teaching, the use of this medium in Christianity is nearer its use in the Greco-Roman world by philosophers, moralists, and rhetoricians.

Turning to Christian literature, we find that the second and third centuries were a time in which a rich apocryphal literature was produced. Apocryphal Acts especially flourished. The earliest are the Acts of John, of Peter, of Paul, of Andrew, and of Thomas, all except the last probably to be dated before 200. The apocryphal Acts may not strictly be pseudonymous, for the titles pertain to subject, not author. Nevertheless the *Acts of Paul* makes explicit what is perhaps intended by all; the manuscript ends with the statement "Acts of Paul by the Apostle."[15] This work is a special case also because there is external testimony concerning its composition. Tertullian relates,

> But if the writings which wrongly go under Paul's name claim Thecla's example as a license for women's teaching and baptizing, let them know that in Asia the presbyter who composed that writing, as if he were augmenting Paul's fame from his own

Greco-Roman Education, esp. 199–201, 213–28.

12. Malherbe, "Ancient Epistolary Theorists."

13. New translations in Charlesworth, ed., *The Old Testament Pseudepigrapha*, 1:525–59, 621–52. Other apocalypses perhaps of the same period are *2 Enoch* and *Apocalypse of Abraham*. These and others are also included in Charlesworth.

14. Yadin, *Bar Kokhba*, 124–253.

15. Speyer, *Die literarische Fälschung*, 211.

store, after being convicted, and confessing that he had done it
from love of Paul, was removed from his office. (*De bapt.* 17)

Since the *Acts of Paul* is orthodox in doctrine (Tertullian's objection
was only that it allowed a woman to teach and baptize), the only explanation for the presbyter's removal from office seems to be that the book was a
fraud, falsely bearing Paul's name.[16] The *Acts of Peter and the Twelve Apostles* (NHC VI, 1) from Nag Hammadi and *The Act of Peter* (BG 8502, 4)
from the Berlin Gnostic Codex add to the extensive Petrine apocrypha in
the second century. The former maintains a first-person apostolic standpoint throughout. The latter is perhaps related to the previously known
Acts of Peter. Indeed, whatever the pious motives, all the apocryphal Acts
are forgeries with frequent use of the first person singular for an apostle's
words and intentions, so that it is fair to say that the same impulse was
behind these productions as behind pseudonymity. Their popularity demonstrates an interest in early Christianity in this kind of writing: a desire
for additional information about famous figures in the church, an interest
in collecting and manufacturing traditions or stories, and the existence of
a market to read the resultant productions—the kind of setting in which
pseudonymous literature can flourish.

With the apocryphal Gospels the pseudonymity becomes more explicit and the situation thereby more problematic. We have preserved from
the second century an infancy Gospel (*Protevangelium of James*, which
supplements the sparse New Testament information on Mary), a sayings
Gospel (the Coptic *Gospel of Thomas*, to be distinguished from the infancy
Gospel of the same name, which itself contains traditions reaching back to
the second century), and a passion gospel (*Gospel of Peter*). We know the
names of many others.[17] The *Gospel of Peter* is the subject of a well-known
incident where doctrinal orthodoxy was determinative in acceptance.

> Another book has been composed by [Serapion of Antioch]
> *Concerning What Is Known as the Gospel of Peter*, which he has
> written refuting the false statements in it, because of certain
> in the community of Rhossus, who on the ground of the said
> writing turned aside into heterodox teachings . . . "For I myself,
> when I came among you, imagined that all of you clung to the
> true faith; and, without going through the Gospel put forward
> by them in the name of Peter, I said: If this is the only thing that
> seemingly causes captious feelings among you, let it be read. But

16. Guthrie, "Acts and Epistles in Apocryphal Writings," 330–34.

17. Hennecke, *New Testament Apocrypha*, vol. 1; 2nd ed. Schneemelcher.

> since I have now learned, from what has been told me, that their
> mind was lurking in some hole of heresy, I shall give diligence
> to come again to you . . . But we, brethren, . . . were enabled by
> others who studied this very Gospel, that is by the successors
> of those who began it, whom we call Docetists (for most of the
> ideas belong to their teaching)—using [the material supplied]
> by them, were enabled to go through it and discover that the
> most part indeed was in accordance with the true teaching of
> the Savior, but that some things were added." (Eusebius, *H.E.*
> VI.12.3–6)

Stuart Currie, in one of his virtuoso performances before the Seminar on the Development of Early Catholic Christianity,[18] noted the absence of episodic material from the ministry of Jesus in surviving second-century traditions, quite the opposite of the situation concerning the apostles' ministries in the various Acts. There continued to be interest, however, in expanding and collecting traditions about other phases of Jesus' career. These were increasingly difficult to promote in the face of the Four Gospel canon, already well established by the time of Irenaeus[19] and presumably Tatian.[20] Gnostic literature offers several works termed Gospels but all are of a different genre from the canonical Gospels (even John) and those apocryphal Gospels mentioned above. *The Gospel of Philip* (NHC II, 3) from Nag Hammadi and the *Gospel of Mary* from the Berlin Gnostic Codex (BG 8502,1) are so identified by colophons at the end. The title *Gospel of Truth* (NHC I, 3) is supplied from the work's opening words. The *Gospel of the Egyptians* (NHC III, 2, and IV, 2) is really a life of Seth.

Are these apocryphal Gospels pseudonymous? Some definitely are. An actual claim to be written by James (not further identified) is made by the *Protevangelium* 25 and by Thomas at the beginning of the *Gospel of Thomas*, and *Gospel of Peter* 14:60 (cf. 7:26) makes a first person reference to Simon Peter. It might be possible, even in these cases, to regard the works as an attempt to summarize traditions associated with a certain person

18. Currie, "The Scarcity of Extra-Biblical Episodic Tradition about the Ministry of Jesus in Second-Century Christian Literature."

19. *Adv. haer.* III.11.8. The reference to four zones of the earth and four winds is an argument "after the fact," not an argument for the four; he used these illustrations because four was the number of Gospels he had; if he had had a different number he could have been equally creative (and persuasive?) as to the fittingness of that number.

20. His *Diatessaron* has been argued both ways: he wouldn't have exercised freedom with the text if the Gospels were truly "canonical," or since they were "canonical" he had an interest in putting them in one narrative. At any rate, the fact that he demonstrably used only four is significant.

without the deception implied in forgery or to regard the ascriptions as later (mistaken) guesses. Some of the same considerations are posed about the titles of the canonical Gospels. But the circumstances are different. The canonical Gospels make no explicit claim to authorship, and such express statements about the writer as are found in the *Protevangelium* and *Gospel of Thomas* were a characteristic of forgeries.[21] Moreover, the early church did not hesitate to attribute canonical Gospels to non-apostolic authors, viz. Mark and Luke, even if their authenticity was defended on the basis that they preserved the preaching of Peter and Paul respectively.[22]

Christians in the second century forged reports of Pilate to Tiberius. The fifth-century *Gospel of Nicodemus* begins with *Acts of Pilate*; these, however, seem to be a Christian response to pagan *Acts of Pilate* forged in 311 or 312 to stir up animosity against Christians.[23] The pagan version, in turn, may have been suggested by earlier Christian claims that the official acts of Pilate supported their position.[24] Some of the Christian *Sibylline Oracles* belong to the second century.[25] Outright forgery, therefore, was not unknown to second-century Christians.

Apocalypses were apparently not too popular in orthodox circles. This may be a reflection of the move in Christianity from a Jewish to a Greek milieu, or especially the move from circles in which apocalyptic flourished. The *Apocalypse of Peter* is the only orthodox apocryphal apocalypse from the second century, and it presents a revelation of the future state, rather a different concern from the traditional Jewish apocalypses and the canonical Apocalypse of John. The text makes the express claim to be from "I, Peter" (ch. 2). The *Vision of Paul* belongs later.[26] The *Shepherd of Hermas* uses revelatory form for quite a different kind of message. The same is true, for yet another kind of content, for the Gnostic apocalypses. Several of the Nag Hammadi tractates bear the title "Apocalypse," and several others under another title have a similar setting: a post-resurrection revelatory discourse by Jesus and dialogue with his disciples.[27]

21. Speyer, *Die literarische Fälschung*, 45–56.

22. Tertullian, *Adv. Marc.* IV.2.2; 5.3–4.

23. Eusebius, *H.E.* IX.5.1.

24. Justin, *Apol.* I, 35; 48; Tertullian, *Apol.* 5.2; 21.24.

25. Hennecke, *New Testament Apocrypha*, 2:707–8; Schneemelcher, 2nd ed., 2:652ff.

26. Ferguson, "Psalm-Singing at the Eucharist"; included in this collection.

27. Perkins, *The Gnostic Dialogue.*

The situation in regard to epistles in second-century Christian literature is quite different from what has been found in regard to other kinds of writings. The paucity of pseudonymous epistles is analogous to the situation in orthodox circles in regard to apocalypses, but the reason here would be different, for we remember the relative absence of Jewish epistles.

Genuine epistles continued to be written. *First Clement* is a letter from the church of Rome to the church at Corinth. The ascription to Clement as the actual writer seems to be correct; the evidence of the manuscripts is confirmed by the testimony of Dionysius of Corinth.[28] Clement did not write in his own name but in the name of the church, but there is no pseudonymity involved. The message is really from the church (or its leadership), but someone had to compose it. *Second Clement* is not a letter but a sermon; nor is it pseudonymous, for the ascription to Clement is secondary. Seven letters of Ignatius are generally regarded as genuine.[29] These genuine letters were interpolated and supplemented by six spurious letters to form the long rescension in the fourth century. If Polycarp, *Philippians* is made up of two letters,[30] there is no question that both come from Polycarp. The so-called *Epistle to Diognetus* is actually an apology, perhaps joined to part of a sermon; it is anonymous. The letter form reported accounts of martyrdom from one church to another—*Martyrdom of Polycarp*; *Letter of the Churches of Lyons and Vienne*. Accounts of martyrdom were a fruitful field for producing forgeries, but this came later.[31]

A large number of authentic letters from the church fathers are known. From Eusebius we learn of an extensive correspondence of Dionysius of Corinth,[32] as well as of other bishops.[33] Some letters of Irenaeus are known.[34] The letter of Clement of Alexandria about Secret Mark may be

---

28. Eusebius, *H.E.* IV.23.11, "your letter written to us through Clement."

29. The conflicting efforts of Weijenborg, *Les lettres d'Ignace d'Antioche*; Ruis-Camps, *The Four Authentic Letters of Ignatius the Martyr*; and Joly, *Le Dossier d'Ignace d'Antioche*, have not shaken the modern consensus. See Schoedel, "Are the Letters of Ignatius of Antioch Authentic?"; and Hammond Bammel, "Ignatian Problems." The reviews that I have seen have been uniformly negative.

30. Harrison, *Polycarp's Two Epistles to the Philippians*. Professor Farmer's suggestion about an earlier date for Marcion's teachings removes an important external argument for a later dating of the main body of the surviving letter.

31. Delehaye, *Les passions des martyrs et les genres littéraires*.

32. Eusebius, *H.E.* IV.23.

33. Quasten, *Patrology*, 1:278ff.

34. Ibid., 293.

accepted as genuine; if pseudonymous, it belongs very much later than our period.[35] The anti-Montanist writer Apollonius reproached the Montanist, Themiso, for drawing up a catholic epistle in imitation of the apostle (probably referring to 1 John),[36] but the imitation seems to be of the idea of a general epistle rather than an attempt at pseudepigraphy. The most extensive collection from the ancient church is that of Cyprian—fifty-nine letters from him plus six from councils under his leadership and sixteen from others to him.

It is time now to survey "epistles" where there is a question of pseudepigraphy. There are very few Christian pseudepigraphal epistles in the second century and a virtual absence of epistles associated with apostolic names. The so-called *Epistle of Barnabas* is not truly a letter, little more so than the so-called First Letter of John. It is a doctrinal treatise. Moreover, modern scholarship is unanimous in the conclusion that the author was not the New Testament Barnabas,[37] but pseudonymity is not the only alternative to that identification. The author does not give his name, and the ascription to Barnabas may be secondary, a later effort to enhance the authority of the writing, or simply an "(un)educated guess." Confusion may have arisen from a homonym. Was the companion of Paul the only person in the ancient church to bear the name Barnabas? Perhaps we should not be too quick to consider *Barnabas* pseudonymous. Nor is the *Epistle of the Apostles* properly an epistle. It, however, claims to be a letter written by the apostles (chap. 1–2), but in fact it is a post-resurrection revelation of Christ to his apostles of the type now best known from Nag Hammadi but with orthodox content. It is presumably an orthodox reply to just such documents as the numerous Gnostic apocalypses. In the *Epistle of the Apostles* there is not just an effort to summarize the apostolic preaching but a claim to joint apostolic composition. The apostles are not individual personalities (the names given in ch. 2 are inaccurate), but a "dogmatic fact,"[38] standing for correct doctrine.

35. Smith, *Clement of Alexandria and a Secret Gospel of Mark*. A caution about authenticity is expressed by Osborn, "Clement of Alexandria: A Review of Research 1958–1982," 223–25. A considerable literature has ensued: representative affirmative arguments by Brown, "On the Compositional History of the Longer ('Secret') Gospel of Mark"; competing views by Hedrick, Stroumsa, and Ehrman, "The Secret Gospel of Mark: A Discussion"; negative on authenticity are Carlton, *The Gospel Hoax*; Jeffery, *The Secret Gospel of Mark Unveiled*.

36. Eusebius, *H.E.* V.18.5.

37. The manuscript designation is simply Barnabas, but the identification with the New Testament Barnabas is old—Clement of Alexandria, *Strom.* II.7;20; V.10.

38. Brox, "Zum Problemstand in der Erforschung," 23.

This is an appropriate place for a digression on the phenomenon of claims to apostolicity. This claim is especially evident in the church order literature. One of the earliest surviving, perhaps the earliest, non-canonical Christian writing is the *Didache*, "The Teaching of the Lord through the Twelve Apostles to the Nations." Nothing in the contents suggests actual apostolic authorship or forgery. I take it that the title represents a claim to summarize the content of apostolic teaching and directions to the church. In a broad sense the document could be considered a pseudepigraph, but I do not consider it pseudonymous in a deceptive sense. Since there was a desire to preserve the legitimation of apostolicity for developments in the organization and liturgy of the church, there may be various layers in the surviving *Didache* and thus an erroneous claim to apostolicity. The *Apostolic Tradition* of Hippolytus is further removed from apostolic content, but the situation is still the claim to represent apostolic instructions and not apostolic authorship. That latter stage is reached in the mid-third century with the Syriac *Didascalia* and carried even further in the fourth-century *Apostolic Constitutions* (e.g., VI.14; 16; book VIII assigns different decisions to different apostles). Omitting several other church order documents claiming apostolic authority, we note the ultimate claim in the fifth-century *Testament of our Lord*.

As the *Didache* was an effort to present apostolic directions on church order,[39] I assume that the "Apostles' Creed" (*Symbolum Apostolicum*) originated in a similar way as an attempt to summarize the apostolic faith. The text remained fluid for some time, but through frequent use the title was taken seriously as indicating origin. The *Commentary on the Apostles' Creed* (Symbol) by Rufinus at the end of the fourth century reports the tradition that the twelve apostles before going forth on their missionary efforts met and agreed on this summary of Christian faith, each contributing one clause.[40] The legend was elaborated so as to identify the contribution by each apostle.[41] Such emphasis on the apostolicity of the church's faith, organization, discipline, and liturgy is, at least in part, a reaction to the Gnostic controversy.

Embedded in the *Acts of Paul* is a letter from Corinth to Paul reporting a Gnostic-like teaching which was troubling the church and Paul's reply, the so-called *3 Corinthians*. We know that it had an independent

---

39. Brox, *Falsche Verfasserangaben*, 35–36.

40. Chapter 2. Cf. Ambrose, *Expl. Symb.* 2; chapter 8 notes that as there are twelve apostles so there are twelve articles.

41. Pseudo-Augustine, *Sermo suppos.* 240:4; 24:5 from sixth century.

circulation apart from the *Acts of Paul*[42] and attained a kind of canonical status for a time in the East Syrian church (Ephraim wrote a commentary on it), from whence it passed into the Armenian Bible. Testuz argued that *3 Corinthians* was an independent production incorporated into the *Acts of Paul*,[43] but it seems more likely that the author of the *Acts* himself created the correspondence, which in spite of the exposure as forgery had enough success to gain an independent existence. Either way, we have an illustration of one of the regular ways of giving authentication to a forgery: an accompanying letter, either introducing or incorporated in the work.[44] *Third Corinthians* is such a subordinate production, designed to lend credibility to the larger forgery. It furthermore allowed Paul to speak directly against the Gnostic teaching which is combated in the *Acts of Paul.*

The *Letter of Peter to James* and *Letter of Clement to James* in the Pseudo-Clementines are like *3 Corinthians*, forgeries that are part of a larger pseudonymous production.[45] The source analysis of the Pseudo-Clementines is so complicated that little can be said with confidence; but *Peter to James* probably belongs to the original second-century Ebionite production, and *Clement to James* is part of the orthodox reworking in the third-century *Grundschrift* of our present *Homilies* and *Recognitions* (fourth century).[46] These works thus are not to be seen as ordinary pseudepigraphal epistles but as subordinate to a larger corpus.

Clement of Rome was a favorite foster parent for anonymous (*2 Clement* above) and pseudonymous works (*Apostolic Constitutions* through Clement). Besides the Pseudo-Clementines there are two letters *On Virginity* handed down under Clement's name. They are in reality one work and date to the third century.[47]

There was an even more abundant Petrine apocrypha, a fact which increases the likelihood of pseudepigraphical epistles under Peter's name, and this phenomenon belongs to the second century. Already noted are the *Gospel of Peter*, the *Acts of Peter* (plus the Coptic *Acts of Peter and the*

---

42. Testuz, *Papyrus Bodmer X–XIII.*

43. Ibid., 23–25. Klijn, "The Apocryphal Correspondence between Paul and the Corinthians," finds evidence both for the author of the *Acts* incorporating an existing correspondence into his work and for the influence of the *Acts* on the correspondence (16).

44. Speyer, *Die literarische Fälschung*, 79ff.

45. Ibid., 8.

46. Schmidt, *Studien zu den Pseudo-Clementinen*, 316, for *Peter to James*; and Strecker, *Das Judenchristentum in den Pseukoklementinen*, on *Clement to James.*

47. Quasten, *Patrology*, 1:58–59.

Twelve Apostles and *The Act of Peter*), and the *Apocalypse of Peter*. There are to be added the apologetic work *Preaching of Peter* (*Kerygma Petrou*), known from quotations in Clement of Alexandria,[48] and the different Jewish-Christian *Preachings of Peter* (*Kerygmata Petrou*), identified within the Pseudo-Clementines.[49]

Eusebius accepted the correspondence of Abgar with Jesus as authentic, but it was a forgery from not too many years before he wrote.[50] It too was part of a larger work—*Acts of Thaddaeus*.

The Nag Hammadi library has not added greatly to the number of second-century epistles. *The Letter of Peter to Philip* (NHC VIII, 2) gets its title from the first paragraph, which is something of a cover-letter introducing the tractate, itself actually another account of a dialogue between the resurrected Christ and his disciples. The letter form in connection with a post-resurrection apocalypse is similar to the *Epistle of the Apostles*. Peter is the leader of the disciples, but after the brief opening letter the narrative proceeds in the third person. The whole is part of the usual Christian Gnostic claim to a secret tradition. The *Epistle to Rheginus* (NHC I, 4) is a *Treatise on the Resurrection*. Lacking any identification of its author, the work is not pseudepigraphal. Another letter treatise from Gnostic circles is the genuine *Letter of Ptolemy to Flora*, quoted by Epiphanius.[51]

Paul is remembered as the most prolific early Christian letter writer, but no apocryphal letters (apart from *3 Corinthians*) from the second century were ascribed to him.

The Muratorian Fragment records two Marcionite forgeries in Paul's name—letters to the Alexandrians and Laodiceans.[52] Nothing is known of the former, but a letter from antiquity has come down under the name *Epistle to the Laodiceans*. It was written no later than the fourth century, but a more precise date cannot be determined from the contents. Harnack thought the Muratorian Fragment referred to this letter, and Quispel has argued that it is Marcionite and is to be dated 160–90.[53] Such opinions have rightly not won favor. The *Epistle to the Laodiceans* is a feeble effort

48. Reagan, *The Preaching of Peter*.

49. Schoeps, *Theologie and Geschichte des Judenchristentums*, 51ff.

50. Eusebius, *H.E.* I.13; II.1.6–8.

51. *Haer.* XXXIII.3–7; English translation in Grant, *Second-century Christianity* (1946) 30–37; 2nd ed. (2003) 63–68.

52. Muratorian Fragment, line 64. See Ferguson, "Canon Muratori: Date and Provenance," 681 (see chap. 16 above).

53. "De Brief aan de Laodicenbsen een Marcionitische vervalsing," 43–46, cited in Speyer, *Die literarische Fälschung*, 229 n. 3.

to supply the letter mentioned in Col 4:16. As a cento of Pauline phrases, especially from Philippians, it has the negative value of showing what an uninspired forger would produce. Of course, there are good and bad forgers, as there are good and bad authors, but if this is typical of what one working with Pauline materials would come up with, it only increases our respect for the canonical letters.

The *Epistle to the Laodiceans* exists only in Latin but may have been written in Greek. The *Correspondence between Paul and Seneca* was written in Latin, later than the second century. These letters seek to commend Paul to Roman literary circles which might be offended by his style.[54]

By way of summary, we have found that epistles were a favorite form of Greek pseudepigraphy and apocalypses were the favorite form of Jewish pseudepigraphy. Christianity in the second century made minimal use of either form of pseudepigraphy. The favorite forms of pseudepigraphy in second-century Christianity were gospels and acts of apostles. There was a considerable Christian pseudepigraphy and a considerable epistolary literature in the second century, but the two categories rarely coalesce. Our canvas has turned up very few pseudonymous letters surviving from the second century, and if the explanations offered are accepted, no independent pseudonymous epistle ascribed to an apostle. The result is quite different for other genres of literature—gospels, acts, apocalypses, apologies, poetry. What are we to make of this?

The New Testament, in contrast, offers a nearly reverse situation. There twenty-one of the twenty-seven books are designated epistles. A representative introduction to the New Testament considers only seven (is the number significant?) of the thirteen Pauline epistles as definitely genuine.[55] Of the seven catholic epistles, none passes critical scrutiny, and if we omit the three Johanine epistles which give no name of an author in the text, there are still four commonly considered pseudepigraphical.[56]

---

54. Against Quasten's judgment of "not later than the third century" (*Patrology*, 1:155), Speyer gives a date at the end of the fourth century (*Die literarische Fälschung*, 258). For studies, see Lightfoot, *St. Paul's Epistle to the Philippians*, 271, 329–33; Sevenster, *Paul and Seneca*; and Herrmann, *Sénèque et les premiers chrétiens*.

55. Kümmel, *Introduction to the New Testament*, 178, considers the Pastorals as later than Paul, and Ephesians, Colossians, and 2 Thessalonians as doubtful; Koester, *Introduction to the New Testament*, 2:242, 263–70, removes the last three altogether from Paul's pen.

56. Kümmel, *Introduction to the New Testament*, 290–91, 297–98, 301, 304, 311–12, 315–16.

How are we to explain this?[57] (1) The only pseudepigraphical epistles produced in the early generations of Christianity were so well done and so useful that they are all preserved in the canon. (2) Any others, if there were others, or the only ones, were so poorly done that they were not preserved; or they were not preserved because they failed to make the canon. Either of these two explanations is difficult to accept, for numerous gospels and acts were both preserved and excluded from the canon. Age of writing and accident of transmission must be taken into account, but the numbers are sufficiently large to make the probabilities for the existing distribution slim. (3) Epistles were found to be hard to forge and so were not attempted or were quickly rejected when produced. That seems unlikely since the pseudepigraphical letter was much developed in Greek philosophy and in rhetorical education. (4) Or was pseudepigraphy widely practiced by Christians in the first century but not in the second? That is possible, but no explanation for the change is immediately obvious. (5) The New Testament undoubtedly has been studied more than the second-century literature. Does this mean that it has been studied more carefully or that the scrutiny of the second-century literature has been less critical and skeptical? (6) Does the second-century evidence raise questions about too hasty conclusions about the presence of pseudepigraphical epistles in the New Testament? (7) Or do we need some category other than pseudepigraphy to describe the phenomenon?

---

57. James, *The Apocryphal New Testament*, 476, notes the paucity of apocryphal epistles and offers the following explanations: "it does appear that the Epistle was on the whole too serious an effort for the forger, more liable to detection, perhaps, as a fraud, and not so likely to gain the desired popularity as a narrative or an Apocalypse." Whatever degree of truth there is in these observations, the present study calls for further qualification.

19

Factors Leading to the Selection and Closure of the New Testament Canon

A Survey of Some Recent Studies

THE EARLY FOLLOWERS OF Jesus began with a set of scripture, the sacred writings of the Hebrew Bible, but known to most in their Greek translation. The recognition of the Jewish scriptures may have been a barrier to Christians creating their own scriptures, but it may just as well have served as a pattern for that development. The recognition of a canon of New Testament writings placed alongside the scriptures of Judaism was primarily a result of the internal dynamic of the Christian faith. The conviction of a new saving work of God in Christ, its proclamation by apostles and evangelists and the revelation of its meaning and application by prophets and teachers, led naturally to the writing of these messages and their acceptance as authoritative in parallel with the books already regarded as divine scripture. External factors did not determine that there would be a New Testament canon nor dictate its contents. These external factors, however, had an influence on the process of definition and likely hastened that process. But, first, let us consider what those on the inside of the church thought about the situation.

THE INTERNAL DYNAMICS

The testimony of the first Christian writers to comment on which books were regarded as authoritative described these books as those "handed down" and "received." This standard language for "tradition" was used about the canonical books. In reference to the Gospels, for instance, Irenaeus spoke of "The Gospels handed down to us from the apostles" (*Adv. Haer.* 3.11.9), with which we may compare, "The Gospel handed down to us by the will of God in scriptures" (3.1.1). Clement of Alexandria specified "The four Gospels that have been handed down to us" (*Strom.* 3.13.93). Serapion of Antioch rejected the *Gospel of Peter* as "pseudepigrapha," "knowing that we [orthodox Christians] did not receive such writings" (Eusebius, *H.E.* 6.12.3). The early ecclesiastical writers did not regard themselves as deciding which books to accept or to reject. Rather, they saw themselves as registering which books had been handed down to them.[1] While they could have been self-deceived or have written to deceive others, but the first task of the historian is to determine what the participants understood about the circumstances. The consistency of usage across a broad spectrum of the early church is noteworthy.

Authority, Memory, and Scripture

Several internal needs of the new community favored the special recognition of certain books. The collecting and preserving of certain writings was a natural result of remembering and transmitting the testimony of the apostles and other eyewitnesses to Jesus and the stories about the early activities of his disciples. Authoritative materials were needed for various purposes.

As early communities developed, there was a need for guidance in the moral life of members. The *Didache* 1–6 shows a compilation built around the theme of the "Two Ways" used in the instruction of candidates for baptism. The teachings of Jesus on various questions were collected, preserved, and incorporated in the Gospels, and considerable sections of the letters of Paul and others address such topics.

What did it mean to believe in Jesus? Confessional materials used on many occasions, notably at baptism and codified in what was later called the "Apostles' Creed," required and led to the fixing of a consistent

---

1. This was still the usage of Athanasius (*Ep. fest.* 39): "handed down to our ancestors."

narrative framework for the life of Jesus. Accounts of conversion and the growth in the number of disciples, during and after the personal ministry of Jesus, served to strengthen faith and steadfastness in Jesus' followers.

Distinctive Christian worship practices also served as preconditions for a canon of scripture. The eucharist involved the remembrance of the passion of Christ and particularly the institution narrative. Prayers and confessional statements were grounded in the teachings of Jesus and the proclamation of his apostles. Christian materials were read in the assemblies from quite early (Mark 13:14; Rev 1:3; and see below on Paul's letters). The church did not have to wait until the end of the second century (and certainly not the fourth century) to know what books to read in church. Necessarily, it took some distance in time to focus on writings more than on the oral message.

Material accepted as divine revelation would have been authoritative from its reception. This is evident in the book of Revelation. It presents itself as a "revelation" and a written "prophecy" (Rev 1:1–3). As divinely inspired revelation, its words could neither be added to nor taken away from (Rev 22:18–19). This principle applied to other revelations (e.g., Eph. 3:5).

Authoritative materials were not transmitted exclusively in scripture. Baptismal instructions, confessions of faith, liturgical formulae, and similar materials were means of communicating Christian beliefs and practices. But writings were part of this transmitted material that from the beginning had a quasi-canonical status in Christian communities. The increasing passage of time left direct contact with living witnesses rarer and put more premium on written records as aids to memory and a standard by which to evaluate teachings.

Papias lived toward the end of the time when the appeal to eyewitnesses was still possible. His words have commonly been taken as reflecting the decided preference for the oral tradition over written scriptures. The ancient world did value the oral word over the written word, but more may be read by modern interpreters into Papias' statement than he intended.

> I will not hesitate to take into account along with my interpretations whatever I learned well and remember well from the presbyters, confirming the truth by them. For I did not rejoice, as many do, in those who talk a lot but in those who teach the truth, nor in those who recall alien commandments but in those who recall what was given in faith by the Lord and was derived from the truth itself. If ever someone who had accompanied the presbyters should come, I examined carefully the words of

> the presbyters, [to learn] what Andrew, Peter, Philip, Thomas,
> James, John, Matthew, or any other of the disciples of the Lord
> said and what things Aristion and the presbyter John, disciples
> of the Lord, are saying. For I did not suppose the contents of
> books would profit me so much as the words of the present and
> living voice. (Quoted by Eusebius, *H.E.* 3.39.3–4, from Papias,
> *Interpretation of the Lord's Oracles*)

It is not at all clear that Papias is juxtaposing oral reports of apostolic teaching and apostolic writings. In fact it may be written documents that he was interpreting in his "Interpretations of the Lord's Oracles," for "oracles" (λόγια) could be used of books.[2] Matthew and Mark certainly, and perhaps Luke and John,[3] had canonical status for him (Eusebius, *H.E.* 3.39.14–16). His concern was arriving at the truth, so his preference was for a primary over a secondary source.[4] Truth was found in apostolicity, so the contrast is between the teachings derived from the Lord and his disciples by way of the presbyters who had direct contact with them and the writings of heretical teachers.[5]

There are many early indications of the recognition of authoritative Christian writings. The acknowledgement of the scripture principle, although not yet a "canon," implicitly contained the idea of canon.[6] Paul expected his written instructions as well as his oral teaching to be received as authoritative (1 Cor 14:37; 2 Thess 2:15; 3:14). One of the documents accepted into the New Testament canon, 2 Peter, places Paul's letters on a level with the Old Testament scriptures (2 Pet 3:15–16). Moving to other early Christian literature we find that Clement of Rome, Ignatius, and Polycarp made extensive use of Paul's letters and drew on them as authoritative. If the Latin version is reliable, Polycarp quoted Eph 4:26 as "scripture" (*Phil.* 12.1).[7] More significant overall than a citation of Paul as scripture is the overwhelming use Polycarp (and others) made of New

---

2. So the Jewish scriptures: Josephus, *B.J.* 6.311; and *1 Clem.* 53.1; 62.3

3. Hill, "What Papias Said about John (and Luke)."

4. Baum, "Papias, der Vorzug der Viva Vox."

5. Walls, "Papias and the Oral Tradition."

6. See my comments in the "Introduction," to *The Bible in the Early Church*, xi–xii.

7. Affirmed by Nielsen, "Polycarp, Paul, and the Scriptures"; so also Dehandschutter, "Polycarp's Epistle to the Philippians," 281–83. Bauer (*Die Polycarpbriefe*, 69–71) understands the first part of *Phil.* 12.1 as saying that he has no authority to command as scripture does; he then surveys various interpretations of the quotation and suggests it is a combination of Ps 4:5 and Deut 24:14–15, and not an ascription of "scripture" status to Ephesians.

Testament writings. Polycarp wove together the phraseology of Paul's letters together with 1 Peter and 1–2 John for his own letter to the Philippians. The *Didache* several times appeals to the "Gospel" as authoritative (8.2; 11.3; 15.3 and 4). It is debated whether he means only the message or also has a written document in mind; in each case the material referred to is found in Matthew.[8] Ignatius puts together the "Prophecies, the Law of Moses, and the Gospel" (*Smyr.* 5.1); since the first two are written, the presumption is that the third is also, but his addition of "our own individual sufferings" may weaken the connection.[9] Both *Barnabas* (4.14) and *2 Clement* (2.4) quote Matthew—the former introducing Matt 22:14 as "it is written," and the latter quoting Matt 9:13 as "another scripture." It may be argued that the authority is the Lord and not a written document, but his words are found in a writing, and they are quoted from this writing in a manner that puts it on the same level with the Old Testament.[10]

Although second-century Christian authors accepted the Old Testament as scripture, they used the New Testament writings, in relation to their quantity, much more than they did the Old Testament.[11] Citation as "scripture" appears to be less significant than the overwhelming use and importance attached to the writings that form the core of our New Testament. It may claim too much "to say that the canon was fixed" already at the end of the first century,[12] "since its edges were still quite fuzzy"; yet it would be equally mistaken to say that "there was no Christian scripture other than the Old Testament" at this time, "for much of the core [of the New Testament] already had as high a status as it would ever have."[13] In

---

8. Tuckett "Synoptic Tradition in the Didache," concludes that the *Didache* presupposes the finished gospels of Matthew and Luke. For further bibliography see my "Love of Enemies and Nonretaliation in the Second Century," 84–85 nn. 12–13.

9. Goulder ("Ignatius' 'Docetists,'" 16–17 n. 4) argues from this verse, from the possible quotation of John 3:8 in *Phld.* 7.1, and from the juxtaposition of the Prophets and the Gospel in *Phld.* 9.2 that the "Gospel" in *Phld.* 8.2 is written, as were the "archives" (Old Testament?). Hill ("Ignatius and the Apostolate") sees Ignatius's view of the apostles as testimony to the regard in which their writings were held.

10. Beatrice ("Une citation de l'Evangile de Matthieu," 232–34) argues that the identical theological and ecclesiological contexts confirms that *Barnabas* is indeed quoting the Gospel of Matthew.

11. Barton, *The Spirit and the Letter*, 18–19, with reference to the statistics gathered by Stuhlhofer, *Der Gebrauch der Bibel von Jesus bis Eusebios*.

12. Cf. Zahn, *Geschichte des neutestamentlichen Kanons*; supported by Swarat, "Das Werden des neutestamentlichen Kanons."

13. Barton, *The Spirit and the Letter*, 19.

terms of the significance of scriptural status, there is no time when Christians did not treat the New Testament as scripture.[14]

It may be urged that the inexactitude in quotations indicate that second-century authors either were not quoting New Testament documents or, if they were, did not hold them in high regard. There are several problems with this reasoning.[15] Quotations may take various forms: in addition to verbatim quotations, there are interpretive quotations, intentional changes to affect the meaning, paraphrastic quotations, quotations accommodated to sentence structure, and simply loose quotations when the point does not depend on exact words. None of these need imply a lack of respect for the quoted text. To the contrary, if there were lack of respect, there would be no quotation or allusion; and the greater the respect for the text the more need for deliberate changes to make it appear to say what one wants it to say. Comparable variations are found in second-century authors' quotations from the Old Testament, and there is no question that its text was fixed in writing (even though there were different forms of the text) and was considered authoritative scripture. Quoting from memory is not the same as quoting from an oral tradition.

Mary Carruthers' study of memory in medieval culture is applicable to ancient culture, whose understanding and practices in regard to memory it followed, as her references to Cicero and Quintillian demonstrate.[16] For the ancients a book was a support for memory, and more confidence was placed in the memory than in books. Authoritative texts were often not quoted verbatim, for "memory for things" was preferred to "rote iteration" (memory of words), even when the speaker had accurate command of the original words.[17]

Another perspective to be considered is that a written text actually gives a speaker or writer more freedom in quotation than an oral message does. Something preserved only orally must be quoted, if not verbatim, with great faithfulness. There is not the same need for exactitude in regard to written materials, for the writer can assume that the reader knows the text and only needs to be reminded of it or can always consult the original text. The presence of a written text provides a standard of reference that permits the one quoting to play with variations.

14. Ibid., 134–35.

15. Various ramifications of orality and textuality are broughtout by Barton (ibid., 87–104, 123–30).

16. Carruthers, *The Book of Memory*, esp. 26–27, 31–32, 160, 189–94.

17. Jaffee in a review, "Oral Culture in Scriptural Religion," 227–28.

Other indications of the acceptance of some New Testament writings as scripture may be briefly indicated; their force will be variously evaluated as to their significance. Papyrus fragments from Egypt, notably the John Rylands fragment of John (P[52]), show an early circulation of the Gospels that may be indicative of their authority, certainly of their use. Apocryphal writings from the second century tend to fall into the same literary genres as the canonical books—Gospels (*Gospel of Peter, Protevangelium of James*), Acts (*Acts of Peter, Acts of Paul, Acts of John*), Letters (*Epistle of the Apostles*), and Apocalypses (*Apocalypse of Peter*). This phenomenon may be indicative that certain forms of writing had already imprinted themselves on the Christian consciousness as the way Christian books were to be written if special authority for them was desired. The translation of writings that came to make up the New Testament into other languages began quite early—Latin and Syriac before the end of the second century and Coptic not much later. The language in which Tatian undertook his harmony of the Gospels (the *Diatessaron*) is debatable, but in his time or shortly thereafter Syriac translations of some New Testament books were available.[18] The same had happened in Latin. There may not have been a "canon" to determine which books to translate, but there certainly was a special need felt and widespread use to justify such undertakings. A literary confirmation of the Latin translation is found in the *Acts of the Scillitan Martyrs* from North Africa in 180. One of the martyrs, Speratus, carried a case containing "books and letters of a just man named Paul" (12). The "books" is probably a reference to Gospels, although the text may mean, "books, that is letters of Paul."[19]

Wherever Paul and his associates labored, there was an interest in his letters and there were those who respected them as authoritative. As part of his apostolic mission, Paul wrote letters as more than occasional correspondence. The letters of Paul were read and reread in the assemblies of the churches to which they were addressed, and he expected them to be read by others (1 Thess 5:27; Col 4:16), a practice that continued or was

---

18. The canon of the Syriac church is a special problem, because it later did not include the General Epistles and Revelation. Siker ("The Canonical Status of the Catholic Epistles") points out that these letters were in the Philoxenian and Harclean versions; they were not included in the Syriac canon because of their absence from the Peshitta, which increasingly became the authoritative version of the Syriac New Testament.

19. Bonner ("The Scillitan Saints and the Pauline Epistles") takes the books as gospels; but den Boeft and Bremmer ("Notiunculae martyrologicae IV," 116–17) translate "books of epistles."

resumed quite early, so he and others had copies from the beginning.[20] It is probable that several collections were made.[21] Paul's letters were collected by the end of the first century at the latest.[22] This is evident from their use by authors as widely separated geographically as Clement of Rome, Ignatius of Antioch, and Polycarp of Smyrna. The only question is the extent of the collection. Marcion's edition of the letters of Paul did not contain the Pastoral epistles, but Polycarp clearly used them, so much so that von Campenhausen thought Polycarp wrote them, a view that did not gain much favor.[23] Hebrews was a special case, and its varying position among the letters of Paul reflect hesitation about accepting it as Paul.[24]

Harry Gamble suggested that the collection of Paul's letters was the impetus for the Christian adoption of the codex.[25] The collection and preservation of Paul's writings obviously occurred in the Pauline circle and thus near the lifetime of the apostle. May it go back even earlier? E. Randolph Richards has carried Gamble's proposal a step further. He suggests that Paul, like other letter writers of his time, kept a copy of the letters he wrote. Since the codex was the common form for an author's notebooks, this personal set of copies Paul had with him in Rome (cf. the *membranas* of 2 Tim 4:13) passed at his death to his disciples, who saw to its copying and distribution in the same form.[26] The theory is unprovable but offers an explanation for the early knowledge of Paul's letters and the early use of the codex by Christians.

20. Hartman, "On Reading Others' Letters."

21. Gamble (*Books and Readers in the Early Church*, 59–62) cites evidence for three different orders in which the letters were collected: (1) Marcion's collection that begins with Galatians and ends with Philemon; (2) Papyrus 46, dated about 200, that follows the order that became established except for reversing Ephesians and Galatians; and (3) the letters to seven churches, treating those to the same church as one letter and basing the order on length, so that Corinthians is first and Colossians (perhaps including Philemon) is last.

22. Foster, "The Earliest Collection of Paul's Epistles") suggests that Luke made the earliest collection of Paul's letters as a third volume to go with his Gospel and Acts. Zuntz (*The Text of the Epistles*), drawing on textual criticism (working from P[46]), concluded that "the archetypal *Corpus* [*Paulinum*] was produced about A.D. 100" (279).

23. Von Campenhausen, *Polykarp von Smyrna und die Pastoralbriefe*.

24. W. H. P. Hatch ("The Position of Hebrews") surveys the different positions of Hebrews in the manuscripts and canon lists; Anderson ("The Epistle to the Hebrews") argues that it is more plausible that Hebrews was incuded among the letters of Paul before the formation of the corpus as a whole than that it was added to an existing Pauline corpus.

25. Gamble, *Books and Readers in the Early Church*, 58–66.

26. Richards, "The Codex and the Early Collection of Paul's Letters."

Early Regard for the Gospels

An earlier suggestion on the Christians' adoption of the codex appealed to the authority of the Gospels.[27] The words of Jesus carried authority from the beginning (1 Cor 7:10, 12; Acts 20:35),[28] and the passion narrative was the core of the apostolic preaching (1 Cor 15:1–8). A four-Gospel canon was in place by the time of Irenaeus.

> It is not possible that the Gospels can be either more or fewer in number than they are. For since there are four zones of the world in which we live, and four principal winds, while the church is scattered throughout the world, and the "pillar and ground" [1 Tim 3:15] of the church is the Gospel and the Spirit of life; it is fitting that she should have four pillars . . . The Word . . . who was manifested to humanity has given us the Gospel under four aspects but bound together by one Spirit. (Irenaeus, *Against Heresies* 3.11.8)

Irenaeus continues with other instances of the number four—the four living creatures of Revelation "among whom Christ is seated"[29] and the four principal covenants made by God (from Noah, from Abraham, the law by Moses, and the Gospel through Christ). He names the four Gospels as John, Luke, Matthew, and Mark. It is often stated that Irenaeus was arguing for something new and had quite weak arguments for his position. This approach misunderstands the importance of number symbolism in the ancient world and Irenaeus's use of it. He does not argue for four Gospels because there are four winds or four corners of the universe. He appeals to this symbolism because he has four Gospels. If he had three, five, or some other number, he would have found an appropriately fitting analogy. Irenaeus does not see himself as an innovator but as champion of a traditional position in the church over against the Marcionite narrowing down and Valentinian expansion of the Gospel canon.

27. Roberts and Skeat, *The Birth of the Codex*, 57–61.

28. Dungan, *The Sayins of Jesus in the Churches of Paul.*

29. Skeat ("Irenaeus and the Four Gospel Canon") explains the anomalies in Irenaeus's remarks (like the unusual order of the four gospels) as deriving from an earlier source that had interpreted the four creatures of Ezekiel and Revelation. The remarks presuppose a four-gospel canon and a four-gospel codex, and since earlier than Irenaeus, point to a date of 170 at the latest. Blanchard (*Aux Sources du Canon*), on the other hand, argues that the gospels had not acquired normative status.

The significance of Tatian's *Diatessaron* (c. 170?) has been argued both ways.[30] It is commonly said that if the Four Gospels were regarded as sacred scripture, he would not have treated them so freely as to weave them together into a separate narrative (it is worth noting that the Gospel of John serves as the chronological framework). On the other hand, why would he have bothered unless the works were considered important? Because they were authoritative, Tatian was concerned enough to do the study involved in reducing the four authorities to one unified account.

Tatian may have received the idea and indeed the basis for his project from his teacher Justin. Several scholars find the best explanation for the wording of Justin's Gospel quotations to be a harmony of the teachings of Jesus that he produced in his school.[31] Justin testifies that the "Memoirs of the Apostles" (a title his pagan readers would recognize from the *Memoirs of Socrates*), called by Christians "Gospels" (*1 Apol.* 66.3), were read in the Sunday assemblies of Christians on a par with the Old Testament (*1 Apol.* 67.3). Many think these were only the Synoptic Gospels and profess to find no evidence that Justin knew the Fourth Gospel, but this reflects a curious scholarly blindness.[32] If we may press the exact words of Justin, "the memoirs, which I say were composed by his apostles [plural] and their followers [plural]" (*Dial.* 103.8), he knew at least two Gospels by

30. The most comprehensive study is Petersen, *Tatian's Diatesseron*, whose interests are textual and not canonical. Petersen calls attention to reports of two other harmonies near the time of Tatian, or a little later: "Theophilus [bishop of Antioch] . . . put together into one work the words of the four Gospels" (Jerome, *Ep.* 121.6), and "Ammonius the Alexandrine has left us the gospel as a diatessaron," in which he placed alongside the Gospel of Matthew the parallel pericopes of the other three gospels (Eusebius, *Ep. Carp.* 1) (32–33). These undertaking would seem to presuppose the special authority of the four gospels.

31. Notably Bellinzoni, *The Sayings of Jesus in the Writings of Justin Martyr*; Bellinzoni, "The Gospel of Matthew in the Second Century," esp. 239–42, which accepts Koester's further elaboration: Koester, *Ancient Christian Gospels*, 360–402; also, Osborn, *Justin Martyr*, 123–24. Others think a compilation for catechetical purposes (and not a harmony) sufficiently accounts for the passages cited by Justin: Hagner, "The Sayings of Jesus in Apostolic Fathers and Justin Martyr," 249; Strecker, "Eine Evangelienharmonie."

32. In a nuanced study, Pryor ("Justin Martyr and the Fourth Gospel") discounts some of the evidence adduced for Justin's use of the Fourth Gospel, concluding that Justin knew the work, but not as scripture or the work of an apostle. Cosgrove ("Justin Martyr and the Emerging Christian Canon") sees Justin as devaluing the canonical authority of the New Testament, including the Gospels; Hill ("Justin and the New Testament Writings") counters by referring to Justin's apologetic purpose and high evaluation of apostolic authority (note esp. *Dial.* 119.6, "God's voice spoken by the apostles").

apostles and two by their associates. Quotations drawn from Matthew and Luke are frequent; there is a quotation from Mark 3:16–17 ascribed to the "Memoirs of Peter" (*Dial.* 106.3).[33] Moreover, one passage may put John among the Memoirs: "For I have already proved that he was the only begotten of the Father of all things, being begotten in a peculiar manner as Word and Power by him, and having afterwards become man through the Virgin, as we have learned from the Memoirs" (*Dial.* 105.1). The virgin birth comes from Matthew and Luke, but the language of "only begotten" (μονογενής) and designation as "Word" (λόγος) are found only in John.[34]

Contemporary with Justin, the *Martyrdom of Polycarp* by his church in Smyrna emphasized martyrdom "according to the Gospel" (1.1; 19.1; cf. 4.1) in such a way as at least to include the teachings of written Gospels.[35]

Recent study is pushing the collection of a four-Gospel canon back to the early second century.[36] Irenaeus could have been familiar with four-Gospel codices. P[45] from the first half of the third century is the earliest codex of the four Gospels and Acts.[37] P[75] from around 200 contains Luke and John, a combination that suggests it may have originally been combined with a codex of Matthew and Mark.[38] The fragments of P[4], P[64], and P[67] are from the same codex, dated late second century, and contain Matthew and Luke, making it possibly our earliest four-Gospel codex.[39] Since these three codices are independent of one another, they are evidence for the four-Gospel canon at the end of the second century, and unless the idea was independently arrived at by different compilers, there must have been predecessors. This consideration takes us back at the latest to the mid-second century.

Moody Smith's 1999 presidential address to the annual meeting of the Society of Biblical Literature in Boston carries us back to the very

33. The whole context of this passage (*Dial.* 97–106) is a dialogue between the Old Testament and the New Testament (primarily the Gospels, but there are parallels to Paul and Hebrews) in interpreting Psalm 22.

34. The absence of an exact reference earlier in the *Dialogue* where Justin has done this does not carry much weight in view of Justin's rambling style, and he may be substituting Johannine language here to express the claims he has made for another being besides the Supreme God in the creation account and in the theophanies of the Old Testament.

35. Buschmann, *Das Martyrium des Polykarp*, esp. 49–58.

36. Stanton, "The Fourfold Gospel"; Heckel (*Vom Evangelium des Markus*) dates the formation of the fourfold collection ca. 110–120.

37. Kenyon, *The Chester Beatty Biblical Papyri*.

38. Skeat, "The Origin of the Christian Codex."

39. Skeat, "The Oldest Manuscript of the Four Gospels?"

composition of the Gospels.[40] Accepting the distinction between scripture and canon, Smith examined the Gospels themselves for indications that the authors understood themselves to be writing scripture. He finds appreciable evidence in Matthew and Luke that they were continuing the Old Testament story, were imitating it, and were writing a definitive account of the coming of Jesus and his place in the history of salvation. The intent of Mark and John in this regard was less obvious, but there is evidence that they too were functioning as scripture from quite early. This is implicit, according to Smith, in the commonly accepted view that Matthew and Luke used Mark and in the way that 1 John presupposes the Fourth Gospel and was engaged in exegetical controversy over its meaning. The continuity of these Gospels with the Old Testament story contrasts with the apocryphal gospels, notably the *Gospel of Thomas*. This finding coincides with the fact that there is no time in Christian history after the writing of the four Gospels when one can find evidence of their not being accepted as scripture.

Supportive of this claim is Richard Bauckham's contention that the Gospels were written not just for one community but for any and every church which they might reach.[41] The early Christian movement was a network of communities in close communication with one another, their leaders traveled widely, Christianity was viewed as a worldwide movement, and early Christian literature circulated rapidly (indeed, the purpose of writing was to reach people beyond those with whom one had personal contact). All these factors support the interpretation of the contents of the Gospels as written for all Christians. Such broader audiences and purposes than narrow, local ones are consistent with, although not necessarily requiring, the writing of authoritative "scripture." Their early acceptance by Christians was the presupposition of their later preeminence.

The evidence of textual criticism is against the four canonical Gospels having undergone a long period of development with several stages in their composition. Positively stated, the history of the text shows the Gospels were composed in the form in which they exist today.[42] This situation in turn allows the time for them to be accepted and brought together in a collection by the early second century.

Codices P[66] and P[75] from about 200 give the titles of the Gospels, "The Gospel [singular] According to . . . ," that is, the one gospel in multiple written forms. These titles require a period of time during which the

40. D. M. Smith, "When Did the Gospels Become Scripture?"
41. Bauckham, "Introduction," and "For Whom Were Gospels Written?"
42. Victor, "Was ein Texthistoriker."

individual Gospels were circulated together and belong to an early stage of their transmission, likely going back to the early second century.[43]

An indirect testimony to the four-Gospel collection is the separation of Luke from Acts. These books were two volumes of one work, but there is no point in the transmission history of the two volumes where they are joined. If they were written on two scrolls, their separation would have been easy to effect, but when the codex came into use, why were they not put in the same codex? The most plausible explanation is that the two works were separated in order for Luke to become part of a Gospel collection. And this separation presumably occurred before Marcion, for he accepts Luke but not Acts.[44]

If other gospels such as the *Gospel of Thomas* and the *Gospel of Peter* were as early as the canonical Gospels, then the need for differentiation between what was authentic and correct and what was not was equally early; if those works are later, they represent alternatives produced in part under the influence of the canonical Gospels.

Early Christian Terminology for the Authoritative Writings

Early Christian writers made frequent reference to a threefold expression of authority: "the Prophets, the Lord, and the Apostles."[45] The pattern is already reflected in Clement of Rome, whose exhortation against schism includes examples and quotations ("it is written") from the Old Testament, followed by, "Remember the words of the Lord Jesus," and the admonition, "Take up the epistle of the blessed Paul the Apostle" (*1 Clem.* 45–47).[46] One of the earliest explicit statements is from Polycarp: "As [Christ] himself commanded us and the apostles who preached the gospel to us and the prophets who announced beforehand the coming of our Lord" (*Phil.* 6.3). Ignatius made a similar combination of "apostles, prophets,

---

43. Hengel, "The Titles of the Gospels and the Gospel of Mark." Koester disagrees and puts the use of these titles at the end of the second century ("From Kerygma-Gospel to Written Gospel," esp. 373 n. 2).

44. Farmer and Farkasfalvy (*The Formation of the New Testament Canon*, 64 and 73) suggest that Marcion's Gospel and Apostle (the letters of Paul) were modeled on and a substitute for Luke and Acts.

45. Van den Eynde, *Les normes.* Eno (*Teaching Authority in the Early Church*) concerns more the offices from which teaching was given.

46. A similar "history of salvation" view appears in *Barnabas* 6.5–9, "The prophets prophesied" of Christ, and while teaching and doing miracles "he chose out his own apostles who were to preach his gospel."

and the church," but the distinctive feature of the gospel is the "coming of the Savior, our Lord Jesus Christ" (*Philad.* 9.1–2; cf. 5.1–2). Both Ignatius and Polycarp had persons in mind, but the messages of these authorities were found in books (see above at n. 9 on Ignatius's other formulations). The same goes for Irenaeus: "The utterances of the prophets, of the Lord, and of the apostles" (*Adv. haer.* 2.2.5) or more fully, "The preaching of the church, which the prophets proclaimed . . . but which Christ brought to perfection, and the apostles have handed down, from whom the church received [it]" (ibid., 5.pref.).[47] Irenaeus certainly implied books, as other statements, to which we shall come, make clear.[48] Clement of Alexandria explicitly refers to books. In a discussion of the scriptures as the demonstration of truth, "giving a complete exhibition of the scriptures from the scriptures themselves," Clement declares: "We have as the source of teaching the Lord, both by the Prophets, the Gospel, and the blessed Apostles" (*Strom.* 7.16.95, 97).[49] The Lord was the authority, but he made his teaching known in a threefold collection of writings—Prophets, Gospel, and Apostles. Prophets were taken by Christians as a comprehensive designation of their Old Testament, so that Moses and David were cited as "prophets." Elsewhere Clement exhorts, "Let one believe the Prophecies, Gospels, and Apostolic Words" (*Quis dives* 42.17). Origen began his work on *First Principles* by affirming that Christ is the truth, whose words include not only what he spoke while in the flesh but also what he spoke through Moses and the prophets and through the apostles (*Princ.* 1.pref.1).[50] This threefold summary of authority was a natural expression of the Christian periodization of the history of salvation. But it is worth raising the question if the Jewish three-part canon of Law, Prophets, and Writings influenced Christians to posit their own authorities in a three-

47. Almost identical wording in *Epid.* 98. Cf. *Haer.* 3.9.1, "Neither the prophets, the apostles, nor the Lord Christ in his own person"; 3.17.4 "The Lord testifies, as the apostles confess, and as the prophets announce"; and 1.8.1 quoted below.

48. His contemporary Theophilus of Antioch certainly had books in mind: "Concerning the righteousness that the law enjoined, confirmatory utterances are found both with the prophets and in the Gospels, because they all spoke inspired by one Spirit of God"; and he quotes 1 Tim 2:12 and Rom 13:7–8 as "the divine word gives instructions" (*Autol.* 3.12, 14).

49. *Strom.* 6.15 refers to the scriptures containing "the teaching of the Lord by his apostles and what was announced by "prophecy and the Savior himself."

50. Cf. "Gospels, Apostles, and Prophets" (*Comm. Jo.* 1.23). It may be noted that the Pseudo-Cyprian, *De aleatoribus* 10 cites its authorities in the order, "the prophet" (1 Kings), "the blessed apostle" (Paul), "the Lord in his gospel" (Matthew), and "the apostle John" (1 John).

fold form. This threefold summary continued in use at a time when only by an extension of meaning could the terms cover the contents of scripture,[51] an illustration of how terminology from an early time remained in use with an altered or accommodated meaning and was not evidence for the limitation of the canon to the books properly so named.

There was from early times another formulation of the Christian authorities in a fourfold formulation, and this more obviously a reference to writings. This formulation balanced two collections from the Old Testament and two from the New: the Law, Prophets, Gospels, and Apostles. The "Law and the Prophets" often stood for the whole Old Testament canon (e.g., Matt 22:40; John 1:45; Acts 24:14; 28:23; Rom 3:21; and frequently later). Christians soon paralleled this with the Gospels and Apostles. Thus, Irenaeus could put the "writings of the Evangelists and the Apostles" alongside "the Law and the Prophets" (*Adv. haer.* 1.3.6).[52] The *Epistle to Diognetus* 11.6 states, "The fear of the Law is sung, the grace of the Prophets is known, the faith of the Gospels is established, the tradition of the Apostles is kept, and the grace of the church exults." Clement of Alexandria, in a context discussing "reading the scriptures of the Lord," speaks of his four part Bible as "the ecclesiastical harmony of the Law and the Prophets together, and the Apostles also along with the Gospel" (*Strom.* 6.11.88.5). Tertullian includes in the faith of the church at Rome that "She combines the Law and the Prophets with the writings of Evangelists and Apostles, from which she drinks in her faith" (*Praescr.* 36).[53] This fourfold summary of scripture finds frequent expression in Origen. Note his listing, "Law, Prophets . . . Gospel Writings, and Apostles' letters" (*Comm. S. of S.* 2.3).[54] He affirms the agreement "of the Old Scriptures

51. The formulation continued in use as late as the early fifth century, e.g., "Prophets, Gospels, and Apostolic Writings" in Nicetas, *Utility of Hymn Singing*, 3.

52. Cf. "The preaching of the apostles, the authoritative teaching of the Lord, the announcements of the prophets, the writings [dictated words] of the apostles, and the ministry of the law" (*Haer.* 2.35.4). Irenaeus had various twofold formulations: "Law and Prophets" for the Old Testament (*Haer.* e.g., 3.9.2; 4.5.1; 4.64); "the entire scriptures, the Prophets and the Gospels" (2.27.2); "The Mosaic law and the grace of the new covenant" (3.12.11); "Law" and "Gospel" as two covenants (4.9.1; cf. 4.12.3– 4). Threefold formulations: "the prophets, the apostles, and the Spirit himself" (3.19.2) "prophets, apostles, and all the disciples" (3.24.1); prophets, Christ, and the law (4.2.1).

53. For the latter pair, cf. *Praescr.* 4, "the sayings of the Lord and the letters of the apostles." Tertullian more often makes a twofold classification, as "Law and Gospel": Marc. 1.19 (where they are described as "two documents"); 4.1; 4.11; 5.2, 13; this classification is frequently expressed as a distinction of the Old and New Testaments, for which see below.

54. In the *Comm. Cant.*, as elsewhere, "Law and Prophets" stands for the Old

with the New, of the Law with the Prophets, of the Gospels with the Apostolic Scriptures, and of the Apostolic Scriptures with each other" (*Comm. Mt.* 2). The scriptures "inspired by the Holy Spirit" were "the Gospels and Apostolic writings, and the Law and the Prophets" (*De princ.* 1.3.1).[55] He also spoke of "the Scriptures of the Law and Prophets and Apostles and Gospels" (*Hom. Ex.* 12.4).

A shorthand expression for the authorities recognized by Christians was "prophets and apostles," it being understood that the Lord's authority stood behind both. This appears already in 2 Peter 3:2, "Remember the words spoken in the past by the holy prophets, and the commandment of the Lord and Savior spoken through your apostles." It serves as a summary of the scriptures read in church according to Justin, *1 Apology* 67.3 (cf. *Dial.* 119.6) and the two categories for public reading that the *Shepherd* could not belong to in the *Muratorian Fragment* lines 77–78. Compare the "prophetic and apostolic meadow" as Clement of Alexandria's summary of the sources of knowledge (*Strom.* 1.1). This terminology may be seen as sketching a theology of the "pre-Canon" or "proto-Canon."[56] Such an anticipation of the two-part Christian Bible may also be seen in the reference to "the books and the apostles" in *2 Clem.* 14.2.

The terminology, however, that came to prevail was that of Old Covenant (Testament) and New Covenant (Testament). This usage began before the end of the second century.[57] Melito of Sardis reported going to Palestine where he "learned accurately the books of the Old Covenant" (Eusebius, *H.E.* 4.26.3), wording that might imply there were also books of a New Covenant but not necessarily with this title. An anonymous opponent of Montanism spoke of "the word of the new covenant of the gospel" (Eusebius, *H.E.* 5.16.3) but apparently with reference to the message more than to a collection of books (see further below). Irenaeus made frequent use of the terminology of old and new covenants, but it is not clear that he used "New Covenant" as a designation for a collection of books, although some statements approximate this.[58] "The old would be that previous giving of the law; and the new points out that manner of life according to the

---

Testament. Cf. 3.12 for "Old Testament Scriptures" and "Gospels."

55. Cf. *Princ.* pref. 4: "God . . . gave the Law, the Prophets, and the Gospels, being also the God of the apostles and of the Old and New Testaments."

56. Farkasfalvy, "'Prophets and Apostles,'" 120.

57. Kinzig ("*Kainē diathēkē*") provides more references. See n. 87 for the use of the terminology in the Montanist controversy.

58. See Ferguson, "The Covenant Idea in the Second Century," 140–48 (on Irenaeus) and 150–51 (on Covenant as a title for books); see chap. 14 above.

gospel" (*Adv. haer.* 4.9.1). The two covenants came from the same God, a thrust against Marcion and some Gnostics, and contained the highest and best laws in common (*Adv. haer.* 4.12.3). In other passages Irenaeus makes more of a contrast between the covenants (*Adv. haer.* 4.11.3; 4.13.1–2), and in some of these he comes closer to an identification of the new covenant with books. Thus, after quoting from 1 Corinthians 7, Irenaeus says the apostles "granted certain precepts in the new covenant" similar to what God did in the old covenant (*Adv. haer.* 4.15.2). In speaking of the Scriptures and the "difference of the covenants," he puts the "Mosaic law and the grace of the new covenant" together as both suited to their respective times (*Adv. haer.* 3.12.11–12). However, even if we could be sure that Irenaeus was associating books with the new covenant, that does not make New Covenant a title for the books.

No uncertainty attaches to the use by writers after Irenaeus of Old and New Covenants as titles for collections of books. Clement of Alexandria says, "In both Covenants mention is made of the righteous" (*Str.* 5.6.38), and "It is preached and spoken by the Old and New Covenant" (*Str.* 5.13.85). He quotes Matt 5:27–28 as "the voice of the Lord in the New Covenant" (*Str.* 3.11.71). The "ecclesiastical rule," as stated by Clement, is "the concord and harmony of the Law and the Prophets with the Covenant delivered at the coming of the Lord" (*Strom.* 6.15).[59] Tertullian's Latin gave "testament" (*testamentum*) as the equivalent to covenant in western European languages. His usual word for the scriptures was *instrumentum*,[60] and he used this word also for "covenant," but he recognized that "testament" was the common Christian term: "each Instrument, or Testament, as it is more usual to call it" (*Adv. Marc.* 4.1).[61] He referred to written passages in the Old Testament and New Testament in confirmation of his views on the Trinity (*Adv. Prax.* 15) and quotes prohibitions issued by Paul and Jesus in the "New Testament" (*De pud.* 6.5).[62] These passages make it likely that Tertullian, in the context of discussing the two dispensations of the Law

---

59. For Clement's use of "covenant" language, see Ferguson, "The Covenant Idea," 151, 152–54 (see chap. 14 above); and Kinzig, "*Kainē diathēkē*," 529.

60. E.g., *Apol.* 21.1; *Res.* 21.1; 33:1; 39.8; 40.1; *Herm.* 19; 20; *Praescr.* 38.8; *Marc.* 4.2; 4.6.7. Especially notable is *Pud.* 10 where he notes that the *Shepherd* had failed to find a place in the *divino instrumento* ("divine Instrument"), the scriptures.

61. Ferguson, "The Covenant Idea," 148–50; and Kinzig, "*Kainē diathēkē*," 529–30, 536–41. Kinzig suggests that it was Marcion who usually called his Bible *testamentum* (539–40).

62. *Pud.* 1.5 refers to the judgments in "each Testament" and *Jejun.* 15 contrasts the teachings of the "Old Testament" and "New."

and the Gospel, is using New Testament of a collection of books when he writes, "The New Testament is made very concise and is disentangled from the intricate burdens of the Law" (*Adv. Marc.* 4.1).

Hippolytus in likening the church to a ship compared its tillers to "the two testaments" (*Antichr.* 59): the statement is not unambiguous between "agreements" or "written records" of the agreements, but the latter is more likely, especially in view of the usage of his predecessors and contemporaries. For him "holy scriptures" included books that we know as Old Testament and New Testament.[63] Cyprian a few years later used the terminology of "old and new" without the word "covenant" in reference to the scriptures: "As you examine more fully the scriptures, old and new, and read through the complete volumes of the spiritual books" (*Test.* pref.).

Origen followed what was by his time already common Christian usage to designate the two parts of scripture as "Old and New Covenants," but his philological training made him recognize the novelty of this usage, so he spoke of "the divine scriptures of the so-called Old and New Covenant" (*De princ.* 4.1.1).[64] When Eusebius spoke of "covenantal" writings (*H.E.* 3.3.3), he was not coining a new term for what was not yet called the canon, but making an adjective of the title that had been in use for at least a century for those books that we now call the canon. If there was a name for a collection of books as the New Covenant (Testament), there must have been some recognizable entity to which this name referred, and it must have been set over against another body of writings known as "Old Testament."[65]

Whatever internal factors provided the motive for the recognition of a canon, what external factors hastened the process and sharpened the definition of the canon?

63. "Whatever things, then, the holy scriptures declare, at these let us look" (*Noet.* 9), and in the following exposition he quotes not only from the Prophets and Psalms but also from Acts (specifically identified as scripture: 13, 14), John, Matthew, and Revelation.

64. The same qualification occurs in *Comm. Jo.* 5.8; also for the Old Testament in *Or.* 22.1, and even for covenant in reference to God's agreements (*Mart.* 12). Kinzig ("*Kainē diathēkē*," 530–32, 543) attributes the reluctance to the Marcionite origin of the terminology (I understand "unaware of the [the title's] origin" in his his statement to be a misprint for "aware"), but Origen's qualification "so-called" even for "agreements" may reflect the common Hellenistic usage for "last will and testament." For Origen's distinction between the Old and New Testaments see also *Princ.* 3.1.16; *Comm. Jo.* 1.4–5 (where he includes Acts and the Epistles in "Gospel"); *Comm. Matt.* 10.12 ("Old and New Scriptures").

65. Kinzig, "*Kainē diathēkē*," 536.

EXTERNAL INFLUENCES

Many of the debates in the post-apostolic church were over the question of where to find the authentic voice of revelation and authentic Christianity. The church's struggle with false teaching and the consequent definition of the boundaries of right belief carried with them the recognition of certain books as the source of authentic teaching.

Marcion

The conflict with Marcion takes pride of place in the history of the formation of a canon of scriptures. Marcion had the first collection of authoritative Christian writings of which we are aware. Because of this, many ascribe the idea of a New Testament canon to him,[66] but others doubt this claim.[67] This claim is possible only by not recognizing the authority that New Testament books already had in the church. The letters of Paul were already collected by Marcion's time; the four Gospels were written, in circulation, and perhaps already being brought together. The new contribution of Marcion, as far as evidence now available goes, was to bring a Gospel (Luke) and the letters of Paul into one collection. His introduction to this collection, the *Antitheses*, set forth the contrast between the Old Testament and the Gospel, a contrast that makes plausible the suggestion that Marcion was the one who first gave the designation Old Covenant and New Covenant to bodies of writings.[68] However, his explicit rejection of the Old Testament as Christian scripture raises doubts about this suggestion.

Marcion's combination of the Gospel and the Apostle is often seen as the impetus for his opponents to begin the process of bringing together more Gospels and other writings, notably the Acts and perhaps some of the General Epistles, as a counterweight to his exclusive Paulinism. This was not the way his opponents saw the situation. Perhaps, writing from a later time, they saw the situation from the perspective of that later time, but the historian should allow for the possibility that they recorded what

66. Von Harnack, *The Origin of the New Testament*; Knox, *Marcion and the New Testament*.

67. Barton (*The Letter and the Spirit*, 35–62) refutes Harnack's thesis that Marcion created the idea of the Christian canon and also its more plausible modified version, that Marcion expedited the process of canonization.

68. See nn. 57 and 64. Tertullian said, "The whole aim . . . of his *Antitheses* centers in establishing a diversity between the Old and New Testaments" (*Marc.* 4.6).

had been the reaction from an earlier time. What the early church remembered about Marcion, and repeatedly criticized him for, was his rejection of the God of the Old Testament, not a putative role in creating the New Testament.[69] Memories are not always accurate or complete, but the collective consciousness shows what was thought to be important.

The criticism of Marcion included his limiting the Gospel to Luke alone and revising the letters of Paul. Irenaeus had this to say on the subject:

> Marcion [besides abolishing the prophets and the law] mutilates the Gospel that is according to Luke . . . He likewise persuaded his disciples that he himself was more worthy of credit than are those apostles who have handed down the Gospel to us, furnishing his followers not with the Gospel but merely a fragment of it. In like manner, too, he dismembered the letters of Paul. (*Adv. haer.* 1.27.2)

Most of our detailed knowledge of Marcion's position comes from Tertullian's refutation.

> Marcion ought to be called to a strict account concerning these other Gospels [he has mentioned John, Matthew, and Mark] also, for having omitted them, and insisted in preference on Luke; as if they, too, had not had free course in the churches as well as Luke's Gospel from the beginning. (*Adv. Marc.* 4.5)

He elsewhere says:

> Since Marcion separated the New Testament from the Old, he is necessarily subsequent to that which he separated, inasmuch as it was only in his power to separate what was previously united. Having been united previous to its separation, the fact of its subsequent separation proves the subsequence also of the man who effected the separation. (*Praesc.* 30)

With reference to Paul, Tertullian counters Marcion's giving the title of Laodiceans to Ephesians with the church's true tradition, but he then dismisses the significance of the title with a statement that clearly reflects a longstanding "canonical" authority for Paul's letters: "In writing to a certain church the apostle did in fact write to all" (*Adv. Marc.* 5.17.1),[70] since he was a divine spokesman.

---

69. Barton, *The Spirit and the Letter*, 56. Irenaeus, *Haer.* 1.27.2; 4.38.1–5; Tertullian, *Praescr.* 30; 38.

70. Cf. *Mur. Frg.* lines 41–59.

In the context of his statement about the four Gospels, quoted earlier, Irenaeus noted the preference of various false teachers for one Gospel:

> So firm is the ground upon which these Gospels rest that the very heretics themselves bear witness to them, and starting from them, each endeavors to establish his own peculiar doctrine. For the Ebionites . . . use Matthew's Gospel . . .; Marcion mutilates that according to Luke . . . ; those who separate Jesus from Christ [Docetists]. . . prefer the Gospel by Mark . . .; those who follow Valentinus make copious use of that according to John . . . (*Adv. haer.* 3.11.7)

The idea of having only one, or one principal, Gospel had great appeal. That may have been behind Tatian's production of the *Diatessaron*, to keep the material from the four Gospels but to make explicit that they tell one story.

Justin Martyr tells us that he wrote against Marcion and other heretics (*1 Apol.* 26; cf. 58). The treatise was not preserved, whether from accident, from limitations in its argument, or from the taking up of what was of value in later refutations. If the last, may the argument against a narrowing down of the apostolic witness have also been affirmed by Justin? Was Marcion's use of only Luke a factor in Justin compiling collections of the teachings of Jesus from both Luke and Matthew? At any rate, it is clear that Tertullian was not the first to realize that there was a problem with Marcion's Bible and try to answer his claims. The classic statements of a position and (negatively) the classic responses usually come a generation or two later as a result of conflict and preliminary debates. Tertullian was a highly original thinker and writer, but the main issues were defined well before him by such as Justin and Irenaeus.

At any rate, the four-Gospel canon, for whatever difficulties it may give theologians, was seen as a defense against heresy.[71] Moreover, it is a great boon to the historian to have multiple witnesses to the life of Jesus and to the Christian story. Not only the four-Gospel canon and the addition of some of the other non-Pauline writings but the whole New Testament as a unified collection of writings may go back to the Marcionite crisis; so argues a significant new study by David Trobisch.[72]

---

71. Cullmann, "Die Plurality der Evangelien" = "The Plurality of the Gospels"; Merkel (*Die Pluralität der Evangelien*) has a collection of texts.

72. Trobisch, *Endredaktion*, 122–23, 158. See also the recently published English version of this volume: Trobisch, *The First Edition of the New Testament*.

Instead of taking the usual history of theology approach of tracing the development by examining literary sources, Trobisch argues that the proper approach is to examine the history of the Christian Bible as a book. The four oldest manuscripts of the New Testament—Sinaiticus, Vaticanus, Alexandrinus, and Ephraemi Rescriptus—are from the fourth and fifth centuries. Each manuscript is independent of the others, but their agreement in extent and order of contents means we must assume a common archetype.[73] The external identifying characteristics of the witnesses to the text of the Christian Bible—the type of abbreviation of the *nomina sacra*, use of the codex, a common pattern of names for the individual books (Gospel according to . . . ; General Epistle of . . . ; Epistle of Paul to . . .), and a uniform name for the two parts of the whole collection (New Testament and Old Testament)—all go back to the earliest stage of transmission. They show the work of a single redaktor who produced the canonical edition of the New Testament as part of a total Christian scripture.[74] The internal contents show an interest in unity and a harmonizing feature, between Paul and Peter and between Paul and the Jerusalem apostles. These features fit the time of the Marcionite conflict, and the inclusion of the Synoptic Gospels together with the Gospel of John suggest the context of the Easter controversy, when differences in custom were accepted as not inconsistent with the one faith. These considerations point to the middle of the second century at the latest for the production of the canonical edition of the Bible.[75] Trobisch does not venture a specific place, person, or circle where this edition originated, but its widespread acceptance in the Christian world at the end of the second century and beginning of the third attests its success in orthodox circles. The independent literary attestation for use of (some of) the General Epistles is not so strong as for the other writings by the mid-second century, and the degree of uniformity in the order of books in the manuscript tradition may be exaggerated by Trobisch; but the uniform manuscript features and the way in which Trobisch ties the contents of the collection together support his overall thesis of a concrete circle that brought the individual writings together in a literary unity.[76] He raises the question: Is not one forced to understand the early church's discussion about the authenticity of individual writings a reaction

73. Trobisch, *Endredaktion*, 35–39, 54, 58.

74. Ibid., 16–35, 58–71.

75. Ibid., 124, 158–99.

76. Ibid., 11–16.

to a completed book (rather than stages on the way to the collecting of a book)?[77]

Gnostic Teachers

By the time of Marcion some of the early teachers of those now lumped together under the term "Gnostics" were active. The charge was lodged against some Gnostics of enlarging the canon to include more books than the great church recognized. Irenaeus contrasted the approach of Marcion and the Valentinians:

> Marcion, rejecting the entire Gospel, yea rather, cutting himself off from the Gospel, boasts that he has part in the Gospel. . . . Those who are from Valentinus, being, on the other hand, altogether reckless, while they put forth their own compositions, boast that they possess more Gospels than there really are. Indeed, they have arrived at such a pitch of audacity as to entitle their comparatively recent writing "the Gospel of Truth," though it agrees in nothing with the Gospels of the apostles. (*Adv. haer.* 3.11.9)

He mentions the *Gospel of Truth*, which he contrasts with the Gospels "handed down from the apostles" that he classifies as "scriptures." In more summary fashion, however, he says that apart from Marcion and his followers, who mutilate the scriptures, "all the rest, inflated with the false name of `knowledge,' do certainly recognize the scriptures, but they pervert the interpretations" (*Adv. haer.* 3.12.12). Tertullian too contrasted Marcion's reductionism with what he considered Valentinus's expansion of the Gospel material:

> Of the scriptures we have our being before there was any other way, before they were interpolated by [heretics] . . . One man perverts the scriptures with his hand, another their meaning by his exposition. For although Valentinus seems to use the entire volume, he has nonetheless laid violent hands on the truth only with a more cunning mind and skill than Marcion.

77. Ibid., 57. The situation may be parallel to the discussions of the Jewish rabbis concerning Ecclesiastes, Song of Solomon (*m. Yadaim* 3:5) and Esther (*b. Meg.* 7a). They were not considering whether certain books should be admitted to the collection of holy writings, but why they had these books Cf. Barton, *The Spirit and the Letter*, 108–31, for a plausible explanation of the rabbinic discussions. See also Barton's and Gamble's contributions to this volume for alternative explanations of the influence of Marcion on the origins of the New Testament canon.

> Marcion expressly and openly used the knife, not the pen, since
> he made such an excision of the scriptures as suited his own
> subject-matter. Valentinus, however, abstained from such exci-
> sion, because he did not invent scriptures to square with his own
> subject-matter . . . and yet he took away more, and added more,
> by removing the proper meaning of every particular word . . .
> (*Praescr.* 38)

Tertullian's argument presupposes an entity that he calls the "Christian scriptures" (ch. 37) and "our scriptures" (ch. 38). The Old Testament is not the subject of this discussion. In passing, we note that Valentinus was using "the whole volume," so there must have been an identifiable body of Christian writings that could be treated as a single book (*integro instrumento*). Valentinus achieved his purposes by the pen, reinterpretation, but Marcion by the knife, excision.

The "Gnostics" provide some of the earliest testimony to the authority of New Testament writings. Some of them employ terminology in their titles from the usage of other Christians (*Gospel of Truth, Gospel of Philip*), but the significant element to be noted is the wide acquaintance with and use of documents now considered canonical. The way in which the *Gospel of Truth*, for example, draws on language and gives a "Gnosticizing" interpretation seem to imply a recognition of authoritative scripture.[78] The somewhat later *Gospel of Philip* uses citation formulas to introduce quotations from New Testament books.[79] Early Gnostic teachers offered their own interpretations of New Testament books. Basilides (c. 117–138) quotes the Gospels of Matthew, Luke and John and Paul's letters (Romans, 1 and 2 Corinthians, and Ephesians) as scripture and wrote exegeses of the Gospel.[80] He is our earliest full witness to the New Testament as scripture, but the offhand way he speaks shows that he was not the first to do this and was reflecting common usage. Lloyd Patterson has concluded that the unity of scripture that Irenaeus found in the history of salvation was not his discovery but was expressed by the Valentinians. Irenaeus took over the pattern of the Valentinain interpretation but gave it a different content.[81] It seems possible to push the argument one step further back:

78. Van Unnik ("The 'Gospel of Truth' and the New Testament," esp. 108–26) finds acquaintance with the Gospels, Pauline Epistles, Hebrews, and Revelation, and traces of Acts, 1 Peter, and 1 John, used in such amanner that proves they had authority for the author and had enjoyed that authority for a considerable time.

79. Stroud, "New Testament Quotations in the Nag Hammadi Gospel of Philip."

80. Grant, *The Formation of the New Testament*, 121–24.

81. Patterson, "Irenaeus and the Valentinians."

The Valentinians could not have cited and used scripture the way they did unless the scriptures read and honored in the church had already created the notion of Christian scriptures. The use of the scriptures in a different way from that of the church forced an examination of scripture as a whole, as is done by Irenaeus (see further below). The first commentary on a New Testament book was by the Valentinian Heracleon on John. Since Gnostics had their own writings, presumably they would not have used New Testament books unless a consensus of earlier usage constrained them.

This constraint, of course, was not felt by those groups further removed from catholic Christianity, but for those closer to the orthodox, such as the Valentianians, the issue was not so much one of scripture as the interpretation of scripture, as the quotations from Irenaeus and Tertullian above indicate. Is there a plan within scripture (the rule of truth)[82] by which scripture is to be interpreted, or does one bring a plan from outside scripture and rearrange its contents to fit that plan? Irenaeus and the orthodox said there was a plan or plot within scripture itself. It is all the more significant that this plot derived from placing the Christian sources of authority alongside the Old Testament. Irenaeus, after identifying the triple authority of prophets, Lord, and apostles as "scriptures," used a graphic illustration from mosaic art to describe the situation:

> Such, then, is their [disciples of Ptolemaeus] system, which neither the prophets announced, nor the Lord taught, nor the apostles delivered, but . . . they gather their views from reading non-scriptural writings . . . , while they endeavor to adapt with an air of probability to their own peculiar assertions the parables of the Lord, the sayings of the prophets, and the words of the apostles in order that their scheme may not seem altogether without support. In doing so, however, they disregard the order and the connection [*taxis kai heimon*] of the scriptures, and so far as in them lies, dismember and destroy the truth . . . Their manner of acting is just as if one, when a beautiful image of a king has been constructed by some skillful artist out of precious jewels, should then take this likeness of the man all to pieces, should rearrange the gems and so fit them together as to make them into the form of a dog or of a fox and even that but poorly executed; and should then maintain and declare that this was the beautiful image of the king that the skillful artist constructed pointing to the jewels that had been admirably fitted together by the first artist to form the image of the king but have been with

82. Ammundsen, "The Rule of Truth in Irenaeus."

> bad effect transferred by the latter one to the shape of a dog, and
> by thus exhibiting the jewels should deceive the ignorant who
> had no conception what a king's form was like and persuade
> them that the miserable likeness of the fox was in fact the beau-
> tiful image of the king. (*Adv. haer.* 1.8.1)

The scriptures must have been regarded as a sacred book for these heretics (in Irenaeus's estimate) to have used them in this way or have felt that they had to find their doctrine in them. Moreover, for Irenaeus there was already an established "order and connection" that was violated by the Valentinian interpretation.

Tertullian in his *Prescription against Heretics* argues the question of who has the right to interpret the scriptures. "They [heretics] treat of the scriptures and recommend their opinions out of the scriptures. To be sure, they do. From what other source could they derive arguments concerning the things of the faith, except from the records of the faith?" (ch. 14). He denies to the heretics this right because the scriptures belong to the catholic Christians (ch. 15; 19). He charged Valentinus wth tampering with the scriptures "by his different expositions and acknowledged emendations" (*Praescr.* 30).

The Gnostic controversy made imperative a clarification of what writings accurately expressed apostolic teaching and apostolic authority. Against the secret tradition claimed by certain Gnostic Christians, Irenaeus appealed to the public teaching of the churches. This included the teaching of the scriptures, as can be seen by Irenaeus's refutation in Books 3–5 of *Adversus haereses*. As is recognized, Irenaeus is the first orthodox Christian author whose works argue from scripture as a whole. After setting forth the views of the heretics (book 1) and giving a rational refutation (book 2), he declares that he will devote a special book to the "scriptures of the Lord" (2.35.4), referring to the immediately mentioned preaching and teaching of the apostles, Lord, prophets, and law. As he begins to adduce "proofs from the scriptures" (3.pref.), he appeals to the Gospel first proclaimed in public and "at a later period by the will of God handed down to us in the scriptures to be the ground and pillar of our faith" (3.1).[83] He starts with the Old Testament (3.6) but then quickly turns to the Gospels of Matthew (3.9), Luke (3.10.1–4), Mark (3.10.5), and John (3.11.1–6). He finds the doctrine of the "other apostles" in the book of Acts—Peter

---

83. Sesboüé ("La preuve par les Ecritures chez S. Irénée," in examining *Haer.* 3.5.1 concludes that by "scriptures" Irenaeus primarily means the Old Testament, although he did regard the New Testament as scripture.

(3.12.1–7), Philip (3.12.8), Paul (3.12.9), Stephen (3.12.10), the letter of the apostles in Acts 15 (3.12.14), and Paul again (3.13–15). From the witness of the apostles in book 3, Irenaeus turns in book 4 primarily to "the words of the Lord," supplemented from the prophets and Paul.[84] The eschatological treatment in book 5 makes much use of Revelation (esp. 5.34–36).

Montanism

The principal criticism of Montanism concerned its manner of ecstatic prophesying.[85] The church affirmed in principle that prophecy continued in the church but found examples lacking as time went on and in regard to the Montanists found their claims did not measure up to scriptural standards. The standard by which to judge authentic prophesy was found in scripture, the New Testament as well as the Old Testament. We could wish to be able to identify the source used by Epiphanius in his description of Montanism, but critical opinion puts it in the second or third century.[86] The author judges Montanist prophecy false when compared with "the prophecies which exist in truth and came to be in truth in the Old and New Testaments."[87] The earliest evidence is not unambiguous on how the Montanists related their prophecies to the New Testament. Did they supplement or interpret it? Their opponent Apollonius at the end of the second century says of a Montanist confessor named Themiso that he "composed a general epistle [*katholikēn epistolēn*] of the apostle," but there seems no claim of "scriptural" authority intended.[88] Another opponent of about the same time, Gaius in Rome, is described by Eusebius as "curbing the rashness and daring of [the Montanists] in composing new scriptures" (*H.E.* 6.20.3), but how much does this wording depend on Eusebius? The question may turn on what was acknowledged theoretically and what functioned practically in regard to authority. In the early third century Hippolytus characterized the Montanists as saying that "They have learned something more through them [Montanus, Priscilla, Maximilla] than

---

84. For the unity of book 4, see Bacq, *De l'ancienne*, usefully summarized by Donovan, "Irenaeus in Recent Scholarship," 221–23.

85. Heine, *The Montanist Oracles and Testimonia.*

86. See the comments on earlier study in ibid., x.

87. Epiphanius, *Pan.* 48.3.2. Cf. the Anonymous quoted by Eusebius, "They will not be able to prove that any prophet either of those in the Old Testament or the New was inspired in this [ecstatic] way" (*H.E.* 5.17.3).

88. Quoted by Eusebius, *H.E.* 5.18.5.

from the Law and the Prophets and the Gospels" (*Ref. haer.* 8.19).[89] And so the Montanists came to be criticized also for expanding the realm of revelation beyond the apostolic age. The Pseudo-Tertullian charges, "They say that the Paraclete said more in Montanus than Christ revealed in the Gospel, and they say he has said not only more, but things that are better and greater" (*Adv. omn. haer.* 7).

The opponents of Montanism, therefore, expressed the conviction that the period of revelation had ended. There may be a question about referring the statements to written records, but they seem to be included in what the anonymous author quoted by Eusebius said.

> For a very long and considerable time, dear Avircius Marcellus, you have enjoined me to compose a treatise against the heresy of those who follow Miltiades. I was rather hesitant until now, not because I lacked the ability to refute the lie and bear testimony to the truth, but from fear and concern lest in any way I appear to some to add a new writing or add to the word of the new covenant of the gospel to which one who has chosen to live according to the gospel itself can neither add nor subtract. (*H.E.* 5.16.3)

The unknown author's profession of modesty is a conceit, but he may have chosen to express the literary convention of modesty in the way that he did because the Montanist oracles were adding "to the new covenant" and were being collected in writing. Van Unnik was correct to withdraw this passage as a witness to a completed New Testament to which nothing could be added or taken away, but he was right to see in it a connection of the new covenant with writings that recorded it.[90] Such is implicit in the Anonymous's professed reason for his reluctance to write, and the wording is pointless unless the "new covenant of the gospel" was now to be found in writings. Elsewhere, he speaks of "Old and New Testaments,"[91] possibly eras of time but also possibly collections of writings.

The consciousness brought to the surface by the Montanist controversy that the era of revelation was closed and that there was a qualitative

---

89. Cf. *Haer.* 10.25, "They go astray by paying more attention to their [Montanus, Priscilla, and Maximilla] words than to the Gospels when they appoint new and unusual fasts."

90. He argued for this passage as a witness to a fixed corpus of writings in "De la regle"; in "*Hē kainē diathēkē*," he concludes that it refers rather to the total message, but he does suggestthat the Anonymous was the first to link the name "New Testament" with a collection of books.

91. See n. 87 above.

difference between the church's origins and the present had definite implications for the recognition of a canon of scripture. Henning Paulsen has argued that the aspects of "normativity, exclusiveness, and fixed interpretation," which emerged in the Montanist controversy, "when taken together mark the meaning of Montanism for the formation of the New Testament canon."[92] One could understand this as making explicit what was latent in the tradition and faith of the church.

Persecution and Martyrdom

Marcionites, Montanists, and mainstream Christians knew the experience of martyrdom. Little attention has been paid to the factor of persecution in the history of the canon, but William R. Farmer has called attention to how suitable the New Testament canon was for strengthening Christians facing martyrdom.[93] The four canonical Gospels witnessed to the real flesh and blood martyrdom of the Son of God; the letters of Paul witnessed to the same gospel, told of Paul's sufferings, and set the cross of Jesus as a norm for Christian conduct; the Acts of the Apostles told of the triumphant sufferings of the early church; Revelation held out the hope of victory in the face of suffering and martyrdom; and other letters (especially 1 Peter and 1 John) set the humanity and sufferings of Jesus at the center of faith.

By the time of the Diocletian persecution in 303 Roman authorities included in their campaign to confiscate Christian property the requirement that Christian books be handed in and burned. In the words of Eusebius, "We saw with our very eyes . . . the inspired and sacred scriptures committed to the flames in the marketplaces" in response to the imperial letter "ordering the destruction by fire of the scriptures" (*H.E.* 8.2.1 and 4). The requirement showed that the authorities knew Christians had an identifiable set of holy writings and knew their importance to the Christian communities.[94] Hierocles, governor of Bithynia and the chief promoter of the persecution, was knowledgeable of the Christian Bible and had already attempted in two books against the Christians "to prove the falsehood of sacred scripture," by which was meant Christian sacred writings as the

---

92. Paulsen, "Die Bedeutung des Montanismus," esp. 43 and 52.

93. Farmer and Farkasfalvy, *The Formation of the New Testament Canon*, 22–26, 31–43, 55–56; on the canon of the Martyrs of Gaul (Eusebius, *H.E.* 5.1–2), see further Farkasfalvy, "Christological Content."

94. Gamble, *Books and Readers*, 144–50.

reference to Paul and Peter makes clear.[95] Christians themselves thought they had an identifiable set of scriptures, for they immediately were exercised over the morality of giving up documents to the authorities, an issue that became the occasion for the Donatist schism. Christians might hide writings, try to pass off apocryphal and heretical texts, or decide in some cases what to hand over and what not to, but for the most part they knew what books the soldiers were looking for.

Particularly impressive is the size of the library of the church in Cirta, capital of Numidia in North Africa. The chief official asked that the "writings of the law [the Christian 'law'?] and anything else you have here" be brought out. The subdeacon Catullinus surrendered "one very large codex" (a text of the Gospels?) but explained that the lectors possessed most of the books. The authorities then searched the homes of seven lectors with the command to give up the "Scriptures" and found thirty-six more books of varying size.[96] We are not told the contents of these volumes. However, it may be noted that the Donatist schism, which arose out of conflicts resulting from different responses to the command to hand over scriptures, had no different canon from the Catholic churches of North Africa according to the testimony of Augustine.[97]

After Constantine

When the situation reversed under Constantine, the Roman government financed the multiplication of copies of scriptures instead of destroying them. Constantine directed Eusebius to have prepared for the churches in Constantinople fifty copies "of the sacred scriptures which you know to be especially necessary for the restoration and use in the instruction of the church."[98] Eusebius says his prompt fulfillment of the request was acknowledged by letter from Constantine (*V. Const.* 4.37). Constantine knew there was such an entity as the Christian scriptures required for public reading in the new churches being built in Constantinople, and certain books were copied and others left out. Constantine's commis-

---

95. Lactantius, *Inst.* 5.2.

96. *Gesta apud Zenophilum* (ET in Vassal-Philipps, *The Work of St. Optatus*, 353, 355–58) for this information.

97. *Cresc.* 1.37; cf. the definition of these in *Unit. Eccles.* 19.51: "The canonical scriptures of the Law and the Prophets to which are added the Gospels, the Apostolic Epistles, the Acts of the Apostles, and the Apocalypse of John."

98. Eusebius, *Vit. Const.* 4.36; cf. 4.34, "providing copies of the sacred oracles."

sion did not require that Christians decide what the contents of scripture were; it was intended to replace those copies of the scriptures destroyed in the persecution. In complying with Constantine's request, Eusebius was not allowed the nuance of his historical groupings; books were either copied or not.

What did Eusebius include? From his *H.E.* 3.25.1–7 we learn what Eusebius concluded to be the "acknowledged" (*homologoumenai*) or "covenantal" (*endiathēkai*) writings (the two terms are synonymous) in the churches. These were twenty-two books, lacking James, 2 Peter, 2–3 John, and Jude from the present canon. Following the literary criticism of the time, Eusebius had three categories: acknowledged, disputed, and spurious books.[99] Within the "disputed" books (*antilegomenai*) he distinguished those that met the criteria of deriving from apostolic times and authorship by apostles or apostolic men from other works that, although not being "spurious" (*nothoi*), did not. Eusebius' own canon (his word for what we call the canon was "covenantal")[100] included the church's acknowledged books, with the exception of Revelation,[101] plus the writings that he accepted as apostolic in the disputed group.[102] Eusebius's canon was essentially what he found in Origen.[103] Origen while at Alexandria had doubted 2 Peter, 2–3 John, James, and Jude, the same books Eusebius listed as "disputed," but apparently during his stay in Caesarea these

99. Baum, "Der neutestamentliche Kanon bei Eusebios." His thesis is that these categories employed by Eusebius were taken over from Greek criticism of authenticity (321). The latter two terms were not equivalent (337–38). For Eusebius genuine apostolic writings were "canonical" (315), but the list of candidates for canonicity included also writings from the apostolic epoch (316, 326–27). Eusebius had three criteria for grading the church's reception of writings, and all three had to be met for a writing to be "covenantal": use by church writers, evaluation by church writers, and public reading in church (328–33). Writings were classified as spurious on the basis of style and content (335–37).

100. Ibid., 333–34.

101. Mazzucco ("Eusèbe de Césarée et l'*Apocalypse de Jean?*") refers to Eusebius's abundant use of Revelation outside the *Church History* and argues that Eusebius objected to an apocalyptic interpretation of the book, not an allegorical or historical use of it. He applied its apocalyptic elements to the coming of Christ, the destruction of Jerusalem, and the persecutions of Diocletian and Galerius. His political understanding of the Roman empire precluded an apocalypticinterpretation of a millennial reign on earth after Jesus came again.

102. Baum, "Der neutestamentliche Kanon bei Eusebios," 333–34 (for the church's canon); 341–42 (for Eusebius's canon).

103. *H.E.* 6.25.3–14; Origen, *Comm. Jo.* 1.4–6; 5.3; Eusebius also cites the *Comm. Matt.* and the *Fr. Heb.* Baum, "Der neutestamentliche Kanon bei Eusebios," 322.

doubts were removed, for his writings from this later time include these books in the "scriptures."[104] Moreover, Origen considered the writing of scripture had ceased and regarded its contents as "complete."[105] Presumably Eusebius would have had copied in addition to the Septuagint his twenty-six book New Testament.[106] That fact may have contributed to the frequent Greek lists of the scriptures that correspond to our New Testaments but lack Revelation.

Much information has been uncovered in our investigation without reference to the Muratorian Canon. Trobisch in his brief mention of the *Canon Muratori* as not understanding itself to describe the extent of the Christian Bible quotes Hans Lietzmann to the effect that the document is "a kind of introduction to the New Testament."[107] As a corollary of that perspective, it presupposes a canon rather than seeking to establish one.

David Brakke studies external factors in Athanasius's famous *Festal Letter* 39 for the year 367, which first uses "canonized" (*kanonizomena*) scriptures and lists an explicitly closed New Testament canon of twenty-seven books.[108] He argues that Athanasius's disputes with Arians and Melitians reflected "fundamental conflicts between competing modes of Christian authority, spirituality, and social organization."[109] The bishop of Alexandria was not trying to impose a canon where one was lacking or to close a canon that others preferred to leave open. Rather the conflict was "between two competing and distinct canon types,"[110] with Athanasius contending for an authoritative canon that functioned in connection with

104. Oliver ("Origen and the New Testament Canon") citing Origen, *Hom. Exod.* 13.2 and *Hom. Josh.* 7.1. For Origen's New Testament canon, see also Bardenhewer, *Geschichte der altkirchlichen Literatur*, 2:152–56, who defends the reliability of Rufinus's translation of Origen's passages on the canon. Kalin ("Re-examining New Testament Canon History"), by defining canon as a closed list, denies that Origen had a New Testament canon list. He asserts rightly that Eusebius has compiled a list from Origen's writings; but his position on Origen's "canon" depends on discrediting Rufinus's translation of *Hom. Josh.* 7.1 and not considering the sequence of Origen's writings and the possibility that Origen changed his views.

105. *Hom. Jes. Nav.* 7.1 and *Comm. Matt.* 10.12. Cf. the end of his Prologue to the *Comm. Cant.*, where Prov.22:28, "Do not remove the ancient landmark that your ancestors set up," is quoted in support of not giving a place to apocryphal writings.

106. Baum, "Der neutestamentliche Kanon bei Eusebios," 342–44.

107. Trobisch, *Endredaktion*, 57 n. 149, citing Lietzmann, *Wie Wurden die Bücher*, 53.

108. Brakke, "Canon Formation and Social Conflict."

109. Ibid., 399.

110. Ibid., 409.

an episcopally organized Christianity in order to restrain and control both an "academic" Christianity based on the authority of independent teachers whose canon was not precise and an "enthusiastic," "martyr" Christianity that drew inspiration from "apocryphal" books. Such may accurately describe the social context that prompted Athanasius to provide his list of canonical books for the Egyptian churches without depriving Athanasius of a significant place as a witness to a consensus that had long been emerging in the churches.

The councils of the church played little part in the canonization of scripture. When councils did speak on the subject, their voice was a ratification of what had already become the mind of the church.[111] Canon 60 of the Council of Laodicea (c. AD 363) is likely a later insertion into the decrees of the council; it lists a twenty-six book New Testament, lacking Revelation. The first councils certainly to speak on the subject of the canon were in North Africa—Hippo (393) and Carthage (397 and 419). They were under the influence of Augustine, for whom the canon was closed: "For the canon of the sacred writings, which is properly closed" (*Civ. Dei* 22.8).[112]

---

111. Metzger, *The Canon of the New Testament*, 97.

112. His New Testament list, our twenty-seven, is in *Doctr. chr.* 2.8.13.

Bibliography

Achelis, Hans. *Die Canones Hippolyti.* TU 6. Leipzig: Hinrichs, 1891.

Adler, Nikolaus. *Taufe and Handauflegung: Eine exegetisch-theologische Untersuchung von Apg 8, 14–17.* Neutestamentliche Abhandlungen 19/3. Münster: Aschendorf, 1951.

Amann, Émile. "Réordinations." In *Dictionnaire de Théologie Catholique,* edited by Alfred Vacant et al., 13:2390–92. Paris: Letouzey & Ané, 1936.

Ammundsen, Valdemar. "The Rule of Truth in Irenaeus." *JTS* 13 (1912) 574–80. Reprinted in *Orthodoxy, Heresy, and Schism in Early Christianity,* edited by Everett Ferguson, 138–44. Studies in Early Christianity 4. New York: Garland, 1993.

Anderson, C. P. "The Epistle to the Hebrews and the Pauline Letter Collection." *HTR* (1966) 429–38.

Aristotle. *Constitution of Athens.* Edited by J. E. Sandys. London: Macmillan, 1912.

Armstrong, Jonathan J. "Victorinus of Pettau as the Author of the Canon Muratori." *VC* 62 (2008) 1–34.

Arnold, William Rosenzweig. *Ephod and Ark: A Study in the Records and Religion of the Ancient Hebrews.* Harvard Theological Studies 3. Cambridge: Harvard University Press, 1917.

Atchley, E. G. Cuthbert F. *On the Epiclesis of the Eucharistic Liturgy and in the Consecration of the Font.* London: Oxford University Press, 1935.

Attridge, Harold W. *First-Century Cynicism in the Epistles of Heraclitus.* Harvard Theological Studies 29. Missoula, MT: Scholars, 1976.

Avigad, Nachman, and Yigal Yadin, editors. *Genesis Apocryphon: A Scroll from the Wilderness of Judaea.* Jerusalem: Magnes, 1956.

Bacq, Philippe. *De l'ancienne à la nouvelle alliance selon S. Irénée: Unité du livre IV de l'Adversus Haereses.* Sycomore: Série Horizon. Paris; Lethielleux, 1978.

Baehrens, W. A. *Origenes Werke.* Vol. 6–7, *Homilien zum Hexateuch in Rufins Übersetzung.* GCS. Leipzig: Hinrichs, 1927.

Balás, David L. "Marcion Revisited: A 'Post-Harnack' Prespective." In *Texts and Testaments: Critical Essays on the Bible and Early Church Fathers,* edited by W. Eugene March, 95–108. San Antonio, TX: Trinity University Press, 1980.

Baltzer, Klaus. *Das Bundesformular.* 2nd ed. Wissenschaftliche Monographien zum Alten und Neuen Testament 4. Neukirchen Kreis Moers: Neukirchener, 1964. (ET = *The Covenant Formulary: In Old Testament, Jewish, and Early Christian Writings.* Translated by David E. Green. Philadelphia: Fortress, 1971.)

Bardenhewer, Otto. *Geschichte der altkirchlichen Literatur*, Vol. 2, *Vom Ende des zweiten Jahrhunderts bis zum Beginn des vierten Jahrhunderts.* 2nd ed. Freiburg: Herder, 1914. Reprinted, 1962.

Bardtke, Hans. "Die Rechtstellung der Qumran-Gemeinde." *TLZ* 86 (1961) 94–104.

Barlêa, Octavian. *Die Weihe der Bischöfe, Presbyter, and Diakone in vornicänischer Zeit.* Acta philosophica et theological 3. Monachii: Societas Academica Dacoromana, 1969.

Barthelemy, D., and J. T. Milik, editors. *Qumran Cave 1.* Discoveries in the Judaean Desert 1.

Barton, John. *The Spirit and the Letter: Studies in the Biblical Canon.* London: SPCK, 1997. (= *Holy Writings, Sacred Text: The Canon in Early Christianity.* Louisville: Westminster John Knox, 1997.)

Bauckham, Richard. "For Whom Were Gospels Written?" In *The Gospels for All Christians: Rethinking the Gospel Audiences,* edited by Richard Bauckham, 9–48. Grand Rapids: Eerdmans, 1998.

———. "Introduction." In *The Gospels for All Christians: Rethinking the Gospel Audiences,* edited by Richard Bauckham, 1–7. Grand Rapids: Eerdmans, 1998.

Baudissin, Wilhelm. "Priests and Levites." In *Dictionary of the Bible,* edited by James Hastings, 4:67–97. New York: Scribners, 1902.

Bauer, Johannes Bapt. *Die Polykarpbriefe.* Kommentar zu den Apostolischen Vätern 5. Göttingen: Vandenhoeck & Ruprecht, 1995.

Baum, Armin D. "Der neutestamentliche Kanon bei Eusebios: (*Hist. eccl.* 3.25.1–7) im Kontext seiner literaturgeschichtlichen Arbeit." *Ephemerides theologicae lovanienses* 73 (1997) 307–48.

———. "Papias, der Vorzug der Viva Vox, and die Evangelienschriften." *NTS* 44 (1998) 144–51.

Beardslee, William. "The Casting of Lots at Qumran and in the Book of Acts." *NovT* 4 (1960) 245–52.

Beatrice, P. F. "Une citation de l'Evangile de Matthieu dans l'Epître de Barnabé." In *The New Testament in Early Christianity,* edited by J.-M. Sevrin, 231–45. BETL 86. Leuven: Peeters, 1989.

Beckwith, Roger. *The Old Testament Canon of the New Testament Church: And Its Background in Early Judaism.* London: SPCK, 1985.

Behm, Johannes. *Der Begriff Diathēkē im Neuen Testament.* Leipzig: Deichert, 1912.

———. *Die Handauflegung im Urchristentum in religions-geschichtlichen Zusammenhang untersucht.* Naumburg: Pätz, 1911.

Bellinzoni, A. J. "The Gospel of Matthew in the Second Century." *SecCent* 9 (1992) 197–258.

———. *The Sayings of Jesus in the Writings of Justin Martyr.* NovTSup 17. Leiden: Brill, 1967.

Benoit, André. *Saint Irénée: Introduction a l'étude de sa théologie.* Paris: Presses universitaires de France, 1960.

Best, Ernest. "Acts XIII.1–3." *JTS* n.s. 11 (1960) 344–48.

Billerbeck, Paul. *Kommentar zum Neuen Testament aus Talmud und Midrasch.* Vol. 2. Munich: Beck, 1924.

Black, Matthew. *An Aramaic Approach to the Gospels and Acts.* 3rd ed. Oxford: Clarendon, 1967.

Blanchard, Yvés-Marié. *Aux Sources du Canon: Le Temoignage d'Irenee.* Cogitatio Fidei 175. Paris: Cerf, 1993.

Blanchetière, F. "Aux sources de 1'anti-judaïsme chrétien." *RHPR* 53 (1973) 353–98.

Boak, A. E. R. "The Organization of Guilds in Greco-Roman Egypt." *Transactions and Proceedings of the American Philological Association* 68 (1937) 212–20.

Boeft, Jan den, and Jan Bremmer. "Notiunculae martyrologicae IV." *VC* 45 (1991) 105–22.

Bokser, B. Z. "Justin Martyr and the Jews." *JQR* 64 (1973/74) 97–122, 204–11.

Bonner, Gerald. "The Scillitan Saints and the Pauline Epistles." *JEH* 7 (1956) 141–46.

Botte, D. B. "L'authenticité de la *Tradition Apostolique de saint Hippolyte.*" *Recherches de Theologie ancienne et medievale* 16 (1949) 177–85.

Bradshaw, Paul F., editor. *The Canons of Hippolytus*, with a translation by Carol Bebawi. Bramcote, UK: Grove, 1987.

Brakke, David. "Canon Formation and Social Conflict in Fourth-Century Egypt: Athanasius of Alexandria's Thirty-Ninth *Festal Letter.*" *HTR* 87 (1994) 395–419.

Braun, René. *Deus Christianorum.* Paris: Presses universitaires de France, 1962.

Bright, William. *Notes on the Canons of the First Four General Councils.* Oxford: Clarendon, 1882.

Brightman, F. E. "The Sacramentary of Serapion of Thmuis." *JTS* 1 (1900) 247–77.

Brooks, E. W. *The Sixth Book of the Select Letters of Severus Patriarch of Antioch.* 2 vols. in 4. London: Williams & Norgate, 1903.

Brown, Colin, editor. *The New International Dictionary of New Testament Theology.* 4 vols. Grand Rapids: Zondervan, 1975.

Brown, Scott G. "On the Compositional History of the Longer ('Secret') Gospel of Mark." *JBL* 122 (2003) 89–110.

Brox, Norbert. *Falsche Verfasserangaben: Zur Erklärung der frühchristlichen Pseudepigraphie.* Stuttgarter Bibelstudien 79. Stuttgart: KBW, 1975.

———. "Zum Problemstand in der Erforschung der altchristlichen Pseudepigraphie." *Kairos* 15 (1973) 10–23.

Buchanan, George Wesley. *The Consequences of the Covenant.* NovTSup 20. Leiden: Brill, 1970.

Buell, D. K. *Why This New Race: Ethnic Reasoning in Early Christianity.* New York: Columbia University Press, 2005.

Burrows, Millar. *The Dead Sea Scrolls.* New York: Viking, 1955.

Buschmann, Gerd. *Das Martyrium des Polykarp.* Kommentar zu den Apostolischen Väter 6. Göttingen: Vandenhoeck & Ruprecht, 1998.

Busolt, Georg. *Griechische Staatskunde.* 2 vols. 3rd ed. Handbuch der Klassischen Altertmnswissenschaft. Munich: Beck, 1920–1926.

Cabrol, Fernand. "Imposition des mains." In *Dictionnaire d'archéologie chrétienne et de liturgie*, edited by Fernand Cabrol and Henri Leclercq, 7:391–413. Paris: Letouzey & Ané, 1926.

Campenhausen, Hans von. *The Formation of the Christian Bible.* Translated by J. A. Baker. Philadelphia: Fortress, 1972.

———. *Polykarp von Smyrna und die Pastoralbriefe.* Heidelberg: Winter, 1951

Carlton, Stephen C. *The Gospel Hoax: Morton Smith's Invention of Secret Mark.* Waco: Baylor University Press, 2005.

Bibliography

Carruthers, Mary J. *The Book of Memory: A Study of Memory in Medieval Culture.* Cambridge Studies in Medieval Literature 10. Cambridge: Cambridge University Press, 1990.

Cary, M. *A History of Rome down to the Reign of Constantine.* 2nd ed. New York: St. Martins, 1954.

Charles, R. H. *The Apocrypha and Pseudepigrapha of the Old Testament in English.* Oxford: Clarendon, 1913.

Charlesworth, James H. editor. *The Old Testament Pseudepigrapha.* Vol. 1. Garden City, NY: Doubleday, 1983.

Chase, Frederic Henry. *The Old Syriac Element in the Text of Codex Bezae.* London: Macmillan, 1893.

Christo, G. G. *The Church's Identity Established through Images according to Saint John Chrysostom.* Rolli, NH: Orthodox Research Institute, 2006.

Cirlot, Felix L. *The Early Eucharist.* London: SPCK, 1939.

Clark, Donald Lehman. *Rhetoric in Greco-Roman Education.* New York: Columbia University Press, 1957.

Coleborne, W. "The Shepherd of Hermas: A Case for Multiple Authorship and Some Implications." *Studia Patristica* 10 (1970) 65–70.

Congar, Yves. *Jalons pour une théologie du laïcat.* Unam Sanctam 23. Paris: Cerf, 1954.

Connolly, R. Hugh. *Didascalia Apostolorum.* 1929. Reprinted, Ancient Texts and Translations. Eugene, OR: Wipf & Stock, 2010.

———. *The So-called Egyptian Church Order and Derived Documents.* Texts and Studies 8/4. Cambridge: Cambridge University Press, 1916.

Cooper, James, and J. J. Maclean. *The Testament of Our Lord.* Edinburgh: T. & T. Clark, 1902.

Coppens, Joseph. *L'imposition des mains et les rites connexes dans le Nouveau Testament et dans l'eglise ancienne: Études de théologie positive.* Universitas catholica Lovaniensis II/15. Paris: Gabalda, 1925.

Coquin, René-Georges. *Les Canons d'Hippolyte.* Patrologia Orientalis 31/2. Paris: Firmin-Didot, 1966.

Cosgrove, C. H. "Justin Martyr and the Emerging Christian Canon." *VC* 36 (1982) 209–32.

Cotsonis, Jerome. "A Contribution to the Interpretation of the 19th Canon of the First Ecumenical Council." *Revue des études Byzantines* 19 (1961) 184–97.

Coyle, J. Kevin. "The Laying on of Hands as Conferral of the Spirit: Some Problems and a Possible Solution." *StPatr* 18 (1989) 339–53

Cross, Frank Moore. *The Ancient Library of Qumran.* Garden City, NY: Doubleday, 1958. 3rd ed. Minneapolis: Fortress, 1995.

Cullmann, Oscar. "Die Pluralität der Evangelien als theologisches Problem im Altertum: Eine dogmengeschichtliche Studie." *Theologische Zeitschrift* 1 (1945) 23–42. Translated as "The Plurality of the Gospels as a Theological Problem in Antiquity: A Study in the History of Dogma." In *The Early Church*, edited by Oscar Cullmann. London: SCM, 1956.

Cureton, William, editor. *Ancient Syriac Documents Relative to the Earliest Establishment of Christianity in Edessa and the Neighbouring Countries: From the Year of Our Lord's Ascension to the Beginning of the Fourth Century.* 1864. Reprinted, Eugene, OR: Wipf & Stock, 2004.

Currie, Stuart Dickson. *Koinonia in Christian Literature to 200 A.D.* Ann Arbor: University Microfilms, 1962.

———. "The Scarcity of Extra-Biblical Episodic Tradition about the Ministry of Jesus in Second Century Christian Literature." Paper presented to the Seminar on the Development of Early Catholic Christianity, 1967.

Dabin, Paul, SJ. *Le Sacerdoce Royal des Fidèles dans la tradition ancienne et moderne.* Paris: Universelle Verselle, 1950.

Damme, Dirk van. *Pseudo-Cyprian Adversus Iudaeos: Gegen die Juden-christen.* Paradosis 22. Freiburg: Universität Verlag, 1969.

Danby, Herbert. *The Mishnah.* Oxford: Oxford University Press, 1933.

Daniélou, Jean. *The Origins of Latin Christianity.* Translated by David Smith and John A. Baker. Development of Christian Doctrine before the Council of Nicea 3. Philadelphia: Westminster, 1977.

———. *Primitive Christian Symbols.* Translated by Donald Attwater. Baltimore: Helicon, 1964.

———. *The Theology of Jewish Christianity.* Translated by John A. Baker. Development of Christian Doctrine before the Council of Nicea 1. London: Darton, Longman, & Todd, 1964.

Daube, David. *The New Testament and Rabbinic Judaism.* 1956. Reprinted, Eugene, OR: Wipf & Stock, 2011.

Davies, J. G. "Deacons, Deaconnesses and the Minor Orders in the Patristic Period." *JEH* 14 (1963) 1–15.

Davies, W. D. *Paul and Rabbinic Judaism.* 2nd ed. London: SPCK, 1955.

D'Costa, Gavin. "One Covenant or Many Covenants? Toward a Theology of Christian-Jewish Relations." *Journal of Ecumenical Studies* 27 (1990) 441–52.

DeBruyne, Luciano. "L'imposition des Mains dans l'art Chrétien ancien." *Rivista di Archeologia Christiana* 20 (1943) 113–278.

Deferrari, Roy J., translator. *Early Christian Biographies.* FC 15. New York: Fathers of the Church, 1952.

Dehandschutter, B. "Polycarp's Epistle to the Philippians: An Early Example of 'Reception.'" In *The New Testament in Early Christianity*, edited by Jean-Marie Sevrin, 275–91. BETL 86. Leuven: Peeters, 1989.

Delehaye, Hipplyte. *Les passions des martyrs et les genres littéraires.* Brussels: Bureaux de la Société des Bollandistes, 1921.

Dibelius, Martin, and Hans Conzelmann. *Die Pastoralbriefe.* Handbuch zum Neuen Testament. Mohr/Siebeck: Tübingen, 1955. (ET = *The Pastoral Epistles.* Translated by Philip Buttolph and Adela Yarbro. Hermeneia. Philadelphia: Fortress, 1972.)

Dix, Gregory. "The Ministry of the Early Church." In *The Apostolic Ministry: Essays on the History and Doctrine of Episcopacy*, edited by Kenneth E. Kirk, 183–303. New York: Morehouse-Gorham, 1947.

———. *The Treatise on the Apostolic Tradition of St. Hippolytus of Rome.* 2nd ed. Corrections, preface, and bibliography by Henry Chadwick. London: SPCK, 1968.

Dölger, Franz Joseph. *Sol Salutis: Gebet und Gesang im christlichen Altertum, mit besonder Rücksicht auf die Ostung in Gebet und Liturgie.* Liturgiegeschichtliche Forschungen 4/5. Münster: Aschendorff, 1925.

Dombrowski, Bruno W. "*Ha-Yahad* in 1QS and *to koinón*: An Instance of Early Greek and Jewish Synthesis." *HTR* 59 (1966) 293–307.

Donovan, Mary Ann. "Irenaeus in Recent Scholarship." *SecCent* 4 (1984) 219–41.

Dulles, Avery. *Models of the Church*. Garden City, NY: Doubleday, 1974.

Dungan, David L. *The Sayings of Jesus in the Churches of Paul: The Use of the Synoptic Tradition in the Regulation of Early Church Life*. Philadelphia: Fortress, 1971.

Easton, B. S. "Jewish and Early Christian Ordination." *Anglican Theological Review* 5 (1923) 308–19.

Ehrenberg, Victor. "Losung." In *Paulys Realencyclopädie der classischen Altertumswissenschaft*, edited by Georg Wissowa, 13,2:1451–504. Stuttgart: Metzler, 1927.

Ehrhardt, Arnold. *The Apostolic Succession in the First Two Centuries of the Church*. London: Lutterworth, 1953.

———. "The Gospels in the Muratorian Fragment." In *The Framework of the New Testament Stories*, 11–36. Cambridge: Harvard University Press, 1964.

———. "Jewish and Christian Ordination." *JEH* 5 (1954) 125–38.

Elderenbosch, Pieter Adriaan. *De Oplegging der Handen*. 'Gravenhage: Boekencentrum, 1953.

Elfers, Heinrich. "Neue Untersuchungen über die Kirchenordnung Hippolyts von Rom." In *Abhandlungen über Theologie und Kirche: Festschrift für Karl Adam*, edited by Marcel Reding, 169–211. Duesseldorf: Patmos, 1952.

Ellard, Gerald. *Ordination Anointings in the Western Church Before 1000 A.D.* Monographs of the Mediaeval Academy of America 8. Cambridge, MA: Mediaeval Academy of America, 1933.

Ellis, E. Earle. *The Old Testament in Early Christianity: Canon and Interpretation in Light of Modern Research*. WUNT 54. Tübingen: Mohr/Siebeck, 1991.

Emerson, Everett H. "Calvin and Covenant Theology." *Church History* (1956) 136–44.

Eno, Robert B., SS. *Teaching Authority in the Early Church*. Message of the Fathers of the Church 14. Wilmington: Glazier, 1984.

Epp, Eldon Jay. *The Theological Tendency of Codex Bezae Cantabrigiensis in Acts*. SNTS Monograph Series 3. 1966. Reprinted, Eugene, OR: Wipf & Stock, 2001.

Epstein, I. *The Babylonian Talmud*. 34 vols. London: Soncino, 1935–1952.

Evans, Ernest. *Tertullian Adversus Marcionem*. Oxford Early Christian Texts. Oxford: Clarendon, 1972.

———. *Tertullian's Homily on Baptism*. London: SPCK, 1964.

Evetts, B. *History of the Patriarchs of the Coptic Church of Alexandria*. 4 vols. Patrologia Orientalis. Paris: Firmin-Didot, 1904–14.

Eynde, Damien van den. *Les normes de l'enseignement chrétien dans la littérature patristique des trois premiers siècles*. Universitas catholica lovaniensis. Dissertationes ad gradum magistri in Facultate theologica consequendum conscriptae II/25. Gembloux: Duculot, 1933.

Farkasfalvy, Denis M. "Christological Content and Its Biblical Basis in the Leter of the Martyrs of Gaul." *SecCent* 9 (1992) 5–25. Reprinted in *Christianity in Relation to Jews, Greeks, and Romans*, edited by Everett Ferguson, 279–99. Recent Studies in Early Christianity 2. New York: Garland, 1999.

———. "'Prophets and Apostles': The Conjunction of the Two Terms before Irenaeus." In *Texts and Testaments: Critical Essays on the Bible and Early Church Fathers*, edited by W. Eugene March, 109–34. San Antonio: Trinity University Press, 1980.

Farmer, William R., and Denis M. Farkasfalvy. *The Formation of the New Testament Canon: An Ecumenical Approach*. Theological Inquiries. New York: Paulist, 1983.

Farrer, A. M. "Ministry in the New Testament." In *The Apostolic Ministry: Essays on the History and Doctrine of Episcopacy*, edited by Kenneth E. Kirk, 133–42. New York: Morehouse-Gorham, 1947.

Ferguson, Everett. "Attitudes to Schism at the Council of Nicea." *History 9: Schism, Heresy and Religious Protest*, edited by Derek Baker, 57–63. Cambridge: Cambridge University Press, 1972.

———. *Baptism in the Early Church: History, Theology, and Liturgy in the First Five Centuries*. Grand Rapids: Eerdmans, 2009.

———, editor. *The Bible in the Early Church*. Studies in Early Christianity 4. New York: Garland, 1993.

———. "Canon Muratori: Date and Provenance." *Studia Patristica* 17.2 (1982) 677–83.

———. "Christian Use of the Old Testament." In *The World and Literature of the Old Testament*, edited by John T. Willis, 346–57. Austin: Sweet, 1979.

———. *The Church of Christ: A Biblical Ecclesiology for Today*. Grand Rapids: Eerdmans, 1996.

———. "Community and Worship." In *Routledge Companion to Early Christian Thought*, edited by D. Jeff Bingham, 313–30. London: Routledge, 2012.

———. "The Covenant Idea in the Second Century." In *Texts and Testaments: Critical Essays on the Bible and Early Church Fathers: A Volume in Honor of Stuart Dickson Currie*, edited by W. Eugene March, 135–62. San Antonio: Trinity University Press, 1980.

———. "Eusebius and Ordination." *JEH* 13 (1962) 139–44.

———. "Introduction." In *The Bible in the Early Church*, edited by Everett Ferguson, xi–xii. Studies in Early Christianity 4. New York: Garland, 1993.

———. "Jewish and Christian Ordination." *HTR* 56 (1963) 13–19.

———. "Laying on of Hands in Acts 6:6 and 13:3." *ResQ* 4 (1960) 250–52.

———. "The Laying on of Hands: Its Significance in Ordination." *JTS* n.s. 26 (1975) 1–12. Reprinted in *Church, Ministry, and Organization in the Early Church Era*, edited by Everett Ferguson, 147–58. Studies in Early Christianity 13. New York: Garland, 1993.

———. "Love of Enemies and Nonretaliation in the Second Century." In *The Contentious Triangle: Church, State, and University: A Festschrift in Honor of Professor George Huntston Williams*, edited by Rodney L. Petersen and Calvin Augustine Pater, 81–95. Kirksville, MO: Thomas Jefferson University Press, 1999.

———. "Ordination in the Ancient Church." PhD diss., Harvard University, 1959.

———. "Ordination in the Ancient Church (4 parts)." *ResQ* 4 (1960) 117–38; 5 (1961) 17–32; 67–82; 130–46.

———. "Origen and the Election of Bishops." *Church History* 43 (1974) 26–33.

———. "Psalm-Singing at the Eucharist: A Liturgical Controversy in the Fourth Century." *Austin Seminary Bulletin* 98 (1983) 52–77.

———. "Qumran and Codex D." *RevQ* 8 (1972) 75–80.

———. Review of G. M. Hahneman, *The Muratorian Fragment* in *JTS* n.s. 44 (1993) 691–97.

Ferrua, Antonio. *Le pitture della nuova catacomba di Via Latina*. Monumenti di antichità Cristiana 2/8. Vatican: Pontif. Istituto di archeologia cristiana, 1960.

Fitzmyer, Joseph A. "The Qumran Scrolls, The Ebionites, and Their Literature." *Theological Studies* 16 (1955) 335–72. Reprinted in *Essays on the Semitic Background of the New Testament*, 435–80. Grand Rapids: Eerdmans, 1997.

Foakes-Jackson, F. J., and Kirsopp Lake, editors. *The Beginnings of Christianity*. Vol. 4. London: Macmillan, 1933.

Flusser, David. "Healing through the Laying-on of Hands in a Dead Sea Scroll." *Israel Exploration Journal* 7 (1957) 107–8.

Foster, Lewis. "The Earliest Collection of Paul's Epistles." *Bulletin of the Evangelical Theological Society* 10 (1967) 44–55. Reprinted in *The Bible in the Early Church*, vol. 3, edited by Everett Ferguson, 150–61. Studies in Early Christianity 3. New York: Garland, 1993.

Freedman, David Noel. "Canon of the Old Testament," In *Interpreter's Dictionary of the Bible, Supplementary Volume*, edited by Keith Crim, 130–36. Nashville: Abingdon, 1972.

Frey, J. B. "Les communautea Juives a Rome aux premiers temps de l'Eglise." *RSR* 21 (1931) 129–68.

Funk, F. X. von. *Didascalia et Constitutiones Apostolorum*. Paderborn: Schoeningh, 1905.

Gaechter, Paul. "Die Wahl des Matthias (Apg. 1, 15–26)." *Zeitschrift für Katholische Theologie* 71 (1949) 318–46.

Gager, John. *Origins of Anti-Semitism: Attitudes Toward Judaism in Pagan and Christian Antiquity*. Oxford: Oxford University Press, 1985.

Galtier, Paul. "Imposition des mains." In *Dictionnaire de Théologie Catholique*, edited by Alfred Vacant et al., 7:1302–1425. Paris: Letouzey & Ané, 1923.

———. "Imposition des mains et bénédictions au bapteme." *Recherches sciences religieuse* (1937) 464–66.

Gamble, Harry Y. *Books and Readers in the Early Church: A History of Early Christian Texts*. New Haven: Yale University Press, 1995.

Gaster, Moses. "Ordination (Jewish)." In *ERE* 9 (1917) 552–55.

Gerke, Friedrich. *Die Stellung des Ersten Clemensbriefes innerhalb der Entwicklung der Altchristlichen Gemeindeverfassung und des Kirchenrechts*. TU 47. Leipzig: Hinrichs, 1931.

Giet, Stanislas. *Hermas et les pasteurs: Les trois Auteurs du Pasteur d'Hermas*. Paris: Presses universitaires de France, 1963.

Giversen, Søren. "The Covenant—Theirs or Ours?" In *The New Testament and Hellenistic Judaism*, ed. Peder Borgen and Søren Giversen, 14–18. Peabody, MA: Hendrickson, 1997.

Göller, Emil. "Die Bischofswahl bei Origenes." In *Ehrengabe Deutscher Wissenschaft*, edited by Franz Fessler, 611–15. Freiburg: Herder, 1920.

Gore, Charles. *The Church and the Ministry*. Rev. ed. London: Rivingtons, 1949.

Goulder, Michael D. "Ignatius' 'Docetists.'" *VC* 53 (1999) 16–30.

Gräbe, Petrus J. *Der Neue Bund in der frühchristlichen Literatur: Unter Berücksichtigung der alttestamentlich-jüdischen Voraussetzungen*. Forschung zur Bibel 96. Würzburg: Echter, 2001.

Graffin, R., and F. Nau, editors. *Revue l'Orient Chrétien*. Paris: Leroux, 1896.

Grant, Robert M. "The Book of Wisdom at Alexandria: Reflections on the History of the Canon and Theology." *Studia Patristica* 7 (1966) 462–72.

———. *The Formation of the New Testament*. New York: Harper & Row, 1965.

———. *Second-century Christianity: A Collection of Fragments*. London: SPCK, 1946. 2nd ed. Louisville: Westminster John Knox, 2003.

Grayston, Kenneth. "The Significance of the Word 'Hand' in the New Testament." In *Mélanges bibliques en hommage au R. P. Béda Rigaux*, edited by Albert Descamps and André de Halleux, 479–88. Gembloux: Duculot, 1970.

Grobel, Kendrick. *The Gospel of Truth: A Valentinian Meditation on the Gospel.* Nashville: Abingdon, 1960.

Guthrie, Donald. "Acts and Epistles in Apocryphal Writings." In *Apostolic History and the Gospel: Biblical and Historical Essays Presented to F. F. Bruce on His 60th Birthday*, edited by W. Ward Gasque and Ralph P. Martin, 328–45. Grand Rapids: Eerdmans, 1970.

Haenchen, Ernst. *Die Apostelgeschichte.* 13th ed. Göttingen: Vandenhoeck & Ruprecht, 1961. (ET = *The Acts of the Apostles: A Commentary.* Philadelphia: Westminster, 1971.)

Hagen, Kenneth. *A Theology of Testament in the Young Luther: The Lectures on Hebrews.* Studies in Medieval and Reformation Thought 12. Leiden: Brill, 1974.

Hagner, Donald A. "The Sayings of Jesus in Apostolic Fathers and Justin Martyr." *Gospel Perspectives* 5 (1985) 233–68.

Hahneman, Geoffrey Mark. *The Muratorian Fragment and the Development of the Canon.* Oxford Theological Monographs. Oxford: Clarendon, 1992.

Halton, Thomas P. *The Church.* Message of the Fathers of the Church 4. Wilmington, DE: Glazier, 1985.

Hammond Bammel, Caroline P. "Ignatian Problems." *JTS* n.s. 33 (1982) 62–97.

Hanson, R. P. C. "The Ideology of Codex Bezae in Acts." *NTS* 14 (1968) 282–86.

———. "The Provenance of the Interpolator in the 'Western' Text of Acts and of Acts Itself." *NTS* 12 (1965–66) 211–30.

Harnack, Adolf von. *Der Kirchengeschichtliche Ertag der Exegetischen Arbeiten des Origenes.* 2 vols. TU 42. Leipzig: Hinrichs, 1918.

———. *The Origin of the New Testament and the Most Important Consequences of the New Creation.* Translated by J. R. Wilkinson. New Testament Studies 6. London: Williams & Norgate, 1925.

———. *Die Quellen der Sogenannten Apostolischen Kirchenordnung: Über den Ursprung des Lectorats und der anderen niederen Weihen.* TU 2/5 (1886) 6.

———. "Über den Verfasser und den literarischen Charakter des Muratorischen Fragments." *ZNW* 24 (1925) 1–16.

Harrison, P. N. *Polycarp's Two Epistles to the Philippians.* Cambridge: Cambridge University Press, 1936.

Hartman, Lars. "On Reading Others' Letters." *HTR* 79 (1986) 137–46.

Hatch, Edwin. "Ordination." In *Dictionary of Christian Antiquities*, edited by William Smith and Samuel Cheetham, 2:1501. London: Murray, 1893.

Hatch, William H. P. "The Position of Hebrews in the Canon of the New Testament." *HTR* 29 (1936) 133–51.

Hawthorne, Gerald F. "A New English Translation of Melito's Paschal *Homily.*" *Current Issues in Biblical and Patristic Interpretation*, edited by Gerald F. Hawthorne, 147–75. Grand Rapids: Eerdmans, 1975.

Hayman, Henry. "The Position of the Laity in the Church." *JTS* 5 (1904) 499–516.

Heckel, Theo K. *Vom Evangelium des Markus zum viergestaltigen Evangelium.* Tübingen: Mohr/Siebeck, 1999.

Hedrick, Charles W., Guy G. Stroumsa, and Bart D. Ehrman. "The Secret Gospel of Mark: A Discussion." *JECS* 11 (2003) 133–63.

Hefele, Charles Joseph, and H. Leclercq. *Histoire des conciles d'après les Documents Originaux.* Paris: Letouzey, 1907.

Heine, Ronald E. *The Montanist Oracles and Testimonia.* Macon, GA: Mercer University Press, 1989.

Hengel, Martin. "The Titles of the Gospels and the Gospel of Mark." In *Studies in the Gospel of Mark,* 64–84. Translated by John Bowden. London: SCM, 1985.

Henne, Phillipe. "La Datation du Canon de Muratori." *Revue biblique* 100 (1993) 54–75.

Hennecke, Edgar. "Zur Apostolischen Kirchenordnung." *ZNW* 20 (1921) 241–48.

Hennecke, Edgar, and Wilhelm Schneemelcher, editors. *New Testament Apocrypha.* Translated by R. McL. Wilson. 2 vols. London: SCM, 1965.

Herrmann, Leon. *Sénèque et les premiers chrétiens.* Collection Latomus 167. Brussels: Latomus, 1979.

Hess, Hamilton. *The Canons of the Council of Sardica A.D. 343: A Landmark in the Early Development of Canon Law.* Oxford Theological Monographs 1. Oxford: Clarendon, 1958.

Hild, J. A. In *DAGR* 2 (1908) 504.

Hill, Charles E. "The Debate over the Muratorian Fragment and the Development of the Canon." *Westminster Theological Journal* 57 (1995) 437–52.

———. "Ignatius and the Apostolate: The Witness of Ignatius to the Emergence of Christian Scripture." *StPatr* 36 (2001) 226–48.

———. "Justin and the New Testament Writings." *StPatr* 30 (1997) 42–48.

———. "What Papias Said about John (and Luke): A 'New' Papian Fragment." *JTS* n.s. 49 (1998) 582–629.

Hillers, Delbert R. *Covenant: The History of a Biblical Idea.* Seminars in the History of Ideas. Baltimore: Johns Hopkins University Press, 1969.

Hinson, E. Glenn, translator and editor. *Understandings of the Church.* Sources of Early Christian Thought. Philadelphia: Fortress, 1986.

Hitchcock, F. R. Montgomery. *Irenaeus of Lugdunum: A Study of His Teaching.* Cambridge: Cambridge University Press, 1914.

Hoffman, Lawrence. "Jewish Ordination on the Eve of Christianity." *Studia Liturgica* 13 (1979) 11–41.

Horbury, William. "Jewish-Christian Relations in Barnabas and Justin Martyr." In *Jews and Christians in Contact and Controversy,* 127–61. Edinburgh: T. & T. Clark, 1998.

Horner, Timothy J. *Listening to Trypho: Justin Martyr's Dialogue Reconsidered.* Contributions to Biblical Exegesis and Theology 28. Leuven: Peeters, 2001.

Hruby, Kurt. "La notion d'ordination dans la tradition juive." *La Maison Dieu* 102 (1970) 30–56.

Hughes, John J. "Hebrews 9:15ff. and Galatians 3:15ff.: A Study in Covenant Practice and Procedure." *NovT* 21 (1979) 27–96.

Hvalvik, Reidar. *The Struggle for Scripture and Covenant: The Purpose of the Epistle of Barnabas and Jewish-Christian Competition in the Second Century.* Wissenschaftliche Untersuchungen zum Neuen Testament 2/82. Tübingen: Mohr/Siebeck, 1996.

Instinsky, Hans Ulrich. *Bischofsstuhl und Kaiserthron.* Munich: Kösel, 1955.

Irenaeus. *Proof of the Apostolic Preaching.* Translated and annotated by Joseph P. Smith. Westminster, MD: Newman, 1952.

Jaffee, Martin. "Oral Culture in Scriptural Religion: Some Exploratory Studies." *Religious Studies Review* 24 (1998) 223–30.

James, M. R. *The Apocryphal New Testament*. Corrected ed. Oxford: Clarendon, 1953.

Jeffery, Peter. *The Secret Gospel of Mark Unveiled: Imagined Rituals of Sex, Death, and Madness in a Biblical Forgery*. New Haven: Yale University Press, 2007.

Johnson, Maxwell E. *The Prayers of Sarapion of Thmuis: A Literary, Liturgical, and Theological Analysis*. Rome: Pontificio Istituto Orientale, 1995.

Joly, Robert. *Le Dossier d'Ignace d'Antioche*. Travaux 69. Brussels: Éditions de l'Université de Bruxelles, 1979.

———. "Hermas et le pasteur." *VC* 21 (1967) 201–18.

Karpp, Heinrich. *Die frühchristlichen und mittelalterlichen Mosaiken in Santa Maria Maggiore zu Rom*. Baden-Baden: Grimm, 1966.

Kemp, E. W. "Bishops and Presbyters at Alexandria." *JEH* 6 (1955) 125–42.

Kenyon, F. G. *The Chester Beatty Biblical Papyri*. London: Walker, 1933.

Kinzig, Wolfram. "*Kainē diathēkē*: The Title of the New Testament in the Second and Third Century." *JTS* n.s. 45 (1994) 519–44. Reprinted in *Norms of Faith and Life*, edited by Everett Ferguson, 59–84. Recent Studies in Early Christianity 3. New York: Garland, 1999.

Kirk, Kennth E., editor. *The Apostolic Ministry: Essays on the History and Doctrine of Episcopacy*. New York: Morehouse-Gorham, 1947.

Klausner, Theodor. "Studien zur Entstehungsgeschichte der christlichen Kunst." *JAC* 3 (1960) 112–33.

Klijn, A. F. J. "The Apocryphal Correspondence between Paul and the Corinthians." *VigChr* 17 (1963) 2–23.

———. *A Survey of the Researches into the Western Text of the Gospels and Acts. Part Two: 1949–1969*. NovTSup 21. Leiden: Brill, 1969.

Knox, John. *Marcion and the New Testament*. Chicago: University of Chicago Press, 1942.

Koester, Helmut. *Ancient Christian Gospels: Their History and Development*. Philadelphia: Trinity, 1990.

———. "From Kerygma-Gospel to Written Gospel." *NTS* 35 (1989) 361–81.

———. *Introduction to the New Testament*. Vol. 2, *History and Literature of Early Christianity*. Philadelphia: Fortress, 1982.

Krauss, Samuel. *Synagogale Altertümer*. Berlin: Harz, 1922.

Kuhn, Karl Georg. *Konkordanz zu den Qumrantexten*. Göttingen: Vandenhoek & Ruprecht, 1960.

———. "Nachträge zur *Konkordanz zu den Qumrantexten*." *RevQ* 4 (1963) 163–234.

Kümmel, Werner Georg. *Introduction to the New Testament*. Translated by A. J. Mattill Jr. Nashville: Abingdon, 1966.

Laing, Gordon J. "Priest, Priesthood (Roman)." In *ERE*, 10:325–35. New York: Scribner, 1922.

Lampe, G. W. H. *A Patristic Greek Lexicon*. Oxford: Clarendon, 1968.

———. *The Seal of the Spirit: A Study in the Doctrine of Baptism and Confirmation in the New Testament and the Fathers*. 2nd ed. 1967. Reprint, Eugene, OR: Wipf & Stock, 2004.

Lawson, John. *The Biblical Theology of Saint Irenaeus*. London: Epworth, 1948.

Lauchert, Friedrich. *Die Kanones der wichtigsten altkirchlichen Concilien.* Sammlung ausgewählter kirchen- und dogmengeschichtlicher Quellenschriften 12. Leipzig: Mohr/Siebeck, 1896.

Lauterbach, Jacob Z. "Ordination." In *The Jewish Encyclopedia*, edited by Isidore Singer, 9:428–30. New York: Funk & Wagnalls, 1916.

Leaney, A. R. C. *The Rule of Qumran and Its Meaning: Introduction, Translation, and Commentary.* New Testament Library. Philadelphia: Westminster, 1966.

Lécuyer, Joseph. "Le problème des consécrations épiscopales dans l'Eglise d'Alexandrie." *BLE* (1964) 241–57.

———. "La succession des evêques d'Alexandrie aux premiers siècles." *BLE* (1969) 80–99.

Ledegang, F. *Mysterium ecclesiae: Images of the Church and Its Members in Origen.* BETL 156. Leuven: Peeters, 2001.

Legrand, Phippe-Ernest. "Sacerdos. Grece." In *DAGR* 4 (1908) 938–46.

Leiman, Sid Z. *The Canonization of Hebrew Scripture: The Talmudic and Midrashic Evidence.* Transactions—The Connecticut Academy of Arts and Sciences 47. Hamden, CT: Archon, 1976.

Lengeling, Emil Joseph. "Der Bischof als Hauptzelebrant der Messe seiner Ordination." In *Kyriakon: Festschrift Johannes Quasten*, edited by Patrick Granfield and Josef A. Jungman, 2:886–912. Münster: Aschendorff, 1970.

Lewis, Jack. "What Do We Mean by Jabneh?" *Journal of Bible and Religion* 32 (1964) 125–32.

Liebenam, Wilhelm. *Zur Geschichte und Organisation des römischen Vereinswesen.* Leipzig: Teubner, 1890.

Leitzmann, Hans. *Wie Wurden die Bücher des Neuen Testaments heilige Schrift? Fünf Vorträge.* Lebensfrage 21. Tübingen: Mohr/Siebeck, 1907.

Lightfoot, J. B. *The Apostolic Fathers.* 2nd ed. London: Macmillan, 1885.

———. *St. Paul's Epistle to the Philippians.* London: Macmillan, 1913.

Lindars, Barnabas. "Qumran and the Christian Ministry." *Church Quarterly Review* (1959) 335–44.

Lindblom, Johannes. "Lot-casting in the Old Testament." *Vetus Testamentum* 12 (1962) 164–78.

Lohfink, Norbert, SJ. *The Covenant Never Revoked: Biblical Reflections on Christian-Jewish Dialogue.* New York: Paulist, 1991.

Lohse, Eduard. *Die Ordination im Spätjudentum und im Neuen Testament.* Göttingen: Vandenhoeck & Ruprecht, 1951.

Lowy, S. "The Confutation of Judaism in the Epistle of Barnabas." *Journal of Jewish Studies* 11 (1960) 1–33.

Luneau, Auguste. *L'Histoire de salut chez les Pères de l'Église: La Doctrine des Ages du Monde.* Théologie Historique 2. Paris: Beauchesne, 1964.

Macalister, A. "Anointings." In *Dictionary of the Bible*, edited by James Hastings, 1:100–102. New York: Scribners, 1900.

MacDonald, J. "Imposition of Hands in the Letters of Innocent I." *StPatr* 2 (1957) 49ff.

MacLennan, Robert S. *Early Christian Texts on Jews and Judaism.* Brown Judaic Studies 194. Atlanta: Scholars, 1990.

Malherbe, Abraham J. "Ancient Epistolary Theorists." *Ohio Journal of Religious Studies* 5 (1977) 3–77.

———. *The Cynic Epistles: A Study Edition*. SBL Sources for Biblical Study 12. Missoula, MT: Scholars, 1977.

Manson, T. W. *The Church's Ministry*. Philadelphia: Westminster, 1948.

Mantel, Hugo. "Ordination and Appointment in the Period of the Temple." *HTR* 57 (1964) 325–46.

Marrou, H. I. *A History of Education in Antiquity*. Translated by George Lamb. 1956. Reprinted, New York: New American Library, 1964.

May, Gerhard. "Marcion in Contemporary Views: Results and Open Questions." *Second Century* 6 (1987–88) 129–51.

Mazzucco, Clementina. "Eusèbe de Césarée et l'*Apocalypse de Jean*?" *StPatr* 17 (1993) 317–24.

McCarthy, Dennis J. *Old Testament Covenant: A Survey of Current Opinions*. Growing Points in Theology. Richmond: John Knox, 1972.

———. *Treaty and Covenant: A Study in Form in the Ancient Oriental Documents and in the Old Testament*. 2nd ed. Analecta biblica 21. Rome: Pontifical Biblical Institute, 1978.

Mendenhall, George E. "Covenant." In *Interpreter's Dictionary of the Bible*, edited by George Arthur Buttrick, 1:714–23. Nashville: Abingdon, 1962.

Menoud, Philippe-H. "Les additions au groupe des Douze Apôtres d'après le livre des Actes." *Revue d'histoire et de philosophie religieuses* 37 (1957) 71–80.

Merkel, Helmut. *Die Pluralität der Evangelien als theologisches und exegetisches Problem in der Alten Kirche*. Traditio christiana 3. Bern: Lang, 1978.

Metzger, Bruce M. *The Canon of the New Testament: Its Origin, Development, and Significance*. Oxford: Clarendon, 1987.

———. "Literary Forgeries and Canonical Pseudepigrapha." *JBL* 91 (1972) 3–24.

Minear, Paul. *Images of the Church in the New Testament*. Philadelphia: Westminster, 1960.

Moll, Sebastian. *The Arch-Heretic Marcion*. Tübingen: Mohr/Siebeck, 2010.

Molland, Einar. "Irenaeus of Lugdunum and the Apostolic Succession." *JEH* 1 (1950) 12–28.

Mommsen, Theodor. *Römisches Staatsrecht*. Vol. 1. Leipzig: Hirzel, 1887.

———. "Die Stadtrechte der lätinischen Gemeinden Salpensa und Malaca in der Provinz Baetica." *Abhandlungen der philologisch-Historischen Classe der Königlisch Sächsischen Gesellschaft der Wissenschaften* 3 (1857) 361–507.

Moore, George Foot. *Judaism*. Vol. 3. Cambridge: Harvard University Press, 1954.

Morrice, William G. "New Wine in Old Wine-Skins: XI. Covenant." *Expository Times* 86 (1975) 132–36.

Müller, Karl. "Kleine Beiträge zur alten Kirchengeschichte." *ZNW* 28 (1929) 274–96.

Musurillo, Herbert. "History and Symbol: A Study of Form in Early Christian Literature." *Theological Studies* 18 (1957) 357–86.

Neusner, Jacob. *Aphrahat and Judaism*. Studia Post-Biblica 19. Leiden: Brill, 1971.

Newman, Julius. *Semikhah (Ordination): A Study of Its Origin, History, and Function in Rabbinic Literature*. Manchester: Manchester University Press, 1950.

Nielsen, Charles Merritt. "Polycarp, Paul, and the Scriptures." *Anglican Theological Review* 47 (1965) 199–216.

Nilgen, Ursula. "Brotvermehrung." In *Lexikon der christlichen Ikonographie*, edited by Engelbert Kirschbaum, 1:326–30. Rome: Herder, 1968.

Nilsson, Martin P. *Geschichte der griechischen Religion*. Handbuch der klassischen Altertumswissenschaft. Munich: Beck, 1950. (ET = *A History of Greek Religion*. Translated by F. J. Fielden. Oxford: Clarendon, 1952.)

Nock, Arthur Darby. "Intrare sub Iugum." *Classical Quarterly* 20 (1926) 107–9.

O'Hagan, Angelo P. "Early Christian Exegesis Exemplified from the Epistle of Barnabas." *Australian Biblical Review* (1963) 33–40.

Oldenberg, Hermann. "De inauguratione sacerdotum Romanorum." In *Commentationes Philologae in Honorem Theodori Mommseni*, 159–62 Berlin: Weidmann, 1877.

Oliver, William G. "Origen and the New Testament Canon." *ResQ* 31 (1989) 13–26.

Osborn, Eric F. "Clement of Alexandria: A Review of Research 1958–1982." *SecCent* 3 (1983) 219–44.

———. *Justin Martyr*. Beiträge zur historischen Theologie 47. Tübingen: Mohr/ Siebeck, 1973.

Paget, J. Carlton. "The Epistle of Barnabas and the Covenant of the Lord." Paper delivered at the Eleventh International Conference on Patristic Studies, Oxford, 21 August, 1991.

Patterson, L. G. "Irenaeus and the Valentinians: The Emergence of the Christian Scriptures." *StPatr* 18.3 (1989) 189–220.

Paulsen, Henning. "Die Bedeutung des Montanismus für die Herausbildung des Kanons." *VC* 32 (1978) 19–52.

Peebles, Bernard M. "Sulpicius Severus: 'Life of St. Martin.'" In *Niceta of Remesiana: Writings; Sulpicius Severus: Writings; Vincent of Lerins: Commonitories; Prosper of Aquitaine: Grace and Free Will*. FC 7. New York: Fathers of the Church, 1949.

Penella, Robert J. *The Letters of Apollonius of Tyana*. Leiden: Brill, 1979.

Perelmuter, Hayim Gorem. *Siblings: Rabbinic Judaism and Early Christianity at Their Beginnings*. Mahwah, NJ: Paulist, 1989.

Perkins, Pheme. *The Gnostic Dialogue: The Early Church and the Crisis of Gnosticism*. Theological Inquiries. New York: Paulist, 1980.

Petersen, Erik. "Das Schiff als Symbol der Kirche: Die Tat des Messias im eschatologischen Meeressturm in der jüdischen und altchristlichen Ueberlieferung." *Theologische Zeitschrift* 6 (1950) 77–79.

Petersen, W. L. *Tatian's Diatessaron: Its Creation, Dissemination, Significance, and History in Scholarship*. Supplements to Vigilae Christianae 25. Leiden: Brill, 1994.

Phillips, George, editor. *The Doctrine of Addai, the Apostle*. London: Trübner, 1876.

Ploeg, J. van der. "La Regle de la Guerre: Traduction et Notes." *Vetus Testamentum* 5 (1955) 373–420.

Plumpe, Joseph C. *Mater Ecclesia: An Inquiry into the Concept of the Church as Mother in Early Christianity*. Studies in Christian Antiquity. Washington, DC: Catholic University Press, 1943.

Pohlmann, H. "Diatheke." In *Reallexikon für Antike und Christentum*, edited by Franz Joseph Dölger and Hans Lietzmann, 3:982–90. Stuttgart: Hiersemann, 1957.

Poland, Franz. *Geschichte des griechischen Vereinswesens*. Leipzig: Teubner, 1909.

Porter, Harry Boone. *The Ordination Prayers of the Ancient Western Churches*. London: SPCK, 1967.

Preus, J. Samuel. *From Shadow to Promise: Old Testament Interpretation from Augustine to the Young Luther*. Cambridge, MA: Belknap, 1969.

Prigent, Pierre. *L'epître de Barnabé I–XVI et ses sources*. Etudes bibliques. Paris: Lecoffre/ Gabalda, 1961.

————. *Justin et l'ancien testament: L'argumentation scripturaire d traité de Justin contre toutes les heresies comme source principale du Dialogue avec Tryphon et de la première Apologie.* Etudes bibliques. Paris: Lecoffre, 1964.

Prigent, Pierre, and Robert A. Kraft. *Epître de Barnabé.* Sources chrétiennes 172. Paris: Cerf, 1971.

Pryor, J. W. "Justin Martyr and the Fourth Gospel." *SecCent* 9 (1992) 153–69.

Quasten, Johannes. *Patrology.* Vol. 1: *The Beginnings of Patristic Literature.* Utrecht: Spectrum, 1950.

————. *Patrology.* Vol. 2: *The Ante-Nicene Literature after Irenaeus.* Utrecht: Spectrum, 1953.

Quispel, Gilles. "De Brief aan de Laodicensen een Marcionitische vervalsing." *Nederlands Theologisch Tijdschrift* 5 (1950) 43–46.

Rabin, Chaim. *The Zadokite Documents.* 2nd ed. Oxford: Clarendon, 1958.

Rankin, David. *Tertullian and the Church.* Cambridge: Cambridge University Press, 1995.

Reagan, Joseph N. *The Preaching of Peter: The Beginning Christian Apologetic.* Chicago: University of Chicago Press, 1923.

Rehm, Bernhard. *Die Pseudoklementinen.* GCS. Berlin: Akademie, 1953.

Reicke, Bo. "The Constitution of the Primitive Church in the Light of Jewish Documents." In *The Scrolls and the New Testament,* edited by Krister Stendahl, 143–56. New York: Harper, 1957. [Translated from *Theologische Zeitschrift* 10 (1954) 95–113.]

Remus, Harold. "Justin Martyr's Argument with Judaism." In *Anti-Judaism in Early Christianity,* vol. 2, *Separation and Polemic,* edited by Stephen G. Wilson, 59–80. Waterloo: Wilfrid Laurier University, 1986.

Rengstorf, Karl Heinrich. "ἀπόστολος." In *TDNT* 1 (1964) 407–47.

Richard, Marcel. "Florileges spirituels grecs." In *Dictionnaire de Spiritualité,* edited by Marcel Viller, SJ et al., 5:494ff. Paris: Beauchesne, 1964.

Richard, Marcel, and Bertrand Hemmerdinger. "Trois nouveaux fragments grecs de l'*Adversus Haereses* de Saint Irénée." *ZNW* 53 (1962) 252–55.

Richards, E. Randolph. "The Codex and the Early Collection of Paul's Letters." *Bulletin for Biblical Research* 8 (1998) 151–66.

Riedel, Wilhelm. *Die Kirchenrechtsquellen des Patriarchats Alexandrien.* Leipzig: Deichert, 1900.

Rikhof, Herwi. *The Concept of Church: A Methodological Inquiry into the Use of Metaphor in Ecclesiology.* London: Sheed & Ward, 1981.

Roberts, C. H., and T. C. Skeat, *The Birth of the Codex.* London: British Academy, 1983.

Robinson, J. Armitage, editor. The *Demonstration of the Apostolic Preaching.* Translations of Christian Literature. IV: Oriental Texts. London: SPCK, 1920.

Rokéah, David. "The Church Fathers and the Jews in Writings Designed for Internal and External Use." In *Antisemitism through the Ages,* edited by Shmuel Almog, 39–70. Elmsford, NY: Pergamon, 1988.

————. *Justin Martyr and the Jews.* Jewish and Christian Perspective Series 5. Leiden: Brill, 2002.

Ropes, James Hardy. *The Text of Acts. The Beginnings of Christianity.* Edited by F. J. Foakes-Jackson and Kirsopp Lake. Vol. 3. London: Macmillan, 1926.

Rudorff, Adolfus Fridericus. *Zeitschrift für geschichtliche Rechtswissenschaft* 15 (1850) 232–40.

Ruis-Camps, H. *The Four Authentic Letters of Ignatius the Martyr*. Translated by Kathleen England. Orientalia Christiana analecta 213. Rome: Pontificium Institutum Orientalium Studiorum, 1980.

Sandgren, L. D. *Vines Intertwined: A History of Jews and Christians from the Babylonian Exile to the Advent of Islam*. Peabody, MA: Hendrickson, 2010.

Schermann, Theodor. *Die allgemeine Kirchenordnung: Frühchristliche Liturgien und kirchliche Überlieferung*. Studien zur Geschichte und Kulture des Altertums. Paderborn: Schoeningh, 1914.

Schlier, Heinrich. "Die Ordnung der Kirche nach den Pastoralbriefen." In *Glaube und Geschichte: Festschrift für Friedrich Gogarten*, edited by Heinrich Runte, 38–60. Giessen: Schmitz, 1948. (Reprinted in: *Aufsätze zur Biblischen Theologie*. Leipzig: St. Benno, 1968.)

Schmidt, Carl, editor. *Acta Pauli aus der Heidelberger koptischen Papyrushandschrift Nr. 1*. Veröffentlichungen aus der Heidelberger Papyrus-Sammlung 2. Leipzig: Hinrichs, 1904.

———. *Studien zu den Pseudo-Clementinen*. TU 46.1. Leipzig: Hinrichs, 1929.

Schmidt, Francis. "Election et triage au sort (1QS VI, 13–23 et Ac 1, 15–26)." *Revue d'histoire et de philosophie religieuses* 80 (2000) 105–17.

Schmidt, Joseph. "L'organisation de l'église primitive et Qumrân." In *La Secte de Qumrân el les origines du Christianisme*, edited by J. P. M. van der Ploeg, 217–31. Recherches bibliques 4. Paris: de Brouwer, 1959.

Schneemelcher, Wilhelm. *New Testament Apocrypha*. 2 vols. 2nd ed. Cambridge: James Clarke, 1992.

Schoedel, W. R. "Are the Letters of Ignatius of Antioch Authentic?" *Religious Studies Review* (July, 1980) 196–201.

Schoeps, Hans Joachim. *Theologie und Geschichte des Judenchristentums*. Tübingen: Mohr/Siebeck, 1949.

———. *Jewish Christianity: Factional Disputes in the Early Church*. Translated by Douglas A. Hare. Philadelphia: Fortress, 1969.

Schroeder, H. J., OP. *Disciplinary Decrees of the General Councils: Text, Translation, and Commentary*. St. Louis: Herder, 1937.

Schürer, Emil. *Geschichte des jüdischen Volkes im Zeitalter Jesu Christi*. 3 vols. Leipzig: Hinrichs, 1907.

Schwartz, Eduard. *Eusebius*. GCS. Leipzig: Hinrichs, 1902–.

Segal, Alan F. "Covenant in Rabbinic Writings." *Studies in Religion* 14 (1985) 53–62.

———. *Rebecca's Children: Judaism and Christianity in the Roman World*. Cambridge: Harvard University Press, 1986.

Sesboüé, Bernard. "La preuve par les Ecritures chez S. Irénée: A propos d'un texte difficile du Livre III de l'*Adversus haereses*." *NRTh* 103 (1981) 872–87.

Sevenster, J. N. *Paul and Seneca*. NovTSup 4. Leiden: Brill, 1961.

Sevrin, Jean-Marie. *The New Testament in Early Christianity*. BETL 86. Leuven: Peeters, 1989.

Siker, J. S. "The Canonical Status of the Catholic Epistles in the Syriac New Testament." *JTS* n.s. 38 (1987) 311–40.

Simon, Marcel. *Verus Israel: Études sur les relations entre chrétiens et juifs dans l'empire romain (135–425)*. Bibliothèque des écoles francaises d'Athènes et de Rom 166. Paris: de Boccard, 1964. (ET = *Verus Israel: A Study of the Relations between*

Christians and Jews in the Roman Empire (135–425). Translated by H. Keating. Littman Library of Jewish Civilization. New York: Oxford University Press, 1986.)

Siotis, Markos Antonios. "Die klassische und die christliche Cheirotonie in ihrem Verhältnis." *Theologia* 20 (1949) 314–34, 524–41, 725–40; 21 (1950) 103–24, 239–57, 458–59; 22 (1951).

Skarsaune, Oskar. *The Proof from Prophecy: A Study of Justin Martyr's Proof-Text Tradition*. NovTSup 56. Leiden: Brill, 1987.

Skarsaune Oskar, and Reidar Hvalvik, editors. *Jewish Believers in Jesus: The Early Years*. Peabody, MA: Hendrickson, 2007.

Skeat, T. C. "Irenaeus and the Four Gospel Canon." *NovT* 34 (1992) 194–99.

———. "The Oldest Manuscript of the Four Gospels?" *NTS* 43 (1997) 1–34.

———. "The Origin of the Christian Codex." *Zeitschrift für Papyrologie und Epigraphie* 102 (1994) 263–68

Smith, D. Moody. "When Did the Gospels Become Scripture?" *JBL* 119 (2000) 3–20.

Smith, Morton. *Clement of Alexandria and a Secret Gospel of Mark*. Cambridge: Harvard University Press, 1973.

Smith, R. Payne. *Thesaurus Syriacus*. 2 vols. 1901. Reprinted, Ancient Language Resources. Eugene, OR: Wipf & Stock, 2007.

Smith, Thomas, editor and translator. "The Clementina." In *Ante-Nicene Fathers*. Vol. 8. Reprint, Grand Rapids: Eerdmans, 1951.

Sokolowski, F. "Partnership in the Lease of Cults in Greek Antiquity." *HTR* 50 (1957) 133–43.

Speyer, Wolfgang. *Die literarische Fälschung im heidnischen and christlichen Altertum: Ein Versuch ihrer Deutung*. Handbuch der Altertumswissenschaft 1/2. Munich: Beck, 1971.

Spicq, C. *Saint Paul: Les Epîtres Pastorales*. Etudes biblique. Paris: Gabalda, 1947.

Stanton, Graham N. "The Fourfold Gospel." *NTS* 43 (1997) 317–46. Reprinted in *Norms of Faith and Life*, edited by Everett Ferguson, 1–30. Recent Studies in Early Christianity 3. New York: Garland, 1999.

Staveley, E. S. *Greek and Roman Voting and Elections*. Aspects of Greek and Roman Life. London: Thames & Hudson, 1972.

Steinwenter, A. "Ius iurandum." In *Paulys Realencyclopädie der classischen Altertumswissenschaft*, edited by Georg Wissowa, 10:1256–57. Stuttgart: Metzler, 1917.

Stendahl, Krister. "ΑΞΙΟΣ im Lichte der Texte der Qumran-Höhle." *Nuntius* 7 (1952) 53–55.

Stengel, Paul. *Die griechischen Kultusaltertümer*. Handbuch der klassischen Altertums-Wissenschaft 5/3. Munich: Beck, 1920.

Stommel, Eduard. "Bischofsstuhl und höher Thron." *JAC* 1 (1958) 52–78.

Strack, Hermann L., and Paul Billerbeck. *Kommentar zum Neuen Testament*. Vol. 2, *Das Evangelium nach Markus, Lukas und Johannes und die Apostelgeschichte*. Munich: Beck, 1924.

Strecker, Georg. "Eine Evangelienharmonie bei Justin und Pseudoklemens?" *NTS* 24 (1978) 297–316.

———. *Das Judenchristentum in den Pseudo-Klementinen*. 2nd ed. TU 70. Berlin: Akademie, 1981.

———. "On the Problem of Jewish Christianity." Appendix 1 to the English translation of Walter Bauer, *Orthodox and Heresy in Earliest Christianity*, edited by Robert A. Kraft and Gerhard Krodel, 241–87. Philadelphia: Fortress, 1971.

Stroud, William J. "New Testament Quotations in the Nag Hammadi Gospel ot Philip." In *SBLSP 1990*, 68–81. Atlanta: Scholars, 1990.

Stuhlhofer, Franz. *Der Gebrauch der Bibel von Jesus bis Eusebios: Eine statistische Untersuchung zur Kanongeschichte*. Wuppertal: Brockhaus, 1988.

Stylianopoulos, Theodore. *Justin Martyr and the Mosaic Law*. SBL Dissertation Series, 20. Missoula, MT: Scholars, 1975.

Sundberg, Albert C., Jr. "Canon Muratori: A Fourth-Century List." *HTR* 66 (1973) 1–41.

———. "Revised History of the New Testament Canon." *Studia Evangelica* 4 (1968) 452–61.

Swarat, U. "Das Werden des neutestamentlichen Kanons." In *Der Kanon der Bibel*, edited by G. Maier, 25–51. Giessen: Brunnen, 1990.

Sykutris, J. "Epistolographie." In *Paulys Realencyclopädie der classischen Altertumswissenschaft*, Supplement 5. Stuttgart: Metzler, 1931.

Szikszai, Stephen. "Anoint." In *Interpreter's Dictionary of the Bible*, edited by George Arthur Buttrick, 1:138–39. Nashville: Abingdon, 1962.

Tanner, Norman P., and G. Albergio, editors. *Decrees of the Ecumenical Councils*. Washington, DC: Georgetown University Press, 1990.

Tcherikover, Victor A., and Alexander Fuks, editors. *Corpus papyrorum Judaicarum*. Vol. 1. Cambridge: Harvard University Press, 1957.

Telfer, W. "Episcopal Succession in Egypt." *JEH* 3 (1952) 1–13.

Testuz, M. *Papyrus Bodmer X–XIII*. Geneva: Bibliotheca Bodmeriana, 1953.

Thesleff, Holger. *An Introduction to the Pythagorean Writings of the Hellenistic Period*. Acta Academiae Aboensis. Humaniora XXIV/3. Abo: Abo Akademie, 1961.

Thistelton, Anthony C. "The Supposed Power of Words." *JTS* n.s. 25 (1974) 283–99.

Thompson, N. H. "The Covenant Concept in Judaism and Christianity." *Anglican Theological Review* 64 (1982) 502–24.

Thornton, L. S. "The Choice of Matthias." *JTS* 46 (1945) 51–59.

Tipei, John Fleter. *The Laying on of Hands in the New Testament: Its Significance, Techniques, and Effects*. Lanham, MD: University Press of America, 2009.

Tod, Marcus N. *Sidelights on Greek History: Three Lectures on the Light thrown by Greek Inscriptions on the Life and Thought of the Ancient World*. Oxford: Blackwell, 1932.

Tollinton, R. B. *Selections from the Commentaries and Homilies of Origen*. London: SPCK, 1929.

Torrey, Charles Cutler. *Documents of the Primitive Church*. New York: Harper, 1941.

Toutain, J. "Sacerdos. Rome." In *Dictionnaire des Antiquités Grecques et Romaines*, edited by Charles Daremberg et al., 4:942–46. Paris: Hachette, 1908.

Trakatellis, Demetrios. "Justin Martyr's Trypho." *HTR* 79 (1986) 287–97.

Trinterud, Leonard J. "The Origins of Puritanism." *Church History* (1951) 37–57.

Trobisch, David. *Endredaktion des Neuen Testaments: Eine Untersuchung zur Entstehung der christlichen Bibel*. Göttingen: Vandenhoeck & Ruprecht, 1996.

———. *The First Edition of the New Testament*. Oxford: Oxford University Press, 2000.

Tuckett, C. M. "Synoptic Tradition in the Didache." In *The New Testament in Early Christianity*, edited by J.-M. Sevrin, 197–230. BETL 86. Leuven: Peeters, 1989.

Turner, C. H. "Apostolic Succession." In *Essays on the Early History of the Church and the Ministry*, edited by H. B. Swete, 93–214. London: Macmillan, 1918.

———. "The Early Episcopal Lists II." *JTS* 1 (1902) 529–53.

———. "The Ordination Prayer for a Presbyter in the Church Order of Hippolytus." *JTS* 16 (1915) 542–47.

———. "Χειροτονία, Χειροθεσία, Ἐπίθεσις Χειρῶν." *JTS* 24 (1923) 496–502.

Ullmann, Walter. Significance of the *Epistola Clementis* in the Pseudo-Clementines." *JTS* n.s. 11 (1960) 295–317.

Unnik, W. C. van. "The 'Gospel of Truth' and the New Testament." In *The Jung Codex: A Newly Recovered Gnostic Papyrus*, edited by F. L. Cross, 81–129. London: Mowbray, 1955.

———. "*Hē Kainē Diathēkē*—A Problem in the Early History of the Canon." *StPatr* 4 (1961) 212–27.

———. "De la règle mete prostheinai mete aphelein dans l'histoire du canon." *VC* 3 (1949) 1–36.

Vassal-Philipps, O. R. *The Work of St. Optatus against the Donatists*. London: Longmans, Green, 1917.

Verheyden, J. "The Canon Muratori: A Matter of Dispute." In *The Biblical Canons*, edited by J.-M. Auwers and H. J. de Jonge, 486–556. BETL 163. Leuven: Peeters, 2003.

Victor, U. "Was ein Texthistoriker zur Entstehung der Evangelien sagen kann." *Biblica* 79 (1998) 499–514.

Vogel, C. "L'imposition des mains dans les rites d'ordination en Orient et en Occident." *La Maison Dieu* 102 (1970) 57–72.

Vouaux, Léon. *Les Actes de Pierre*. Les Apocryphe du Nouveau Testament. Paris: Letouzey & Ané, 1922.

Walls, A. F. "Papias and Oral Tradition." *VC* 21 (1967) 137–40. Reprinted in *Orthodoxy, Heresy, and Schism in Early Christianity*, edited by Everett Ferguson, 107–10. Studies in Early Christianity 4. New York: Garland, 1993.

Watkins, Oscar D. *A History of Penance: Being a Study of the Authorities*. Vol. 1: *The Whole Church to A.D. 450*. London: Longmans, Green, 1920.

Weijenborg, Reinoud. *Les lettres d'Ignace d'Antioche: Étude de critique littéraire et de théologie*. Translated by Bartélemy Héroux. Leiden: Brill, 1969.

Weinfeld, Moshe. "*berith*." In *Theological Dictionary of the Old Testament*, edited by G. Johannes Botterweck and Helmer Ringgren, 2:253–79. Grand Rapids: Eerdmans, 1975.

Wengst, Klaus. *Tradition und Theologie des Barnabas Briefes*. Arbeiten zur Kirchengeschichte 42. Berlin: de Gruyter, 1971.

Wernberg-Møller, P. *The Manual of Discipline*. Studies on the Texts of the Desert of Judah 1. Leiden: Brill, 1957.

Westcott, Brooke Foss. *A General Survey of the History of the Canon of the New Testament*. 4th ed. London: Macmillan, 1875.

Wilcox, Max E. *The Semitisms of Acts*. Oxford: Clarendon, 1965.

Wilder, Terry L. *Pseudonymity, the New Testament, and Deception: An Inquiry into Intention and Reception*. Lanham, MD: University Press of America, 2004.

Williams, A. Lukyn. *Adversus Judaeos: A Bird's-Eye View of Christian Apologies until the Renaissance*. Cambridge: Cambridge University Press, 1935.

Wilpert, Josef. *Le Pitture delle Catacombe Romane*. Rome: Desclée, Lefebvre, 1903.

Wilson, Stephen G., editor. *Anti-Judaism in Early Christianity*. Vol. 2, *Separation and Polemic*. Studies in Christianity and Judaism 2. Waterloo, ON: Wilfrid Laurier University, 1986.

Bibliography

Wissowa, Georg. *Religion and Kultus der Römer.* 2nd ed. Handbuch der Klassischen Altertumswissenschaft. Munich: Beck, 1912.

Woodhouse, W. J. "Priest, Priesthood (Greek)." In *ERE* 10:305.

Wordsworth, John. *Bishop Sarapion's Prayer-Book: An Egyptian Sacramentary Dated Probably about A.D. 230–356.* 2nd ed. London: SPCK, 1923.

Vloberg, Maurice. *L'Eucharist dans l' art.* Grenoble: Arthaud, 1946.

Yadin, Yigal. *Bar Kokhba: The Rediscovery of the Legendary Hero of the Second Jewish Revolt against Rome.* New York: Random House, 1971.

Yoder, James D. "Semitisms in Codex Bezae." *JBL* 78 (1959) 317–21.

Zahn, Theodor. *Geschichte des Neutestamentlichen Kanons.* 2 vols. Erlangen: Deichert, 1890.

Zeitlin, Solomon. "The *Semikah* Controversy between the Zugoth." *Jewish Quarterly Review* 7 (1917) 499–517.

Ziebarth, E. "Eid." In *Paulys Realencyclopädie der classischen Altertumswissenschaft,* edited by Georg Wissowa, 5:2075–83. Stuttgart: Metzler, 1905.

Zuntz, Günther. *The Text of the Epistles: A Disquisition upon the Corpus Paulinum.* London: British Academy, 1953.

———. "A Textual Criticism of Some Passages of the Acts of the Apostles." *Classica et Mediaevalia* 3 (1940) 20–46.

Index of Ancient Sources

NEW TESTAMENT

❧

APOCRYPHA AND PSEUDEPIGRAPHA

∾

JOSEPHUS

∾

MISHNAH, TALMUD, AND RELATED LITERATURE

MURATORIAN FRAGMENT

NEW TESTAMENT APOCRYPHA AND PSEUDEPIGRAPHA

❧

GREEK, LATIN, AND SYRIAC WORKS

CYRIL OF JERUSALEM

Catecheses

DIDASCALIA APOSTOLORUM

EPHREM THE SYRIAN

Hymns against Heresies

EPIPHANIUS

Refutation of All Heresies

EPISTLE OF BARNABAS

EUSEBIUS

Ecclesiastical History

Demonstration of the Apostolic Preaching

JEROME

Commentary on Isaiah

PRISCILLIAN OF SPAIN

Tractates

PSEUDO-ANTONIUS MELISSA

Loci Communes

PSEUDO-AUGUSTINE

Sermons

PSEUDO-CHRYSOSTOM

PSEUDO-CLEMENTINES

Epistle of Peter and James

Homilies

Letter of Clement to James

Recognitions

PSEUDO-CYPRIAN

Adversus Iudaeos

De Aleatoribus

De Montibus Sina et Sion

Index of Subjects

Aaron, installation of, 119, 120, 122
Abraham
    Christ and, 24
    forecasting covenants, 186, 215
acclamation, 30, 50, 79, 115–16
Act of Peter, 237, 244
Acts of Paul, 236–37, 242–43
Acts of Peter, 82, 243
Acts of Peter and the Twelve Apostles,
    237, 243–44
Acts of Pilate (Christian), 238
Acts of Pilate (pagan), 238
Acts of the Scillitan Martyrs, 253
Acts of Thaddaeus, 244
Adam, as Christ figure, 7
Adler, Nikolaus, 99
Adversus haereses (Irenaeus), 272–73
Adversus Iudaeos, 193–94
Afrahat, 162
Against Celsus (Origen), 198–99
Against Heresies (Irenaeus), 192, 199,
    214
Against the Jews (Tertullian), 189, 200
Against Marcion (Tertullian), 189, 190,
    191, 200
agreement, 202
Alexander, 88, 144, 147
Alexandria
    bishops entering office in, 151
    Co-option in, 112
    Naming in, 125–26
    ordination procedure at, 86–91
Alogi, the, 224
Ambrose
    Election of, 66

ordination of, 63
Annals (Eutychius), 87–88
anointing, 35, 36, 123–24. *See also*
    Chrismation
anti-Gnostic fathers, 184
anti-Montanism, 221
Antitheses (Marcion), 190, 191, 265
Apocalypse of John, status of, 219, 222
Apocalypse of Peter, 222, 239, 244
apocalypses, 236, 239
apocryphal literature, 236
    apocryphal Acts, 236–37
    apocryphal gospels, 237–38, 258
    Petrine apocrypha, 243–44
    following NT genres, 253
Apollonius of Tyana, 235, 241, 273
Apologia contra Arianos (Athanasius),
    62
apostles
    as congregational representatives,
        95–96
    Jewish, 49
    selecting a successor to Judas, 90
    successors of, 93–94
"Apostles' Creed" (*Symbolum Apostoli-
    cum*), 242
Apostolic Church Order, 91
Apostolic Constitutions, 18 , 53–54 ,
    55n3, 56, 66, 67, 105, 123, 157–
    58, 166, 242
apostolic succession, 93–94, 134,
    153–54
apostolicity, claims to, 242
apostolic teachings, 250

office, duties of, performing, 120
officers, elections of
   in Greek associations, 31, 34
   in Roman associations, 31
oil, anointing with, 123–24. *See also* chrismation
Old Covenant, 262–63.
Old Testament
   canon of, 229
   chrismation in, 123
   covenants in, 175, 178
   precedents in, for ordination, 37–41, 96, 108, 161
   priestly traditions in, Christianity's break with, 35, 125
   prophesying a new covenant, 190
   used as Christian book, 195–97
omens, significance of, 148
On Baptism (Tertullian), 14
On the Passover (Melito of Sardis), 193, 199
open canon, 228–30
oral tradition, preferred over written scripture, 249–50
ordained, exclusive jurisdiction of, 42
ordination, 52
   as act of God, 68
   appointments to, 16
   in Asia Minor (3rd cent.), 80–82
   as blessing, 20–21
   ceremonies of, significance of, 108
   ceremony of, 53–63
   changing authority for, 40–41
   Christian-Jewish differences in, 43
   as communal affair, 42
   considered at the Council of Nicaea, 15–20
   in the *Didascalia*, 85–86
   as God's action, 78, 79
   hands associated with prayer in, 165
   illustrating the church functioning as the body of Christ, 108
   indelibility of, 15–19
   irrevocable, 43
   inspired designations and, 152
   linguistic divergence and, 97–98
   meaning of, in Judaism, 42
   mystical, 17

new, 70–71
North Africa's practices of, 79
part and conditional, 43
people at, reasons for, 148
power of, 170–71
prayer as constitutive part of, 119
as prayer and laying on of hands, 20
prayers in, 60–61
presence of people at, reasons for, 90
priestly interpretation of, 70
private, 46, 47–48
rabbinic, model for, 126
in rabbinic literature, 40–45
reception at, of grace of the Holy Spirit, 69
restricted to the Holy Land, 42–43
resulting in sacramental change, 69
secret, 148n33
special gift in, 69
special powers attached to, 107
Syriac terms for, 162
in Syrian Orthodox church, 162
terminology for, Jewish and Christian, 162
theological meaning of, 170
Origen, 86, 159, 170, 223, 229, 230, 231
   advocating divine guidance sought through prayer, 152
   canon of, 277–78
   on covenant, 196–97, 198–99
   expressing authority of scripture, 260, 261–62
   images used by, for church, 2
   on Joshua's appointment, 90
   ordination of, 90
   on the presence of people at an ordination, 148
   priests in writings of, 151
   on selection of church officers, 142–44
   on scriptures of the Old and New Covenant, 264
   using ark imagery for the church, 12
   using body imagery for the church, 2–4, 8
   using bride image for the church, 4

using building image for the church, 8

using mother image for the church, 5, 6

using people of God imagery for the church, 10–11

using temple image for the church, 8–10

Palestine, dying bishops appointing their successors in, 82–83

Palestinian Talmud, 40–41, 125

Papias, 249

parish system, 150

Parochial Election, 52, 80

Patterson, Lloyd, 270

Paul, authority of, 250–51

Paulianists. *See* Paul of Samosata, followers of

Paul of Samosata, 154

followers of, 15, 18–20

Paulicianists, 71–72

Pauline canon, 230–31

Pauline letters, significance of, 253–54

Paulsen, Henning, 275

penitents, reconciliation of, 18, 66, 97, 104, 105

three-stage cycle in, 169n50

people of God, church as, 10–12

personality, transfer of, 129, 166

Peshitta, 130, 141, 226–27, 253n19

Peter I, 151

Peter II, 144

Peterson, Erik, 14

petition, 163, 164

Petrine apocrypha, 243–44

Phalaris, 235

Philippians, 240

Philo, 101, 102, 107–8, 158, 159

Philostratus, 235

Plato, 155

Plumpe, Joseph C., 5

Polycarp, 230, 240, 250–51

career of, 58–59

expressing authority of scripture, 259, 260

installation of, as bishop, 59–60

Polycarp of Smyrna, 254

pontifex maximus, 30, 113

Pontius, 80

popular election, 63

Porrection, 30, 36, 52, 54, 106, 109, 122–23

power, transfer of, 97

prayer, 25–26, 32, 52, 54

absent from Jewish ordination descriptions, 96

appointing and, 100–101

bestowing spiritual gifts, 103

central in Christian ordination practice, 96

as constitutive part of Christian ordination, 119, 171

designated for each new ministerial grade, 119–20

divine invocation taking the form of, 119

as element of ordination, 20, 60–61, 119

elements of, 105

emphasis on, 68

hands associated with, 164–65

Holy Spirit descending in response to, 75

imposition of hands and, 105, 110, 131, 161, 165, 170–71

for presbyter, omitted from *Apostolic Tradition*, 89

seeking divine guidance through, 152

significance of, for explaining ordination's meaning, 105

silent, 119

"Prayerbook" (Serapion), 165–66

Preaching of Peter (*Kerygma Petrou*), 244

Preachings of Peter (*Kerygmata Petrou*), 244

Presbyteral Election, 52

presbyters, 145

activities of, 59

in the Alexandrian church, 112

bishops' selection of, 145

college of, 103

distinguished from bishops, 89

electing bishops, 148–49